THE POLITICAL USE OF MILITARY FORCE IN
US FOREIGN POLICY

This book is dedicated to Kimi King with whom all things are possible.

The Political Use of Military Force in US Foreign Policy

JAMES DAVID MEERNIK

LONDON AND NEW YORK

First published 2004 by Ashgate Publishing

Reissued 2018 by Routledge
2 Park Square, Milton Park, Abingdon, Oxon OX14 4RN
711 Third Avenue, New York, NY 10017, USA

Routledge is an imprint of the Taylor & Francis Group, an informa business

© James David Meernik 2004

James David Meernik has asserted his right under the Copyright, Designs and Patents Act, 1988, to be identified as the author of this work.

All rights reserved. No part of this book may be reprinted or reproduced or utilised in any form or by any electronic, mechanical, or other means, now known or hereafter invented, including photocopying and recording, or in any information storage or retrieval system, without permission in writing from the publishers.

A Library of Congress record exists under LC control number: 2004007712

Notice:
Product or corporate names may be trademarks or registered trademarks, and are used only for identification and explanation without intent to infringe.

Publisher's Note
The publisher has gone to great lengths to ensure the quality of this reprint but points out that some imperfections in the original copies may be apparent.

Disclaimer
The publisher has made every effort to trace copyright holders and welcomes correspondence from those they have been unable to contact.

ISBN 13: 978-0-815-39808-0 (hbk)
ISBN 13: 978-1-351-14572-5 (ebk)

Contents

1	Introduction	1
2	Security, Power and Realist Explanations of the Political Use of Military Force	20
3	Economic Interests and the Political Use of Military Force	76
4	Liberal Idealism and the Political Use of Military Force	119
5	Diversionary Theory and the Political Use of Military Force	157
6	Comprehensive Analysis of the Political Use of Military Force in US Foreign Policy	206
7	Conclusion	231
Bibliography		*245*
Index		*257*

Chapter 1

Introduction

Operation Vigilant Warrior

On October 7, 1994, Saddam Hussein ordered a substantial deployment of his military forces to Iraq's border with Kuwait. The US had only three years prior decisively defeated Iraq in the Persian Gulf War, but Saddam Hussein remained in power with a significant military capability still intact. Now he was threatening Kuwait and its oil fields again and testing the resolve of the US. How would the US respond to this threat to the nation of Kuwait and to the stability of the Middle East? Would President Clinton use the US' military might to deter Iraq from threatening its neighbors? That is the question that lies at the heart of this book and it is one that is important not just to international relations and foreign policy scholars, but the American public and indeed, the world at large. When does the US use military force to influence other governments, and for what reasons? There is no shortage of reasons why President Clinton might have used the US military to deal with Saddam Hussein and Iraq's threat to Kuwait. In fact, there are four principal explanations for the use of military force short of war that are the subject of this book and that might explain this particular case: 1) security and power interests, 2) economic interests and objectives, 3) the promotion of democracy and human rights, and 4) domestic, political interests. Which one explains why President Clinton did use force to respond to the Iraqi government's actions? More importantly, why do all presidents use force to achieve the aims of US foreign policy?

First, in the Iraqi case, decision makers in the US government perceived a great many issues and interests at stake in this crisis that could affect the stability of the Middle East and US national security. The US had staked a great deal of its credibility on containing Saddam in the Middle East and preventing him from threatening his neighbors. US forces patrolled the Persian Gulf, the skies over southern and northern Iraq and were stationed throughout the region. If the US was not prepared to utilize its advantages at this time to meet this challenge, countries around the world might well question America's willingness to live up to its other commitments. A move by Iraq to recapture Kuwait, or to attack Saudi Arabia would have upset the balance of power in the region and allowed Iraq to assume a much more prominent role in Middle East politics. This in turn would have jeopardized moderate Arab regimes with whom the US was on good terms, such as Egypt and Jordan. Thus, Saddam Hussein's latest Kuwaiti gambit engaged vital, national interests for the US.

2   The Political Use of Military Force in US Foreign Policy

Of course, Persian Gulf oil was never far from any discussion of what Saddam's move might mean to the US. The US, its European allies and Japan imported tremendous quantities of oil from and through the Gulf region. US oil prices had increased dramatically in the summer of 1990 when Saddam invaded Kuwait. Certainly, if Iraq could seize Kuwait and intimidate Saudi Arabia, Saddam Hussein would have incredible leverage over world oil prices. No one needed to emphasize the consequences of such a development for the US and global economy to President Clinton.

One can also find a justification for the US deployment in the desire to promote democracy and human rights. During and immediately after the Persian Gulf War, the US government sought the overthrow of Saddam Hussein and his replacement by a more legitimate and representative government. It encouraged separatist movements in northern and southern Iraq, funded various opposition movements inside and outside of Iraq, and used the Central Intelligence Agency to foment resistance within the Iraqi regime. If it did not expect that a Western style democracy was anywhere in the offing, President Clinton certainly spent substantial time and money trying to overthrow and ultimately liberalize the Iraqi government. The US had acquired a vested interest in Iraqi politics and any opportunity that presented itself to destabilize Saddam Hussein's brutal regime could be exploited to ultimately create a friendlier, less repressive government.

And if Saddam Hussein was not creating enough headaches for President Clinton, his administration was experiencing a number of problems at home that might make a foreign adventure just the right antidote. Clinton was in the process of losing the battle over revamping the nation's health care system, the corner piece of his domestic agenda. Other legislative initiatives were also stalled in a gridlocked Congress. President Clinton's support among the public, which had never been that great, had declined in the weeks prior to the Iraqi moves to only 42 percent. Congressional elections, in which Republicans were forecast to do very well (they eventually took over both chambers for the first time since 1953), were just a few weeks away. A timely display of American power and executive leadership might have been just what Clinton needed at the time to demonstrate strong leadership and rally the public behind him.

So why did President Clinton dispatch 170 planes and 6500 personnel to the Persian Gulf?[1] Take your pick of explanations for they are all plausible, supported by evidence and backed by extensive theoretical justification. If there are multiple, potential explanations to our research question, we should analyze this case and others where the US has used military force for political objectives utilizing all the explanatory tools at our disposal. That is, to understand why presidents engage in these types of military actions, we must examine the ability of each of the explanations to account for these events, for Operation Vigilant Warrior is but one of hundreds of such uses of force that have occurred throughout US history. Before we begin this assessment, however, we must be clear about the

---

[1] http://www.fas.org/man/dod-101/ops/vigilant_warrior.htm as found on August 20, 2003.

Introduction 3

definition of these uses of military force. For while many Americans are acquainted with the very few, but very significant wars the nation has been involved in, we tend to be less familiar with the many uses of force short of war.

Defining the Political Use of Military Force

The subject of this book is the political use of military force, short of war, in US foreign policy. It is a study of the use of force as a diplomatic weapon. The events I explore are those military operations that have been designed to influence change in and among foreign countries. Political uses of force short of war involve attempts to *persuade* other nations and their leaders to do or not do things US foreign policy makers desire. The US has used its military in actions short of war hundreds of times since the founding of the Republic to accomplish all manner of foreign policy aims. They are among the most frequent, significant and far-reaching tools in US foreign policy. From actions in the Caribbean during the Quasi War in the late 18th century, the deployment of the naval armada under Commodore Perry to open up Japan, the use of naval force to help stop the slave trade, and the more extensive gunboat diplomacy in the Caribbean in the first part of this century, instances of the use of military force short of war have been replete in the pre modern era. Since World War II the US has embarked on hundreds of military missions abroad, including a number of prominent incidents like the naval quarantine around Cuba during the 1962 missile crisis, the world wide nuclear alert during the 1973 Middle East War, the 1983 invasion of Grenada, the 1986 bombing of Libya, the invasions of Panama (1989), Haiti (1994) and the deployment in Bosnia in 1995. These operations involve high-level crisis politics and struggles over some of the most salient issues of the day. American lives have been lost and much treasure has been expended. The course of politics within the US and around the world has been altered by these events.

Such activities have been called by scholars, 'political uses of military force'. So that we may be explicit at the outset regarding the subject matter of this book, I quote here the definition of a political use of military force that has been adopted by many scholars in this research area:

> A political use of the armed forces occurs when physical actions are taken by one or more components of the uniformed military services as part of a deliberate attempt by the national authorities to influence, or to be prepared to influence, specific behavior of individuals in another nation without engaging in a continuing contest of violence (Blechman and Kaplan, 1978, p.12).

To understand fully the implications of this definition for the present study, it is necessary to analyze each of its component elements. I begin with what is perhaps the most contentious issue involved in the definition of a political use of military force–the distinction between such actions short of war, and actual wars. There have been hundreds of such events in the years after World War II, while in the preceding 150 years of history, presidents also found cause to frequently use force

4   *The Political Use of Military Force in US Foreign Policy*

to attain diplomatic ends (Blechman and Kaplan, 1978; Congressional Research Service, 1993). Wars, however, have been fairly rare in US history. Therefore, I do not analyze the causes of US participation in the following wars: The War of 1812, the Mexican-American War, the Spanish-American War, World War I, World War II, The Korean War, The Vietnam War, and the Persian Gulf War (the 2003 Iraq War lies outside the time frame of this analysis).

Blechman and Kaplan make two critical distinctions between political uses of military force and wars in their definition. First, there is the key clause that limits the definition of political uses of military force to situations where US decision makers sought to achieve their goals, 'without engaging in a *continuing* contest of violence' (emphasis added). As Blechman and Kaplan (1978, p.13) write, 'Although a war may result from a use of the armed forces, which otherwise meets the terms of the definition, the initiation of war must not have been the *intent* of the action' (emphasis in the original). Thus, presidents may order the deployment of Army or Marine forces to a hostile or friendly nation, such as Somalia in 1992 or Lebanon in 1958, but the goal is not to engage another's armed forces in a long-term contest that culminates in military surrender, but to influence political developments. Given that in a political use of military force the intent of US leaders is to avoid a continuing contest of violence, these events are much less violent than wars in US history. There may be US casualties initially, or some comparatively low level of combat deaths over time, but when presidents authorize political uses of military force, they do not do so with the intention or expectation that there will be long-term fighting. Thus, while US wars have involved thousands of American deaths, as well as the deaths of many others, political uses of military force rarely even approach such levels. Political uses of military force differ from wars most fundamentally in the qualitatively different amount of violence involved. Wars are called 'wars' in large part because of this violence.

The second, critical distinction between political uses of military force and wars involves the notion of 'influence'. Like all nations, the US has employed its sea, land and later air forces in situations short of war, not so much to impose its will on others, but rather to influence the behavior of foreign actors. Wars, on the other hand, involve violence designed to impose one's will upon the enemy so that he has no choice but to do as he is told. In war one seeks a position from which to dominate one's enemies to the point where they have no choices. When using force short of war, the objective is to change the adversary's *perception*, as well as the actual costs and benefits of various courses of action so that the target selects one's preferred policy. In war if the military successfully completes its mission–if it is victorious–the state's immediate, foreign policy goals are essentially realized. In the use of force short of war the military may flawlessly complete the tasks set out for it by the civilian leadership (e.g., show the flag), but the operation may still fail to change the behavior of the target. In war the opponent is the enemy. A use of force short of war, however, may be directed at friends, enemies or neutrals–any actor whose behavior one is seeking to change. Not surprisingly, given the finality and destructiveness of war and the commensurate malleability of force short of war, the latter has been the preferred instrument of American foreign policy.

Introduction 5

Despite these critical distinctions between political uses of military force and wars, there is still a zone of ambiguity between the two in which scholars might reasonably disagree about the proper placement of some events. The invasion of Panama in 1989 might be seen as a war by some since President Bush Sr. essentially sought to impose US will on the Panamanian government of Manuel Noriega to force him out of power. Different phases of the Vietnam War in which President Johnson sought, through bombings and bombing pauses, to influence North Vietnamese leaders to reach accommodation with the US, share much in common with the definition of the political use of military force. And how can we ever know whether it was the 'intent' of US national authorities to avoid going to war when they authorized a military invasion? Simply put, we may never truly know such intentions and we may never arrive at a definition that objectively and perfectly divides political uses of military force from wars for there may be some amount of ambiguity in some cases. I argue that we should strive for a definition that provides us with the most reasonable and thorough criteria for studying military actions short of war.

The Blechman and Kaplan definition of the political use of force and the data set derived from that definition are superior to other data sets using different definitions of such types of military action. There are three other data sets used in international relations research that might be relevant. The Correlates of War project, focuses on war, and is therefore not appropriate for this study. The International Crisis Behavior project focuses on international crises and not uses of force and thus substantially undercounts the number of relevant events (Meernik, 2000). The Militarized Interstate Dispute project also contains data on uses of force and distinguishes between wars and military actions short of war. However, in a 2001 study, Fordham and Sarver analyze all data sets involving military actions that might be used to study the political use of military force. They conclude that the Blechman and Kaplan data set is the most inclusive, and that the Militarized Interstate Dispute data set, '...is not appropriate for testing theoretical arguments about US decisions to use force...' (Fordham and Sarver, 2001, p.456). If we wish to study the political use of military force in as thorough a fashion as is possible, we should utilize the Blechman and Kaplan definition.

In addition to distinguishing between political uses of military force and wars, Blechman and Kaplan also describe the various types of military operations and their goals that fall within their definition. Operations have included the following: provision of a US presence, visits to foreign ports, naval patrols, reconnaissance and surveillance, non-routine military exercises, demonstrations of right of naval passage, transportation of military equipment or forces to assist another actor (such as a foreign government or rebel force), movement of a foreign actor's military forces or equipment, evacuation of US and other citizens, the use of firepower to influence foreign events, the emplacement of US ground forces or occupation of territory to influence events, the interposition of US military forces between foreign actors, naval blockades or 'quarantines' and other civil-military functions (Blechman and Kaplan, 1978, p.54).

The foreign policy objectives US officials seek to attain embrace a variety of situation-specific as well as more general goals. In their analysis, Blechman and

6 *The Political Use of Military Force in US Foreign Policy*

Kaplan group together these disparate objectives into four, broad 'modes'. These are, to deter, compel, assure and induce targets. The objectives of deterrence and compellence refer to attempts to influence the behavior of adversaries. Deterrence involves military activities designed to persuade an adversary *not* to undertake some action, such as invading its neighbor. As we saw, the US moved troops to the Persian Gulf in the fall of 1994 to deter Saddam Hussein from attacking Kuwait or Saudi Arabia. Compellence entails persuading an adversary to perform some behavior. The US naval quarantine of Cuba during the 1962 Cuban Missile Crisis was designed to compel the Soviets to remove their nuclear missiles. Assurance and inducement refer to attempts to convince friendly states to perform analogous types of behavior. For example, the US has sought to assure nations of its commitment to their security (such as South Korea in 1969 after North Korea shot down a US, EC-121 plane), and it has also sought to induce its allies to take measures to counter both internal and external foes (such as in many uses of force in Central America in the 1980s). Additionally, Blechman and Kaplan find a fifth classification of 'latent' goals where US objectives remain rather murky and are not immediately obvious to the ostensible targets.

It is also useful to define these actions by showing what they are not. Such actions are undertaken against foreign targets rather than actors within the US. Political uses of military force short of war do not include the ongoing basing of military troops in foreign countries or the routine rotation of personnel in and out of these bases. Routine basing of troops is just that–routine and ordinary. Political uses of military force are extraordinary and discrete operations designed to accomplish a specific aim. For example, the permanent stationing of US troops in Europe, Japan and South Korea does serve to deter aggression, but it is generally not related to changing specific behavior in an immediate situation. An augmentation of these forces in response to say, specific North Korean provocations would quality as an attempt to influence the behavior of the North Korean government. The deployment of US forces to Kuwait to deter Iraqi aggression would qualify. Political uses of military force also do not encompass covert or paramilitary operations whose personnel, methods and objectives are designed to be kept secret. We simply have no way of knowing where, when and why these operations occurred. We often do not even know that they have occurred. While such operations are not impossible to analyze (e.g., Johnson, 1989), they do not lend themselves to the type of thorough, systematic empirical inquiry I adopt in this book.

The limited use of force is one among many foreign policy tools the president has it his disposal. In some sense we can view these tools as existing along a continuum from peaceful to forceful action the president can take to influence the actions of foreign governments. At one end of the continuum there is diplomacy, much of it routine (meetings between US ambassadors and foreign governments) and some of it extraordinary (e.g., the Camp David negotiations in 1978 and 2000). Somewhere in the middle lie the carrots and sticks of economic, military and other forms of assistance presidents can manipulate to encourage change in other countries' foreign policies. At the other extreme are all-out wars, such as World War II, which are comparatively rare events in US history. I would

Introduction 7

place the limited use of force somewhere between the middle of this continuum and the end represented by war, as it shares characteristics with both diplomacy and military action.

When confronted by an international crisis, a president may influence events by gradually moving along this continuum to exert greater and more sustained pressure on foreign governments. After Iraq invaded Kuwait in 1990 the US reacted with words, then economic sanctions, military deployments, and finally war. Or the president may opt to do several things simultaneously. We often see limited uses of force accompanied by diplomacy as US foreign policy makers communicate in words what the military is supposed to demonstrate in deeds. And sometimes, especially when international crises occur quite rapidly, presidents may move straightaway to the use of force because there is insufficient time for international conferences or economic sanctions to take effect. And because the president is commander-in-chief, he can deploy the military about the globe fairly quickly. In so doing he underscores the seriousness of an international situation to the US in a way words sometimes cannot. Not surprisingly, given the relative ease and visibility of these actions, presidents throughout history have relied upon military action to realize the most vital aims of US foreign policy.

Curiously, however, few scholars have sought to systematically analyze these events across time to understand why presidents use force. The scholarly community in political science and history has often focused on one theory, one case or one period of time. From these studies we can learn much. But as long as they remain discrete, relatively unintegrated explanations we cannot understand, as much as it is possible, the whole scope of these events. We should build upon all the work that has been done to date to study the political use of military force in a systematic and empirical manner. We should study all uses of force short of war by the US since the founding. We should set our sights high for though this book may not realize the objectives I have just described, the next batch of scholars who examine this topic will hopefully be further advanced in their understanding than we are now. Having laid out my ambitions, I should next like to briefly describe my approach. To do so, I must first describe the four dominant theories of the political use of military force.

Four Theories of the Political Use of Military Force

Research on US foreign policy and international relations provides us with four principal theories that seek to explain the use of force as a response to different security and power goals, economic interests, liberal idealist aims, and domestic political interests held by the president and US foreign policy makers. There are other explanations, and certainly individual uses of military forces may be driven by idiosyncratic factors that do not belong to any of the four theories I discuss. I believe, however, that we should systematically and empirically assess the strengths and weaknesses of these four, major theories across time, determine to what extent they can be integrated and ultimately attempt such a synthesis. As in any empirical endeavor, we should begin our analysis with the better-established accounts of the phenomena we seek to understand.

Many scholars contend that security and sovereignty interests are the paramount goals of foreign policy in general and the use of force in particular (Gilpin, 1987; Huntington, 1993; Morgenthau, 1973; Waltz, 1979). Perhaps the most preeminent school of thought regarding the importance of security in international relations is realism. Realist theory generally assumes that states are the dominant actors in international relations; power is the primary currency; and security is the ultimate objective. The classical realist model treats the state as a unitary, rational actor concerned primarily with military and security issues and motivated almost exclusively by external events rather than internal interests. States utilize their militaries as a means to exploit opportunities to advance international security objectives or to respond to threats to those interests. Force is used to protect one's own, key allies, strategic choke points, vital resources and prevent aggression. The realist model has the advantage of being intuitively understandable and supported by a great deal of prima facie evidence. Indeed, it is rare that we cannot find at least one security concern cited to justify some use of force. Yet, despite the dominance of realists in policymaking positions and the field of international relations, scholars have developed other explanations for these events. In contrast to realist explanations, which stress the importance of national security and external events, these theories are more concerned with what transpires inside rather than outside the US to explain foreign policy.

Marxist and leftist scholars have long argued that capitalist nations, including the US, use force to advance and protect economic interests, especially those of multinational corporations (Dos Santos, 1970; Frank, 1969; Galtung, 1971; Kolko, 1969; Odell, 1974; Rosen, 1974; Wallerstein, 1974, 1988). Other scholars have also emphasized the importance of economic factors in states' foreign policies (Gilpin, 1987; Kennedy, 1987; Keohane and Nye, 1989; Krasner, 1983). They contend that monetary and trade policy, control of strategic resources, and the flow of international investments can be as important as security interests, and that economic dominance is a key determinant of international power. As well, the ultimate justification for the use of force may be the protection of a society's economic prosperity. Indeed, from the time of the Napoleonic wars through American interventionism in Central America and the Caribbean early in the 20th century, to the repeated use of force in the oil-rich Persian Gulf, one finds a long and storied history of military might employed on behalf of economic objectives. Scholars have developed broad, theoretical models of the role of economic forces in American foreign policy, but to date, there has been comparatively little testing of quantitative models of such research.

Recently, many academics and foreign policy practitioners have addressed the role of military force in advancing goals associated with liberal idealism, such as democracy and human rights (Fossedal, 1989; Hermann and Kegley, 1998; McDougall, 1997; Meernik, 1996; Peceny, 1996, 1999; Smith, 1994; Whitcomb, 1998). With the collapse of the US' primary ideological opponent and the near-universal consensus that democratic states do not war on one another, we see ample justification for a foreign policy aimed at exporting American ideals abroad–

Introduction 9

what I will term 'liberal idealism'. In Panama (1989), Haiti (1994) and Bosnia (1995) US military force secured the conditions necessary to establish and maintain democracy. Yet, this not just a recent phenomenon. Woodrow Wilson repeatedly dispatched the military to Latin America to oversee elections and influence internal politics. The US diverted a significant portion of its naval fleet in the 1840s to try to halt the illegal slave trade off Africa, the Caribbean and South America. Indeed, as many international relations scholars have pointed out, powerful states have good reason to export their ideologies and the political systems that embody them to create similar, and thus friendly, foreign governments (Krasner, 1978; Ikenberry and Kupchan 1990).

Finally, there is veritable cottage industry of research that seeks to find evidence of a relationship between domestic political factors and the use of force (DeRouen, 1995, 2000; Fordham, 1998a, 1998b; Gelpi, 1997; James and Hristoulas, 1994; James and Oneal, 1991; Leeds and Davis, 1997; Meernik, 1994; Meernik and Waterman, 1996; Miller, 1995; Morgan and Bickers, 1992; Ostrom and Job, 1986; Richards et al, 1993; Smith, 1996a, 1996b 1998, 1999; Yoon, 1997; Wang, 1996). Despite these many studies, however, we still cannot say with any precision just what effect domestic conditions have on the president's desire to use military force. Some argue presidents are more likely to use force when times are bad, other scholars argue presidents will more likely refrain from deploying the military in these periods. Still other researchers find little if any linkage between the internal and the external. In many ways the problems in the literature on the diversionary use of force are a microcosm of the difficulties we see in general in analyzing the political use of military force. Often researchers focus their attention on investigating one set of explanatory factors instead of empirically, systematically and comprehensively analyzing the diverse theories on the political use of military force.

Despite all this research, I would argue that we have not succeeded in explaining why presidents use force short of war. Why, despite the loss of many a tree to produce the plethora of books and articles on the subject, have we come up short? I see several fundamental weaknesses in many of our analyses. First and foremost, we will find it difficult to achieve any comprehensive understanding of this subject as long as so much research is focused on testing single theories of the use of force. For example, many of the quantitative studies of the use of force by American presidents in political science journals are almost exclusively concerned with the role of domestic factors in decision making. The literature on the diversionary use of force is replete with models that test a multiplicity of measurements of presidential popularity and the US economy, but are relatively less developed with respect to other potential explanations. Therefore, it is unlikely we will be able to assess the relative impact of all potential explanatory factors as long as we study one theory at a time.

Second, in many of the quantitative studies of the use of military force, rather than investigating to what extent US foreign policy goals were engaged in particular crises, scholars have focused much attention on the nature of the domestic and international *environment* at the time force was used. What was the level of US unemployment at the time? What was the level of US tension with the

Soviet Union at the time? What was the president's popularity at the time force was used? Why would researchers concentrate their energies on the timing rather than the context of uses of force? Given the nature of their research designs, most are left with no alternative. Among scholars studying quantitatively the political use of military force by American presidents, most predict whether presidents deploy the military or not in some given period of time, such as a month, quarter or year. The dependent variable measures the presence or absence of a use of force during a unit of time. This measurement scheme does not tell us what international events precipitated a use of force, nor does it tell us if a president used force on more than one occasion during some period of time. Therefore, scholars are forced to rely on information about the state of the domestic and international environments rather than information about a particular crisis to which the president may or may not respond. By using a period of time as the unit of analysis we can measure the general amount of war in the international environment, but not the presence or absence of war in a particular crisis. We can measure whether or not there was some incident somewhere at that time in which American lives were threatened, but not whether they were threatened in some particular crisis. In short, by employing a period of time as the unit of analysis we lose a great deal of information. Instead, we must structure our research designs to test theories of US foreign policy goals, not just the characteristics of the domestic and international environments at the time of uses of force. To determine what motivates presidents to use force we must be able to determine what threats or opportunities to advance US interests were present in individual, international crises.

Another problem with our analyses is that too often we test our hypotheses using Cold War era data and do not analyze the use of force before World War II. We know that there were many occasions in the period from 1789 through 1941 when presidents sent US forces into Central and South America, the Middle East and the Far East for all manner of economic, liberal idealist and perhaps political purposes. These incidents should be examined as well using available evidence to ascertain what factors were most prominent in motivating military missions. The only way we can evaluate the true depth of concern for security, economic interests, liberal idealist goals or domestic politics in presidential decision-making is by testing the models across a broad expanse of time.

The net result of these various problems is that while we have witnessed an accumulation of findings about the political use of military force by the US, we have not been blessed with an integration of evidence. We lack a holistic picture. Any account of the political use of military force in US foreign policy is incomplete and deficient without the incorporation of all four of these theories. We must be aware that the ultimate purpose of the use of military force in response to international events is to protect the values, institutions and prosperity the nation enjoys. We cannot understand the use of force separate from those things it is supposed to safeguard—whether it is national security, economic prosperity, fundamental political values, or political survival. While I do not wish to trace the

Introduction

11

origins of every political use of force back to the more distant and fundamental values it seeks to attain, neither can we ignore these basic objectives. Even though we are unlikely to find that any theory can provide a thorough account for all political uses of force, we should not set the evidentiary standard so high. The conditions and events that these theories assume influence the use of force will be much more likely to contribute to rather than determine the use of force. Therefore, our standard of proof should be that the influences identified by these models should decisively contribute toward the decision to use force even if they do not always dictate it. They should provide the primary explanation for some number of political uses of force even if they do not provide the dominant explanation for all such events. At the risk of showing my cards to the reader early on, however, I will argue throughout this book that throughout history presidents use force primarily to protect/advance US security; often to promote economic interests; occasionally to advance liberal idealist goals; and seldom to advance their own domestic political interests.

The Use and Opportunity to Use Force

Having defined the concept of the political use of military force by the US, and highlighted the dominant theories on the subject, we must now turn to an empirical measurement, or operationalization of these events to prepare the way for the analyses that follow. There is not one comprehensive data set on the political use of military force by the US throughout history. Rather, there are several data sets that cover discrete time periods. The Congressional Research Service (1993) study, 'Instances of Use of the US Armed Forces Abroad, 1798-1993' includes a listing of all major uses of force.[2] It does not, however, contain a great deal of information on these events and so is not always suitable for multivariate statistical analysis. Nonetheless, the Congressional Research Service data set is the only comprehensive listing of all uses of force from the 18th century through the years prior to World War II. And it does contain enough information to gain some understanding as to the purposes for which the military was deployed, as well as when and where these events occurred. Therefore, I will use these data and some fairly simple, descriptive statistics to provide the reader with an accounting of the reasons why force was used in the period 1798-1941. While such data do not lend themselves to precise statistical analyses, they do acquaint us with US military actions in a period of time for which we ought to have a greater understanding than currently exists.

After World War II we see researchers make a systematic effort to collect data on all the different circumstances and conditions surrounding the use of force. Of particular importance is the *Force Without War* study by Blechman and Kaplan (1978). This analysis of the political use of military force by the US from 1946 through 1976 was the first, systematic inquiry into these events, and many scholars

---

[2] http://www.fas.org/man/crs/crs_931007.htm as found on August 20, 2003.

12 *The Political Use of Military Force in US Foreign Policy*

have used these data ever since. Zelikow (1984), followed up the Blechman and Kaplan study with data for the years 1977-1984. Until the advent of the Internet, however, no one scholar, group or institution sought to gather all such data for the years after 1984. Instead, researchers relied on one-shot studies done by various think tanks and components of the Defense Department, such as, The Center for Naval Analyses. Its study, 'The Use of Naval Forces in the Post-War Era: US Navy and US Marine Corps Crisis Response Activity, 1946-1990' is one of the most comprehensive since a majority of uses of force entail some sort of naval deployment. The Air Force also contracted out for a study of its crisis involvement, 'Toward the Future: Global Reach-Global Power, US Air Force'. Beginning in the late 1990s, The Federation of American Scientists created a web site that contains a thorough listing of all recent uses of force and a fairly good listing of Cold War and pre Cold War uses of force.[3] I relied upon all these sources to compile one, comprehensive data set for the years 1948-1998 covering all US political uses of military force. I do not include uses of force associated with the Vietnam War between 1965 and 1972, the Persian Gulf War of January, 1991 to March, 1991, and all uses of force that involved friendly 'port of call' visits by the US Navy. I use these data in Chapters 2 through 5 in multivariate, statistical analyses to test hypotheses derived from each of the four theories individually, and in Chapter 6 to test all these hypotheses together.

If we are to understand why presidents use force, we must also understand why presidents sometimes *do not* use force. We must also search for information on instances where no force was used. While the universe of such cases may be infinite, since presidents could theoretically decide to use force whenever and wherever they wished, for practical reasons, presidents are limited, and so too should our search for decisions not to use force. I argue simply that scholars should analyze whether or not presidents use force, given some opportunity, or international crisis. I must also note that I confine my search for such events to the post World War II era. Identifying all these events across the whole of US history is a daunting task beyond the ambitions of this book.

Opportunities to use force are defined as those situations we can reasonably suppose that the president considered the use of military force as a policy option. The opportunities to use force I consider are events that seemed likely to attract the president's attention. This does not imply that there was in every case actual evidence of a foreign threat to the US, only that the events were of such magnitude that there is reason to believe the president perceived a threat. The criteria that were used to define and identify international events likely to be perceived as containing such threats are borrowed from Job and Ostrom (1986, p.10). Please note that this is a separate and very different paper from their well-known 1986 article in the *American Political Science Review*. Their criteria are:

> 1) the situation involved a perceived current threat to the territorial security of the U.S., its current allies, major clients or proxy states;

---

[3] http://www.fas.org/man/dod-101/ops/#post as found on August 20, 2003.

Introduction 13

2) the situation posed a perceived danger to US government, military or diplomatic personnel; to significant numbers of US citizens or to US assets;
3) events were perceived as having led, or likely to lead to advances by ideologically committed opponents of the US (i.e., communists or extreme leftists broadly defined) be they states, regimes or regime contenders;
4) events were perceived as likely to lead to losses of US influence in regions perceived as within the US sphere of influence, especially viewed as Central and South America;
5) events involved inter-state military conflict of potential consequence; in human and strategic terms; or events, because of civil disorder, threatened destruction of substantial number of persons.

Job and Ostrom justify this set of events as worthy of inclusion in the data set because they are generalized to be a 'syndrome of characteristics commonly found in use of force situations' (1986, p.9). That is, attributes of situations where presidents used force in the past as defined by Blechman and Kaplan (1978) and Zelikow (1986) were used as the search criteria for opportunities to use force. Thus, by generalizing from these characteristics backward and forward across time and nations they were able to construct a data set of events that combine opportunities to use force and uses of forces. This method of 'criterion matching' was one of several which might have been employed to justify the search for and inclusion of events in the data, but it is the most empirically defensible. The following discussion borrows heavily from my previous work on this subject (Meernik, 1992).

One possible alternative to criterion matching is to examine the historical record to determine what nations and events US presidents and foreign policy leaders identified as vital interests. These situations would define opportunities to use force. Historical induction, however, is fraught with numerous complications. First, as Job and Ostrom note, such a methodology is afflicted with a paradox of US foreign policy: 'US interests are what US decision makers perceive them to be from moment to moment' (1986, p.9). Interests and opportunities end up defining one another. Thus, a lack of permanently defined interests precludes establishing search criteria that are not dependent upon the nature of each, individual opportunity. Secondly, the historical record is littered with examples of presidents asserting one policy while following another. Dean Acheson's declaration of a Far East defense perimeter excluding South Korea, US denial of military involvement in Guatemala in 1954, and the Reagan policy of no deal making with terrorists are all part of a common trend of incongruity between declared and actual policy. Thus, while the historical record can provide clues to determine which events threaten American interests, it does not provide the explicit guidance an empirically justifiable methodology requires.

A second alternative is to utilize the work of other researchers and data sets to build a classification of opportunities to use force. Unfortunately, much of the work in international conflict has examined only those *events that were likely to lead to war* (which is a feature Blechman and Kaplan definitively rule out of their definition of the political use of force), rather than a limited use of force. While some of these events undoubtedly merit inclusion in this data set, the data collected

14   *The Political Use of Military Force in US Foreign Policy*

by the COW Project, Brecher and Wilkenfeld (1997) and others generally does not include the many minor and moderately important events that lead to political uses of military force (e.g., military coups in Third World nations, isolated but noteworthy attacks on US military personnel, etc.).

Criterion matching is the most empirically justifiable method for creating an opportunity data set. By specifying a set of conditions under which uses of force may occur, the search criteria are not complicated by the alterations and inconsistencies of American foreign policy and the incomplete definitions of other data sets. While this methodology appears to reduce the probability of making errors of commission, the possibility of errors of omission cannot be overlooked. There are no satisfactory solutions to this dilemma, however, since no matter what methodology is chosen there is always the possibility that a use of force was considered under highly peculiar and/or secret conditions. The challenge for the researcher lies in determining exactly where and when these threats are present. Some scholars (Clark and Regan, 2003) have argued that there is a near tautology between the definition of an opportunity to use force and a use of force. Obviously these events must necessarily share similarities with one another. If one studies crisis escalation and war, one must also analyze two types of events, one of which results from the other, that share many things in common. To argue otherwise would be to assert that there are no differences between international crises and war. Since wars, like the political use of military force, emerge from crises, there will be similarities between crises and the event of interest. It is the responsibility of the researcher to articulate why some crises lead to war, or to force short of war, and why others do not.

I was able to use data Job and Ostrom (1986) had already collected on opportunities to use force between 1948 and 1984. Their data provide the same information on crisis characteristics for all incidents regardless of whether or not the president used force. I supplemented these data for the years 1985 through 1998 by following Job and Ostrom's data collection procedures. I reviewed several yearly almanacs of important, international events, including *The Statesman's Yearbook*, and *Political Handbook of the World* in search of situations that resembled the types of crises to which presidents had at other times responded with force. Having compiled a list of potential opportunities, I examined more detailed event summaries for further validation and information including: *Facts on File, Keesings Contemporary Archives* and the *New York Times Index*. Those events that did meet these specifications were added to the list of opportunities compiled by Job and Ostrom (1986). Information was collected on the specific events, actors and military action surrounding opportunities 1948-1998. I use these opportunities as the unit of analysis with which to analyze the political use of force in the period 1948-1998. These data build upon and extend my previous research in this area (Meernik, 1994).

Table 1.1 Presidents, Opportunities and the Use of Force

President	Opportunities	Uses of Force	Frequency
Truman	40	11	27.5%
Eisenhower	82	50	60.9%
Kennedy	55	35	63.6%
Johnson	66	39	59.0%
Nixon	54	16	29.6%
Ford	25	8	32.0%
Carter	20	45	44.4%
Reagan	110	74	67.2%
Bush	51	24	47.0%
Clinton	77	41	53.2%
Total	605	318	52.5%

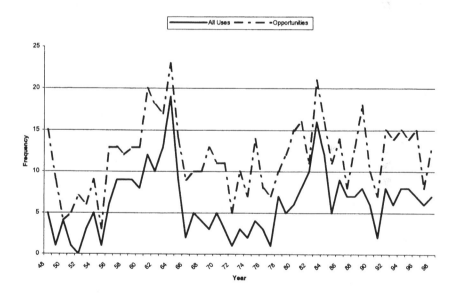

Figure 1.1 Opportunities to Use Force and Uses of Force, 1948-1998

Table 1.1 provides a brief summary of the frequency of uses of force, given an opportunity for the post World War II presidential administrations. Figure 1.1 charts the ebb and flow of uses of force and opportunities to use force from 1948-1998. Overall, in the period 1948-1998 I found that there were 605 crises, or opportunities to use force, and that presidents used force in 318 of these events. Presidents Eisenhower, Kennedy, Johnson and Reagan were most likely to use

16   *The Political Use of Military Force in US Foreign Policy*

force. Indeed, the period between the end of the Korean War and the beginning of the Vietnam War averaged 8.6 uses of force per year. These involved many well-known international crises, such as the 1958 intervention in Lebanon, the 1962 Cuban Missile Crisis, the civil war in the Belgian Congo in the early 1960s and several of the showdowns with the USSR over the status of West Berlin. There were also many lesser known uses of force that may not have captured much attention at the time, or are remembered now, but are nonetheless indicative of US foreign policy strategy and behavior. For example, there were several uses of force involving US relations with Indonesia as foreign policy makers sought to keep that nation out of the communist sphere of influence. There were also multiple uses of force that occurred in the Dominican Republic in the early 1960s immediately before and after the June, 1961 assassination of long time dictator, Rafael Trujillo. We might expect as much in an era when the battle for superpower supremacy was at its height; crises were still occurring in Europe and the Cold War battleground was extending into the third world. These were also the years of bipartisan consensus in Congress and amongst the public that the war on communism should be waged vigorously and should be led by the president. Subsequently, the protracted US involvement in Vietnam appears to have dampened presidential willingness to use force elsewhere–uses of force averaged roughly four per year during the war years from 1965-1972.

Less well-known and remembered are the many instances in this era where presidents did not deploy the military–the dog that did *not* bark in the night. But these events too provide revealing insights about the limitations of the use of force. For example, despite having encouraged the Hungarians to revolt against communist rule in the fall of 1956, and despite making 'rollback' of communism a center piece of his foreign policy, Dwight Eisenhower chose not to use force in any active or passive way to assist the Hungarians who fought against their communist government even as Soviet tanks rolled into Budapest. Presidents were certainly willing to entertain countering communism in the third world with military force, but not in those areas where they might confront Soviet forces. The US also resisted the use of force to assist the Tibetan revolt against the Chinese in 1959, although the CIA was involved in training Tibetan exiles. The US also did not use force in any manner after the 1961 Soviet shootdown of the U2 spy plane flown by Gary Powers. Presidents have generally tended to avoid using force when an operation would necessarily involve them in a military confrontation with the Soviet Union (Meernik, 1994).

The other type of situation where presidents generally do not use force are those more obscure events that do not 'seem' to present any serious threat to the US, although occasionally we find presidents using force in these situations. For example, while President Kennedy did authorize the use of force against Zanzibar in 1961 after instability there, he did not do so in the case of Angola in 1961. Many times presidents would deploy US warships to Central or South America to 'demonstrate' US interest in some nation that was going through or had just emerged from a military coup, such as in Brazil in 1964. On many other occasions, however, presidents were not so inclined and chose not to deploy the US Navy to 'signal' its preferences after coups in Bolivia in 1964 or in Argentina

Introduction 17

when Juan Peron was toppled from power in 1955. Sometimes the feasibility of using force plays a role as in the case of landlocked nations like Bolivia, while at other times, presidents may have used other means to express US interests, such as diplomacy or foreign aid.

Uses of force declined considerably after the years of fighting in Southeast Asia drained away the bipartisan foreign policy consensus and resources, and led to the Vietnam Syndrome. Presidents Nixon, Ford and Carter were all less likely to use force than not, given an opportunity. They did use force in some well-known instances like the 1973 Yom Kippur War in the Middle East, the 1975 capture of the US ship, Mayaguez, by the Cambodian government, and when the US 'discovered' Soviet troops in Cuba in 1979. But there were more cases where the US chose not to get involved that again demonstrate the limits of US foreign policy, and likely the US public. Extensive involvement in third world civil wars was decidedly out of vogue, and thus the US refrained on many occasions from using force in Central America and Africa in the late 1970s. Even the wars between Vietnam and Cambodia in 1978-1979, and Vietnam and China in early 1979, and the killing fields of Cambodia during the reign of the Khmer Rouge, 1975-1978, did not elicit displays of US military might. After several years of retrenchment and the failure of détente, however, the public signaled its readiness for a more assertive American presence on the international scene. The Reagan administration's greater willingness to confront communist forces abroad, and its desire to re-energize the military contributed to a substantial increase in the use of force. In fact, Reagan is nearly 20 percent more likely to use force than Jimmy Carter and 30 percent more likely than Nixon and Ford. The 1982-1984 intervention in Lebanon, the 1983 intervention in Grenada, the 1986 bombing of Libya and 1987-1988 reflagging of the Kuwaiti oil tankers are all well-known. But Reagan also used force to influence the war between Chad and Libya during the mid 1980s on more than one occasion; he repeatedly authorized naval exercises in Central America in the 1980s to signal US power to those fighting in the various wars in that region, and to assert the US Navy's rights of passage around Albania (1981), in the Black Sea (1986 and in 1988).

We remember Presidents George Bush Sr. and Bill Clinton for many of their large-scale military operations, such as the actions in Panama, the Persian Gulf, Somalia, Haiti, Bosnia, and Kosovo. Their propensity to use force (47 percent and 52 percent, respectively), however, follows very closely the average across all presidential administrations (53 percent). Following in the tradition of earlier American reluctance to use force in regard to events in Eastern Europe, however, George Bush Sr. did not authorize any military operations in the fall of 1989 as communist governments fell in East Germany, Czechoslovakia and Romania. Both presidents Bush and Clinton were fairly preoccupied with events in the Persian Gulf region and in the Balkans to use force elsewhere, despite many critical events in world politics. The US did not use force in relation to coups in the USSR (1991) or, Ethiopia (1991), an attempted coup in Venezuela (1992), the 1994 Zapatista revolt in Mexico, the 1996 confrontation between Greece and Turkey in the Mediterranean, the final overthrow of Mobutu in Zaire in 1997, and the nuclear weapons testing incidents in Pakistan and India in 1998. What is most

The Political Use of Military Force in US Foreign Policy

interesting is that the US had used force many times in the past in very similar circumstances in Ethiopia, Venezuela, Greek/Turkish confrontations, Zaire, and in regard to events on the Indian subcontinent. Such events may have been of great interest in the bipolar world of the Cold War, but the importance of many of these developments was substantially diminished in today's world where the US is deploying forces by the tens of thousands elsewhere. But while it might be fascinating to explore here why presidents used force on some of these occasions and not on others, rather than explaining these differences on an ad hoc basis, we must examine and test the different theories that purport to explain these differences. For though we see in Table 1.1, that there is almost an even chance that any president will use force in any given international crisis, we know that presidential decision making does not proceed as if it were a coin toss. Thus, the task ahead is specify exactly what factors precipitate a decision to use the military for political purposes.

The Plan of the Book

My plan is to address each of the four theories in separate chapters as well as together in a comprehensive analysis. Accordingly, Chapters 2 through 5 of the book are in-depth examinations of the four theories of the political use of military force–the realist/security and power explanation, the economic interest model, the liberal idealist explanation, and diversionary theory. Each of these chapters is organized in a similar fashion. I first outline the theoretical explanation at the center of the chapter. I discuss the literature and research on the theory and assess its utility. I then present a brief overview of three different incidents where presidents used military force to promote these various, foreign policy goals. The three cases I detail in each chapter are selected because there seems to be strong prima facie evidence that interests pertaining to the theory highlighted in the chapter were important considerations in the military operations. Because I am looking for cases where there is strong evidence in favor of a given theory, I have chosen cases that have already been researched by others, and so rely principally upon these secondary analyses for the historical background. Thus, my purpose is not to bring to light new, documentary evidence in these case studies, but rather to apply a particular theory to our interpretation of already well-known (at least from a scholarly perspective) events. In effect, these are intended to be 'easy' tests for each of the four theories of US foreign policy behavior. I have no doubt that there are plenty of cases that could falsify any of the theories I examine, given the variety of military interventions and complexity of US foreign policy. Indeed, we may conclude that even the 'best' cases for a particular theory are still insufficient or weak. Nonetheless, it seems reasonable to let each theory put its 'best foot forward' and determine if these cases can withstand more rigorous scrutiny after their presentation. Having described three cases in each chapter that are likely candidates for supporting the various theories, I then assess the relative strengths and weaknesses of the cases to determine how powerful each theory is in explaining presidential decision making.

Introduction 19

The next step in each of these chapters is an analysis of historical data on the use of military force short of war in the pre-modern era, roughly 1798-1941. The information from these years is not as extensive and detailed as more recent data, but broad trends are often quite revealing. Subsequently I turn to the data-rich, post World War II era to test each of the theories in multivariate, statistical analyses. I outline several, specific predictions regarding the influence of variables related to each of the four theories in the period 1948-1998. Using the information or variables from each of the theories, I predict whether or not presidents will use force, given my definition of an 'opportunity to use force'. While these statistical models are necessarily incomplete without the inclusion of variables from the other theories, they do provide us with an indication of the explanatory power of each of the four theories taken individually. I conclude these chapters with an assessment of the theory's overall explanatory and predictive value.

I test all four of the theories together in Chapter 6 using the same methodology, but with all the heretofore separated variables brought together into one model. After testing the comprehensive model and assessing its strengths and weaknesses, as well as those of the four theories, I analyze the cases where the model performed well and performed poorly to better understand how it might be improved. I conclude in Chapter 7 by summarizing the findings, analyzing the strengths and weakness of the theories and their ability to explain the use of force in the future. By the end of this book the reader should know well the story of the political use of force in US foreign policy. Whether she begins with only the most cursory knowledge of the subject, after finishing the final page, she should understand that these phenomena are at once complex and predictable. Complex, because of the long and varied history of these operations. Predictable, because presidents have behaved in very similar and explainable ways across time when confronted with international crises.

In the end, we must ask why it is so important to explain these events. In addition to their importance in US foreign policy, their effects on all nations involved, and the scholarly confusion that cries out for clarity, I believe there is one other, important purpose served by this book. I believe that if we can understand why force is used, we also learn something about what it is to be an American. We learn what issues are important enough to the US that presidents would risk lives and devote much time and money to influence events outside the US. Is the US a nation of hardheaded realists interested only in protecting American security and assuring that no nation can ever challenge our independence? Or, is it a nation of idealists, trying to implant its notions of the good and the just on foreign cultures? Are American leaders men and women who look upon foreign policy as a means to enrich big businesses or bolster their own careers? Whatever the answer is, ultimately the use of force is not just an extension of US power, it is an extension of US values as well. How we define the goals behind these endeavors is the picture the US presents to the world of itself, lingering long after the troops have come home.

Chapter 2

Security, Power and Realist Explanations of the Political Use of Military Force

Introduction

When George W. Bush was campaigning for the White House in 2000 he asserted that he would not use military force unless it was in the national strategic interest. Presumably he was attempting to explain that he would only use force for important reasons, and perhaps by implication, his opponent, would not. Few chose to question what, exactly, the Republican candidate meant by this, including the Democratic contender, Vice President Al Gore. Bush did not elaborate on his definition of the term 'national strategic interest'. Presidents, almost without exception, explain their military deployments on the basis of national security or national interest. But what exactly do presidents mean by national security? How can we determine when national security is *not* driving the use of force if presidents always justify their behavior on that basis? Is there some method that we might use to objectively measure this term? Can we identify national security interests before they are acted upon or must we always resort to post hoc reasoning? These are just a few of the many questions that attach to this particular explanation of the use of force. In this chapter I will wade into the thicket of controversy concerning the role of security and power interests in the use of military force short of war by US presidents. What we find is that the security rationale is ubiquitous and powerful, yet highly manipulable and constantly evolving. The quest for security and power can explain many if not most uses of force through American history, but a security-oriented explanation succeeds at the price of being ill defined.

There is no one theory of the role of security and the use of force, although the international relations theory of realism comes closest. Thus, unlike diversionary theory or theories of economic imperialism and domination, we are not testing one particular theory of the political use of military force. Many scholars who have written histories of and conducted empirical inquiries into US foreign policy have stressed the importance of a variety of international developments and interests that we might agree have something to do with US security. Historical accounts often stress the importance of power and the acquisition of foreign territories to explain gunboat diplomacy. But, many of those who have written histories or analyzed the relevance of security in foreign policy have deliberately, and sometimes unwittingly, been more concerned with prescription than description. As Zakaria (1998, p.183) writes, '...most realist

Security, Power and Realist Explanations of the Political Use of Military Force 21

theories of foreign policy *entreat* states to act in certain ways' (emphasis added). That there is no general or grand 'theory' of security and foreign policy (again with realism as the next best thing) makes it difficult to test one. Instead, I will refer throughout this chapter to security and power 'explanations' of the use of force to scoop up realism and the various mid-level theories and other accounts of this foreign policy behavior. I join together the terms 'security' and 'power' as the two concepts are closely connected in international relations, and are often linked together. Still, I tend to use the term 'security' to encompass both and to avoid having to use the cumbersome conjunction of the two terms at all times.

Because the quest for security–to be secure in one's prosperity and freedom–is at the heart of US foreign policy, those threats that impinge upon national security in specific situations (e.g., threatening moves by North Korea along its demilitarized border with South Korea), or those more broad-spectrum challenges to US security (e.g., the Soviet threat during the Cold War) are often key to explaining the political use of military force. National security interests are generally the necessary and sufficient conditions for most uses of force. Other objectives typically can only be advanced to the extent to which they do not conflict with national security–it can 'trump' all other goals. As such, we must knit together the external forces and conditions that pose threats to the power and national security of the US into an integrative theory of the political use of military force. In this chapter I explain why national security and power are the central elements of our quest for an integrative and comprehensive theory of the political use of military force. I attempt to bring together many of the concepts identified by scholars studying national security policy into this theory while leaving room for the foreign policy objectives discussed in other chapters.

I first discuss various theories and accounts of the use of force that focus on security and power interests, especially realism. I then discuss three case studies of presidential decision-making and the use of force where we would expect that security considerations played a major role. These are: the 1818 invasion of Spanish Florida, the 1899 US intervention in Samoa and the 1948-1949 Berlin Airlift. Next, I review the history of these US security and power goals and interests, and the role of military force short of war in achieving these ends. I pay particular attention to the expansion and contraction of security interests, US power and the use of military force. Along the way, I review the empirical evidence on the use of force and security goals through descriptive statistics in the pre World War II era. Subsequently, I analyze the post World War II period and develop a multivariate model of the political use of military force using security and power indicators. I conclude with a discussion that suggests one method by which we might integrate security interests, power and the use of force in theories of foreign policy behavior.

Studies of Security and Power Interests and the Use of Force

Because there is no one theory of security/power and the use of force, but a wide variety of theories, histories, and statistical analyses, a review of the literature on

22   *The Political Use of Military Force in US Foreign Policy*

this subject must be widespread. I have attempted below to group these perspectives under various labels, although this categorization should not be considered determinative. It is merely suggestive as there is a great deal of overlap among the different categories. Hopefully, the reader will begin to understand just how diverse our understanding of this subject is.

Realism and its Relatives

To understand how security considerations affect the behavior of states, one necessarily turns first to realism, the long dominant, theoretical paradigm in the field of international relations. While it is not possible to describe the work of every realist scholar that bears on this subject, I will highlight those who have made the more substantial contributions to modern realism. There is no longer one strand of realist thought, but the original and its several variants that seek to extend and improve upon it. Recent realist-oriented theories of international relations and foreign policy include: neorealism (Gilpin, 1987; Waltz, 1979), offensive realism (Mearsheimer, 1990; Schweller, 1998; Zakaria, 1998) and defensive realism (Snyder, 1991). Increasingly, however, the lines are blurred between these new realist theories and other theories of foreign policy. Some incorporate the impact of domestic politics (e.g., offensive realism) on international behavior into their theoretical framework and so utilize many of the same hypotheses about state behavior we find in economic and diversionary theories. I will focus on the contributions made by these theories that enhance our understanding of how the international environment and security concerns affect a state's–the US–foreign policy.

Traditional or classical realism (or just plain 'realism') is a parsimonious theory of international relations premised on several assumptions or observations about the international environment. While most succinctly illustrated in the work of Hans Morgenthau, political theorists (e.g., Machiavelli, 1999; Hobbes, 1968), historians (e.g., Thucydides, 1996; Carr, 1946), diplomats (e.g., Kennan, 1951; Kissinger, 1994) and political scientists (e.g., Wolfers, 1962) have contributed to its theoretical development. The first assumption of realism is that the international environment is anarchic in that there is no superordinate body to control the actions of sovereign states. Second, these sovereign states are first and foremost interested in their security vis a vis other states. Without a superordinate international organization to protect them, states must rely on their own capabilities and exertions to safeguard their territory and independence. Security-seeking ultimately creates conflict as states take defensive measures that appear offensive to other states (i.e., the security dilemma). Third, states are conceived of as unitary actors with fixed preferences. That is, each state pursues its own, objectively determined national interest, regardless of changes in internal political or societal forces. A state's behavior internationally is determined by its capabilities, relative to other powers. Fourth, capabilities are the crucial determinant of international behavior and outcomes. They determine the type of polarity in the system, alliance configurations, conflict propensity and conflict outcomes. The more powerful the state, the more successful it is. Thus, power is what defines and separates realism

Security, Power and Realist Explanations of the Political Use of Military Force 23

from other schools of thought that would explain or prescribe state behavior based on economic, moral or legal factors. As a theory of international relations, realism is primarily focused on behavior that is jointly determined by the actions of two or more states. This also distinguishes realism from nation-specific and cross-national studies that explain the actions of individual units. Yet while the idealized theory of realism may admit little or no consideration of the affect of forces internal to the state (Legro and Moravcsik, 1999), one finds the writing of individual realists replete with analyses of the foreign policy making process.

The doyen of contemporary realism, Hans Morgenthau wrote extensively on the realist interpretation of American national interests. National interest, defined in large part in terms of power, is at the core of foreign policy and international relations. No matter what a state's ultimate objectives are in the world, power is always the immediate aim. Morgenthau also argues that wittingly or unwittingly, states strive to maintain an equilibrium or balance of power in international relations as the most natural and efficient way of securing peace (Morgenthau, 1973). Yet it is never clear in his writings whether he envisioned the concept of the balance of power as a prescription for security, or an inevitable result of states jockeying for primacy in international affairs. Morgenthau (1982) is clear in his criticism of the influence of subnational groups on foreign policy. Statesmen who confuse the interests of business, religion or world federalism with the national interest do so at the peril of their state's existence, for in an anarchic world, the state has only itself to defend against other states. The use of force is predominantly and should always be dictated by the pursuit of national security.

For Henry Kissinger (1994), 19th century, European diplomats like Richelieu, Metternich, Castlereigh, and Bismarck epitomized the ideal, foreign policy leader who recognizes the objective needs of the state and acts on the basis of national security. They understood that to survive in the world, one must take one's enemies and allies, as they are, not how one might like them to be. Kissinger stresses the importance of balances of power in maintaining peace and stability in the world, and the role of foreign policy makers in achieving this sort of equilibrium of forces. Naturally, he credits Richard Nixon and the foreign policy they engineered as one of the few attempts at bringing interests and actions into harmony (he 'concedes' that much of their work was thwarted or undone by the Congress and others). Like many realists, Kissinger's work informs our understanding of the use of force insofar as he describes when force *ought* to be used. But he also shares with many realists an unfortunate tendency to elaborate upon these criteria in an overly abstract manner. Maintaining a balance of power, protecting vital interests and ensuring the security of allies are all important interests, but can only be discerned on a case-by-case basis.

George Kennan is typically cast as a realist because of his sober and critical appraisals of US foreign policy. He is most famously known as the original author of the Cold War strategy of containment. Trained as a diplomat in the days of the elitist foreign policy establishment, Kennan has often criticized US foreign policy for being excessively legalistic, moralistic and overly influenced by capricious, public opinion. Without a corps of foreign policy practitioners protected against these vicissitudes of the body politic by strong-minded executives

24   *The Political Use of Military Force in US Foreign Policy*

and a compliant Congress, the nation's interests could not be prudently safeguarded. Kennan (1985, p.282) argued for a policy, '...founded on recognition of the national interest, reasonably conceived, as the legitimate motivation for a large portion of the nation's behavior' and a pursuit of '...that interest without either moral pretension or apology'. His inclusion in the realist camp thus has more to do with his opposition to idealistic foreign policy doctrines than a development of a unique, realist doctrine.

In response to those who would turn realism into a theory of foreign policy making, Kenneth Waltz (1979) developed neorealism. It shares many of the same assumptions of realism, but accords primacy to the role of the international system. Neorealism emphasizes the manner in which the balance of power internationally–determined by the distribution of capabilities–dictates international outcomes. At a minimum all states seek security and at a maximum, strive for universal domination (Waltz, 1979, p.118). Waltz emphasizes that in an anarchic environment, dominated by functionally similar units (sovereign states), we should observe naturally occurring balances of power and states becoming more alike over time as they mimic each other's successful international strategies. Neorealism is not, however, a theory of state behavior. In Waltz's words (1979, p.73), a systemic theory, 'can tell us what pressures are exerted and what possibilities are posed by systems of different structure, but it cannot tell us just how, and how effectively, the units of the system will respond to those pressures and possibilities'. As well, Waltz argued that balances of power occur in the international environment in much the same way as economic competition creates a degree of equilibrium among firms. It is more an inevitable consequence of the aggregated strategies of the component units of the system than a goal-directed outcome desired by these units. Many of Waltz's critics accused his theory of being overly deterministic, and even self-perpetuating. Subsequent scholars sought to expand the domain of realist and neorealist inquiry so that it could make better predictions about state behavior. This led to the study of many factors internal to states and international outcomes beyond those associated with conflict.

Taking Waltz to his logical conclusion, offensive realists argue that states seek to capitalize on power differentials to achieve greater levels of influence in world politics (e.g., Zakaria, 1998). Rose (1998, p.147) summarizes the offensive realist depiction of foreign policy activity as:

> the record of nervous states jockeying for position within the framework of a given systemic power configuration. To understand why a state is behaving in a particular way, offensive realists suggest, one should examine its relative capabilities and its external environment, because those factors will be translated relatively smoothly into foreign policy and shape how the state chooses to advance its interests.

Zakaria's study of US foreign policy behavior from 1865 to 1908 seeks to explain why early in this period the US refrained from an expansionist foreign policy, while later it embarked on numerous international undertakings. His central premise is that 'nations try to expand their political interests abroad when central

Security, Power and Realist Explanations of the Political Use of Military Force 25

decision-makers perceive a relative increase in state power' (Zakaria, 1998, p.38). State power is more than just material capabilities for it encompasses the ability of the state to extract resources from society. Christensen (1996) argues that state power also explains changes in US-Sino relations. Each side exploited conflict with the other to help justify its mobilization of resources. Extrapolating from this research, we might expect that as relative capabilities and state power expand, conflictual behavior, like the use of force short of war, will increase as well.

Defensive realism emphasizes the security dilemma of international politics. Because the anarchic, international environment forces states to take measures to protect themselves, any increase in one state's level of security compromises the security of other states. Defensive realism emphasizes the importance of factors other than the distribution of capabilities, such as the level of threat and the power of domestic political actors, in determining international outcomes. Because there is a great deal of uncertainty about states' power, strategy and preferences, leaders' beliefs and biases are important, and should be modeled along with the foreign policy making process. Snyder (1991) also argues that great power over expansion results from the demands of domestic, political coalitions with a stake in military spending and economic autarky on government (see also Kennedy, 1987; Olson, 1982). These groups tend to believe that a failure to expand ultimately weakens the state and their power over it. Such strategies are typically self-defeating, unless a state possesses a capacity for learning and attaining a balance between resources and commitments. Democracies are thought to have a better capacity for this type of learning and balancing.

Applying any of these realist theories to the study of a particular, US foreign policy activity, however, is difficult or inappropriate. Classical realism provides us with a useful framework for studying international relations, but its concept of the national interest, which might conceivably be used to explain state behavior, is necessarily vague and abstract. Indeed, there is a tautology in many analyses of this concept, for often the national interest is defined by identifying where the US does act. But if the national interest is where the US uses force, and if the US uses force to advance the national interest, we have learned very little about either concept. Waltz (1979) argues that his neorealism was not designed to make predictions about what nations will do at any point in time. Research into international activism by offensive and defensive realism scholars is more promising. Here we find that US international activity can be explained by domestic political institutions and power levels (Zakaria 1998) and rent-seeking, special interest groups. There is one area in which realists tend to be in agreement. Most accept the argument that increasing levels of power lead to greater foreign policy activity–a notion I will expand upon later.

Historical Research on US Military Intervention

Under this rubric one finds many historical accounts of particular military interventions as well as more comprehensive studies. I have chosen to focus on those works that specifically address the limited use of force and which take a more systematic approach to the subject. In an early, ambitious study of American interventionism, Tillema (1973) developed a framework with which to predict interventions and non-interventions. He argues that many theories and explanations for US interventions are inadequate because they are too universal and determinative. Theories based on imperialism, or simple anti-communism seem to imply that the US intervenes whenever its economic or political interests are threatened. Such theories cannot tell us when and why the US does not intervene in many cases. Tillema proposes the notion of decision-making restraints as a crucial factor in foreign policy deliberations. He argues that, '...there are restraints upon an ever-present tendency to resort to military force in crises, and that intervention will occur unless it is restrained' (1973, p.37). Tillema (1973, p.179) finds that large-scale interventions occur:

> When they [American leaders] believed that a communist government might be established in a country that did not have one. And military intervention has occurred when, and only when, restraints of the international system, the top-level decision-making process, and the shared moral values of foreign policy leaders have not operated.

Tillema only considers the Korea War, the 1958 Lebanon intervention, the 1965 Dominican Republic intervention and the Vietnam War cases as sufficiently large to be considered interventions, but his framework is still useful for studying other, smaller-scale uses of force. Most importantly, he highlights the importance of studying occasions when interventions were likely contemplated, but did not occur. Studies of the use of force short of war often do not explain cases where force might have been considered, but was not chosen. Tillema's work demonstrates that theories unable to account for the absence of the event being studied suffer from a form of selection bias, and ultimately are more difficult to falsify.

Richard Betts' analysis of nuclear diplomacy (1987) also provides an important advancement of the field. While Betts is chiefly interested in investigating the episodes in which the US utilized nuclear-capable units of its armed forces or threatened to use nuclear weapons, his inquiry has several implications for this study. He finds that more than anything else presidents focused on 'the political imperative of blocking the adversary's advance than on the danger of war if the enemy refused to desist and the dispute intensified' (Betts, 1987, p.213). Betts' analysis of the secondary importance of avoiding military confrontation with the Soviet Union when the US feels particularly aggravated by Soviet advances is also important. We would expect that presidents would refrain from using military force under such dangerous circumstances, as they often did during the Cold War (e.g., Hungary 1956; Czechoslovakia 1968).

In their ground-breaking study of the political use of military force, Blechman and Kaplan (1978) devote most of their attention to describing the location, time, type of deployment and the success of uses of military force from 1946-1976. In addition, the authors developed a simple model predicting the annual frequency of uses of the military. Utilizing only the presence and lingering effects of the Korean and Vietnam wars, national confidence and the number of opportunities to use force to predict the frequency of uses of force from 1946 through 1976, the authors are able to show a reasonably good fit for their model. Interestingly, however, they conclude that it is nearly impossible to predict military actions on a case-by-case basis without access to decision making participants and relevant documents. Nonetheless, in the case-study portion of their study, Blechman and Kaplan highlight the role of communist involvement in crises in alerting presidents to threats to American interests.

Brands (1987) examines three noteworthy American military interventions (Dominican Republic, Lebanon and Grenada) to highlight the types of factors presidents consider when confronted with an international crisis. He concludes that the most critical factors inducing an application of force include a history of instability in a region, a rapid progression of events, which encourages bureaucratic consensus, endangered American lives, and the shadow of past failures or problems elsewhere. While Brands is able to shed additional light on the concerns weighing on presidents, his selection of just the well-known cases, like many others who study these phenomena, inhibits somewhat the external validity of his work. While it is very important for any model to be able to predict these major military operations, their prominence should not obscure the insights to be gained from examining less well-known cases.

More recently Boot (2002) analyzes the history of US involvement in the 'savage wars of peace'. These are variously defined as 'low-intensity' operations, small wars, or 'military operations other than war' (Boot, 2002, p.xv). Boot seems to have in mind operations generally more violent than most of the post World War II political uses of force, but less violent than all-out war. While his event histories are more germane to understanding the value and wisdom of these operations, he does also provide insight into their causes and frequency. Most tellingly, Boot argues that one of the principal determinants of the frequency of these uses of force is their cost, particularly in terms of the likelihood of escalating to full-scale and violent war. When such perceived costs or probabilities are low, demand for such interventions grows. In the pre and post Cold War era such costs were relatively low, but during the Cold War when it was feared larger military operations might result in a nuclear confrontation, their numbers declined. This observation seems to apply primarily to those violent or at least more aggressive operations Boot considers. Given the hundreds of military operations the US engaged in during the Cold War that did not rise to this level, his conclusions seem to pertain to a much smaller universe of events.

Conflict Strategy

In the 1950s and 1960s conflict strategists (George and Smoke, 1974; Kaufman, 1955; Schelling, 1960, 1966) analyzed a variety of reasons why states would resort to force short of war and how force might be used as a bargaining tool. They were primarily interested in understanding the dynamics of crisis escalation and resolution and how states could best manage and win in these situations. But while there is a considerable prescriptive angle to their work, their analyses of what leads states to become involved in crises is insightful. First, many argue that there is an interdependence of US commitments such that a threat to one is a threat to all.

The Political Use of Military Force in US Foreign Policy

Few parts of the world are inherently worth fighting over, but defending them or running risks to protect them will help preserve other commitments in other parts of the world. Schelling (1960) finds brinkmanship–manipulating the shared risk of war–a useful policy, especially in the nuclear age. He argues that state leaders have an incentive to take limited, but nonetheless risky actions to demonstrate commitment. Because it is so difficult to make a costly commitment believable (e.g., nuclear retaliation), states must find ways to demonstrate their resolve. Many researchers argue that states may restrict their freedom of action or take dangerous risks to solidify in an adversary's mind the certainty of a commitment. Discrete uses of military force are particularly effective in communicating one's willingness to run risks and protect interests, hence deterring future aggression.

Other scholars have documented the US concern over the maintenance of credibility. Johnson (1985), for example, argued that US foreign-policy makers moved away from the classical model of national interest making when making commitments, to a Cold War model of interest formation. In the classical realist model, nations establish some objective criteria of foreign-policy interests that determine commitments abroad. After determining the extent of their interest, nations project resources to conquer or defend, which in turn determine the credibility of their promise to protect these interests. In the Cold War model, however, commitments were made not because some state or region was intrinsically of value, but because a failure to act might have led other nations to believe the US would not respond with military force when similar situations arose in the future. Interests were determined by the quantity of resources a nation poured into another state to maintain its credibility. Presidents used force to demonstrate credibility, not necessarily to protect or advance tangible, national interests.

According to Gaddis (1982) the salient debate in US foreign policy over credibility has been over whether the military should be used to deter almost all forms of communist aggression (a constant concern for credibility), or just where the US has local superiority (concern for credibility in only some areas). Similarly, Schell writes that the aim of US foreign policy makers was, 'to establish in the minds of peoples and their leaders throughout the world an image of the US as a nation that possessed great power and had the will and determination to use it in foreign affairs (1976, p.342). The concern for credibility is especially prominent in a hegemon's foreign policy since would-be challengers are continually probing for signs or points of weakness. We will return to these arguments later when I discuss the importance of past uses of force, and their implied commitment and engagement of US credibility, on presidential decision making.

Quantitative Studies

Several scholars conducting empirical studies of the use of force, principally focused on domestic political calculations, have included select, 'security' variables in their analyses. Beginning with Ostrom and Job (1986), researchers have examined the impact of various aspects of the international environment on presidential decision-making and the political use of military force. Ostrom and Job (1986), James and Oneal (1991) and James and Hristoulas (1994) all found that when the public is concerned about foreign policy, there is a positive relationship between US-Soviet tension and the likelihood of a major use of force. Presidents are less likely to use force when the nuclear balance favors the US and the public rates foreign policy issues as important. These scholars, like almost all others, also find that when the US was involved in the Korean and Vietnam wars, the probability of a use of force declined as logged, cumulative US battle deaths rose. Measures like these convey a great deal of information about broad incentives and constraints on the use of force. The intensity of the US-Soviet competition during the early years of the Cold War seemed to have played a crucial role in encouraging US involvement in many heretofore obscure places. Involvement in war limited US ability to intervene and probably dampened enthusiasm for such endeavors as well. These variables can tell us that presidents were more likely to use force during particular periods, but not which crisis-specific factors may have led presidents to deploy the military during some crises and not others.

In order to identify these factors, we must look to other studies that examine US behavior in international crises. Using a rational choice model, Wang (1996, p.85) finds that a, 'higher expected value for war and greater costs for backing down are associated with higher severity levels in US responses to crises'. The choice to use force short of war may be conceptually similar to the decision to go to war–both lie on a continuum of aggressive, foreign policy behavior. Thus, Yoon (1997) shows that the US is more likely to intervene in third world, internal wars when an ally of the Soviet Union is involved and when there is a communist presence in the conflict. Few other factors, including USSR intervention, US military assistance to the nation, the distance between the US and the conflict, as well as US economic interests are statistically significant predictors of US intervention behavior. DeRouen (2000) also finds that USSR crisis activity is positively related to the use of force. Meernik (1994, 2000) in studies of presidential decision-making during international crises shows that crisis-specific factors are highly predictive of the use of force. Anti-American violence, the number of actors in a crisis, and a prior use of military force by the US in the crisis locale are positively related to the use of force. Using similar data, Meernik and Waterman (1996) find that environmental variables, like superpower tension, the nuclear balance and US war deaths influence the likelihood of a use of force.

These studies tell us a great deal about the impact of macro and micro-level forces that affect presidential decision-making. This knowledge can be built into a broader theory of security and the political use of military force. But since

30   *The Political Use of Military Force in US Foreign Policy*

few of these scholars were actually testing a theory of security and the use of force (Wang [1996] is probably the best exception of those cited above), it is difficult to place their findings into a theoretical context. There exists a cumulation of findings, but not an integration. Until such time as we sort out this evidence and assemble it into a meaningful whole, the task of explaining how security interests influence the decision to use force will remain difficult. Therefore, we must weave together disparate strands of research to identify factors that are likely important in these decisions, and to move toward a more integrative framework or theoretical basis for studying the limited use of force. In the absence of general theory, this is probably the best we can manage. The silver lining is that we have greater flexibility in testing security explanations and no scholarly dogmas to dominate our research.

Security and Power and the Use of Force: Three Case Studies

As I will do in all chapters, I select three notable uses of force short of war for more intensive study. Each of these cases, the 1818 invasion of Spanish Florida, the 1899 intervention in Samoa, and the 1948 Berlin airlift, seem to involve matters of critical importance to US security. The first involved the protection of its borders, the second concerned the defense of territory believed to be vital to the needs of the US Navy, and the last involved the defense of a key ally. A strong case can therefore be made that in each instance the US used force primarily to defend or advance national security, instead of ideological, political or economic interests. After reviewing the history of each event and the security rationale for the use of force, I assess the utility of the 'security/power' explanation.

The Invasion of Florida

There have been few occasions in the nation's history since the War of 1812 when US territory has been attacked. The US has enjoyed unparalleled security at home given its weak neighbors and the vast oceans around it. One of the most nettlesome territorial issues affecting the US in the early years of its history involved the Spanish presence in Florida. Divided into an East Florida that extended from the Atlantic to the Apalachicola River, and a West Florida that then ran out to the Perdido River, just east of Mobile, the Spanish possessions were viewed as ripe for the plucking. Spain scarcely had a presence in the territory and was preoccupied with revolts in Latin America. Florida's location on the border of the most southern US state, Georgia, seemed to make it more naturally a part of the US than a European empire. But negotiations between the US envoy to Spain, George Erving, and the Spanish government had made little progress since they began in 1815. Three years later, President James Monroe was ready to apply additional pressure to the Spanish to disgorge their lands. He ordered the occupation of Amelia Island, which lay just inside West Florida at the mouth of

Security, Power and Realist Explanations of the Political Use of Military Force 31

the St. Mary's River on the Atlantic. Spanish revolutionaries, pirates, slave traders and smugglers used the island as a staging point for their activities and Spain proved unable to stop them. But when President Monroe's move did not cause Spain to fully meet US demands, Monroe decided to take more forceful action to help the negotiations along. He authorized General Andrew Jackson, the vain, temperamental hero of the Battle of New Orleans, to launch operations against Seminole Indians in Florida who had been attacking settlers in Georgia, supposedly with Spanish connivance. Jackson was given authority to attack and pursue the Indians into Spanish territory, but he was not to attack them if they took refuge in Spanish forts. That would be tantamount to an act of war, which only the Congress could declare. Jackson, however, was not one to worry about such legalistic niceties.

The General thought he had a better idea and wrote directly to the President. He proposed that, 'The whole of East Florida [should be] seized and…this can be done without implicating the government. Let it be signified to me through any channel, (say Mr. J. Rhea) that the possession of the Floridas would be desirable…and in sixty days it will be accomplished' (quoted in James, 1938, p.283). After Jackson had left Tennessee in February of 1818, with an advance party of two mounted companies, he received a letter from the President, although it could not have been written before Monroe received Jackson's letter given the vast distances involved. Monroe wrote, 'The mov'ment…against the Seminoles…will bring you on a theatre where you may possibly have other services to perform…Great interests are at issue…This is not a time for repose…untill (sic) our cause is carried triumphantly thro'' (quoted in James, 1938, pp.283-284). Jackson believed that these veiled hints constituted all the authority he needed to take whatever action was necessary to pacify the Floridas. He and Monroe had been of like mind about the inevitable ceding of the Floridas to the US. As well, his orders from the Secretary of War, John Calhoun ordered Jackson to, 'Adopt the necessary measures to terminate….the conflict' (quoted in James, 1938, p.283). After he joined up with the main force of his army in southern Georgia, Jackson headed straight into Florida with 3000 men and 2000 Native Americans allies.

He had received word that the Seminoles in Florida had demanded arms from the commander of the Spanish fort at St. Marks and were probably controlling the town. As well, there were supposed to be many runaway slaves who were hiding in the area. The Spanish commander, who did not have the forces to contest Jackson, surrendered the fort without a shot, but there were no Indians or runaway slaves. Jackson, who said he needed the fort as a base of operations, commandeered it from the Spanish and raised the American flag. Jackson and his forces then plunged further into Florida, burning and destroying villages and taking whatever supplies they wanted. They next attacked the village of Chief Boleck, but found it deserted too. It was a successful campaign of terror, for the Indians continued to flee deeper into the Florida swamps. On May 5, 1818 Jackson notified Calhoun that he would invade West Florida and probably take Pensacola. He had received information that hundreds of Indians were massing there and with

Spanish aid, were getting ready to attack American settlements. As Jackson's forces neared the town the Spanish governor warned him away and said that if Jackson persisted, there would be a battle. Unconcerned, Jackson began his attack on May 25 and by May 30 the garrison surrendered (James, 1938). Then in a brazen display of power and contempt for international and political conventions, Jackson 'seized the royal archives, appointed one of his colonels military and civil governor, and declared in force the "revenue laws of the U. States"' (James, 1938, p.291). Feeling ill after the taxing campaign through the swamps, Jackson retired back to Tennessee. It did not take long before the political fallout began.

The Spanish protested that what Jackson had done amounted to an act of war. They demanded the forts back and that Jackson be censured for his conduct. The President and cabinet deliberated for many days about the most judicious course of action. On the one hand, no one was desirous of a war with Spain since they feared the other European powers would come to the aid of their royal friends. And some members of the cabinet were shocked at Jackson's willingness to ignore his instructions and appoint a military government without the approval of Washington. But, everyone, especially President Monroe, was mindful of the general's great popularity. After his case was aggressively made by John Quincy Adams, the cabinet finally decided that since Jackson had acted on his own, he would not be censured, but that the forts would be returned to the Spanish. Fearing an explosion of Jackson's volcanic temper when he found out that his position and conquest would not be completely supported, Monroe wrote a very deferential letter to the general. He tried to make Jackson understand that he agreed with what ultimately was done by saying, 'I am aware that cases may occur when the commanding general, acting on his own responsibility, may safely pass the limit...[of his orders] with essential advantage to his country' (quoted in James, 1938, p.293). And while the general's gains might have to be reversed in the short term, Madison opined, 'There is much reason to presume that this action will furnish a strong inducement to Spain to cede the territory. The manner in which we propose to act will exculpate you from censure, and promises to obtain all the advantages you contemplate' (James, 1938, pp.293-294). In the end, Spain continued to negotiate with the US over the fate of Florida. On February 22nd, 1819, a treaty was signed ceding Florida to the US for five million dollars.

President Monroe and his cabinet pursued one primary objective throughout Jackson's invasion, even if at times they questioned his methods. They believed that the security of the US and the defense of its citizens required the acquisition of Florida from Spain. When they perceived that peaceful negotiation was not working, they agreed that a more forceful demonstration of US power and Spanish weakness was necessary. Why was Spanish Florida so important to a country that already was expanding in multiple directions? First, there was the matter of the Seminole raids from Florida and the use of Florida by runaway slaves. The Indian attacks into US territory did not exactly constitute a foreign invasion, but they were a problem to the settlers in Georgia who demanded that the government take action. Jackson himself claimed that, 'So long as Spain has not the power...to preserve the Indians within her territory at peace with the U States, no security can be given to our Southern frontier...' (quoted in Remini, 1977,

Security, Power and Realist Explanations of the Political Use of Military Force   33

p.360). The safe haven for runaway slaves was also a thorn in the side to the slave holding states in the South, although the number of slaves numbered only in the low hundreds.

John Quincy Adams, who had been charged with defending Jackson's actions to the Spanish argued that in all its operations the US had rightfully acted in self-defense. Because the Spanish were unable to exercise control over the Floridas, the US was entitled to pursue the Indians, smugglers and runaway slaves under international law (from the US point of view). Furthermore, Adams argued, since Spain could not administer her lands, she ought to cede them. The president, his cabinet and most members of Congress wanted to take possession of Florida because they believed that the land naturally belonged to the US. It was part of the mainland of the US and touched upon many rivers and harbors that would prove vital to American commerce in the coming years. And while the chances were slight that Spain might enlist the aid of other European powers to retain Florida or cede it to one of them, presidents felt they had to guard against even this remote possibility. In addition, as long as the Floridas remained in European hands, the lands could be used as a staging point for an invasion of the US by any of the European powers. Even the question of recognizing the independence of Spain's other colonies in the New World was made subservient to the acquisition of Florida. Throughout the 1810s the US had refrained from providing any material aid to the rebels for fear of angering the Spanish and hurting the negotiations over Florida. Therefore, we can make a compelling argument that this military operation was undertake to advance American security.

Taking Sides in Samoa

The US entered one of its more isolationist periods after the Civil War. Despite the best efforts of several presidents and their expansionist-minded secretaries of state, Congress repeatedly rebuffed attempts at obtaining new territories, whether by purchase or outright annexation. That the US should take an interest in the Pacific Samoan islands in the years right after the war was rather unusual. That it would enter into a power-sharing arrangement with Great Britain and Germany that many in the US characterized as an 'entangling alliance', was even more remarkable. The military intervention in Samoa that I will discuss took place later, in 1899, but it is enlightening to first cover the events that led up to this incident. I am indebted to and borrow heavily from Kennedy's (1974) excellent analysis of US involvement in Samoan politics for this case study.

The Samoan islands, which lie roughly 2300 miles southwest of Hawaii, were not considered as strategically or economically important as those islands, but there was an excellent harbor at the smaller Samoan island of Tutuila—Pago Pago. Pago Pago was thought to be an ideal coaling station for naval vessels as the US became more involved in Asian, especially Chinese trade. The Commander of the USS *Narragansett* concluded a treaty with a Tutuilan chief on February, 14, 1872 for the exclusive privilege of establishing a naval station. The US Senate, however, refused to act on the treaty. A similar treaty was signed in 1878, but this

34   *The Political Use of Military Force in US Foreign Policy*

time the House of Representatives declined to appropriate the money to build the naval station (Kennedy, 1974, p.14). Under the terms of this treaty, however, the US was given the power to provide its good offices if problems occurred between Samoa and other countries. While the power itself was not substantial, it did place the US government squarely in the middle of the turbulent Samoan politics along with the British and German governments. All three governments were maneuvering for special rights to own land and interject their preferences into the continual problems of Samoan succession. These are the disputes that ultimately led to the US military intervention.

There was no recognized manner of succession to be the chief king in Samoa. There were four royal lines and when one king held all four titles he was considered to be paramount chief, but these titles could be given and taken away by the tribal groups (Kennedy, 1974). Such arrangements had worked reasonably well for the Samoans, but they created ample opportunity for meddling by the whites seeking to advance the cause of this or that chief most compliant to their interests. The roots of the US intervention in 1899 have their beginnings in succession problems in August of 1887 when the US, Great Britain and Germany squared off over which leader was entitled to be paramount chief. The Germans were pushing one candidate for the throne, Tamasese, and after the current king backed by the US and Great Britain refused to step down, 700 German marines were landed and the Germans set up a new government under Tamasese (Kennedy, 1974, pp.76-87). The British and American consuls protested these German machinations even while the German government was negotiating in Washington D.C. over a tripartite arrangement for governing the islands. Eventually the presence of German warships attracted considerable media attention in the US, especially on the West Coast. With an election coming up, something needed to be done. President Grover Cleveland sent a warship to the islands to protest German actions. This, coupled with German Chancellor Bismarck's desire not to make an enemy of the US, caused the Germans to back down. A conference was called to resolve all the Samoan issues. But the agreement that the conference produced was just another recipe for gridlock as all three nations maintained a role in Samoan politics (Kennedy, 1974).

In 1898 conflicts over succession to the throne erupted once again with the Germans backing one faction and the US and Great Britain another. When the succession controversy began, both the US and British representatives counseled their governments not to back the German plan to bring in their favored leader, Mata'afa, from exile. But these two consuls departed soon after and their replacements agreed to the German plan to place Mata'afa on the throne. Just as Mata'afa was returning from the Marshall Islands, the old king died and several contenders began vying for the throne. The US and British governments soon grew suspicious of German motives and decided to advance their own candidate, Tanu, the son of the dead king. The two countries feared that Germany would use the succession controversy in order to finally annex the islands. The dispute over the throne was submitted to a special, European judge provided for in the Berlin agreement that had ended the dispute in 1888. On New Year's Eve, 1898, the judge awarded the throne to Tanu. Mata'afa and the Germans would not accept the

Security, Power and Realist Explanations of the Political Use of Military Force 35

verdict and war broke out (Kennedy, 1974). Then the USS *Philadelphia*, under the command of Rear Admiral Albert Kautz appeared to protect Americans and their interests. After reviewing the recent events, on March 11, 1899 Kautz declared that a government led by Mata'afa was in violation of the Berlin agreement (Kennedy, 1974, p.152). He ordered the government dissolved, but the Germans refused to accept his ultimatum.

Several of Mata'afa's canoes went to occupy strategic points along the coast, but were shelled by the *Philadelphia*. Kautz requested that the British ship, HMS *Porpoise,* open fire on several villages friendly to Mata'afa. In retaliation, Mata'afa's forces attacked white establishments including the UK and US consulates. Kautz ordered US Marines to go ashore with the British to attack Mata'afa's forces. For several days the US and British ships bombarded coastal villages and sent Marines into the jungles to pursue Mata'afa's force and attack villages friendly to him. The British and US organized native armies under Tanu and continued to attack Mata'afa until they felt strong enough to name Tanu as king. The battles continued until the end of April when a cease-fire was arranged. Germany, the UK and the US agreed to form a three-member commission (one representative from each nation) to investigate the disturbances and report back (Kennedy, 1974).

The Commission decided to pay all the Samoan forces for their weapons in order to disarm the combatants and pacify the islands. While Tanu was ultimately recognized as the legitimate king, he and Mata'afa were persuaded to renounce their claims. Kautz then sailed away. For the time being the governance of Samoa was left in the hands of the three powers, which were supposed to act in concert, but the commissioners encouraged their respective governments to allow for a territorial division of Samoa. Subsequently, an arrangement was adopted and the US gained the island Tutuila, with its port of Pago Pago and some additional islands to the east. Germany acquired the rest of Samoa and Great Britain was compensated with gains elsewhere in the Pacific (Kennedy, 1974).

What explains this long-lasting American involvement and use of force in what for most US citizens at the time was a tiny speck of land in the middle of nowhere? The most obvious and concrete interest was the acquisition of a naval station. While the Congress often proved reluctant to acquire a base, there were many in the Department of the Navy and the White House who recognized the value of such real estate, especially after the US acquired Hawaii and the Philippines. It is no surprise that the US finally agreed to Samoa's annexation shortly after the Spanish-American War. At the same time, the US was becoming increasingly involved in Asian politics, especially in China. If the US wanted to back up its interests and diplomacy, it would need to be able to project naval force in this region, which in turn would require coaling stations.

The US was also highly suspicious of German interests in the region and German foreign policy in general. During the Spanish-American War, there had been a sizeable German naval flotilla around the Philippines. The Germans claimed their presence was due to an administrative change of crews among the ships, but in actuality, the Germans were waiting to see if the US decided to attack

36   *The Political Use of Military Force in US Foreign Policy*

the Spanish presence there. If the US declined the opportunity, the Germans would be ready to move in (Kennedy, 1974, p.139). Even after the Dewey's fleet captured the Philippines, the German warships lingered menacingly. American attitudes toward the German government were also highly suspicious. Many newspapers published scathing editorials about Germany. The *Washington Post* wrote, 'We know by a thousand unmistakable signs and by the experience of years, that in the German government the US has a sleepless and insatiable enemy' (quoted in Kennedy, 1974, p.141). As the US drew nearer to Great Britain after many years of hostility, it began to perceive the Kaiser's colonial intrigues with increasing concern.

Finally, there was a general sense in the government that the US was finally due the respect accorded a great power. As the government's instructions to its delegates during one of the many conferences over the fate of Samoa stated, 'in any question involving present or future relations in the Pacific, this government cannot accept even temporary subordination, and must regard it as inconsistent with that international consideration and dignity to which the US, by its continental position and expanding interest must always be entitled' (quoted in Ryden, 1933, p.429). Such demands for deference may not directly influence security, but they do indicate the extent to which the US government was coming to look upon the Pacific Ocean as an American lake in which its interests ought to be preeminent. Given US interests in projecting naval force and guarding against rival powers, especially Germany, the US had numerous security interests on which to justify its armed intervention in Samoan politics. But are there other possible explanations? I address these below.

The Berlin Airlift

After World War II, the German city of Berlin was divided into four sectors, although it was supposed to be governed as one unit. An Allied Control Council, made up of representatives from the US, the Soviet Union, Great Britain and France, was empowered to make the most important decisions, but the allies allowed for limited administrative control by the Berliners in a City Hall, or Magistrat. From the very beginning, however, the Soviets made life difficult for those in the Western sector. They stripped Berlin clean of anything useful for reparations and as revenge. They insisted that the Western allies would have to provide for their sectors' needs from western Germany and would also have to ensure that western Germany continued to compensate the Soviet Union for all of its losses. To make matters worse, the Soviets were reluctant to provide the Western powers reliable access through the German territory they occupied. When questions first arose over how and where the Western states would travel to Berlin, both the US and British militaries assumed that such technical matters would be worked out on the spot and would not pose significant problems. They evidently thought the Soviets would continue to cooperate with them after the war ended. Additionally, some Americans and British were reluctant to specify certain routes to Berlin as acceptable for fear that any route not listed would become permanently off limits.

Security, Power and Realist Explanations of the Political Use of Military Force 37

After repeated instances where US and British military trains were stopped by Russians demanding to search the cars and occupants–a violation of allied agreements–General Eisenhower and the British general Montgomery sent their deputies to negotiate with the Russians for clearer and stronger assurances of Western access. The two deputies, General Lucius Clay and Sir Ronald Weeks met with the Soviet Marshall Zhukov and demanded two rail routes each, one highway route each and several air corridors (Jackson, 1988, p.18). Zhukov, however, convinced them they could make do with half the land routes and more limited air space. The agreements were reached verbally, and were not even forwarded to Washington D.C. until April of 1948 (Tusa and Tusa, 1988, pp.31-32). Everyone assumed this would be a temporary arrangement and that when the Allied Control Council met later, permanent agreements would be reached. The Allies continued to abide Soviet obstructionism and promises in order to maintain unity and Soviet involvement in the war against Japan.

But while the Allies learned to live with such compromises, West Berliners began to fear that eventually they would be absorbed into the Russian sector. After the war's devastation of their capital, the Soviets' insatiable demands for reparations, severe winters and the difficulties of feeding the city, Berliners were quite pessimistic about their chances for survival. And as their economic problems mounted, so too did Soviet intransigence. The Russians refused to consider any loosening of the restrictions on importing food. Their East Berlin police would reach into the West to beat up and arrest East German residents suspected of being sympathetic to the Western cause. Their allies in the Magistrat began forcing out those who cooperated with the West. All through 1946 and 1947 the pressure continued to increase and the Allied Control Council became completely stalemated. The US and Great Britain began to take unilateral measures to alleviate the suffering in their sectors. Talks were held in London, without the Russians, about integrating Germany, providing limited self-government, and most importantly, getting the German economy moving again to help all of Europe. One key element in the Western plan was to introduce currency reform (Tusa and Tusa, 1988). Hopes for prosperity required new currency backed by a central bank to deal with inflationary pressures.

Events escalated rapidly in the Cold War in the spring of 1948. In February there was a communist coup in Czechoslovakia. On March 20 the USSR representative on the Allied Control Council declared that the Council was finished and walked out (Jackson, 1988, p.35). The Allies assumed the Russians were preparing to squeeze them out of the city, but they did not quite know how. Some thought this might be done by cutting off all communications, seizing roads or taking over city government. General Clay, now in charge of the US sector, wrote to Washington that though he had previously doubted war would come, now it might come with 'dramatic suddenness' (Tusa and Tusa, 1988, p.99). On March 30, the Russians announced they would now inspect everything–people and goods–that came into Berlin, in clear violation of numerous agreements the Allies had reached (Jackson, 1988, p.36). The US insisted that it would only give them passenger lists and that Soviet personnel would not be allowed to board military

38 The Political Use of Military Force in US Foreign Policy

trains. When the US and Great Britain tested the Soviet decree by sending military trains to Berlin, Soviet forces refused to let them pass without boarding. The Allies ordered the trains to turn around and go back.

Though the Russians began putting all sorts of nuisance restrictions on river traffic, mail, roads and the like, they continued to let food and supplies into Berlin. Then on June 1, 1948 the London Conference on Germany ended with the West telling the Germans it was time to organize for self-government and announcing that currency reforms would be introduced shortly in West Berlin. When the reforms were actually implemented on June 18, the Soviets stopped all ground traffic into West Berlin and shut off the supply of electricity. The Allies scrambled to provide for Berlin, but their options for ending or managing the blockade were limited. At first it was believed that the blockade would not last long before the two sides reached some sort of compromise. Few believed that a long-term effort to supply Berlin through the air would work given the vast needs of the city (it was estimated it would need 12,000 tons of supplies a day to survive at the pitifully low, post-war levels [Tusa and Tusa, 1988, p.162]). In addition, extra supplies would be needed for the winter, and in all likelihood, there would be fewer flying days during the bad weather months. What little advance planning had occurred involved the logistics of evacuating the West and its entourage, not supplying the entire city indefinitely. And even though the Soviets had violated numerous agreements, confronting them with military force was not a viable option. The West was not prepared for war. Months would be needed before enough troops and supplies would be ready. Thus, any move that might provoke war, such as sending an armed column of troops and engineers down the Autobahn to test Soviet resolve, might very well end in catastrophe for the West.

Early in the crisis the Truman administration did decide that some show of force was needed to demonstrate that the allies would not be intimidated. As Tusa and Tusa wrote (1988, p.88), 'Nearly everyone had reached the conclusion that if the Western powers were to leave Berlin, it would be a grave blow to their prestige in Europe and would undoubtedly result in the whole of Germany coming under the control of the Soviet Union'. Truman ordered two squadrons of B-29 bombers to Great Britain, one of which would continue to Germany. The B-29's were significant because they were equipped to carry atomic weapons, even though the bombs did not accompany the planes across the Atlantic (Betts, 1987, p.25). Truman had hoped to demonstrate to the Soviets that the West was serious about its rights in Berlin and might be prepared to use tremendous force to protect them. The administration believed the transferal was the appropriate signal–not too weak and not too strong–although given that the blockade lasted over a year after the bombers' redeployment, it is not clear that the message had much effect.

The Allies, primarily the US and Great Britain rose to the challenge of supplying the city. More planes from the US and British armed forces were called into service, as were civilian aircraft. Runways and facilities in West Germany were expanded and improved, and new air traffic control teams were formed and trained in the US. The complex logistics of deciding which supplies to carry on what planes and when were hashed out in the first few months. The West exerted every effort it could to make life bearable for Berliners, who were still worried that

Security, Power and Realist Explanations of the Political Use of Military Force 39

eventually the Allies would be driven out of Berlin. Fortunately for the West, the winter weather of 1948-1949 turned out better than expected and there were many more flying days than originally planned. Thus, by the end of the spring of 1949, aircraft were landing approximately every three minutes, 24 hours a day (Tusa and Tusa, 1988, p.267). By April, 7800 tons of supplies were brought in daily. Confidence grew and soon the question became, not when the West would accede to Soviet demands, but when the Soviets would finally relent. Enough supplies had been laid in that the Allies could plan on airlifting indefinitely. It must have become clear to the Russians that not only were the immediate aims of the blockade failing, for living conditions in West Berlin were superior in many respects to those in the Soviet sector, but the blockade was also encouraging and speeding up the creation of the West German state, Western European economic recovery and US involvement in Europe. A West German state was to come into existence shortly, Marshall plan aid and German recovery were helping the economies of the other Western European nations, and the North Atlantic Treaty Organization agreement was signed in April. And to make matters worse, the limited economic sanctions the Allies had imposed on East Germany were making life there worse than in the West. The blockade turned out to be a huge foreign policy blunder for the Soviet Union. After several months of back channel negotiations, the Russians settled for little in exchange for lifting the blockade. They were given assurances that there would be a Council of Foreign Ministers meetings among the major powers, and that a West German government would not be set up before or during the sessions. The Soviets agreed to lift the blockade on May 12, but the USSR continued to prevent trains from reaching Berlin, forbid the use of the autobahn at night, and interfered with air traffic. The airlift continued through August as the Soviets gradually lessened their interference. By the end of the September, the Berlin Airlift was, for all intents and purposes, over (Haydock, 1999, p.274).

The Berlin Airlift operation seems to provide an easy test case for security-based explanations of the political use of military force. Although the US government initially believed that the blockade was more a temporary nuisance than a major challenge to US interests in Europe, once foreign policy makers understood that the Soviet effort was not a repeat of similar tactics used in the past, they directed all available resources to meet the challenge. The response was two pronged. The US military developed and directed the airlift of supplies, known as 'Operation Vittles'. Second, President Truman took steps to demonstrate American and Allied resolve to the Soviets and the nations of Western Europe. He ordered the B-29 bombers to Europe, and asked Congress for authorization to begin selective service. And if there were some in the government who were willing to discuss the possibility of a Western withdrawal from Berlin, only a few weeks into the crisis, the President, Secretary of State Marshall, General Clay and others were providing unconditional guarantees to the Berliners. President Truman and his closest national security advisers came to understand that a capitulation to the Soviets in Berlin would make their commitment to West Germany open to question. This would encourage those in the West who sought to appease the

Soviets, and would make economic planning and recovery more difficult for all of Western Europe. The Berlin blockade was the first of many tests of Western commitment to the isolated city and to the defense of Western Europe. Once the US concluded that its security depended on a free and prosperous West Europe, including West Berlin, there could be no backing down. Thus, despite many later Soviet demands to resolve West Berlin's status to their satisfaction, the US never relented from the positions it took first during the Berlin airlift.

Assessing the Evidence

In the case of the US invasion of Spanish Florida, there was a fine line between the need for secure borders, and the desire for territorial aggrandizement. Had Monroe been solely concerned with protecting US settlers and slaveholders, he might have provided more explicit orders to Jackson not to seize Spanish lands and to confine his operations to dealing with the Indians. But the President saw larger interests at stake here. The question is whether or not those interests were related to a concern for American security, or a broader drive to expand US territory for reasons other than national security.

First, the Monroe administration looked upon the Floridas, as did many other Americans, as a natural and inevitable part of the US. Monroe was convinced that it was the US' interest and destiny to reign over the continental landmass. Some in Washington even believed that the US was destined to control all of North America, and perhaps even South America. Only the US could bring the benefits of good government and economic prosperity to these lands and their inhabitants. And having been shut out of expanding northward into Canada after US losses in the War of 1812, expansionist politicians naturally looked southward and westward where the opposition was weak. Second, many Americans were interested in the commercial advantages of adding more land, more rivers and more ports to the US. Americans in the far south, who were starting to feel the need to acquire and exploit fresh lands, could expand into these new possessions. Southern politicians recognized that the expansion south and west could be used to attract votes from restless would-be settlers. Third, in light of the coming battles over the expansion of slavery into the frontier, one cannot help but think that many southern states viewed the Floridas as suitable for their 'peculiar institution'. As well, several slave states might be carved out of this region and tip the balance of power in the Congress.

The intermingling of economic, political, imperialistic and security objectives in the drive to acquire Florida makes a final assessment of the reasons for the Monroe administration's use of force somewhat problematic. The security rationale is compelling for what country would wish a weak state with strong friends for its neighbor? Any responsible president would have sought to protect US borders by military means if necessary. But did Monroe attack Spain because it was weak or because it truly constituted a danger to the US? Would the US have been content to leave the Floridas alone had there been no Indian attacks or runaway slaves? The British, with whom the nation had just fought a war, posed more of a threat for they were stirring up trouble among the Indians, patrolling the

Great Lakes with warships and contesting US boundaries all over the continent. Yet, the US did not attack or threaten the British. More importantly, the government did not try to develop its military capabilities to either contest British influence or guard against a possible British attack in the future. Thus, Spain looks like a more convenient target of opportunity than a dangerous threat to American security in comparison. The US made other land grabs in the future using similar military tactics that make the Florida invasion look like part of a larger plan to spread across the continent. We should conclude that while security interests were crucial in motivating the use of force, we cannot rule out the possibility that the Monroe administration was simply trying to expand US territory. Whether American security truly demanded such action is a much larger question beyond the scope of this chapter. Nonetheless, security concerns were still necessary, and perhaps sufficient conditions for the use of force.

Was there a similar quest for aggrandizement tied into the Samoan intervention? Was the US acting like an imperial power driven to carve out an empire in the South Pacific? In the late 19th century, as the European powers relentlessly divided up the world into colonial empires, the US took the opportunity afforded by the Spanish American War to acquire its own territories. A colonial empire could soak up excess production in the home country, and reduce reliance on European and other markets where US products might be subjected to high tariffs. But while American businessmen greedily eyed the Asian markets, US economic interests in Samoa were slight. US firms owned only 7 percent of the land. In fact the US had asserted at one point that its lack of commercial interests in Samoa would make it a perfect, neutral arbiter over Samoan affairs (Kennedy, 1974, p.64).

Was the US motivated to acquire Samoa because of a more fundamental drive to expand? There were many politicians in the US who preached Social Darwinism and argued that the US should promote its political, economic and religious practices in backward regions of the world. Did the US acquire its Samoan territory because of the 'white man's burden'? In fact, the US government defended native rights in Samoa far more than either Great Britain or Germany. It refused partition of Samoa for many years because it did not wish to become involved in 'entangling alliances' and imperialist schemes. Grover Cleveland in particular vigorously defended native rights on Samoa and other Pacific islands (Kennedy, 1974). While much of the American defense of native claims might be dismissed as mere rhetoric disguising US fascination with Pago Pago, the US had very little interest in acquiring Samoa simply to provide it more enlightened administration.

The strongest case for the US military intervention in Samoa in 1899 is based on geopolitical, security objectives. The US used military force in Samoa to ensure its continued right to the harbor at Pago Pago. The government feared that the Germans were using the Samoan civil war as an excuse to annex the islands after which they would drive the US and Great Britain out. If the Samoan power struggle was resolved in favor of the man the US and British feared was a German lackey (the Germans themselves commented upon how well trained Mata'afa was

42 *The Political Use of Military Force in US Foreign Policy*

[Kennedy, 1974, p.149]), Germany would be in a position to dictate Samoan politics. That the US and Britain would attack Mata'afa, not just for a few days, but for several months is an indication of how real they perceived this threat to be. Once Pago Pago was made safe for US use, American military vessels would be able to maintain and expand the US presence in Asia. Security objectives would seem to be if not the sole reason for the use of force, then at least, the overriding one.

Alternative explanations of US behavior during the Berlin crisis are also weak. The US was interested in the economic recovery of Western Europe, which the defense of Berlin seemed integral to in many respects. A prosperous West Europe was vital to the US' own security, but also its economic prosperity. To the extent that the US economy required West European recovery, which in turn depended on American security guarantees to Europe, the defense of West Berlin could be seen as motivated by the demands of the US's own prosperity. Viewed in this light, however, all US actions in Europe would have to be seen as predicated on self-reinforcing security and economic interests.

Alternatively, President Truman may have been motivated by the upcoming presidential elections–in which he was expected to lose–to take strong action. Perhaps the 'little man from Missouri' wished to be seen as a strong leader–a man who could fill the shoes of his brave and confident predecessor. At the time the crisis began, his Gallup approval rating was only 36 percent, and postwar inflation was over eight percent. Truman, however, may have been reluctant rather than eager to take strong action because of his domestic weaknesses. He waited until after the election to begin the NATO negotiations in earnest for fear of alienating an American public that still believed the US would not have to station sizeable numbers of troops on foreign soil. He may have also been hesitant to take stronger action than the transferal of the B-29 bombers to Europe, for fear of adverse public and congressional reaction. If anything, domestic political considerations militated against taking strong action. Ultimately, the severity of the threat to the US in this crisis was such that any president would probably have been forced to respond in some manner, regardless of the domestic, political situation in the US. There was a very real fear that if the US began surrendering its positions in Europe, beginning with West Berlin, the Soviets would quickly move in to fill the void, and the appeasers among the European leaders would convince their exhausted populations that the US was not going to protect them and that they would be better off making the best deal possible with the Soviets.

Security-centered explanations of the political use of military force are quite powerful and provide convincing evidence in each of the three case studies, with the possible exception of the Florida invasion. In particular, I find three common threads in each of these incidents that demonstrate the preeminence of security considerations in the president's decision making. First, in each case presidents authorized uses of force to confront threats from rival states. The Spanish in Florida, Germany in Samoa, and the Soviet Union in Berlin were all adversaries of the US and would have posed significant challenges should the dispute have escalated into war. If the US had permitted any of these rivals to

Security, Power and Realist Explanations of the Political Use of Military Force 43

maintain or expand its position in the conflict, the confrontation may have only been postponed to a later period when the rival's power had grown, and/or the US position had become weaker. Second, each of the conflicts involved geopolitically important locations. Spanish Florida bordered the US. US foreign policy makers believed the Samoan islands would be critical in maintaining US influence in the Pacific. And Berlin lay at the heart of Europe on the edge of the iron curtain. As well, the US had a history of interest in these regions. Presidents had been concerned about the security of US borders with Florida and had sought to acquire those Spanish territories for many years prior to Jackson's incursion. The US had signed treaties (albeit not ratified) and had been involved in Samoan politics for 27 years prior to the use of force in 1899. And the US still had thousands of troops in Germany to guarantee that nation's security. US foreign policy in the three case studies was formulated along the lines of the classical model of national interest described above. Third, the issues at stake in each of these cases were critical. Any president would view the defense of US territorial security, power projection capabilities and the security of major allies as a sufficient cause for using military force short of war, if not war itself. A convincing case can be made security concerns were necessary and most likely sufficient conditions for the political use of military force in these incidents.

The Expansion of Security and Power Interests and the Use of Force, 1798-1941

The evolution of US security policy and the manner in which it has affected the use of military force have been long and varied. As the US grew in power and confidence, the government's conception of what issues and areas touched upon the national security tended to expand as well. I divide my analysis of this evolution into several, distinctive periods according to the level of foreign policy activity, primarily the political use of force, US power demanded or allowed. These periods are: 1) the era of foreign policy prudence, 1798-1895; 2) the period of US interventionism, 1895-1919; and 3) the renewed isolationist phase, 1920-1941. I analyze the post World War II era in a separate section. In the discussion of each historical era I seek to explain how security interests were defined and the role of the political use of military force in advancing these interests. My purpose is to provide an account of these time periods so that the reader might understand both the general extent to which force was used and the reasons why force was employed on behalf of national security objectives.

Because security interests are often malleable and temporary, I will briefly discuss which particular interests or threats I deemed to be relevant to US national security. It bears repeating that there is no one theory or perspective that can guide us in the elucidation of these objectives. Rather, we must make our way inductively based on the event descriptions, theory and history. Therefore, I offer the following inventory of US security and power interests that presidents have sought to protect or advance based upon a general review of US foreign policy: 1)

44   *The Political Use of Military Force in US Foreign Policy*

domestic, material interests including territorial integrity, resources, and people; 2) sovereignty; 3) US citizens [public and private] overseas; 4) nations and regions in the Western hemisphere that affect US territory, sovereignty and citizens; 5) nations and regions in other areas of the globe that affect US territory, sovereignty and citizens; and 6) honor, reputation and credibility. This list is by means definitive or even exhaustive, for I merely seek to summarize what are the largely enduring goals of US foreign policy.

I believe that there exists a hierarchy of security interests that is analogous to an individual's hierarchy of needs (Maslow, 1970). Those interests or needs that are most critical to survival must be attended to first and command whatever resources are required. No one interest can ever be fully satisfied (except perhaps territorial expansion) and so the allocation of foreign policy resources and energy is a dynamic process with each interest being allotted some level of attention depending on its salience at the moment. The physical security of US territory should be considered the most fundamental of all interests. This includes all American people, resources and assets within lands under the jurisdiction of the US government. Maintaining US sovereignty and independence is always vital to the national well-being and the preservation of an 'American' way of life. I would rate the importance of protecting Americans overseas as important, but less so than protecting those at home if only because of the risk and cost involved in looking after hundreds of thousands of US citizens the world over. Sometimes military reprisals taken against those who harmed Americans are undertaken more for symbolic, retributive purposes in part to satisfy domestic constituencies. Nonetheless, there are legitimate security and credibility interests at stake in such operations. The nations in the US's immediate environment, the Western hemisphere, have long been a crucial interest to the US. Therefore, I would rank Latin America and the Caribbean as more important to US security than other regions of the world because of their proximity. Europe, Japan and other East Asian nations are of vital importance, especially when they are at risk while the Western hemisphere is quiescent. The abstract interests of honor, reputation and credibility are conceptually similar as they all pertain to images and appearances of strength and influence. They become increasingly important the more powerful the US becomes for US ability to get other states to behave according to its dictates depends heavily on these actors believing that the US has the ability to force them to follow its wishes. Like any major power, the US would prefer to keep the actual exercise of power to compel states to a minimum so as to conserve its resources. The maintenance of reputation is also important as a means of dissuading potential challengers to US hegemony.

First, a brief review of the evidence regarding the use of force in the 1798-1941 period that I will be using in this and subsequent chapters is in order. I analyze data contained in a 1993 study by the Congressional Research Service for the US Congress entitled, 'Instances of Use of US Forces Abroad, 1798-1993'.[4]

---

[4] These uses of force may be found at http://www.fas.org/man/crs/crs_931007.htm as found on July 7, 2003.

Security, Power and Realist Explanations of the Political Use of Military Force   45

This report contains very brief–no more than a sentence or sentence fragment–descriptions of all limited uses of force in the time I study. I examined each of these event descriptions and based on what was explicitly stated in the report as the goal or goals of each of the interventions, created several binary variables that measure whether or not a particular goal was pursued in each case. I did not try to deduce or guess what US or presidential motives might have been. I simply took the language as given and created variables to reflect it. It is possible that other, more subtle aims motivated presidents. I would rather err on the conservative side and rely on the objective language of the report regarding US foreign policy goals, than use a looser standard that might introduce an excessive degree of personal subjectivity into the analysis. For example, a November 17,1904 intervention in Panama indicated that American intervention was designed, 'To protect American lives and property at Ancon at the time of a threatened insurrection', and nothing else.[5] I coded this intervention as having two goals–to protect American lives and to protect American property. A November 18, 1912 intervention in Turkey describes US activity as involving guarding, '...the American legation at Constantinople during a Balkan War'. I coded this intervention as having one goal–the protection of American lives. The vast majority of the rest were equally as explicit and brief in their accounts of the incidents.[6] It is possible that a use of force involved multiple objectives as well, and if so, each objective was included. These data were also supplemented by cases from Peceny (1999) that involve the promotion of liberal idealism, and which are discussed in more detail in Chapter 4.

---

[5] Ibid.

[6] I exclude all events associated with the War of 1812, the Mexican-American War, the Civil War, the Spanish-American War, and World War I. I do include events that took place prior and subsequent to these wars that clearly took place before the formal initiation of hostilities and after the wars were declared over. For instance, the US undertook several provocative military operations along the Texas-Mexican border before war was finally declared. The US also provided assistance to the White Russian armies in the Russian Civil War that took place after World War I.

Table 2.1 Security Goals and the Use of Military Force, 1798-1941

Goal	Number (Percent of all uses)
Protection of US Territory	19 (11%)
Protection of US Citizens	103 (60%)
Protection of Friendly Governments	25 (14.5%)
War Prevention	1 (.6%)
American Honor	3 (1.7%)
Total of Security-Related Uses	133 (77.3%)
Total of All Uses	172

Note: Column totals to more than 133 because some uses have multiple objectives.

Table 2.2 Uses of Force to Advance Security and Power Interests Across Historical Periods

Objective	Protect US Citizens	Protect/Expand Territory	Protect Govts.	Protect US Honor	Prevent War
Period					
1798-1865	34/60	10/60	1/60	3/60	0
	56.7%	16.7%	1.7%	5%	
1866-1898	25/33	1/33	2/33	0	0
	75.8%	3%	6.1%		
1899-1918	29/48	4/48	12/48	0	0
	60.4%	8.3%	25%		
1919-1941	15/31	4/31	10/31	0	1
	48.4%	12.9%	32%	3.2%	
	103/172	19/172	25/172	3/172	1/172
	60%	11%	14.5%	1.7%	.6%

Cell frequencies and percentages represent the number of uses of force aimed at achieving a particular objective/the total number of uses of force for that period of time.

Table 2.3 Uses of Force to Advance Security and Power Interests Across Historical Periods

Period	Number of Uses	Average Number Per Year	Percent of all Uses for the Period
1798-1865	47	.69	78.3%
1866-1898	26	.78	78.8%
1899-1918	36	1.8	75%
1919-1941	24	1.04	77.4%
Total	133	.92	77.3%

Table 2.4 Uses of Force to Advance Security and Power Interests Across Regions

Region	Number of Uses	Percent of All Uses in Region	Total All Uses in Region
Continental US	10	90.9%	11
Central America/ Caribbean	41	65%	63
South America	17	94.4%	18
North Africa/ Middle East	12	100%	12
Sub-Saharan Africa	2	50%	4
Europe/North Atlantic	6	75%	8
Asia	45	80.4%	56
Total all regions	133	77.3%	172

Security, Power and Realist Explanations of the Political Use of Military Force   49

Table 2.5 Uses of Force to Advance Security and Power Interests Across Region and Time

	1798-1865	1866-1898	1899-1918	1919-1941
Continental US	10 21.3%	0 na	0 na	0 na
Central America/ Caribbean	7 14.9%	5 19.2%	20 55.6%	9 37.5%
South America	8 17%	6 23.1%	2 5.6%	1 4.2%
North Africa/ Middle East	5 10.6%	1 3.8%	4 11.1%	2 8.3%
Sub-Saharan Africa	2 4.3%	0 na	0 na	0 na
Europe/ North Atlantic	1 2.1%	0 na	1 2.8%	4 16.7%
Asia	14 29.8%	14 53.8%	9 25%	8 33.3%
Total	47 100%	26 100%	36 100%	24 100%

Total percentages are based on number of uses of force to advance security and power interests in a region for each period of time.

In my examination of the CRS study, I found the following event descriptions to be relevant to national security: 1) protection and expansion of US territory; 2) protection of US citizens; 3) protection of friendly governments; 4) war prevention; and 5) protection of American honor. From 1789-1941, 133 incidents, or 77.3 percent of the total number of uses (172), involved the use of force on behalf of at least one, and sometimes more of, the foregoing aims. We see in Table 2.1 that the protection of US citizens was the most frequent objective of the use of force (103 such occasions or 60 percent of all uses of force), followed by the protection of friendly governments (25 uses of force or 14.5 percent of all uses); protection/expansion of US territory (19 uses or 11 percent of all uses); assertion of American honor (3 uses or 1.7 percent of all uses), and one occasion

50   *The Political Use of Military Force in US Foreign Policy*

where force was used to prevent war (.6 percent). I provide data on the frequency of times presidents pursued these security/power goals across historical periods in Table 2.2. Tables 2.3 through 2.5 provide breakdowns of uses of force across time and regions of the world.

Foreign Policy Prudence 1798-1898

In the first forty years of its existence, US foreign policy was focused principally on defensive measures designed to protect its people and territory. The American desire to remain free of the illiberal and war-prone European system led to a disengagement from balance of power politics. Even if presidents had wished to involve the US in Europe's quarrels, the need to preserve its democratic experiment, coupled with US military weakness would have stopped them. In the years between 1798 and 1823–before the announcement of the Monroe Doctrine– US foreign policy goals were fairly narrow. Among the most critical was the protection of American citizens in foreign lands and on the high seas. In fact, across the entire period of 1798-1941, the most widely cited reason for using the military short of war is the protection of American lives. We see in Table 2.2 that in the years between 1798-1865, of the 60 times presidents used force, 34 missions involved the protection of US citizens (57.6 percent), while in the years between the Civil War and the Spanish American War, force was used 25 times for such objectives (75.8 percent of the 33 times force was used in this era). Throughout US history these operations have served a dual purpose. The US often sends naval forces offshore in some troubled land to evacuate, be prepared to evacuate, or use firepower to protect US citizens and frequently other, foreign nationals. In earlier years, naval commanders were given some discretion over when, where and how to intervene since they were often out of contact with Washington (Buhite, 1995). Many of these operations became quite aggressive as the Marines stormed ashore to assist endangered Americans. Underlying the specific national interest in protecting one's own, however, is the slightly subtler objective of demonstrating American power as a means of exerting influence over foreign governments. The appearance of American warships has often affected the dynamics of many of the internal struggles for power that give rise to chaos and violence. Such operations were especially critical in the early days of the Republic when foreign states might have been tempted to threaten or attack US citizens and their property given the US's fairly weak military. That such challenges were met with force suggests that presidents were quite mindful of the importance of protection and occasionally retaliation against attacks on Americans.

As well, most presidents and their cabinets agreed that the protection of Americans traversing the world's oceans was of vital importance. One of the most heated issues in the early history of the Republic concerned British impressment of American sailors. The British often stopped American vessels on the oceans and boarded them in search of deserters from the Royal Navy. Many of these men had in fact signed up on US commercial vessels, and many had become American citizens. Others merely pretended to be US citizens. In either case Americans regarded them as their fellow citizens, while the British regarded them as deserters and hauled them all away. Often innocent men were seized by the British in the process. The US Navy could do little to stop impressment by the powerful and ubiquitous British fleet for unless it mobilized for war, the US had little hope of forcing the British to back down. There were certainly opportunities aplenty to use force to protect Americans in this regard, but save for the War of 1812, little military force was applied to the problem. In contrast, the US Navy took many measures against pirates in the Caribbean and Mediterranean who captured American vessels and kidnapped US citizens. Not only did the Navy attack pirates on the seas, US Marines occasionally landed and destroyed the towns that were harboring pirates and their benefactors, especially in Cuba and North Africa.

The most sustained use of force short of war in this period was the Quasi War with France, which was sandwiched between the efforts of Washington and Jefferson to keep the US neutral in the Napoleonic wars. Washington's Neutrality Act and the Jay Treaty with Great Britain angered many Americans, but kept the US out of the European wars during his administration. In 1796 France declared that it would no longer respect the neutrality of ships that traded with Great Britain, and French war ships and privateers began seizing American vessels in the Caribbean. After attempts at reaching a diplomatic settlement with the French minister Talleyrand failed and news of French attempts at bribery during the negotiations reached the US, American opinion became enflamed against France. In the summer of 1798 the Congress, 'declared all French treaties null and void, created a Navy Department, funded the construction of new warships, and increased the regular army' (Paterson, Clifford and Hagan, 2000, p.56). President Adams employed the US Navy to retaliate against the French whenever they attacked American vessels, and the Navy responded by seizing over eighty French ships between 1798 and 1800. The use of force apparently had something of the desired effect, for the French later repealed their commercial decrees and concluded an agreement with the US in the Treaty of Mortefontaine.

At home, the US' borders were still undefined and presidents authorized several military operations to secure and expand them. In the northeast, the US disputed its borders with Canada in Maine and New Brunswick, while the British encouraged separatists in Vermont. In the Great Lakes region the British refused to vacate many of their forts and aided Indian attacks on American settlers. Spanish forces continued to hold onto forts on the Mississippi and, in 1784 closed off the mouth of the river to American commerce. At the same time American citizens began to move into Spanish territories in the south, especially in Louisiana and Florida. Later these settlers began to agitate for union with the US, which American presidents were only too happy to encourage through the movement of arms and armies. The Louisiana Purchase solved many of these controversies, but opened new ones, especially with regard to the Floridas. The boundaries between the US and Spanish East and West Florida were imprecise to say the least. Thomas Jefferson claimed that the Louisiana purchase included West Florida and sent troops to the area to assert American claims. In addition there were now contested boundaries with Great Britain and Russia in the Pacific Northwest. As we see in Table 2.2, the US used military force short of war on ten occasions in the

52   *The Political Use of Military Force in US Foreign Policy*

years 1798-1865 (16.7 percent of all uses of force for this era) to assert its territorial claims or to protect what we now might call its 'homeland security', within the continental US, mostly in Florida, but also in Oregon. Presidents exercised a great deal of prudence in these operations for while they were prepared to confront the Spanish, they refrained from overly aggressive moves against the stronger British.

Later Americans attributed a degree of disengagement to this period in US history, perhaps because of Washington's classic injunction against involvement in European quarrels, that is not really accurate. The US tried to remain aloof from the wars consuming Europe, but it could not and did not pursue a policy of total isolationism. American leaders used military force when it was necessary to protect vital and tangible American interests. They demonstrated a keen appreciation for the utility of force short of war, especially in the Quasi War where President Adams, having forced France to back down from its commercial decrees and despite attacks from those within his own party who wanted war, ceased his limited hostilities. Later Presidents like Jefferson (in North Africa in 1804) and Monroe (in Spanish Florida in 1818) also evinced shrewdness in using force for limited political objectives. As long as US' security in the Western Hemisphere and on the high seas remained precarious and the US was militarily weak, presidents used force in a fairly judicious manner. After US territorial integrity was essentially completed with the acquisition of Spanish Florida in 1819, however, we find American presidents expanding their horizons and discerning new threats to US interests.

After the Napoleonic wars ended in Europe, the US entered a period of prosperity and peace. The US settled its differences with Spain over the Floridas and with Great Britain over the Great Lakes region, which was demilitarized. Europe itself was relatively stable and posed no threat to the US. The nation's westward expansion moved inexorably forward, opposed only by Native Americans. The Spanish presence and vague Russian claims in the far West did not pose significant threats to American security. With its land and sovereignty secured, the US government had few, territorial security interests in need of active defense. Thus, with its fundamental needs satisfied, US foreign policy gradually became more offensive in nature as its conception of national interests took in the lands to the south. Presidents and foreign policy makers gradually expanded their conception of the US defensive perimeter to include all the Western Hemisphere, and while increasing US territory through acquisitions, forcible and otherwise, principally from Mexico.

Most notably, the Monroe Doctrine asserted American preeminence in Latin America and the Caribbean. In Chapter 4, I discuss the ideological implications of that pronouncement, but its consequences for US security were equally far-reaching. The ostensible justification for the Monroe Doctrine was the threat of renewed European intervention in Latin America to reimpose the Spanish monarchy or European control over the rebellious colonies. It became quickly apparent, however, that there was little likelihood of any European armada setting sail for the new world. Nor was there much need for a strong American military presence to back up the President's words, as the British Navy guaranteed the

Security, Power and Realist Explanations of the Political Use of Military Force 53

'sovereignty' of the US' southern neighbors. What makes the announcement of the Monroe Doctrine a turning point in the evolution of American security, and especially the role of military force in upholding it, is that it signaled an expansive view of American interests. Where previously US foreign policy was directed toward ensuring the nation's survival, now the more powerful and confident nation looked over the horizon to appreciate how its security could be threatened indirectly by internal and international events in these nations. Over the course of the 19th century the US gradually came to look upon Latin America as its sphere of influence and, by the end of the century, the US reigned supreme. Fear of European meddling, commercial opportunities and the need for a canal across Central America were the guiding considerations in US foreign policy and the use of force.

Gunboat diplomacy played a major role in demonstrating US power and interest in the region. The US did not meddle in the internal affairs of its southern neighbors to the extent it did in the 20th century, but naval forces continually cruised the Atlantic, Pacific and the Caribbean to protect US citizens and property. As there were a great many violent struggles for power during this era, the US Navy was employed quite often. All during the years 1798-1865, presidents used force seven times in Central America and the Caribbean, and eight times in South America as we see in Table 2.5. These interventions, which often consisted of US Marine deployments, were usually limited to defensive measures. However, as the position of the US government in these struggles was generally known, to the extent that the operations were targeted against the anti-American violence of one or another faction, they undoubtedly served other US foreign policy interests as well. There were several occasions on which the US chose not to use force to back the Monroe Doctrine that demonstrate presidents either did not look upon the Monroe Doctrine as wholly inviolable or exercised caution in their choice of tactics against more powerful states. British seizure of the Falklands in 1838 and Greytown, Nicaragua in 1848, and more importantly, the French conquest of Mexico during the US Civil War were met with diplomatic protests rather than naval warships. Clearly, presidents were still cognizant of US inferiority vis a vis the major European powers and chose not to challenge them in the Western Hemisphere until late in the century.

The US had long entertained hopes of building a canal through Central America, but through the first half of the 19th century it had to contend with a strong British presence in the region. US efforts to acquire rights to build a canal through Nicaragua in the late 1840s soon aroused British anger and Great Britain responded to this threat to its dominance in the region by seizing control of territory sought by the US. The Clayton Bulwer Treaty (1850) put an end to such aggressive and unilateral moves to gain the upper hand in control of an isthmian canal. Both sides renounced the right to build a canal or take territory for a canal without the consent of the other. They pledged to support whatever efforts were made to build a canal and assured its neutrality. Before a canal was built, presidents sometimes used force to protect the railroads in this region, but the looming Civil War dampened whatever expansionist aims presidents might have

54   *The Political Use of Military Force in US Foreign Policy*

had. After the war the Grant administration did assert that any canal should be under US authority, but later when the French took the first steps toward building a canal, the Hayes administration protested loudly, but did little else.

Considerable time and energy was also put into acquiring Cuba and other territories in the Caribbean, albeit to no avail. American presidents going back to Jefferson assumed that, in due course, Cuba would be detached from the Spanish empire. President James Polk had informally offered one hundred million dollars for the island, while later administrations were prepared to name a higher price (Pratt, 1955, p.293). Those most strongly committed to acquiring Cuba were from slaveholding states that wished to extend that practice and see their representation in Congress increase. Their advocacy of Cuban annexation, however, raised the ire of abolitionists from the North and doomed such diplomatic efforts. In 1854, after Spanish authorities seized the American steamer, *Black Warrior*, war over Cuba appeared imminent. Many southerners were ready to launch filibustering attacks in Cuba, but as the nation was already so polarized over the slavery question, an issue like Cuba that divided the country along the same sectional lines was a diplomatic dead end. After the Civil War, there were renewed attempts at acquiring land in the Caribbean for naval bases after the Civil War pointed up Northern weaknesses in its naval blockade of the South. But, few in the country looked favorably upon spending money to purchase tiny islands inhabited by people who shared little in common with most Americans of the day.

The US acquisition of Louisiana and the westward movement of settlers led to a broader conception of the suitable limits of US territory. The notion of Manifest Destiny and the quest for land collided first with Mexican control over Texas, California and other western territories. Even before the Mexican-American War of 1848 resolved territorial questions to US satisfaction, American presidents had authorized several, provocative military operations to test Mexican control over these lands. In 1836 US forces occupied disputed territory in Texas during its war for independence. In 1842, a US naval squadron off the coast of California occupied the town of Monterey, although the force withdrew when it was discovered the US was not at war with Mexico. In 1844, President Tyler deployed US forces to protect Texans against Mexico as part of a bold move to force the issue of annexation of Texas. These actions were not confined to contiguous territories.

Force was also used on three occasions, with some violence, to uphold American honor throughout the world, as we see in Table 2.2. From a contemporary vantage point these actions look quaint at best and jingoistic at worst, but they were a customary method for dealing with nations and peoples who refused to play by the military and diplomatic conventions of the day. Great importance was attached to symbolic issues like an officer's honor and deference to the flag because it was felt that a failure to command respect for such things would encourage more material forms of aggression. Alexander Hamilton went so far as to claim, 'To defend its own rights, *to vindicate its own honor*, there are occasions when a nation ought to hazard even its existence' (quoted in Morgenthau, 1973, p.17, emphasis added). In 1824, Commodore David Perry attacked the town of Fajardo, Puerto Rico after residents had insulted some of his

Security, Power and Realist Explanations of the Political Use of Military Force 55

officers. Greytown, Nicaragua was destroyed by American forces, 'to avenge an insult to the American Minister to Nicaragua' (Congressional Research Service, 1993).[7] And in another incident, force was used to demand redress for a Japanese insult to the US flag. In some sense the quest for honor in this era is analogous to the concern for credibility in modern times for both are essentially abstract matters of consequence primarily because the US has feared what lessons others elsewhere would draw from American behavior. The provocations may have changed, but the fears have not.

The US also frequently used force in Asia, especially in the Pacific Islands throughout the pre Civil War period and the years leading up to the Spanish American War. As we see in Table 2.5, before the Civil War, the US deployed military force, typically the Navy and Marines, 14 times in Asia. The US also used force 14 times from 1866-1899. For example, US Marines assisted in the overthrow of the Hawaiian queen, Liliuokalani in 1893 in order to install a government more pliant to US annexation. The US also used force in 1870, 1874, 1889 in Hawaii to influence internal politics. Several uses of force also grew out of instability in China, problems of succession and European influence in Samoa, described earlier, and in Korea as well.

Throughout much of the 19th century, the US used force as often as its interests seemingly dictated, but when such operations would not involve it in conflicts with European powers. But as American power grew, the frontier settled and the slavery issue resolved, it was inevitable that the US would begin to direct its attention outward and again expand the definition of its security interests. As its power grew, the old prudence wore off and the US became much more assertive in using force whenever presidents thought it necessary.

The Emergence of the US and Foreign Policy Interventionism, 1899-1919

The ascension of the US to global power status really begins in 1895 when the Cleveland administration challenged British dominance in Latin America and after some blustery threats, Great Britain chose to appease the US rather than incur its enmity. The crisis involved a border dispute between British Guiana and Venezuela. Venezuela had been seeking US assistance in convincing the British to submit the entire issue to arbitration, but the US had demurred for many years. The change in attitude in 1895 was due in large part to a skillful public relations campaign on Venezuela's behalf that convinced many Americans that the British were unjustly denying Venezuela's claims. The US Congress unanimously passed resolutions urging the president to become involved. A short time later, Secretary of State, Richard Olney issued an ultimatum to the British demanding that they submit the dispute to arbitration. Olney asserted that the Monroe Doctrine allowed no European nation the right to, '...forcibly deprive an American state of the right and power of self-government and of shaping for itself its own political fortunes and destinies'. He went on to argue that the US, 'is practically sovereign on this

---

[7] As found at http://www.fas.org/man/crs/crs_931007.htm on August 13, 2003.

The Political Use of Military Force in US Foreign Policy

continent, and its fiat is law upon the subjects to which it confines its interposition' (quoted in Pratt, 1955, p.348). The British were dismissive of the US' threats at first, but later decided to appease American interests in order to concentrate their energies on the rising German empire. The case went to arbitration and Venezuela, despite its non-representation among the jurists, was awarded additional land. The US never resorted to force to make its point, but it was willing to escalate the dispute to a point where many on both sides expected war. Henceforth, the US was recognized as the dominant power in the Western hemisphere by the Europeans. This status essentially conferred upon the US the right to intervene in those matters in Latin America in which it took an interest. But presidents also recognized that with such rights, came responsibilities. The US would be expected to ensure that the nations of the Latin America and the Caribbean would conduct themselves in a responsible manner in their dealings with the European powers.

The US solidified its dominance of the Western Hemisphere and its status as a global power with victory in the Spanish-American War in 1898. The US acquired Puerto Rico and the Philippines and a dominant status in Cuba. In this same period it also acquired Hawaii and part of Samoa. The US became an imperial power with a global reach. The geographical and political isolation it once enjoyed was now irretrievably gone for its power in the world was such that the US could never again remain on the sidelines forever in the balance of power politics. It acquired substantial interests in the Far East by taking possession of the Philippines and demanding a role in China. President Roosevelt's successful mediation in the Russo-Japanese war of 1904 further demonstrated increased American stature in this region. In the period leading up to World War I, in Europe and the Middle East, the US took part in the resolution of various, major power crises (e.g., the Agadir incident in 1911). Whether or not the US had a stake in the various foreign policy issues of the era is irrelevant. Presidents might claim that the US was simply a helpful, but neutral bystander in these disputes, but it was a very short journey between the sidelines and the playing field. The acquisition of global interests would inevitably lead to involvement and military intervention.

Altogether we see in Table 2.3 there were 36 uses of force short of war throughout the world in this first period of American internationalism. A large number of these uses of force took place in the Western hemisphere. In Table 2.5, we see that there were 20 interventions in Central America and the Caribbean, and 2 in South America (although both these operations involved Colombia and its control over Panama), from 1899 through 1918 as the US sought to prop up weak governments, protect its citizens and keep the peace. Additionally, if we look back to Table 2.2, we also see the gradual increase in the number of uses of force to protect foreign governments, many in Latin America. Between 1798-1898, the US used force only three times to protect foreign governments or guarantee their sovereignty. In the years 1899-1918, presidents relied on the military to help achieve this objective 12 times, or 25 percent of all uses of force in this period. The powerful and confident US government began its interventionism in Central America where the need for a canal had become all too obvious during the Spanish American war. After the French halted their efforts in Panama the way was clear for the US to build a canal. The US convinced the British to renounce the Clayton-Bulwer Treaty, which prevented either side from exercising exclusive control over a canal. But, the government of Colombia would not agree to US terms for the construction and control of the canal. In particular, the Colombian Senate demanded greater compensation for the use of its territory and more control over the canal courts that were to hear disputes over its administration. Shortly after Colombia rejected a treaty with the US, Panama declared its independence. While Teddy Roosevelt denied aiding or encouraging the rebellion, a timely display of American naval power ensured its success. The pliant Panamanian government acceded to Roosevelt's conditions and a treaty was signed giving the US power over the canal and canal zone. When construction was completed in 1914, the US not only had a vital commercial and military stake in the Panama Canal itself, the canal's importance radiated outward and made the US more concerned than ever with the stability of the nations around it.

Not unexpectedly, soon after it acquired Cuba and the right to build a canal in Panama, US military intervention in Central America increased dramatically. These deployments were often inspired by a plethora of economic and ideological interests, but security concerns always loomed large. In addition to the long-term deployment of ground forces to protect the canal zone and to battle the guerilla forces in Cuba, the US repeatedly sent forces into Nicaragua, Honduras, Haiti, and the Dominican Republic. The US gained the right to interfere when these states agreed not to impair their independence or give their territory to other nations. The US acquired military bases in Panama, Cuba and Nicaragua (Pratt, 1955, p.413). The Wilson administration also used force in Mexico to control its political future. The immediate pretext of most military interventions was political instability, which in turn often grew out of problems with public finance. The US was interested in maintaining stability in this region because of the canal, but it also feared that European states might intervene to collect the money owed to their banks and investors. Presidents Roosevelt, Taft and Wilson looked dimly upon the abilities of the hemispheric governments and so their interventions led directly to the creation of US-led military dictatorships over Nicaragua, Haiti and the Dominican Republic.

Its policies in the Far East, especially the Open Door policy toward China involved the US in balance of power politics, and led to far much more military activity. We see in Table 2.5 that presidents used force nine times in Asia, primarily in China as that nation disintegrated after the 1912 revolution. Time and again US forces, especially the Marines, were called upon to protect the lives of American citizens endangered by the chaos in various Chinese cities. The US also had larger strategic interests in the region. Teddy Roosevelt's mediation of the Russo-Japanese War reflected US interests in seeing to it that no one nation so dominated East Asia as to upset the balance of power. As part of his 'speak softly and carry a big stick' strategy, Roosevelt sent the entire US battleship fleet around the world, including a visit to Tokyo. No doubt the display of force was calculated in part to impress the Japanese with American might, just as earlier US naval armadas had.

The US overcame its old reluctance to become drawn into European quarrels as well, although presidents rarely used force in the context of European politics, save for World War I. World War I involved the US for a time in European power politics, but Woodrow Wilson's desire to portray the US effort as part of an ideological campaign, rather than a military one, ensured that the security implications of that war were downplayed in public statements. I discuss in Chapter 4 how Wilsonian idealism helped lead to US participation in the war and inspired US peace making efforts afterward. While not denying the sincerity with which Woodrow Wilson attempted to make the world 'safe for democracy', other US interests were at stake in the war. German provocations in Mexico and general anti-German sentiment in public opinion led to tremendous ill will toward the Kaiser. At the center of all these controversies was the balance of power in Europe and the issue of German domination of the continent. Foreign policy makers in the US may not have been entirely appreciative of the consequences resulting from such dominance (as they showed again in the late 1930s), but they were mindful of the consequences of a victorious German empire for Latin America. In addition, there was a strong concern that German domination of the European landmass would jeopardize the balance of power and might harm US commercial and political ties with the continent, most especially Great Britain and France.

After the war, Wilson threw himself into creating a just peace, but his expansive view of how peace and justice were to be realized required too much of the American people. Appeals to idealism might justify war, but they could not sustain the peace. Wilson's vision of a global, collective security system managed by the League of Nations would have, at least in the views of its critics, led to American participation in entangling alliances and numerous wars. The first result would have violated one of the central tenets of American foreign policy since the days of Washington and Jefferson (the US had entered the war as an 'associated', not an 'allied' power). The second would have brought the US into disputes over which it had little interest. The US Senate refused to ratify the Versailles Peace Treaty and so the US never became a member of the League of Nations and was forced to conclude its own peace treaties a few years later. Thus, was a period of *relative* US isolationism inaugurated. US involvement in global politics did increase in some areas, even without US participation in the League of Nations. The US sent forces into Russia to aid those fighting the Bolsheviks. Its troops remained in Europe for several years after the war ended. But the upward trajectory of its military involvement in global affairs, and even in Central America, ceased. By the time of Roosevelt's 'Good Neighbor' policy toward Latin America, military interventions to the South had stopped. The US had the power and the opportunity to carve out a role for itself as one of the dominant nations of the world, but the public and the government preferred a less militaristic policy.

Security, Power and Realist Explanations of the Political Use of Military Force 59

The Period of Isolationism, 1920-1941

American foreign policy of the 1920s and 1930s is exceptional not for its isolationism in general, but rather for US unwillingness to use force as its tool, particularly in the 1930s. In many respects, presidents' conception of national security evidenced great continuity from previous years. The US was actively engaged in diplomacy on many fronts including naval disarmament in the Pacific, negotiations over German war reparations, instability and great power meddling in China, and several attempts to end or lessen the impact of war. It remained opposed to the domination by one nation of the European continent, and was still committed to the Monroe Doctrine. As in the lead up to all previous major conflagrations in Europe dating back to the Napoleonic era, the US passed laws in the 1930s designed to maintain neutrality and protect its commerce in the hopes of being spared the ravages of wars. The US had to be dragged into both world wars just at the point at which its power would be decisive.

Nowhere was the newfound reluctance of the US to use force more in evidence than in Franklin Roosevelt's 'Good Neighbor' policy. During the Hoover administration, the Roosevelt Corollary to the Monroe Doctrine–the right of the US to intervene in the internal affairs of Latin American and Caribbean states that were viewed as incompetent or illegitimate–had been renounced, although the US still retained the right to intervene when its interests were threatened. FDR abandoned the military interventionism of the previous Roosevelt, Taft and Wilson presidencies and completed the withdrawl of US forces from the region begun under Warren Harding. The US officially forswore the right of intervention in agreements reached with its southern neighbors at Montevideo in 1933. The Convention on the Rights and Duties of States proclaimed that, 'The High Contracting Parties declare inadmissible the intervention of any one of them, directly or indirectly, and for whatever reason, in the internal or external affairs of any other of the Parties' (cited in Pratt, 1995, p.611). The US liquidated its control over Haitian and Dominican Republic affairs and abrogated the Platt Amendment, which had given it the right to intervene in Cuban affairs. Even in Panama, the US rejected its right to guarantee Panamanian independence. The US did use force nine times in this region during the isolationist years, but several of these involved the US military reentering nations in which it had previously intervened. The US put the goodwill such actions generated among the Latin American states to work by committing them to a common front against Axis aggression at the Eighth International Conference of American States in Lima, Peru in late 1938.

Across the whole period, 1919-1941, we do see one US foreign policy objective becoming more important. Presidents used force ten times to protect friendly governments and their sovereignty (Table 2.2), which constitutes 32 percent of all uses of force for this period. While the raw numbers are still small, it is the only security-related foreign policy objective that increases in proportion in this era. Several of these uses of force pertained to FDR's efforts to protect US interests against Nazi Germany. There were five instances immediately prior to World War II where President Roosevelt assumed the defense of European

60   *The Political Use of Military Force in US Foreign Policy*

possessions in or near the Western hemisphere, such as Greenland, Iceland, and British colonies in the Caribbean, to protect American and British interests. But these were the only uses of force in the Roosevelt administration between 1934 and 1941. That the US used force so infrequently, and only to protect itself, speaks volumes about its desire to remain walled off from the growing calamity in Europe.

But, while isolationists in the US might believe the US could seal itself off from the wars of the world, FDR realized that if those fighting Nazi Germany were not helped, one day Hitler would turn his attention to the New World. And even if the US could reach an accommodation with the dictator, his terms were not likely to be in American interests. Thus, in August of 1941, before the US was even officially at war with Germany or Japan, Roosevelt signed the Atlantic Charter with Winston Churchill and committed the US to the destruction of the Axis powers. The Charter declared that after Nazi Germany was destroyed, the two nations held out for 'wider and permanent system of general security', but that before such could be established, a general disarmament and a renunciation of the use of force was necessary. The two leaders were seeking again what had eluded the victorious powers after World War I. But by the time this war ended, the American people as well as the president were convinced that only the US, the most powerful nation in the world, could lead such an effort. Isolationism could never again be an option.

Global Hegemony, Security and Power Interests and the Use of Force, 1948-1998

The Globalization of American Security: The Cold War, 1948-1989

Perhaps no nation accomplished such an abrupt and thorough transformation of its foreign policy as the US did in the period between 1940 and 1947. In the fall of 1940 the US government and the public stood on the sidelines while Hitler moved to conquer Europe and rained bombs on Great Britain. The Congress and the public did little but offer words of encouragement. Seven years later, however, in the spring of 1947, President Harry S. Truman proclaimed to the world that, 'it must be the policy of the US to support free peoples who are resisting attempted subjugation by armed minorities or outside pressures'. Where in 1940 the US was unwilling to use force to defend any nation outside of its hemisphere, seven years later it was willing to use force everywhere in defense of an abstract principle. The Truman Doctrine was inspired by the need to defend Greece and Turkey against communist machinations, and a skeptical Congress was assured that the president did not intend to use force the world over, but that was what happened. The Cold War with the Soviet Union and its communist allies led presidents to assert American security interests in every corner of the globe, no matter how insignificant. And not only could the US national interest be threatened by actual developments in countries, it could be undermined by perceptions of American strength and reputation. Fearful that if the US appeared weak or indecisive in any of the myriad of wars, crises and confrontations that took place throughout the

Security, Power and Realist Explanations of the Political Use of Military Force 61

Cold War, its influence would decline and its security suffer, presidents came to rely upon the limited use of force to demonstrate US power and protect its interests. Because presidents were concerned that confrontations with the Soviet Union and its allies must be managed to prevent them for escalating to nuclear war, direct military conflict with the USSR would have to be avoided, as would military escalation beyond certain levels in crises and wars with Soviet allies (e.g., Vietnam). Therefore, the limited use of force was that seemingly ideal foreign policy tool–not too strong, but not too weak either.

In the first phase of the Cold War, Europe was the main prize and the key battleground of US and Soviet efforts to dominate the political and ideological competition. The future of the divided Germany and the separated city of Berlin led to several showdowns between the superpowers involving limited uses and displays of military force, but there were also conflicts over Greece, Yugoslavia, Austria and the fate of Eastern Europe in general. The bloodiest war in history had just been fought over the future of this landmass, and the US was determined to prevent another war, this time led by the Soviet Union, from ever occurring. The US stationed tens of thousands of troops and weapons in Europe and created the North Atlantic Treaty Organization. The NATO alliance was an especially momentous event in US foreign policy history for never before had the nation entered into a peacetime alliance with any state. After 160 years the public and politicians realized that US security was tied inexorably to the future of Europe and that American power now demanded that the US take the lead in defending the Old World. The US and the USSR viewed the outcome of the Cold War in Europe as critical to their survival and invested enormous resources and energy into defending their interests. But since neither side would allow the other to gain a decisive advantage in Europe, and with the specter of nuclear war hanging over them, US and Soviet leaders gradually carved out spheres of influence and established explicit and tacit rules of the road for managing their disputes. And after the boundary lines in Berlin became concrete with the construction of the Berlin Wall, presidents seldom used limited force again in Europe. With the battle lines hardened in Europe, the superpowers were naturally drawn to other regions of the world to further their political and military ambitions.

The underdeveloped regions of the world took on enormous importance in the global balance of power during the late 1950s and 1960s as the last of the disputes in Europe were resolved. There had been several instances during the 1950s, including tensions in the Taiwan straits, the 1956 Suez crisis and the US intervention in Lebanon in 1958, where East and West clashed, but the struggle for the hearts and lands of the Third World did not begin in earnest until decolonization and Khrushchev's speech on wars of national liberation. As the colonial powers, chiefly Great Britain, France and Belgium, liquidated their empires in Africa and Asia, new states and untested governments sprang up, literally overnight. A lack of adequate preparation by the colonizers and struggles over the spoils of power generated instability, and in some cases civil war in many of these nations. Several of these states were geopolitically important, like the Congo, but most others were valued not because of their position or resources, but because the Cold War was viewed as a zero-sum game. A gain for one side was

62 The Political Use of Military Force in US Foreign Policy

automatically a loss for the other. And if enough of these heretofore-insignificant nations allied with one side in this competition, many foreign policy makers believed it might be sufficient to tip the global balance of power, or beliefs about it. Whenever either superpower tried to extend its influence anywhere, the other soon followed, as surely as night follows day. Thus did the US find itself using military force to influence events in Korea, Vietnam, Indonesia, Laos, Cambodia, in addition to the Cold War crises in Latin America and the Caribbean. How could American security suddenly turn on events in countries that never before had been of any concern to the US? Why would presidents use force short of war hundreds of times during the Cold War? In addition to the peculiar significance of any one nation, there was a larger issue at stake during the Cold War–credibility.

Early on, American foreign policy makers decided that the fight against communism would be an entirely new kind of struggle. Traditional geopolitical interests would still matter, but the global scope and potentially devastating effects of the Cold War meant that changes in beliefs were just as important as changes in actual fact. According to the authors of NSC 68, the blueprint for US Cold War strategy, the Soviet Union was out, 'to demonstrate to the free world that force and the will to use it are on the side of the Kremlin [and] that those who lack it are decadent and doomed' (NSC-68, pp.263-264). Therefore, the US should not make the same mistake it had with Hitler and appease the Soviet Union and appear weak, for it would only encourage more aggression and subversion. If the US did not confront the Soviet Union and its allies and establish a reputation for using force, it would lead to, '...gradual withdrawals under pressure until we discover one day that we have sacrificed positions of vital interest' (ibid, p.290). Throughout the Cold War, presidents and their advisers saw the conflict in terms of the Munich syndrome (i.e., no rewards for aggression) and domino theory (i.e., the interdependence of commitments). American credibility was at stake in potentially every conflict in the world with dire consequences sure to follow if it was not maintained. For example, in 1958 after he learned of Soviet designs in Lebanon and Iraq, Eisenhower asserted that if the US were to do nothing, '...the dependability of the US' commitments for assistance in the event of need would be brought into question throughout the world' (quoted in Blechman and Kaplan, 1978, p.231). During the war in Vietnam, the under-secretary of Defense wrote a memo in which he declared, 'Why we have not withdrawn is, by all odds, one reason. To preserve our reputation as a guarantor, and thus preserve our effectiveness in the rest of the world' (quoted in Schell, 1976, p.362). In regard to events in Central America in the early 1980s, Ronald Reagan claimed that if the US could not, 'defend ourselves there...our credibility would collapse, our alliances would crumble and the safety of our homeland would be out in jeopardy' (quoted in Destler, Gelb and Lake, 1984, p.81). US security was at stake everywhere and in all manner of situations. All a president had to do was assert that American credibility was threatened, and the nation's reputation was engaged. In addition, because the nuclear and even the military peace in general between the US and the Soviet Union came to rely upon the *incredible* threat of mutual assured destruction, presidents believed they had to find some method by which to demonstrate the credibility of the American threat to retaliate with nuclear weapons in an atomic

Security, Power and Realist Explanations of the Political Use of Military Force 63

showdown. Besides the development of a survivable nuclear deterrent, and a hair-trigger warning system, presidents also relied upon the use of force to signal American strength and resolve. The thinking among many nuclear strategists was that the political use of force could credibly signal the willingness to use force on a more massive scale. It is no wonder that given such momentous stakes, limited force became the favored tool in this quest for physical and theoretical security.

As the Third World struggles of the 1960s were resolved in the 1970s, the Cold War battle lines solidified once again. Each side won some friends and allies, while most of the underdeveloped nations tried to play off the superpowers against one another to help themselves. As conflicts in more important states were resolved, the US and the Soviet Union jousted with each other directly or indirectly in the world's backwaters. In Ethiopia, Somalia, Mozambique, and Afghanistan the two sides battled over comparatively marginal prizes. Only in a world so evenly divided could the US invasion of the tiny island of Grenada in 1983 be treated as such a critical event. But, American interests had expanded throughout the 1950s and 1960s to the point where the government could no longer afford to maintain them. The Nixon Doctrine, which emphasized that the US was prepared to use its wealth, but not its manpower to defend third world client states against the communists, was announced as the US began to wind down its involvement in Southeast Asia. In the aftermath of Vietnam the old defense pacts created during the 1950s were allowed to lapse, and the limited use of force declined (Blechman and Kaplan, 1978; Leebaert, 2002). But seemingly no sooner had the US tired of its global obligations than new hotspots and crises erupted in the late 1970s. The tension between the superpowers increased further under the Reagan administration, along with military spending and the use of force. American presidents had learned from Vietnam that the Congress and the public wanted a forceful foreign policy, although they were unwilling to countenance sustained involvement and casualties in obscure nations. The public still expected presidents to appear and act strong, not get pushed around (as Jimmy Carter did over the Iran hostage affair), and be strongly anti-communist, but bloodlessly if possible. Reagan apparently forgot this lesson in Lebanon in 1982-1984, but applied it against Grenada, Libya and in the 'Reagan Doctrine', which asserted that the US had a right to *aid* those fighting against illegitimate governments (as in Nicaragua, Afghanistan and Cambodia). Reagan backed up this aid with uses of force designed to influence events in Central America throughout the 1980s.

During the Cold War the US saw its national interests at stake the world over and used force to defend and advance these interests. Whether American forces were participants themselves in these battles as in Korea, Vietnam, Lebanon, the Dominican Republic, Grenada and elsewhere, or force was used to signal or assist those fighting communism, US foreign policy objectives were advanced by military actions to an extent heretofore unimaginable. Scholars may claim that foreign policy makers were motivated more by ideology, economics or domestic politics, but all indications are that, however misguided some of their policies were, presidents sincerely believed that US survival was at issue and took military action to protect it. The US's economic, political and military advantages guaranteed it victory in this long struggle over an adversary that lacked the

64   *The Political Use of Military Force in US Foreign Policy*

resources needed to win. After communism collapsed in Eastern Europe in 1989 and in the Soviet Union in 1991, the US found its hegemony unchallenged. With the old threats largely gone, presidents and policymakers had to determine where the new threats were to be found.

Defining National Interests in the Post Cold War World, 1990 Onward

Until the end of the Cold War, US foreign policy had always been predicated upon some fairly simple assumptions about the nature of international relations and the best ways to deal with them. In the early years of weakness and subsequent decades of domestic consolidation and territorial growth, foreign policy makers generally sought to avoid the balance of power politics dominated by European nations. Identifying those areas whose defense was vital to the nation's security was fairly straightforward. Only the Western hemisphere was considered important and since European meddling was fairly minimal, the nation could bask in its relative isolation. For a brief period from 1895-1919 the US played a major, but not dominant role in global politics. Evaluations of the national interest and decisions about when to use force to defend and advance these interests had to be based on more complex calculations involving relative capabilities, geopolitics and the like. We see evidence of this in US policy in the Far East, North Africa and Europe at the time, but we also see the emerging moralistic and legalistic rationales for foreign policy so many scholars have decried. After World War II, the global struggle with the Soviet Union and communism led to a foreign policy based on zero-sum game assumptions. Since almost any gain for the USSR meant an equivalent loss for the US, US interests, whether real or reputational, were perceived to be at stake everywhere. This obviated the need for a foreign policy based on strictly realist and/or objective calculations. In the Cold War's wake presidents again face the challenge of making foreign policy without the luxury of isolation or the demands of zero-sum competition to dictate the national interest. There are obvious interests in European stability, Persian Gulf oil, and Korean security, but having largely avoided dealing with the world's complexity for so long, presidents now were in search of new foreign policy strategies to unite their diverse concerns. Defining when, where and why they would use military force to advance the nation's foreign policy proved just as difficult as ever.

In the first few years after the Cold War we find a variety of competing alarms, ambitions and agendas to guide US foreign policy. During the early 1990s a plethora of articles appeared asserting that the post Cold War world was just as dangerous as the Cold War. Samuel Huntington (1993) argued that we were in era of 'clashing civilization' (1993). John Mearsheimer (1990) predicted that the same old antagonisms that had plagued Europe in the past would return. Policymakers were not immune from such hyperbole. President Clinton's first Director of Central Intelligence, James Woolsey claimed that, 'we have slain a large dragon, but we now live in a jungle filled with a bewildering variety of poisonous snakes' (quoted in Mueller, 1994, pp.356-357). Even someone as cautious and practical as Colin

Powell argued that, 'The real threat is the unknown, the uncertain. In a very real sense, *the primary threat to our security is instability...*' (emphasis added).[8] Presidents struggled to make sense of these threats and develop a new rationale for using force to defend against them. George H. Bush's vision of a New World Order, never precisely defined, worked well enough to justify military intervention against Iraq, but was shelved after the Gulf War as so much rhetoric. In addition to asserting instability as a threat to American security, the Clinton administration elevated the importance of promoting democracy as a means of enhancing US security. Massive interventions in Bosnia and Kosovo were authorized to bring peace and democracy. US security has, in many respects, become just as concerned with how nations treat their people as it is with how states behave toward their neighbors. As well, presidents Bush and Clinton deployed the military to deal with instability in the Balkans and the Horn of Africa, and rogue states in the Middle East and East Asia. Now, the threat of terrorism has assumed primacy in US foreign policy, but that too has been used to justify everything from waging war in Iraq to not driving SUV's. Perhaps fighting terrorism is just the sort of amorphous doctrine–part security-driven and part value-based–that can be stretched to fit any number of contingencies that presidents seem to prefer. And given that security from terrorism requires both substantial military power and reach, and involves the protection of innocent American lives, the likelihood that it will be used to justify all manner of military actions short of war, and war itself is considerable. Nonetheless, we are still unsure just where US interests lie at any given moment in the war on terrorism, for terrorists are (potentially) everywhere. The threat of terrorism has merely postponed the day of reckoning when presidents will once again have to grapple with determining the objective interests of American foreign policy and the role of force short of war in achieving them.

A Model of the Use of Force and Security and Power Interests, 1948-1998

Having briefly explored US security and power interests and the use of force in more recent times, we may use this knowledge, along with what we have learned from other studies of this subject, to develop a more systematic explanation of this foreign policy phenomena. Realism and the various security/power-oriented explanations of US foreign policy describe the many factors that affect presidents' decisions regarding the use of force. We saw that these factors were often discussed in very general terms by many international relations scholars (e.g., the notion of a national interest), but that foreign policy scholars engaging in empirical analysis had more precisely defined and measured many international conditions likely to lead to a use of force. Yet, researchers pursuing this former line of inquiry tended to rely on measures that were identified on a somewhat ad hoc basis–they were not always derived from some larger theory. This, I argued, made it difficult to make claims about the value and utility of security-oriented theories. However,

---

[8] General Colin Powell, testimony, Committee on the Budget, US Senate, February 3, 1992.

66 *The Political Use of Military Force in US Foreign Policy*

we can identify from all the previous analyses in this chapter, several, particular conditions that ought to influence the likelihood that a president will use force in some international crisis.

First, the realist paradigm tells us that the most enduring and powerful predictor of state behavior is power. In particular, US power, relative to other nations is perhaps the key explanatory variable in realism, and the most obvious manifestation of a nation's status in the world. Power in this sense means the resources the nation possesses that allow it to act influentially. Indicators like the size of the US economy, the US population, and the size of its military provide us with a way to compare US power to other nations in a concrete way. We would expect that the greater the power of the US internationally, the more likely a president will be to use force. Increased power not only makes uses of force feasible, it also is an indication of the status of the US in international politics. Only major powers are involved in and can perceive interests at stake in events across the globe. As the US' power in the international system increases, its interactions with other nations increase, as does the likelihood that US foreign policy will, in some manner, conflict with the policies of these other states. In the post World War II era, the US has been one of the two most powerful states, or the most powerful. We would expect that a dominant power would find it necessary to use force on many occasions to protect against challengers and maintain its hegemony. Therefore:

Hypothesis 1: The greater the US share of relative capabilities in the international system, the more often presidents will use force short of war.[9]

The US' status and influence are as much dependent upon perceptions of its power and will as they are on its true capabilities. When other nations trust the threats and commitments the US makes, the President can generally dispose of challenges with actions less aggressive than the use of force. The historical record makes clear that presidents have believed a failure to protect US credibility would create suspicion from uncertain allies and challenges by probing adversaries (Gaddis, 1982; Johnson, 1985; Schell, 1976). Presidents have feared that a failure to uphold US commitments would encourage Hitlerian behavior (the Munich syndrome and domino theory), and lead allies to make peace with America's enemies. As Johnson (1985) argues, presidents have perceived an interdependence of these commitments–a threat to a commitment anywhere is a threat to commitments everywhere. Especially when the commitment involves a prior, military intervention (e.g., the continual use of force against Iraq throughout the 1990s), presidents and their advisers have asserted that US national interests have been

---

[9] I use the US share of global capabilities from the Correlates of War, National Material Capabilities data set for the years 1948-1993 available at http://cow2.la.psu.edu/ (Singer, Bremer and Stuckey, 1972). These data are lagged two years. For the years 1996-1998 I use the last known value of the US CINC score.

Security, Power and Realist Explanations of the Political Use of Military Force 67

engaged. Once engaged, presidents often feel compelled to respond with force to subsequent threats to these explicit or implicit commitments. A failure to respond militarily in international crises that affect these commitments may lead to perceptions of weakness and lack of resolve. Therefore:

Hypothesis 2: When an international crisis occurs where the US has used force in the previous twelve months, presidents will be more likely to use force in the present situation.[10]

Of critical importance to any president will be the gravity of a particular crisis and the extent to which it affects US relations with other nations. The number of international actors a crisis draws in is a key sign of the event's potential impact. As this number increases, the greater and deeper the effects will be, the greater the size of the international audience observing the behavior of the hegemon, and the greater the need for visible action to rise above the cacophony of diplomacy and threats. As the number of crisis actors grows, so too does the number of states who might be targeted by a political use of force. Presidents will be mindful of the need to appear strong and resolute during such international crises. The greater the number of crisis actors, the greater the importance of the crisis to US national interests.

Hypothesis 3: When an international crisis occurs, the US will be more likely to use military force short of war the greater the number of crisis actors.[11]

Attacks on American citizens pose severe challenges to US influence abroad and presidential leadership at home (Brands, 1987; Tillema, 1973). As we have seen, presidents have used force throughout US history to defend and rescue Americans caught in crises overseas. The fundamental need and desire to take care of its own explains many of these American interventions. Aside from the need to protect lives, there are other, broader interests at stake in such crises. If presidents were unwilling to use force to protect their fellow citizens, foreign allies might well wonder to what lengths the US was prepared to go to protect *their* citizens. Presidents might fear that an unwillingness to use force to protect US citizens would be taken as an indication of American unwillingness to use force in general. Therefore:

Hypothesis 4: When an international crisis involves threats or violence to American citizens, presidents will be more likely to use military force.[12]

---

[10] Data on prior uses of force are taken from the 1948-1998 data sets on the political use of military force described in Chapter One.

[11] Data on the number of crisis participants was taken from Blechman and Kaplan (1978) Zelikow (1984), *Facts on File, Keesing's Contemporary Archives*, and the *New York Times Index.*

[12] ibid.

68   *The Political Use of Military Force in US Foreign Policy*

Most scholars seem to agree that the political use of force declines during wartime as the president's attention, military personnel and funds are directed elsewhere (Meernik, 1994; Ostrom and Job, 1986). In particular, US involvement in the Korean and Vietnam Wars altered foreign policy, principally by the diversion of vast amounts of resources and personnel halfway around the world. The materiel and manpower required for these undertakings was so substantial it made military operations in other parts of the globe difficult to mount. More importantly, escalating US casualties in these wars made military involvement in other international crises distinctly less attractive. For example, Mueller (1973) finds that presidential popularity dropped as American casualties increased in Vietnam. Ostrom and Job (1986) find that US uses of force declined as logged, cumulative battle deaths in Korea and Vietnam increased. Therefore, during the time periods between June, 1950 and July, 1953, and August, 1964 (The Gulf of Tonkin incident) and January, 1973, presidents ought to be reluctant to authorize additional deployments of military force in order to conserve personnel for more immediate security needs. I measure the impact of each war by the logged, cumulative number of battle deaths per month.[13] Therefore:

Hypothesis 5: Presidents will be less likely to use force during an international crisis as logged, cumulative battle deaths in the Korean and Vietnam wars increase.

To test these hypotheses, I employ a more complex, statistical model. The objective is to predict what conditions associated with the aforementioned hypotheses are influential in explaining whether or not presidents use force, given an opportunity to do so. I am predicting a 'yes' or 'no' choice by the president, and so I utilize a statistical model that is designed to estimate the likelihood of a binary decision choice using a set of independent variables. The statistical estimation procedure known as probit is designed to do exactly this and its estimates are fairly simple to analyze (Greene, 1993). All of the hypotheses are tested together in one multivariate analysis. To interpret the substantive impact of this and the other coefficients, I rely on the marginal effects coefficients. These coefficients indicate the percentage increase in the probability of a use of force associated with a one-unit increase in an independent variable, while holding all other variables constant at their mean value. The overall fit of this model is quite good. The likelihood that all the coefficients are equal to zero is infinitesimally small. The five security related factors successfully predict 71.9 percent of all cases. The model accurately predicts 71 percent of the non uses of force and 72.60 percent of the uses of force. The proportionate reduction of error is 40.8 percent.

---

[13] From Job and Ostrom (1986).

Table 2.6 Predicting Uses of Force 1948-1998 Using Probit Analysis: The National Security and Power Model

Variable	Coeff.	Standard Error	T Statistic	P Value	Marginal Effect
US International Power	-2.267	1.139	-1.99	0.047	-.9002
Prior Use of Force	.4056	.1276	3.18	0.001	.1580
Number Crisis Actors	.3052	.0395	7.71	0.000	.12118
Anti-US Violence	.9240	.1308	7.06	0.000	.34078
War Deaths.	-.0565	.0173	-3.26	0.001	-.0224
Constant	-.7422	.2540	-2.92	0.003	

N=605
$\chi^2 = 160.3$, p. $< .0001$
Pseudo $R^2 = .191$
Percent Correctly Predicted = 71.9%
Proportionate Reduction of Error = 40.8%

Somewhat surprisingly we see that the US share of international power ('US International Power') is negatively related to the propensity of presidents to use force. As well, the coefficient for this variable is statistically significant. The higher the share of US global power, the less likely presidents are to use force. In the post World War II period, presidents apparently use force more often as the US share of international capabilities diminished. We should remember, however, that in the immediate aftermath of World War II, the US share of international power was artificially high. After several years the war-ravaged economies of Europe, Japan and the Soviet Union recovered to more normal levels and the US share of world power necessarily declined, even though the absolute size of its economy continued to expand. As well, we know from Chapter 1 that Harry Truman used force less often than any other president. The inclusion of those years through the Korean War may be causing this somewhat odd result. After removing all the observations for the years 1948-1953 from the data, I reran the model and this time found that there was no relationship between US relative power and the use of limited force (results not shown). Although this result does not confirm the expectation of a positive relationship, we at least see that presidents did not necessarily act contrary to what most scholars and policymakers would take to be sound advice. That is, the reach of US foreign policy should not exceed its grasp, otherwise imperial overstretch (Kennedy, 1987) may damage the US domestically and internationally over the long run.

We find support for the idea that US presidents were concerned with the preservation of US credibility. Presidents were more likely to use force where they had used it in the past ('Prior Use of Force'). When a crisis occurred in a locale where the US had used force in the previous twelve months, presidents were about 16 percent more likely to use force in the current crisis, according to the marginal effects coefficient. When we examine the simple frequency of such events, we see that presidents used force roughly 72 percent of the time (129 times out of 179 opportunities where force had been used in the previous year). Prior involvement may well have created expectations of future action. Having used force once in a crisis locale, presidents may believe that allies, adversaries and neutrals perceive something of an implicit commitment or interest in developments in the crisis region. These crisis actors will no doubt pay close attention to what the US does the next time a problem arises. If the president is unwilling to use force, these actors may conclude that the US has lost interest in the crisis region and that therefore, they may act with a freer hand.

But what matters most in such situations, may be what presidents think these other states' leaders perceive about the US, rather than what those leaders actually believe. During the Cold War presidents sometimes created artificial expectations of US commitment and engaged US credibility where perhaps it was not at issue, simply by proclaiming that American credibility was at stake. Having done so, they could scarcely afford to ignore such verbal commitments and the costs this might entail to the US reputation as a reliable guarantor. On the other hand, prior uses of military force may just make future uses more feasible as more US forces may be stationed in the region. This in turn may also make future crises more likely. Regardless, we see that the past exercises a powerful impact on the likelihood of future US military operations.

As the number of nations involved in a crisis increases so too does the president's propensity to use military force ('Number Crisis Actors'). For every additional nation involved in an international crisis, the probability of a political use of military force increases by 12 percent, all other things being equal. The number of actors involved plays a major role in presidential decision making by serving as indicator of the importance of the crisis in world politics. It represents the extent to which the crisis will touch upon the interests of other states. It may signal whether a crisis is purely a local affair, a regional matter or an event with global repercussions. The more states involved, the more the US will be cognizant of the audience to which it is performing and the message its actions will send to these states.

As we saw in the historical analysis, presidents often use force to protect or rescue Americans who are being threatened or attacked overseas ('Anti-US Violence'). When such opportunities arise, presidents are 34 percent more likely to use force, according to the marginal effects coefficient. When we examine the overall spread of the data, we see that presidents used force 75 percent of the time when such incidents arose (126 out of 168 incidents). The significance of some of these events in any grand, strategic sense may be limited, but certainly a failure to use force to protect one's own might be perceived by foreign leaders as a sign of weakness. Allies might well conclude that the president was unwilling to use force in general to protect important interests, and enemies might be emboldened to attack Americans elsewhere. We have also seen presidents justify several, major

Security, Power and Realist Explanations of the Political Use of Military Force 71

military interventions, at least in part, in the name of protecting American lives. The 1980 hostage rescue mission in Iran, the 1983 invasion of Grenada and the 1989 invasion of Panama were each premised to some extent on threats to and violence against US citizens. This truly represents one of the more enduring concerns of US foreign policy.

Lastly, note that presidents are less likely to use force as American casualties in Korea and Vietnam mount. As resources and personnel are mobilized to confront the greater threat to the nation, we would expect presidents to be less inclined or able to dispatch US forces elsewhere. Increasing deaths of US military personnel have been associated with diminishing support for the war and for the presidents who presided over them (Mueller, 1973). Not surprisingly, such loss of life in one remote part of the world discourages presidents from engaging in similar operations elsewhere.

Presidents have found no shortage of American security interests in the world and no shortage of reasons to use military force to advance these interests. The globalization of American security interests has essentially been completed. Few domestic or international issues escape the attention of the hegemon. US' foreign policy is predicated primarily on the need to maintain its political and military hegemony, and challenges to this order can come from any state or force hostile to the implicit or explicit rules of the system. While force may be of declining utility against those states that share US values, it remains the ultimate weapon to defend and promote the system against adversary states and terrorist organization. As long as those nations that challenge American hegemony are fairly weak, presidents will find the use of force a convenient tool. But if, in the not too distant future, a more powerful challenger to US hegemony emerges, presidents will again become just as concerned with how force is used in order to preserve its security.

Discussion and Conclusions

We have seen that there is no 'one' security or power *theory* of US foreign policy making and the political use of military force. Realist theories of international relations provide guidance in understanding conflictual behavior, such as wars and militarized disputes, and closely associated phenomena, such as alliance formation. Most such theories are not intended to explain and predict the foreign policy actions of individual states. We can draw general inferences about the kinds of issues and developments that might lead a state to take measures to defend or advance security interests. Yet, even if there were more realist theories concerned with foreign policy making, we still confront a rather intractable problem with specifying a 'security' theory or explanation of the political use of military force. What does 'security' mean? What, exactly, are 'security' interests? Based on these analyses, I outline a definition of 'security' below that can be used to help explain how the US has pursued its more specific, security interests.

A minimalist definition of the term *'security'* would stress its defensive nature. A state of security is one in which the physical territory of the state is at least free of threats to its integrity. But security is also an environment in which policies of the state and its regime type are free from review or limitation by an entity external to the nation. The first aspect of security is the more easy to determine since national territory is a tangible thing that the state occupies in whole and without question, if it is completely secure, or in some part, if it shares control with another nation on actor. The latter element of security, sovereignty, is far more difficult to measure. All states are limited in some manner because they are influenced by and anticipate the reactions of other states. Sometimes this influence results in beneficial cooperation, for states willingly give up their sovereignty on some issues, while at other times it results in costly interference. Security in this minimalist sense can be thought of as a condition in which a state's preferences regarding its physical integrity and sovereignty are realized. Few if any states approach such an ideal condition, free of worries about the actions of other states. Their foreign policies are thus tailored to trying to attain some proximate level of security. Some nations strive ceaselessly to reach this ideal point (perhaps Israel), while others realize its unattainability and so content themselves with realizing some level of security less than ideal (perhaps Finland during the Cold War). Most fall somewhere in between.

If we begin by conceiving of the goal of security as essentially defensive, how does this influence the means by which a state attempts to achieve this condition? Morgan and Palmer (1997) differentiate between proactive and reactive foreign policies that I rely on quite heavily. A minimalist conception of security 'policy' would be reactive in nature. That is, states would take action only in defense and in reaction to what other states are doing in order to protect their security. These distinctions may seem obvious at the theoretical level, but in practical terms it is extremely difficult to find that bright line between the two. To give but one obvious example, would we say that a nation in danger of invasion tomorrow, launches a preemptive attack today is being proactive or reactive? For the sake of argument, however, let us say that a minimalist 'security' policy would be defensive in design and reactive in execution. States would act only when there are clear and present dangers to their territory and sovereignty. They would not seek out enemies, or go casting about for some sort of provocation.

Having illustrated an ideal point at one end of the spectrum of security policies, we must examine the opposite end, which is closer to where we will find the US. A maximalist definition of security would move the zone of interest physically and politically beyond the immediate environs of the state to encompass more, most or all of the world. A state with maximalist security interests would be concerned about all manner of direct and indirect threats. It would be concerned not just with what Wolfers (1962, p.73) calls 'possession' goals–those things that a state acquires (e.g., resources and rights), but also 'milieu' goals–the nature of the environment in which the state exists (e.g., a particular monetary system). Such a state is not just concerned with outcomes, but with the mechanisms by which outcomes are produced and its desire/need to dominate these mechanisms. Correctly or incorrectly, maximalist states view their security as dependent upon

Security, Power and Realist Explanations of the Political Use of Military Force   73

international rules of the game (implicit or explicit) that work to their advantage. For a hegemon whose purview extends to all the most important elements of the international system, survival becomes equivalent to domination. It seeks to dominate the rules in order to perpetuate its hegemony and it strives to maintain hegemony in order to manipulate the rules to its advantage. Security is offensive in nature because national interests have become international interests and because concern for substance has progressed to involvement in process. This is in part why terrorism presents such a threat because terrorists, in addition to the actual human and physical damage they create, are also challenging the nature of the international system.

A maximalist definition of security would be both reactive and proactive in nature. As the zone of interest for a state expands, the need for both reactive and proactive actions will increase. (For a hegemon, a significant portion of its policies will be devoted to reactive policies designed to protect its substantial interests. Such demands will soak up more of its resources and time and make it more difficult to exploit new opportunities for proaction [Morgan and Palmer, 1997].) A state with a proactive orientation to security will be concerned not just with imminent threats and the immediate consequences of its actions, but also long-range threats and consequences. For example, the US has consistently shown an interest in preventing the rise of regional powers inimical to its interests (e.g., Iraq) and in developing measures to counter threats that may arise in the future (e.g., ballistic missile defense). It has been concerned with how its actions affect the outcome of contemporary events and crises, but also how its policies will influence the behavior of nations in the future. The domino theory was but one foreign policy strategy centered on the necessity of preventing not just one outcome, but also an entire series of events. A proactive foreign policy also involves efforts to affect both international developments and their underlying causes. If peace and stability in the world are considered to be intrinsically beneficial, it becomes important to influence those forces that help produce such things. Thus, do we find the US manipulating the internal politics of other nations to make them more peaceful, which in turn is supposed to make the world more pacific. Indeed, the ultimate offensive and proactive conception of security would generate not just an interest in international developments and the mechanisms that produce them, but also intranational politics and the processes that give rise to them.

I have described with a broad brush the most basic conceptions of security and the choices they entail. At this level of abstraction, we can explain and predict foreign policy behaviors only in very general terms. We would expect that as a state's conception of security moves from defensive to offensive and as its policies proceed from reactive to proactive, its foreign policy, including the political use of force short of war, will become more activist. We might also surmise, like most realists, that one of the most important factors influencing the definition of security and security policies, will be a state's power. As states increase in power they will have more resources to implement an activist policy (Morgan and Palmer, 1997; Zakaria, 1998). In addition more powerful states may well come to define their interests based in part on the ability to use their power relationally to affect beneficial, international outcomes. They will seek to preserve and expand the

The Political Use of Military Force in US Foreign Policy

prerogatives that come with power. As the US has grown in power, its foreign policy objectives have expanded. Where once the US devoted most of its scarce resources to the protection of its territory and citizens, since 1898 and especially after 1945, US security interests have moved from being defensive and reactive in nature, to offensive and proactive in nature. Power, as measured in relative capabilities and state strength, has played the major role in causing this transition. The increase in the use of force short of war has been one of its most obvious consequences. Yet, though US relative capabilities are critical in explaining variations in the political use of military over time and in the aggregate, they are not as useful in explaining why presidents resort to using force during particular international crises. Power provides a requisite backdrop, or parameter that makes a use of force more or less likely, but to understand the rationale behind specific decisions to use force, we must turn to situation-specific information. As we saw in the probit analysis of uses of force, these factors, such as anti-American violence, the number of crisis actors and the prior use of force are quite powerful in explaining presidential decision making.

Thus, the quest for security, whether defined defensively or offensively; reactively or proactively, has provided the impetus for a substantial number–probably most–uses of force short of war. From the time of George Washington through the years of George Bush, presidents have nearly always sought to justify these actions, in some manner, as necessary for the preservation of American security. I would make several, general observations regarding what we have learned about security and the use of force. First, we see that security objectives are dynamic. Obvious interests, such as the preservation of the US, are eternal, but much of security policy could be viewed as a malleable vessel which different administrations shape according to a variety of internal and external developments. Threats from foreign governments emerge and disappear–a point the end of the Cold War drove home. New interests especially tend to accumulate around increasing levels of power like iron filings to a magnet. Countries and concerns that once seemed remote suddenly become urgent and intimate. The trajectory of US interests has expanded ever outward geographically from the homelands, to its surrounding neighborhood in the Western hemisphere, and finally to more distant lands. Its power allows the US to be more concerned with such developments and engage in the political use of military force more frequently to meet threats to its interests. But the exact definition of these interests tends to change, sometimes slowly and sometimes quickly, over the course of US history.

Second, throughout its history, most of the issues that affected US security affected it indirectly, and so the linkages between foreign policy crises, US interests and US actions have been indirect. For example, US security may be influenced by developments in the Panama Canal zone, but not nearly to the extent that French security has been affected by Germany, or South Korean security has been affected by North Korea. US power and isolation have made it relatively free of the security concerns that plague most nations, making defense of its actions in terms of national security somewhat less demanding. The recent concern over terrorist actions within the US is a very notable exception to this observation. Given that in its early years the most frequently cited 'security' objective in using limited force was the protection of American citizens abroad (62 percent of all uses), and that territorial security was cited only 11 percent of the time, the US itself has been fairly secure. I do not mean to argue that there have not been real threats to American security or that foreign policy makers are necessarily being disingenuous when they find US security at stake in remote, third world nations. Rather, making the case for the importance of national security in US foreign policy is relatively more difficult compared to other nations. Therefore, we as scholars must look to the manner in which US interests *overseas* have been threatened, and the manner in which US security is affected in myriad ways indirectly through events and developments among and within nations.

Third, a major difficulty involved in using security to explain political uses of military force is that so often security interests are sought to rationalize rather than guide these actions. Few Americans could have located US security interests in Grenada prior to October, 1983, or even locate that nation on a map. Yet, President Reagan defended his intervention, in all probability with sincerity, as a response to a threat to American security from Cuban and communist influence in the region. How can we predict presidential decisions if we do not know what goes into them? The problem of defining security interests a priori are compounded as a state's power increases. A weak nation must confine its interests to the most obvious and proximate. A hegemon like the US, has the ability to involve itself in many more nations and situations. More problematically, foreign policy makers begin to look for threats and assert US interests and commit American credibility where neither was at issue. Such ever-expanding definitions of American national security also make it difficult for the researcher who wishes to explain US actions based on security concerns.

Nonetheless, I believe that such problems can be surmounted. First, by conceiving of the use of force in terms of minimalist/maximalist objectives and reactive/proactive behaviors, we can broadly understand the frequency with which presidents resort to the use of force. Power is certainly a critical factor, but it is more of an environmental condition than a rationale for using force. Second, we must identify recurring national security objectives that help explain political (non) uses of force and justify their importance. Third, we must integrate the other primary objectives sought through the use of military force into a comprehensive understanding of this subject.

Chapter 3

Economic Interests and the Political Use of Military Force

Introduction

Scholars and policymakers have argued long and hard over the extent to which the interests of business have driven US foreign policy. Whether trade follows the flag, or the flag follows trade in some ways makes little difference for we have every reason to suspect an intimate relationship between wealth and power. Not all wealthy states may be powerful, but all-powerful states must be wealthy over the long term, and must therefore be constantly vigilant to threats to and opportunities for economic growth. In the days when governments faced few restraints on their powers and many threats in the world, wars were fought over land, resources, and trade. The US was no exception to this sort of practice. We know the Founding Fathers believed, in the words of George Washington, 'The great rule of conduct for us in regard to foreign relations is, in extending our commercial relations to have with them [principally European states] as little political connection as possible' (quoted in Horsman, 1985, p.69). Yet, even the Framers understood that commercial relations would be difficult without an adequate navy. Indeed, naval vessels, for much of the late 18th and 19th centuries served as floating embassies charged with all manner of diplomatic chores, especially the protection and promotion of American commerce. This much most scholars agree upon. We divide over the extent to which economic interests have influenced foreign policy. Some see foreign policy as nothing more than the international extension of the interests of capitalism, while others perceive in the quest for wealth nothing less than the desire for power and security.

Before proceeding, however, I must define what I mean by economic interests, or more precisely, *economic interest goals*, in foreign policy. Economic interests are those *real and potential sources of wealth and profit held or potentially held by private actors that can be advanced or protected by the state.* The government may act on behalf of the self-interest of a few with policies that provide selective benefits to these actors, or it may act to further the acquisition of wealth generally by society through public policies. It may use force to defend the rights of a single, multinational corporation, or it may use force to extend the broad principles of free market capitalism for the ostensible benefit of all Americans. The president may pursue both objectives simultaneously, and certainly may claim to be engaging in the latter, while actually doing the former. The reader should also understand that although I use the term 'economic interests' as if to suggest that

Economic Interests and the Political Use of Military Force 77

there is a monolithic set of objectives pursued by the US government, in fact there are many and competing economic interests within American society and government. I am interested in exploring those specific and general economic interests that have influenced the US decision to use limited force, regardless of how or over whom their representatives triumphed to have such an impact on foreign policy.

Many more writers used to claim that US foreign policy was driven by the economic self-interest of big business, but such accounts have waned in popularity with the end of the Cold War. In particular, those critical theories of US foreign policy (e.g., Marxism/Leninism) have been discredited for lack of empirical support. Yet, they should not be discounted altogether. The evidence has mostly dispelled the notion that US foreign policy is run by and for the benefit of multinational corporations, but it still is possible that these economic interests play an important role in some decisions to use force. And since international relations scholars applying empirical techniques, especially statistical analyses, have tended to examine the post World War II era, a more thorough analysis of earlier periods of US history may turn up evidence in favor of such explanations. There are also theories of foreign policy that accord economic factors an important role, especially in terms of the US leadership of the global economy, that share some similarities with Marxist and leftist accounts. The works of Robert Keohane, Joseph Nye, Stephen Krasner, Robert Gilpin, G. John Ikenberry, David Lake, Michael Mastanduno and others all emphasize economic interests and issues in shaping US foreign policy, while recognizing the potency of military force. Other research on the impact of interest groups on US foreign policy actions, and the central place of the international economic system in the post World War II era of American hegemony provide important insights as well. Explanations of the use of force based on economic interests deserve the same scrutiny as other theories, for each fits into a larger puzzle.

I contend that economic interests have played a significant role in shaping US foreign policy in general and the political use of military force in particular. The advancement of free market capitalism for the benefit of Americans who engage in commerce and the promotion of private economic interests for the few have been vital concerns of US foreign policy throughout its whole history. Sometimes these objectives have complemented US security interests, as in the Cold War, while at other times they simply *were* US foreign policy, as in the years prior to the Civil War. Economic interests have provided both necessary and sufficient conditions for using force, as we shall see in the analyses below. Yet, despite their prominence in many theoretical works on US foreign policy, they have not received enough attention in empirical, particularly quantitative research on the decision to use force. I aim to fill in as much as possible this deficiency in our understanding of a critical foreign policy action.

First, I review the various theories involving economic factors and foreign policy. Second, as in other chapters, I review three case studies where we have reason to believe economic forces played a strong role in a president's decision to use military force. Third, I describe the evolving role of economic interests in American foreign policy since the founding of the Republic. I pay particular

78 *The Political Use of Military Force in US Foreign Policy*

attention to the role played by military force in protecting US commerce, and discuss the historical trends of such actions in the years 1798-1941. I next analyze the importance of economic interests in explaining the political use of military force in the period 1948-1998 through the use of multivariate analysis. I conclude by assessing the evidence.

Theories of Economic Interests and US Foreign Policy

The development of theories of the economic determinants of the political use of military force by US presidents has not proceeded with the same degree of empirically falsifiable research that we have seen in other theories of military action. Indeed, Mastanduno (1988, p.824) notes that the link between economics and security has been the most neglected area of scholarship in international relations. Nonetheless, there are theories that are generally well recognized and provide useful insights into the economic motivations behind US foreign policy. For our purposes we can identify three different schools of theories on the economic determinants of US security policy and the use of force. These are 1) critical theories including principally Marxism/Leninism, dependency and world system theories, 2) pluralist, or interest group models, and 3) hegemonic theories of the international economic system.

Critical Theories

Despite their differences, I examine several critical theories–Marxism, Leninism, dependency theory, world system theory–together because they generally share a similar orientation and normative (i.e., often critical) perspective on US foreign policy behavior. Many of these theories are not as popular as they once were, but they highlight important actors and interests in the making of US foreign policy, and actually share several features with other economic interest theories of US foreign policy. While Karl Marx was less known for his analyses of international economics, Lenin's *Imperialism, The Highest Stage of Capitalism* takes Marxism as its inspiration and extrapolates the Marxist framework to explain the international behavior of capitalist nations. Domestically, all industries are driven to squeeze as much productivity out of workers as possible, while paying them as little as possible in the drive for ever greater profits. Because workers are not adequately compensated for their labor, however, their lack of buying power results in under consumption. Excessive profit taking by industry leads to a surplus of capital. Industry then begins to look beyond the domestic market to foreign markets to invest the surplus capital, where many argue the rate of return is greater (see Weisskopf, 1974), and to sell goods that cannot be absorbed at home. The state, dominated and run by capitalist interests, goes abroad in search of markets and territories to conquer to alleviate these problems. States use military force whenever necessary to acquire colonies (as in Africa) and force open markets (as in China) on behalf of business. Since markets and territories are finite, Lenin argued that the capitalist nations would ultimately go to war with one another to preserve

Economic Interests and the Political Use of Military Force 79

and extend their domains. Ultimately, however, the drive for markets and the wars over domination of the underdeveloped portions of the world should weaken the imperialist powers. The metropole or center decays as capital is invested elsewhere, and manufacturing plants are transferred to the periphery where labor costs are cheaper. Eventually the heretofore-underdeveloped parts of the world should develop and rival their colonial masters.

Others made similar arguments in the early 20th century, even if their ideological biases were different. Hobson (1902) made many of the same arguments as Lenin, although he argues that businesses are a special, albeit dominant interest in the shaping of international economic policy. The state may conquer lands and wage war on their behalf, but Hobson believed if this damaging influence was exposed, the state could take corrective action before its businesses migrated overseas and bankrupted the nation through colonial wars. Deutsch (1974) points out that there were more than a few conservative capitalists and politicians who also argued that the state needed to find an outlet for surplus capital and find new markets for overproduced goods. In the US, William Taft defended his 'dollar diplomacy' by arguing that 'It is an effort frankly directed to the increase of American trade upon the axiomatic principle that the Government of the US shall extend all proper support to every legitimate and beneficial enterprise abroad' (quoted in Rosenberg [1982], p.59). Scholars differ, however, over just what the US was prepared to do to offer, 'proper support'. Many liberal and critical scholars at the time viewed the US government as dominated by capitalist interests, even though it never developed a colonial empire to the extent of the British or the French dominions. Lenin and Hobson considered military intervention on behalf of capitalism as an inevitable and regrettable result of this domination, while more conservative commentators viewed it as entirely appropriate given the superiority of the industrialized world. But when, despite the Great Depression, two world wars and decolonization, capitalism persisted, modern scholars began to develop new theories of imperialism that could explain capitalist domination.

Dependency theory and world systems theory (Dos Santos, 1970; Frank, 1969; Galtung, 1971; Kolko, 1969, 1988; Odell, 1974; Rosen, 1974; Wallerstein, 1974, 1988) both share many Marxist/Leninist assumptions about the motivations of governments. But, these newer theories emphasized the global, rather than the statist nature of economic domination. In some sense, the capitalist conspiracy becomes an international, rather than simply a national one for these writers argue that the advanced capitalist nations and their multinational corporations share common interests and foreign policy objectives. Both theories analyze economics from a global perspective that emphasizes the 'dependency' of the poor nations of the world on the rich ones and the methods by which the rich nations and multinational corpoations perpetuate their control over the international capitalist 'system'. Kurth (1974, p.5) summarizes their arguments:

> Capitalist systems are propelled outward by three basic drives: the need for raw materials, the need for foreign markets to compensate for inadequate development at home, and the need for foreign investment to absorb surplus capital. These result in capitalist states undertaking expansionist, even imperialist foreign

policies. In particular, it is argued, the foreign interventions and the foreign assistance programs undertaken by the US are primarily determined by the American capitalist system and by economic interests within it.

Dependency theorists divide the world into core and periphery nations. Core nations are those industrialized states that own most of the wealth in the world, manufacture finished products and possess the most advanced technology. Those nations in the periphery are poor, dependent upon a few extractive resources, lack technology and are dominated politically and economically by the core nations. These theorists perceive the international economy as a system devised and maintained by the dominant multinational corporations and most powerful states in the core to perpetuate their economic domination at the expense of the less developed nations. Because the domination is so thorough, core nations are largely spared the need to use military force to subjugate these states (Galtung, 1971). Core states will use force or other means occasionally when faced with major threats to their domination (e.g., the US in Guatemala 1954 and Chile in 1973), but can achieve the same effect through their control of aid, technology and capital. Dependency and world system theorists are quite vague, however, on how a system they perceive as grossly unjust will ever end.

Kolko (1969) applies a similar critique to US foreign policy. He locates the origins of American foreign policy in the systemic needs of capitalism. He notes that while government does not always serve the interests of individual businesses, it does work for the common good of all industries to the detriment of the under-developed nations of the world. 'At every level of the administration of the American state, domestically and internationally, business serves as the fount of critical assumptions or goals and strategically placed personnel (Kolko, 1969, p.26). Similarly, William Appleman Williams (1959) argues that under the guise of the 'Open Door' policy, US decision-makers have sought and gained entry into markets and nations the world over. Once established, the US government defends these gains and protects its 'informal empire' through the use of military force.

Dependency and world systems theories were rather popular in the 1960s and 1970s, but according to Lake (1988), they withered in the 1980s, especially after the collapse of communism. Their greater weakness, however, was a lack of empirical evidence. Kurth (1974, pp.12-13) notes that theories of economic imperialism are hampered by over prediction–they explain events that never happened–(e.g., the US should intervene whenever and wherever its economic interests have ever been threatened) and over determination–other theories can explain the same events. Indeed, most dependency and world systems theorists have been reluctant to test their hypotheses or articulate falsifiable hypotheses. It is especially difficult to disprove an argument that assumes nearly everything that goes on in the international, economic system is manipulated by a capitalist elite. If we cannot find direct evidence linking big business to the economic ills of the third world, we are told it is because the linkages are indirect, and the entire 'system' is benefiting even if some business interests are not satiated in the short-term. Imperialist theories often assume a depth of strategic vision and long-term outlook that few administrations have achieved or even considered. Counter-evidence, like

Economic Interests and the Political Use of Military Force 81

the rise of the Asian tigers, is explained away as the 'core' co-opting some of the periphery in order to maintain the system as a whole. Such theories, because they are vague and subjected to continual adjustment, ultimately become non-falsifiable. Unfortunately there have been only a few empirical studies of the relationship between economic interests and foreign policy actions.

Odell (1974) finds that US military interventions are not related to economic interest in a country or region, but are associated with the level of political instability in the country. Krasner (1978) examined US foreign policy regarding raw materials overseas, and whether US decision makers sought to support the interests of US-based raw materials industries. Krasner tested three different theories of US policy, Marxist imperialism, interest group politics and a statist model. He finds that the US state, principally the executive branch, has been strong enough to resist pressures emanating from domestic lobbies to act on behalf of corporate interests. Instead, US policy has been guided by anti-communism, an ideological objective that transcends societal interests. Krasner argues that this finding tends to discredit both interest group and Marxist/imperialist explanations of US foreign policy that argue the state is either too weak to resist societal pressures, or is thoroughly dominated by capitalists. Gilpin (1975) also argues that there is often a divergence between corporate and national interests and that generally under these circumstances, larger foreign policy goals win out. Smith (1981) reaches similar conclusions. He concludes that to argue the US simply allows the pursuit of wealth to dominate foreign policy is incorrect. The US has taken action where there were no economic interests (e.g., Vietnam), and at other times failed to take strong action where there were (e.g., OPEC 1973-1974; Iran 1979).

As we will see later, there have been linkages between business interests and US military actions. Indeed, even Morgenthau (1973, pp.92-93) writes, '...the liaison of state power and economics in the international field, far from maintaining peace and order, is a source of conflict and war'. Too often, however, theories of economic imperialism assume that all US foreign policy is guided by corporate and capitalist interests. Curiously though, they do share this same feature with security and power-based explanations of the political use of force. Both generally find one dominant factor directly or indirectly guiding and benefiting from US foreign policy. Just as some critical theories of American imperialism have maintained that US economic interests benefit from the assertion of US military might where tangible and direct gains are difficult to locate (e.g., Laos, Chad), so too do power and security rationales contend that US security can be (in)directly threatened by events in the obscure nations of the world (e.g., Angola, Guatemala). In stretching the theory to cover all possible phenomena of interest, the overall argument becomes weaker. The development of an overarching and abstract theoretical framework does not always lead to the derivation of empirically falsifiable hypotheses.

82   *The Political Use of Military Force in US Foreign Policy*

Interest Group/Pluralist Models

Pluralist models of government policymaking assume interest groups are active and influential in lobbying legislators and members of the executive branch on behalf of their special concerns. We know from theory and practice that special interest groups with intensely held preferences are much better able to solve collective action problems and realize their ends (Olson, 1965). In particular, groups that seek private, selective benefits whose costs will be generally distributed among the public (a tax on competitive, foreign products, for example) are likely to be highly active and influential. Many scholars have argued that the US is a 'weak state' that is highly permeated by such rent-seeking, special interests that promote inefficient policies, discourage innovation, and ultimately lead to imperial overstretch (Katzenstein, 1976; Olson, 1982; Skidmore, 1994). Some argue that business enjoys a privileged position (Lindblom, 1977) in certain foreign policy decisions, or that businesses receive preferential treatment with regard to their foreign investments (Lipson, 1985).

Nowhere is this more apparent than in trade policy where industries lobby government to enact or maintain tariffs and other restrictions designed to keep out foreign competition, or even look to the government to force open foreign markets. Schattschneider's (1935) work on protectionist logrolling in the legislative process demonstrates both how active industries are and how susceptible the government is to their demands. Some have argued that business interests are privileged and can even influence government decisions on military intervention. Gibbs (1991, p.5) claims that business interests dominate some foreign policies because of their organization, access to and personal relations with decision makers, the revolving door between the corporate and political worlds and because policymakers are motivated by financial gain. When foreign conflicts do not involve anti-capitalist forces, but do affect foreign investment, government policy will reflect the interests of the dominant business or industry in that particular foreign nation. Gibbs cites US policy toward the Congo in the 1960s as an example. He argues that the US generally sided with the dominant mining interests in the Congo by providing military assistance to Congolese factions in support of these businesses. Such scholars tend to be the minority, however, as many have shown that the US is not always a weak state in foreign policy making. Others like Rodman (1988) are more nuanced and argue that while business does have a privileged position in foreign policy making regarding expropriation and nationalization of natural resource investment overseas, the extent of its influence is difficult to measure. He does, however, note that very few instances of expropriation have led to some sort of US military response (1988, p.330).

In reviewing the findings of a special issue of the journal, *International Organization* on economic statecraft, Ikenberry (1988, p.232) concludes that the interest group model of US trade policy was most accurate throughout much of the post Civil War period, but that the executive began to gain power toward the end of the century and especially in 1934 with the Reciprocal Trade Agreements Act. Lake (1988) argues that the executive branch will be powerful on trade issues because societal pressures cannot cumulate into strategic trade preferences, and because the executive's interests will be shaped by the anarchic international environment and the need for relative power and advantage. Similarly, Krasner (1978) discounts interest group models of influence in raw materials policy because the state can exercise political leadership especially by exploiting societal or corporate divisions, and because key decisions are made by the President and State Department not Congress. Ikenberry (1988, pp.220-221) takes a centrist position and argues that the truth about pressure group vs. state influence in foreign policy is that, 'In the long run, the political institutions that undergird policymaking may well reflect more basic social and international forces'.

Not surprisingly most scholars who advocate or test pluralist models of the influence of economic interests on foreign policy focus on economic policy issues, especially trade and raw materials. Aside from the previously mentioned theorists of economic imperialism, relatively few scholars have chosen to systematically analyze the impact of economic interests on military intervention. Many political scientists would likely agree that military interventions involve crisis policy making where decision time is brief, politics are subordinated to the national interest, and the executive is dominant. In short, these are exactly the sort of policy decisions in which we would expect interest group influence to be weak. But, as we shall see later, there have been many occasions throughout US history where presidents used military force on behalf of commercial interests, not always because the executive was pressured to do so, but because the government considered the protection and expansion of commercial relations abroad as one of its most important responsibilities.

Theories of Hegemony

Systemic theories of the role of economic forces in foreign policy center around the actions of major states, typically hegemons, in maintaining their preferred international economic arrangements. In contrast to Marxist and interest group models of influence that argue policy is a response to social pressures from below; policy in systemic theories is a response to demands and opportunities generated by the international political-economic system (Ikenberry, 1988). Great Britain in the 19th century and the US in the post World War II era both sought to preserve a liberal, capitalist system and were willing to solve collective action problems among the major trading nations by managing currency systems and promoting free markets. As well, the major powers, through foreign investment and foreign aid, supply investment capital and generate development throughout the system (Gilpin, 1975, p.48). Why would hegemons expend resources on maintaining a particular international economic system? As Olson (1965) points out, when the gain exceeds the total cost of providing some amount of the collective good, single actors will absorb all the associated costs. In the case of a liberal, international economic system, the US and Great Britain undoubtedly experienced a net gain from the advantages of open trading and stable currency systems because of their larger, and generally more diverse economies. The more fundamental question concerns whether hegemons provide these collective goods because of economic gain, for more generalized security objectives, or some combination of both.

84   *The Political Use of Military Force in US Foreign Policy*

After World War II, the US devoted significant resources to managing the international capitalist system, and even allowed states like Japan and Western European nations to pursue protectionist policies. The economic recovery of these nations was certainly in the long-term interests of US businesses that needed their export markets, even though it was economically injurious. More fundamentally, however, the US needed a stable and strong Europe and Japan as bulwarks against the Soviet Union. Both economic and security interests would probably have been sufficient to lead the US to accord its allies preferential treatment. But as Gilpin argues, 'other than in a few...exceptional circumstances, societies throughout history have placed much greater emphasis on security values such as social stability or self-sufficiency than on income gains from the free operation of markets' (quoted in Lake, 1988, p.9). Some doubt that hegemons actually work to promote liberal economic systems that are intended to encourage more trade. Mansfield (1992) tests the relationship between hegemony and liberal trade, and finds that it is positive when one uses Robert Gilpin's data (which dates the end of British hegemony as 1914), but insignificant when one uses Immanuel Wallerstein's data (which dates it as 1873).

If hegemons are motivated more by security interests and do not necessarily manage the international economic system in some altruistic fashion for the benefit of all, is there any reason to suppose that systemic economic demands would lead a hegemon to use military force? First, we ought to be skeptical of any notion that would suggest the US would routinely use force for global, economic purposes that do not also provide some tangible benefit. While a president may at times perceive that what is good for the international economic system is good for the US, and vice versa, and use force to protect such interests, these occasions are likely rather infrequent. One could make the case, however, that the preservation of the supply of oil is one such global (or at least Western) interest that the US has been willing to use force to maintain. I discuss this in more detail later. Generally, states use force first and foremost to protect their own interests. Furthermore, testing such all-encompassing relationships is as difficult here as it was for dependency and world systems theories. Second, systemic economic interests are preserved through economic policies that pertain much more directly to the relevant issue. The relationship between systemic economic interests and the use of force, if one should exist, is probably indirect and difficult to test. We should remain alert, but cautious about its impact.

Bringing the Theories Together

I believe that there are areas of convergence between all the theories discussed so far, and that it is possible to develop a model of the role of economic interests in military interventions. But, let us briefly review first where there is divergence among the theories. The critical, pluralist and hegemonic theories differ primarily over why and the extent to which the state acts on behalf of economic interests. Critical theories assume the state, as an appendage of the capitalist system, is wholly responsive to the interests of business and acts always to further them. Latter-day imperialism and dependency theorists seem to agree that the state is

Economic Interests and the Political Use of Military Force   85

dominated and driven by capitalism, but would assert that the state will take action to preserve the system, even if it harms the interests of some businesses in the short-term. Pluralist theories suggest that the weak state structure of the US makes it highly susceptible to the demands of special interest groups that will seek to further their economic interests. Moreover, given that business interests have intensely held preferences, possess substantial resources and are highly organized, government is more likely to act on their interests than on broad or diffuse interests, including, sometimes, the national interest. Despite their power, however, these business groups do not 'own' the system–they are not equivalent to it–in the same manner they do in critical theories. Finally, systemic theories of foreign economic policy suggest that as a hegemon, the US has been able to create and maintain an international economic system advantageous to its own economic interests. Even if US policymakers engineered the institutions, regimes and norms of the system for the America's long-term security interests, they have still worked to preserve a system that generates more wealth for the US than any system that might be designed by another nation. As Gilpin notes, the desire for wealth and power is complementary and self-reinforcing. 'In the short run there may be conflicts between the pursuit of power and the pursuit of wealth; in the long run the two pursuits are identical' (Gilpin, 1975, p.37). In systemic theories, economic interests are driven by the demands of the international system. Weak states must adjust to the system as they find it, while hegemonic states must seize the opportunity to shape it or risk letting a rival dominate global economics.

I find, however, that there is significant convergence among the key elements of all three perspectives. All assert that economic self-interest is a major motivating force in a nation's foreign policy, especially the US'. Each theory contends that states will assist businesses in the furtherance of wealth-generating activities abroad by a variety of means. Whether this drive results from the influence of groups operating within the state or forces operating on the state from without, decision makers will take action to further these economic interests either because of specific pressure, or because of a more general, perceived interest in doing so. There are two, important and unresolved questions that must be addressed in order to explain how the use of military force is influenced by economic considerations.

First, how often does the US government take action to further economic or business interests? Marxist/imperialist theories hold that the interests of capitalism dominate the system; pluralist models suggest that business, special interests are powerful and advantaged groups; systemic theories imply that the preservation of a favorable system is a vital and enduring interest in economic policy making, but are largely silent on the extent to which such macro-level interests influence policy in non-economic crises. Only the more critical theories make some claim about the extent of the relationship between economic interests and the use of force. They argue the relationship is extremely close. The second question concerns the lengths to which the US government is prepared to go to advance economic interests. Actions may range from presidential statements proclaiming a US desire to trade, to technical, economic assistance to underdeveloped nations that open up their markets to the US, to military

86 *The Political Use of Military Force in US Foreign Policy*

intervention to force a government to change its economic policies in favor of US interests. Critical theories would suggest that the US government would go to great lengths to protect business interests, while interest group and systemic economic theories seem to imply that occasionally the US may go to great lengths to protect economic interests. I suggest that both questions can be answered with reference to two, changing circumstances in US foreign policy. These are the level of US power internationally, and the extent to which economic interests overlap or reinforce other interests, primarily security. More specifically, presidents will be more likely to use military force to further US economic interests, contingent on the level of US power, and when economic interests either reinforce or do not conflict with security interests.

The relationship between US power and the promotion of economic interests is complex. On one level, power, as measured by capabilities, provides opportunity. More powerful states, like the US in the late 19th and early 20th centuries, can use military force and other tools to pry open new markets, protect US businesses from nationalization, and fend off foreign rivals. Relatively weak countries do not possess the same ability to forcefully assert their economic interests throughout the world that major powers do. Yet, this very lack of power or capabilities would suggest that weak nations would be especially zealous to protect what little they possess and expand when possible in the interest of political and economic survival. Thus, although we shall see that when the US was fairly weak it often relied on treaties and rhetoric to protect its economic interests, when such interests were significantly threatened, it was forced to take action (e.g., the Barbary pirates). Thus, in times of weakness we should find the US using force when necessary to defend important, economic interests. When American power begins to grow, the weaknesses that had previously tempted foreign actors to threaten US economic interests begin to diminish, but increasing capabilities permit increasing opportunities to advance economic interests. Over time, however, we would expect this relationship to change. With the growth of its economic power and the increasing complexity of international commerce in the post World War II era, we would expect that other methods of influence such as economic assistance and diplomacy would be more conducive to the promotion of US economic interests. Military force becomes too blunt of an instrument, for example, to persuade a country to allow US firms to repatriate more of their profits. Thus, we would expect to find a curvilinear relationship over the course of US history between power and military intervention on behalf of economic interests. As US power increases in the 19th century, we ought to find an increased willingness to use force on behalf of economic interests, *ceteris paribus*. When the US becomes a superpower, we should find less willingness to use force to achieve such objectives as other methods become more appropriate.

The second key variable is the extent to which economic interests reinforce or at least do not conflict with other objectives in US foreign policymaking. Those who argue that security interests generally trump all other objectives may be mostly correct, while those who contend that the state 'is' economic interests or that the US is a weak state dominated by special interests are mostly incorrect. I agree with those who argue the US is not a weak state, but has a

Economic Interests and the Political Use of Military Force 87

strong executive that shapes US foreign policy even on economic issues (e.g., Ikenberry, 1988; Krasner, 1978; Lake, 1987, 1988). I believe that on issues where there is a convergence between economic gain and security, as in US policy toward Latin America and the Caribbean from 1898-1918, presidents will be more likely to use force to further economic interests. In addition, when the US economy is fragile and susceptible to severe downturns due to events overseas, economic interests and national security become nearly indistinguishable, as in the early years of the Republic. Furthermore, when security interests are absent or negligible, as in US policy toward Japan in the mid 1800s, but economic interests are strong, presidents will be more likely to use force. Hence, to understand when presidents use force to promote economic interests we must be generally cognizant of its level of power and specifically aware of the extent to which economic interests complement US security.

I suggest that US presidents are most likely to use force on behalf of economic interests in what I will term, an 'opportunistic' manner. When US power and security objectives converge, presidents become more willing to act on the basis of economic interest. But although I do not believe that economic interests dominate US foreign policy and the decision to use force, I believe they are more powerful than most scholars who have studied the use of force give them credit for. During one long period, 1798-1918, explored in this study presidents were either compelled to use force to protect US economic interests, or seized opportunities to advance economic interests on many occasions. Economic interests were necessary and/or sufficient conditions for frequent political uses of military force. And while subsequent to this era, US economic interests have more often been promoted through less coercive means, the private interests of individual businesses and the public interest of economic prosperity remain fundamental values of foreign policy. As well, they still lead to some major uses of force, most notably interventions in the Persian Gulf to protect the supply of oil.

Economic Interests and the Use of Force: Three Case Studies

Perry's Mission to Japan

In 1638, the Shogun of Japan had issued an edict that read in part, 'So long as the Sun shall warm the earth, let no Christian dare to come to Japan, and, let all know that the King of Spain himself, or the Christian's God...if he violates this command he shall pay for it with his head' (quoted in Lewis and Naojiro, 1923, p.54). While the Japanese had allowed the Dutch to send one ship per year to trade at the port of Nagasaki, no other nation had breached the veil of threats and mystery that surrounded Japan. Some nations like Great Britain, France and Russia had made attempts, but none had succeeded. Thus, it was surprising that the much weaker US should undertake to force the Japanese to open up their nation to trade by sending a naval squadron under Commander Matthew Perry to impress and threaten the Japanese with American military might.

The administration of Millard Fillmore, which authorized the operation, realized from the start that diplomacy without the drawn sword would never succeed in opening up Japanese markets. In the past the Japanese had often fired upon ships that so much as approached their shores. Americans and other sailors who had the unfortunate luck of washing up on Japanese beaches were usually imprisoned and treated cruelly. Many paid for such ill fortune with their lives. But American politicians and businessmen realized that if the US were to become a dominant commercial power in the Pacific region, protect its merchant marine fleet and find coaling stations for its steamships, the island of Japan would play a pivotal role. This commitment to forcing open Japan was made manifest in the presidential instructions by which Matthew Perry was to run his mission (which were largely authored by Perry himself). Although Perry was enjoined to do everything possible to avoid war and to suffer Japanese indignities with grace, he was also told to back up his arguments 'with some imposing manifestation of power' (US Senate, 1854).

Perry was charged with making arrangements for the humane treatment of American sailors and 'the protection of American seamen and property wrecked on these Islands, or driven into their ports by stress of weather', and obtaining permission for American ships to enter Japanese ports for resupply, but the most crucial aspect of his mission was revealed in a very simple declaration in his instructions. He was to obtain permission for, 'our vessels to enter one or more of their ports for the purpose of disposing of their cargoes by sale or barter' (US Senate, 1854). To do this would require more than tact and firmness, however; it would require the omnipresent threat of military force. It would call for the presence of a naval armada bristling with iron guns and steam-driven power to constantly remind the Japanese of their inferior bargaining position.

When Perry entered Edo harbor early in July of 1853 with two steam-powered vessels and two sail-driven ships with 61 guns and 967 men, he was continually alert not to repeat the mistakes of others, including Americans, who had tried and failed to pry open Japan (Wiley, 1990). At first, Japanese officials in junks approached the ships and tried to climb aboard, ostensibly to deliver diplomatic documents and warnings. But the ropes they tried to climb up were cut and rifles pointed in their faces. When the emissaries asked to come aboard the ships, they were directed to communicate only with the flagship, *Susquehanna*. When they asked to meet with the commander of the fleet, they were directed to meet with lesser officers. After the Japanese sent guard boats to surround and intimidate the American squadron, as they had done with other foreign vessels, their ships were warned away. All because, Perry decided that, '...the more exclusive I should make myself and the more exacting I might be, the more respect these people of forms and ceremonies would be disposed to award me' (quoted in Wiley, 1990, p.284). Again and again the Japanese had tried various tactics to confuse, delay, test and ultimately thwart Perry, but on each point Perry resisted. The key to success, he believed was in making clear that while American intentions were entirely friendly and that they had no wish to dominate the Japanese like the European powers had China (of which the Japanese were keenly aware), the Americans were not seeking a favor. The purpose of the visit and the

Economic Interests and the Political Use of Military Force 89

need for the squadron was to issue a demand for the right of any nation to trade with another. Indeed, Perry told the Japanese more than once that he would not be responsible for the consequences should the Japanese refuse his demands (Wiley, 1990, p.62).

When the day finally arrived for Perry to come ashore to meet with appropriately high-ranking Japanese officials in an elaborate ceremony, he took no chances. The Commodore ordered his commanders to position their ships to be able to attack the Japanese with their guns if need be, but also to further reinforce the seriousness of the American demands. An impressive thirteen-gun salute announced Perry as he stepped off the *Susquehanna* to be rowed ashore. After much pomp and circumstance and in a very brief meeting with the Japanese officials, Perry delivered the official copy of the President's letter, which was contained within a very elaborate, solid gold box. He demanded this letter be conveyed to the Emperor and informed the Japanese he would return in the spring with an even larger armada to receive the Emperor's reply. Having accomplished his primary objective, Perry prepared the squadron to set sail, but not before one last display of American military might. Prior to their departure, the squadron was moved in even closer to shore against the wishes of the officials and confronted the Japanese on shore. Finally, on July 17th the Americans set sail and left.

In the spring of 1854, Perry returned to Japan sooner than he and the Japanese expected since Russia had already dispatched elements of its navy to Japan to demand the opening of trade, and other nations were preparing similar expeditions. Once again there was great wrangling over the tedious, but crucial details regarding where and when a meeting was to take place for Perry to receive the Emperor's reply. On March 8, 1854, Perry came ashore for the second time, borne aloft in an elaborate sedan carried by ten Chinese coolies and flanked by an impressive bodyguard, and with 500, fully armed men, three military bands and all his officers. But while the Japanese reply conceded to the first two of the Americans' demands for assistance to ships and sailors in need, and for permission to resupply ships in Japanese ports, Japanese leaders refused to open Japan to regular commerce. Furthermore, the Japanese were not prepared to begin provisioning American ships for another five years. Not to be denied, Perry demanded a treaty with Japan like the US had with China, which opened four ports for trade. The officials demurred and claimed Japan produced what it needed and had no use for trade (Wiley, 1990).

Perry pointedly warned them the US would go to war with Japan like it had with Mexico and that he would return yet again with a larger fleet. The Japanese insisted on no commerce, but said they would provision the Americans with 'gifts'. Sensing an opening, Perry then asked if these gifts could be paid for or returned in kind with other gifts in the form of gold and silver coins. This proved to be the semantic key that unlocked Japan and opened it to trade. The treaty Perry eventually concluded with the Japanese called for the port of Shimoda to be opened for the purchase of supplies at the signing of the treaty. The port of Hakodate was to be opened one year later. In addition, the treaty contained a most favored nation clause granting to the US any trading rights extended to other nations. After Perry's return, the treaty was ratified by unanimous consent in the US Senate.

90 The Political Use of Military Force in US Foreign Policy

There is little reason to doubt that Commodore Perry succeeded where others had failed because of the manner in which he approached the Japanese. Given the importance of ceremony and powerful impressions in Japanese society, Perry was determined to approach the Japanese not as a supplicant, but as an equal. If the Japanese were not prepared to receive him and his squadron as equals, then displaying force and threatening even more force would underline the seriousness of his mission. Perry himself argued that, 'It is very certain that the Japanese can be brought to reason only through the influence of their fears' (US Senate, 1854). Thus did the US cause the Japanese to reverse 200 years of government policy. Not through diplomacy, which had been tried repeatedly by the US and other powers, and not through war and conquest, but through the limited use of military force.

The Invasion of the Tax Collectors

For a brief period between roughly 1900 and World War I, US presidents ordered a surprising number of military interventions to manage unstable and bankrupt governments in Central America and the Caribbean. Most of these interventions followed a predictable script. First, the government in question, having run up a huge debt by dispensing considerable largess to its supporters, would be confronted by angry foreign creditors demanding repayment of loans. Having drained their treasuries of funds, the cliques that ran the regime would be confronted on all sides to pay up or get out. Foreign governments, at the behest of their banks, would threaten intervention should the interest on the loans remain unpaid. Forces from within would demand a new government, partly to deal with the external threat and partly to reward their own clients. The US government would demand financial and political reforms to forestall European intervention. As a last resort, US presidents would order the Marines and a small detachment of financial advisers into these nations to take control of the customs houses where most government revenue was collected. Nicaragua, Haiti, Honduras, Cuba and the Dominican Republic all were targets of the crusading US, bound and determined to take the progressivist cause and reforms to these unfortunate nations. Local resistance was futile and dangerous, as attested to in congressional investigations in 1921 of the abuses perpetrated by US forces in Haiti and the Dominican Republic (Langley, 1980, p.97).

The US intervention in the Dominican Republic in 1916 was perhaps the most thorough-going of all for US forces ran that nation as a military dictatorship for eight years. Teddy Roosevelt had first established a US receivership in the Dominican Republic in 1905, which was later formalized in a treaty signed in 1907. The US controlled the revenue from imports and would set aside 55 percent of the duties to pay off the European powers that loaned money to the government (Langley, 1980, p.77). US involvement in the Republic's financing was keeping in spirit with the Roosevelt Corollary to the Monroe Doctrine in which TR had asserted the US right to intervene in the nations of the Western hemisphere, who because of economic and political mismanagement, might provoke European meddling. But while control of the customs house kept the Europeans at bay, the

Economic Interests and the Political Use of Military Force 91

root causes of the financial mess remained. The personal and patronage-driven politics of the government produced little but corruption and chaos. The assassination of the president of the Dominican Republic in 1911 ushered in a particularly violent era. Despite American tutelage, the Dominican Republic was saddled with a series of short-lived governments.

Woodrow Wilson had campaigned against the 'dollar diplomacy' of his predecessor and was determined to put an end to this perceived favoritism toward corporate interests in US foreign policy. He believed that with US guidance and proper leadership, the Dominican Republic and other nations in the region could be reformed and thereby protected from domestic and foreign predators. But Wilson never seemed to realize that he could not wish away the power of the local politicians and the multinationals through idealistic rhetoric or remove them through military force. When Dominican Republic politics deteriorated further in the spring of 1914, Wilson plunged into the fray.

The incumbent president, Jose Bordas Valdes, was only supposed to preside over new national elections and electoral reform, but having tasted power he sought to succeed himself in office (Healy, 1988, p.192). The opposition, which had been counting on winning the elections and dispensing their own patronage, revolted. While sympathetic to their aims and angered that the current government had broken its promises, US Secretary of State William Jennings Bryan told the opposition that if the rebels overthrew the government, they would receive no revenue from the US-controlled customs. If they stopped their attacks, the US would guarantee fair and timely elections (Healy, 1988, p.193). Wilson dispatched an unofficial team of observers to oversee the election, and the opposition won a majority in the new constitutional assembly. But President Bordas still refused to leave office. With the government's treasury empty and rebellion flaring anew, Bryan demanded that the Dominican Republic accept a US financial adviser. After a few months of fighting and various elections, a new president finally took office in the late summer of 1914. Wilson immediately put the new leader, Horacio Jimenez, in an untenable position. The US president demanded the right to run public works, appoint a comptroller of government finances and provide US assistance in organizing a police force to replace the army (Healy, 1988, p.195). Jimenez was too old and enfeebled to resist US demands, but the heavy-handed pressure made him look like a traitor in the eyes of his countrymen. Local rebellions spread across the country and a movement began in April, 1915 to impeach Jimenez. The new US Secretary of State, Robert Lansing ordered the US Navy to patrol the coast and remind the rebels of US power.

The chaos persisted for over a year as more cabinet ministers defected and took up arms against the Jimenez government. Finally, in April of 1916, Wilson ordered a force of 300 US Marines ashore to prop up the government. Wilson demanded that Jimenez attack the rebels, but Jimenez refused to fire on his countrymen and resigned. The government collapsed and US forces had to occupy Santo Domingo. After several attempts at forming a local government, Wilson gave up and announced the establishment of a military dictatorship in November. No local politician was prepared to be seen as a collaborator with the invading force, no matter how noble its intentions, and so few served. The US continued to

92 *The Political Use of Military Force in US Foreign Policy*

insist that Dominicans would administer the law, although the US government would determine who would be given this responsibility. But, anyone who protested the occupation was deemed unpatriotic and therefore unfit to serve (Healy, 1988, p.197). The US involvement in Dominican Republic politics had begun because of financial issues and problems of political succession. But once Wilson had committed himself to rescuing the Dominicans from themselves, the US government embarked on whole scale reform of Dominican economic policy. The spirit of progressivism that had led to so many reforms at home would be loosened abroad to uplift the downtrodden people of the Dominican Republic. The US military ran the Dominican Republic as a dictatorship until 1924 when the last US forces departed. It would manipulate local politics for many more years to come.

President Wilson's decision to intervene in the Dominican Republic drew inspiration from numerous sources, but though he repeatedly averred that he would not make US foreign policy the tool of corporate interests, his actions nonetheless served their interests in the long run. In each instance from 1905 onward when the US interceded in the domestic politics of the Dominican Republic, one of the most important precipitating factors was the need to control the customs houses to assure the European and US bankers that they would be repaid. In addition, the businesses that invested in the Dominican Republic, especially the sugar plantations, wanted a stable and pliable regime in order to profit from their enterprises. When the island's government collapsed into factionalism there was little law and order. Roving gangs of bandits harassed the sugar plantation owners and forced them to pay protection money. The chaos disrupted the harvests, interfered with the repayment of loans and resulted in the destruction of property. Given that economic forces played a prominent role in presidential decision making and that businesses profited greatly from the US military dictatorship and the reforms and public works projects it initiated, economic interests played a key role in US foreign policy.

The 1954 Coup in Guatemala

In 1944 a coalition of army officers, labor leaders, intellectuals and ordinary middle class citizens overthrew a brutal military dictatorship in Guatemala. The previous president had curried favor with the US and the country's dominant economic force, the United Fruit Company (UFCO) by cracking down on anyone who questioned his domination of politics or UFCO's stranglehold over the economy. The civilian president who eventually took over, Dr. Juan Arevalo, ruled for five years and succeeded in enacting a number of agricultural and labor reforms. His elected successor, Jacobo Arbenz was determined to move further to distribute property to landless peasants and reform the labor laws of the country. UFCO, which had grown accustomed to dictating the terms of its relationship to the Guatemalan government, had opposed the Arevalo reforms, and once company officials fully grasped that their free hand in Guatemala was about to be tied under Arbenz, they launched a full-scale campaign against the regime that ultimately led to its downfall.

Economic Interests and the Political Use of Military Force   93

A few facts reveal the depth of UFCO's power in Guatemala and its attitude toward the Guatemalan people. UFCO had a 99 year lease on almost 1,600,000 acres of land. It was the largest, private landowner in the country and the biggest employer (Gleijeses, 1991, p.90). It did not pay any taxes to the government and did not pay any import duties for the supplies it brought into the country. UFCO owned all but 29 miles of Guatemalan railroad, controlled all the shipping leaving Guatemala's Atlantic Ocean, and controlled most of the power companies. The Guatemalan government had guaranteed there would be no regulation of UFCO's transportation rates, which were calculated by the United Nations to be the highest in the world. On UFCO's plantations all non-white persons had to yield the right of way to whites and remove their hats when talking to them (Immerman, 1982, pp.71-75; Schlesinger and Kinzer, 1999, pp.70-71).

Determined to put an end to this, President Arbenz enacted the Agrarian Reform Law that expropriated uncultivated land with compensation in government bonds. The compensation was set at the listed price of the land according to UFCO for American tax purposes, and UFCO claimed to have lost as much as 18 million dollars through the expropriation (Gleijeses, 1991, p.164). UFCO believed that it was being treated unfairly and refused to comply with the law (Schlesinger and Kinzer 1999, p.76). Luckily for UFCO, known as El Pulpo–the octopus–in Guatemala, its tentacles stretched throughout the US government, especially when the Eisenhower administration took over in 1953. Both Allen Dulles, Director of Central Intelligence and his brother, Secretary of State John Foster Dulles, had worked for UFCO's lawyers in the firm of Sullivan and Cromwell and held substantial amounts of UFCO stock. Eisenhower's National Security Assistant had been chairman of the board. The under-secretary of State, Walter Bedell Smith became a director after he resigned from public service (Immerman, 1982, pp.124-125). UFCO received a favorable hearing from its friends and waged a relentless public relations campaign against the Guatemalan government, which it ceaselessly characterized as being controlled by communists or communist sympathizers.

Eisenhower and Dulles had charged the Truman administration with being soft and complacent toward the global communist threat. Their policy of rollback was ostensibly premised on the need to take more aggressive action to reverse communist gains. Eisenhower realized that such action would be dangerous in Eastern Europe, but feasible and appropriate against nations where the communists were not so firmly entrenched. He was also determined to loosen the reins on the CIA to permit it to go beyond intelligence collection and analysis to covert operations. That the CIA pulled off a successful coup in Iran in 1953 undoubtedly contributed to Ike's optimism that similar machinations would work among the nations to the South. UFCO and others convinced the Eisenhower officials that the communists were about to gain a beachhead in Central America, spread their invidious doctrines, threaten the Panama Canal, and ruin the climate for American businesses. They found a very receptive audience. There were some communists in positions of influence in Guatemalan society, many in the labor unions, and the Arbenz labor and land reforms had the whiff of socialism about them. The Guatemalan National Assembly's moment of silence to acknowledge the death of

94   *The Political Use of Military Force in US Foreign Policy*

Josef Stalin did not endear them to Ike and the Dulles brothers either. In late fall of 1953 Eisenhower authorized the CIA to begin plotting Arbenz's overthrow.

In the old days the US might have simply landed a couple thousand Marines and seized control of the government, but such heavy-handed interventionism was not possible in the new era of decolonization and nationalism. Hence, covert operations became the tool of choice. Indeed, most accounts of US policy toward Guatemala concern the story of the CIA-engineered coup. But, in addition to the coup, Eisenhower also ordered a naval blockade of Guatemala to prevent the importation of arms from the Warsaw Pact. The US had launched an arms embargo against Guatemala in the late 1940s and had pressured its Western European allies to go along with it. But when the Arbenz government heard of the planned invasion it began searching for other weapons suppliers. The US again turned down requests from Arbenz and essentially forced him to go looking for arms in the Eastern bloc. When these small arms were discovered aboard a Swedish freighter in May of 1954 after it docked in Guatemala, Ike ordered the blockade. An Eisenhower directive on the blockade reveals just how far the US was prepared to go to bend the will of the Arbenz government and any foreign country that might aid it. It read, 'To prevent further communist arms build up in Central America, US Navy will stop suspicious foreign-flag vessels on high seas off Guatemala in order to examine cargo. If such vessels will not voluntarily cooperate, they will be taken forcibly to Panama for examination', (quoted in Immerman, 1982, p.159). No vessels were taken against their will to Panama, but the boldness of the plan demonstrated the level of commitment Eisenhower had given to the entire operation. The CIA-led invasion shifted into high gear as well once the story of the arms shipment broke.

The story of the invasion, the massive CIA disinformation campaign and the air attacks by CIA operatives have been recounted elsewhere in fascinating detail (see especially Immerman, 1982), so a lengthy narrative is unnecessary. A few pertinent details, however, are informative. First, the invasion, which was equipped, financed and directed by the CIA, was more a minor incursion than a major military operation. Under the command of Castillo Armas, the 'invasion' force numbered no more than 300 personnel at its height (Schlesinger and Kinzer, 1999, p.114) and stalled after crossing the Honduran-Guatemalan border. Camped six miles within Guatemala the invasion force did little, while fictitious CIA radio reports spread stories of massive troop movements, battles and destruction. Since the CIA was able to jam the signal of the government-run radio station, these wild stories were about the only source of information for the Guatemalan people. Coupled with the occasional air assault on Guatemala City with Coke bottle bombs, the CIA was able to sow panic among the people and alarm in the army. When it became apparent that the US government, primarily in the person of the US Ambassador to Guatemala, John Peurifoy, would settle for nothing less than Arbenz's replacement by a government committed to undoing his reforms, the Guatemalan Army capitulated. Arbenz fled to Mexico and Armas triumphantly entered Guatemala City a few weeks after his 'invasion force' entered the country. It was once again business as usual for UFCO in Guatemala.

Economic Interests and the Political Use of Military Force   95

The United Fruit Company's fingerprints seem to be all over the Guatemalan coup. Not a few commentators have charged that the US government was making foreign policy to serve the interests of a few corporate fat cats at the expense of the poor, long-suffering Guatemalan people (Ayabar de Soto, 1978; Barnet, 1968; Horowitz, 1955). It was an UFCO public relations blitz that put Guatemalan politics on the radar of key public figures in and out of government in the US. UFCO's connections in the government reads like a 'who's who' of the US power elite. The US ambassador, John Peurifoy, acted as UFCO's agent in negotiations with the Arbenz government over land reform and compensation for nationalized properties. According to Schlesinger and Kinzer (1999, p.120), 'Dulles (Allen) promised that whoever was selected by the CIA as the next Guatemalan leader would not be allowed to nationalize or in any way disrupt the company's operations'. UFCO helped smuggle arms and ammunition to Castillo Armas's exile army. And when Castillo Armas took the reins of power, he rescinded the laws passed during the Arbenz regime that had so angered UFCO. As Immerman recounts (1982, p.198),' the new president returned to United Fruit over 99 percent of its expropriated land and abolished all the tax on interest, dividends and other profits payable to foreign investors'. And certainly it seemed that the US was willing to overlook the more important influence of communists in Chile, Costa Rice and Brazil (Gleijeses, 1991, p.362) at the time to focus squarely on Guatemala. The communists in those countries occupied real positions of power, but there seemed to be no giant multinational threatened so much as UFCO was in Guatemala. If ever there was a case in which a multinational corporation instigated, guided and profited from a US military intervention, this would seem to be it.

Assessing the Evidence

Where a multiplicity of goals often obscures presidential motivations in most cases, in the opening of Japan, one goal dominated all others. The US government sent Commander Perry to Japan with one objective–to force Japan to trade. The US government did not seek trade for its own purposes; rather it acted for the benefit of whalers, fur traders, farmers and a myriad of other commercial interests. Perry's orders were explicit in this regard. While Presidents Fillmore and Pierce, who oversaw the mission, were concerned about the safety of US vessels in the region, if Perry had returned without a commercial agreement, the mission would have been judged a failure. Perry would not leave until such terms were agreed upon. Indeed, one looks in vain for some other motivation for the mission to Japan. In some sense the US government was seeking to change the internal policies of the Japanese government to more resemble their own liberal ideals of freedom to pursue economic gain. But aside from opening up treaty ports, Perry made no effort to change the structure or substance of the Japanese government or aid some proliberalization faction in it. One finds even less evidence that somehow US security was at risk. Given that Japan was a completely isolationist nation, it hardly posed any threat to the US. Of all the case studies examined in

96   *The Political Use of Military Force in US Foreign Policy*

this book, the mission to Japan represents the most obvious use of force on behalf of a single aim.

While the US intervention in the Dominican Republic was not driven by greedy businessmen or some, grand capitalist designs, many of the reasons for the intervention, as well as its objectives, were economic. If we examine the entirety of the causal chain, however, we can also appreciate the role played by political instability in the events that led to the US intervention. Rebellions, revolutions, assassinations and other forms of political violence were all too common in the Dominican Republic, Haiti, and other nations in the region. Political instability had been a chronic problem in Latin America for many years, but beginning in the early 20th century, presidents began to perceive a connection between the political upheaval and US economic interests. As trade with the region grew, US military power increased, and Great Britain acknowledged US leadership in the area, the old anti-imperialism and unwillingness to become entangled in the affairs of other nations were pushed aside by those who called upon the US to assume its rightful position in international affairs. Part of being a wealthy and powerful nation meant taking a more active role in these affairs, especially those in one's own backyard. Presidents could hardly argue that the nations of Europe should treat the US with respect if it was unwilling to assume the burdens of power. And nowhere were those burdens more obvious and troublesome than in the Caribbean. At the same time, the key to political stability in the Western hemisphere was financial stability.

Political and economic turmoil and violence harmed US corporations and implicated the European powers with financial interests in these troubled states. A failure to restore financial stability, and guarantee repayment of European loans probably would have resulted in the appearance of British, French, and/or German warships in the Caribbean. Roosevelt justified US military intervention more for security reasons, but Taft's 'dollar diplomacy' was premised on expanding US commercial interests in the region. Woodrow Wilson built upon those military and economic rationales and added a healthy dose of crusading progressivism. Wilson wanted the US to make a more thorough-going effort to reform countries like the Dominican Republic to make it a more fiscally responsible state. Certainly this interest in the credit-worthiness of the Dominican Republic was an interest shared by many in the American business community. The economic interests of private actors and the general interest in the economic well-being of the Dominican Republic for future economic ties are everywhere apparent in US foreign policy making across this era. If leaders in nations like the Dominican Republic and Haiti refused to honor their debts and instead used government funds to reward themselves and their cronies, US economic and political leadership throughout the region might be called into question. That is why inevitably the first step in these US interventions was to control the customs houses that collected the taxes that were to be used to pay back government loans. Thus, we can make a strong case that American economic interests exercised a decisive impact on the decision to use force.

At the time of the 1954 coup in Guatemala and for many years thereafter, some commentators saw the economic rationale behind the US intervention as self-evident (Horowitz, 1955). More recent political science scholars, however, have downplayed the influence of United Fruit Company over US foreign policy. Krasner (1978), Gilpin (1975), Smith (1981) and others have argued that US decision makers' anti-communist ideology drove US foreign policy, not the economic interests of powerful corporations. Even those who have documented the United Fruit Company's extensive part in the Guatemalan coup note that ultimately Eisenhower decided to blockade Guatemala and sponsor an invasion because of a perceived threat to the US. Immerman (1982, p.82) writes, 'The US did not ultimately intervene in Guatemala to protect United Fruit. It intervened to halt what it believed to be the spread of the international Communist conspiracy'. As Gleijeses (1991, p.7) writes regarding the story of the downfall of Arbenz government, 'There is no convenient villain of the piece, but rather a complex interplay of imperial hubris, security concerns, and economic interests'. He (1991, p.362) argues that where during the Arevalo regime, prior to Arbenz, UFCO had been able to strongly influence official Washington views on Guatemala, US foreign policymakers quickly became well-versed in Guatemalan affairs and drew their own conclusions as to the level of communist influence.

There are, unfortunately, many plausible and interconnected rationales that can account for US actions. It is possible UFCO merely alerted the US government to the perceived communist threat to the South. It is possible that UFCO had the ear of many an important foreign policy maker. And it is certainly true that UFCO stood to lose a great deal on its investments if Arbenz had been allowed to remain in power. It is unlikely that Eisenhower would have intervened had the Arbenz government not enacted its economic reforms, but it is equally unlikely that Eisenhower would have acted had there been no communists in Guatemala to serve as at least a pretext. We can say that UCFO's economic interests may have played a necessary, but not sufficient condition in the Guatemalan intervention. Because the economic policies of foreign governments came to be seen as key to locating their sympathies in the Cold War, disentangling these complementary interests is difficult. Unfortunately we can probably never disprove another explanation for the 1954 naval blockade–that anti-communist, security interests merely disguised the baser, and therefore less justifiable, economic interests at stake.

In each of the three histories, we can make a compelling case that the economic interests of private actors played an important role in the decision to use force. In all three instances, the business-unfriendly environment of each nation helped lead presidents to use force to make these regimes more hospitable to American investment and trade. While there was nothing resembling a capitalist, imperialist, or neo-imperialist imperative or conspiracy guiding US foreign policy makers as some critics have alleged, each president recognized the importance of supporting American business abroad. Economic interests played a critical role in two of the three cases, and an important role in the last one.

98   *The Political Use of Military Force in US Foreign Policy*

The Ebb and Flow of Economics in US Foreign Policy

To get a better sense of the extent to which the US used military force to advance economic interests, I use the historical data from the 1993 study by the Congressional Research Service on the use of force to analyze trends in the pre World War II era. When examining these data for evidence of force deployed on behalf of economic interest objectives, I note that whenever the event description mentioned that one of the mission goals was to protect American interests or property, or to influence changes in a foreign country's economic policies, I coded the intervention as promoting economic interests. It should be noted that there may be multiple objectives associated with a use of force. Thus, some of these incidents are also ones that are characterized by anti-American violence as in Chapter 2. We see in Table 3.1 that from 1798-1941, 90 incidents, or 52 percent of the total number of uses (172), can be characterized as involving the use of force to protect/promote American commerce. With the exception of uses of force to protect US security, these are the most numerous types of events. Force is used most often on an annualized basis for such purposes in the years 1899-1918 (averaging 1.23 uses per year), while presidents authorized force at relatively the same rate in the other periods 1798-1865, 1866-1898 and 1919-1941 (.51, .60, and .40 uses per year respectively). The rate is slightly higher in the period 1866-1898, although as a percentage of all uses of force in this period, military operations to advance economic interests are dominant (61 percent of all uses in this period).

Table 3.2 breaks down the uses of force designed to protect or promote commerce by region. We see that 77.8 percent of all uses of force in the South American region had some economic interest component to them–the highest of any region if the world. This is closely followed by Central America and the Caribbean where roughly two thirds of all uses of force were designed, at least in part, to protect or advance commerce. As well, more than 37 percent of the uses of force directed at the North African/Middle East region and Europe aimed to protect commerce. Table 3.3 further breaks down uses force to advance economic interests by time period and region. I discuss each in more detail as we proceed.

Table 3.1 Uses of Force to Advance Economic Interests Across Historical Periods

Period	Number of Uses	Average Number Per Year	Number of all Uses	Percent of all Uses for the Period
1798-1865	35	.51	60	58%
1866-1898	20	.60	33	61%
1899-1919	26	1.23	48	54%
1920-1941	9	.40	31	29%
Total	90	.62	172	52%

Table 3.2 Uses of Force to Advance Economic Interests Across Regions

Region	Number of Uses	Percent of All Uses in Region	Total All Uses in Region
Continental US	1	9.1%	11
Central America/ Caribbean	41	65.1%	63
South America	14	77.8%	18
North Africa/ Middle East	5	41.7%	12
Sub-Saharan Africa	1	25%	4
Europe/North Atlantic	3	37.5%	8
Asia	25	44.6%	56
Total all regions	90	52.3%	172

The Political Use of Military Force in US Foreign Policy

Table 3.3 Uses of Force to Advance Economic Interests Across Region and Time

Region	1798-1865	1866-1898	1899-1918	1919-1941
Continental US	1 2.9%	0 na	0 na	0 na
Central America/ Caribbean	11 31.4%	7 35%	19 73.1%	4 44.4%
South America	7 20%	5 25%	2 7.7%	0 na
North Africa/ Middle East	3 8.6%	1 5%	0 na	1 11.1%
Sub-Saharan Africa	1 2.9%	0 na	0 na	0 na
Europe/ North Atlantic	1 2.9%	0 na	0 na	2 22.2%
Asia	11 31.4%	7 35%	5 19.2%	2 22.2%
Total	35 100%	20 100%	26 100%	9 100%

Total percentages are based on number of uses of force to advance economic interests in a region for each period of time.

Protecting Trade on the High Seas, 1798-1865

Economic issues, and in particular trade, were foremost among the concerns the Founding Fathers confronted in the early years of the Republic. The war with Great Britain won the US its independence, but the break in ties with the mother country created foreign policy problems that plagued the nation for years. As part of the British Empire, the US enjoyed both access to its markets and the protection of the Royal Navy. American farmers and the small, but growing manufacturing sector depended on trade with Great Britain and many of its territories in the Caribbean. The American merchant fleet had relied on the British to protect them from attacks by pirates and warring nations. Now these advantages were gone and the US would have to rely on its own efforts and resources to advance and defend commerce. At few other times in its history was the nation's foreign policy in general and the use of military force in particular so intimately tied to economic interests–a fact that presidents and cabinet officials readily acknowledged. The American Minister to Spain once said in a widely quoted letter to Secretary of State Pickering in 1793, 'If we mean to have a commerce, we must have a naval force to defend it' (Hearth, 1991, p.55). Thomas Jefferson, no fan of a big military proclaimed that, 'We mean to rest the safety of our commerce on the resources of our own strength and bravery in every sea' (quoted in Hagan, 1991, p.54). Some thought privateers and a small coastal defense would be adequate to the task and prevent the nation from developing the imperial ambitions that might accompany the creation of a strong navy. But even Andrew Jackson admitted that the navy required at least, 'no more ships of war than are requisite to the protection of our commerce' (quoted in Schroeder 1985, p.19).

Still, the preferred tool of choice for protecting and promoting US commerce in the very early years of the Republic was international law. US presidents continually emphasized the 'rights' of neutral vessels during the Napoleonic wars. The US insisted on the doctrine of 'free ships make free goods'. That is, ships from non-belligerent nations had the right to trade with any and all nations during wartime and peacetime. But the European powers paid the American rhetoric little heed. The British used their navy to isolate Napoleonic Europe, while France and its allies sought to prevent any trade with the British Empire. Stuck in the middle with no navy to speak of and only high-minded language to make its case, there was little US presidents could do to defend American commerce. This period of weakness did not last long, however, before presidents finally began to order the US Navy into action to protect American commerce on the oceans in the mid 1790s.

Two events conspired to rouse the US out of its reluctance to defend American shipping–the Quasi War with France and the attacks of the Barbary pirates. Both actions have been described previously, so I need not go over them again in great detail. Briefly, as a result of French renunciation of the doctrine of 'free ships make free goods', contained in its 1778 treaty with the US, President Adams ordered the Navy into action to defend American coasts, protect American shipping, especially in the Caribbean, and capture French vessels. Over in the Mediterranean, the Barbary pirates generally acted as the tools of European powers that engaged them to prey upon the commerce of their adversaries. Where once the British had protected US vessels from their depredations, now they encouraged such attacks. The US was rather slow about getting around to retaliating against these kingdoms along the North African coast, but several missions were eventually launched against them (even though in some cases the US continued to pay protection money to the pirates' nominal sovereigns). In each case American presidents ordered the US Navy into action not only to take defensive action to protect US ships, but also to also take offensive action against those who had plundered American vessels. Thus was the born the marriage of the flag and trade. For despite the occasional downsizing of the Navy (as in Jefferson's first term), US leaders realized that a weak navy would only tempt European aggression. As Alexander Hamilton argued, 'A nation, despicable by its weakness, forfeits even the privilege of being neutral', (quoted in Sprout and Sprout 1944, p.16).

102   *The Political Use of Military Force in US Foreign Policy*

Shortly after the War of 1812, in which the US Navy performed exceptionally well, the US began organizing various fleets or squadrons with geographic responsibilities. The Mediterranean Squadron was the first, permanent, naval task force established in 1815 and dealt mainly with the recurring problem of the Barbary pirates. As we see in Table 3.3, several uses of force were directed at North Africa and the Middle East in this period, although they were also aimed at protecting American lives. A short time later the West India Squadron was established 'to police the Gulf of Mexico and the Caribbean Sea against the pirates and 'irregular privateers' which preyed on the lucrative traffic radiating from New Orleans...' (Sprout and Sprout, 1944, p.95). There were ten uses of force in the Caribbean and Central America during this time frame. Many of these were aimed at protecting US ships from attacks by the pirates of the Caribbean, often through the destruction of their bases of operation. The US also established a Pacific fleet to promote and protect the Pacific whaling industry, and monitor the growing problems associated with rebellions in Latin America. Presidents ordered naval deployments to South America periodically to protect US property and lives during outbreaks of violence.

On 11 occasions, uses of force were directed at the protection and promotion of commerce in Asia from 1798-1865–the highest of any region of the world, along with Central America and the Caribbean. Many of these incidents involved operations against island natives in the Pacific in the 1830s and 1840s who attacked US sailors and ships. Looming on the horizon, however, was the potentially profitable trade with China. For most of the 19th century the US had been content to free ride on the gunboat diplomacy of the British (mostly) and the French to keep open the Chinese treaty ports with which the Western powers were allowed to trade. US exporters and importers prospered quite well from the trade– by the time of the Opium War in 1839-1840, only Great Britain carried on more trade with the Chinese than did the US (Van Alstyne, 1973, p.19). US involvement in the opium trafficking was slight, approximately 5 percent according to some estimates (O'Connor, 1969, p.51). But after the Chinese shut the British out of the trade when they refused to pay a bond guaranteeing their non-involvement in opium trafficking, the US picked up the slack. The British were determined to teach the Chinese a lesson and open a few more ports while they were at it. The US was more ambivalent about the propriety of the drug trade, but did send the warships, *Columbia* and *John Adams*, to Canton in 1856 at the height of the crisis to protect American citizens and property and presumably, remind the Chinese of their treaty rights.

More generally, Schroeder (1985, p.20) describes the duties of US Navy captains on the high seas in the first half of the 19th century when, for all intents and purposes, they functioned as American ambassadors abroad, often with considerable discretion given the vast distances separating them from Washington D.C.:

> Once in a distant ocean, navy captains were expected to stop at major ports, contact the American consul there, pay their formal respects to local officials, and collect pertinent economic and political information for government officials in

Economic Interests and the Political Use of Military Force   103

Washington. Occasionally, naval officers protected American commerce by resolving local disputes in which American merchants were involved or by defending the rights of Americans abroad from arbitrary local officials or foreign competitors.

But Navy captains acted as far more than diplomatic envoys on their missions overseas. Often they were ordered, and sometimes took the initiative to deal with attacks on American ships and citizens with more aggressive measures. But their duties extended even beyond military actions to include assisting, '...American traders by receiving and safeguarding funds, issuing bills of receipt which served as negotiable paper, and returning specie to the US' (Field, 1984, 46). In fact, 58 percent of all uses of force in the period 1798-1865 were directed at promoting or protecting US commerce (Table 3.1). Especially after the War of 1812, it was an especially propitious time to use force for such aims. First, the US, while not powerful, did possess a navy of sufficient size to undertake these protection and promotion missions. Indeed, the Navy was largely designed for such purposes as most politicians recognized the necessity of naval protection for the advancement of commerce. Second, these missions did not jeopardize or even conflict with the security goals of the US in any way. Most were directed against far weaker peoples and governments and few interfered with the activities of European powers. As a growing nation the US identified its security very closely with the acquisition of wealth, as many mercantilist nations of the day did. In fact, presidents were becoming increasingly likely to use force to advance commerce as time went on.

The Beginnings of American Style Imperialism, 1866-1898

As we see in Table 3.1, 61 percent of all uses of force from 1866 through 1898 involved economic interests or objectives. This is the highest percentage of any period in the years before World War II. Of these many uses, seven, or 35 percent took place in the US' backyard–Central America and the Caribbean, while seven others occurred in Asia (Table 3.3). The US also embarked on military operations to advance economic interests five times in South America in this era. Most of these uses of force still involved the protection of American assets in foreign countries, or were designed to intimidate those who might or had attacked such property. Often they occurred as rival parties and factions vied for power and American expatriates demanded protection from the fighting and destruction. For example, in 1894 during a civil war in Brazil, the US Navy intervened by stopping one faction from blockading the port in Rio de Janeiro in order to keep it open for American merchant shipping (Hannigan, 2002, p.57).

After the Civil War, presidents continue to use force in many of the same Latin American and Caribbean nations as before, but there are also an increasing number of uses targeting Hawaii, Samoa, Korea, and other territories, especially in the Pacific. Many involved protection of American property during insurrections and wars, as in China in 1894 and Samoa in 1888. Others involved efforts to stop seal poaching in the Bering Strait (1891). Elsewhere in Asia, President Grant tried

104 *The Political Use of Military Force in US Foreign Policy*

to duplicate in Korea the success the US had in opening Japan to trade. The 'hermit' kingdom had long attacked outsiders that dared sail up its rivers in search of commercial opportunities, and many US sailors had been killed as a result of these missions and shipwrecks off the Korean coast. In 1871 President Grant ordered a force totaling 85 guns and 1230 sailors to Korea (O'Connor, 1969). They sailed up the mouth of the Han river and tried to begin negotiations, but the Koreans were in no mood to bargain and tried to fob off the Americans with various delaying tactics. The American commander, Rear Admiral John Rogers, sent some of his gunboats up the river on a surveying mission to more forcefully assert the US position. The Koreans fired on the ships, the ships returned in kind and then went back down the river to join the rest of the squadron. Then, on June 10 Commander Rogers apparently decided he had had enough of Korean recalcitrance and ordered the gunboats back up the river with a landing party of 546 sailors and 105 Marines (O'Connor, 1969, p.153). The force stormed ashore and attacked the Koreans who had fired on them. They razed the Korean fort, killed 350 Koreans, and satisfied that their mission had been accomplished, once again journeyed back to rejoin their comrades. Apparently, Rogers, and his civilian counterpart, Frederick Low the US minister to China, assumed that once the Korean government was apprised of its defeat, US demands would be granted. They waited for word of the loss to reach the Koreans, but nothing happened. Not even when the US offered to exchange some of its prisoners of war with the government did the Koreans show any inclination to parley. Since the US force was not large enough to attack the Korean capitol and demand its capitulation, there was nothing to be done but sail away empty-handed (O'Connor, 1969, p.154).

Despite a fair degree of military activity to advance US business interests, American foreign policy was not nearly so rapacious as the imperialism of the Europeans. While Great Britain, France, Germany and King Leopold of Belgium sought more and more colonial lands, the US largely stayed out of the land grab. The Civil War had interrupted a burgeoning trade with the rest of the world and helps account for something of a turn inward after its conclusion as the war weary nation set about the business of reconstruction. Few in the Congress or the public were in favor of the kind of imperialist passions that gripped Europe in the 1870s through the turn of the century. Some presidents, most notably Ulysses Grant, did try to assist the foreign trade by negotiating for overseas military bases, but were routinely turned down by anti-imperialist Congresses. But if the Civil War did contribute toward a certain isolationism, the industrialization that it spurred ensured that sooner or later the nation would begin looking outward again as its economic power expanded enormously. And when it did, the calls for a strong military, especially a modern, ocean-going navy to lead the way, were stronger than ever.

A few statistics reveal just how impressive the growth of the American economy and its exports was in the post-Civil War period. The US economy as a whole grew at an average annual rate of 5 percent, according to one study (Zakaria, 1998, p.45). Further, Zakaria notes that (1998, p.45):

Economic Interests and the Political Use of Military Force 105

Between 1865 and 1898, American wheat production increased 256 percent, corn 222 percent, and sugar 460 percent. In industrial sectors growth was even greater: coal production rose 800 percent, steel rails 523 percent, and railway track mileage 567 percent. Petroleum production...rose from three million barrels in 1865 to 55 million barrels in 1898.

The US population increased by 230 percent between 1870 and 1910 (Lake, 1988a, p.81). Concomitantly, between 1895 and 1914 there was a 240 percent increase in all exports, while the growth in manufactured products was an incredible 500 percent (Rosenberg, 1982, p.16). From 1897-1914 American direct investments abroad quadrupled from $634 million to $2.6 billion (Rosenberg, 1982, p.25). It was this tremendous economic expansion, coupled with the huge increase in US population and the 'closing of the frontier' that led many to look beyond the US borders to other lands for markets and outlets for American energies. This era of industrialization also figured prominently in many subsequent studies of imperialism that argued surplus US capital required outlets abroad and led to US interventionism in Central America, the Caribbean and East Asia (Kolko, 1969; Williams, 1959). As Rosenberg (1982, p.42) argues 'Economic need, Anglo-Saxon mission, and the progressive impulse joined together nicely to justify a more active role for the government in promoting foreign expansion'.

The growth in the American economy also led many to argue that the US should assume a greater role in world affairs, commensurate with its new-found strength. For if the US were to acquire the new markets and overseas investment opportunities necessary for its continued economic growth, it would have to contend with the European powers that seemed bent on conquering every square mile of the globe. This in turn would require a strong navy. Foremost among the proponents of the need for a strong navy to lead the US into this economic competition was Captain Alfred T. Mahan of the US Navy. Mahan argued that prosperity at home depended on foreign trade and investment, which would depend on a sizeable merchant marine fleet and a strong US presence in foreign markets. The US merchant marine would require security both at sea and in foreign ports, as well as access to supplies on their voyages. These in turn, would require US colonies, coaling stations (before the advent of oil) and a powerful navy. This command of the sea became known as capital-ship theory (Mahan, 1898). The choice, according to Mahan, was simple. Either the US must continue to expand or it must begin to decline and watch others take its place (Sprout and Sprout, 1944, p.214). Mahan's views found eager advocates among ardent nationalist like Theodore Roosevelt and Henry Cabot Lodge. TR's dispatch of the 'Great White Fleet' in 1907 around the world was in many ways a culmination of the journey the US traveled from isolationism to internationalism in this era. And while not all US politicians were ready to make the US a colonial power, most recognized the need for a more modern navy and more visible US presence abroad to assist in the foreign trade. Nowhere was this more aggressive role for the US military in the promotion of economic interests more visible and more far-reaching than in the Central American/Caribbean region and in East Asia. Where previous military interventions typically involved the protection of physical, economic assets owned

106   *The Political Use of Military Force in US Foreign Policy*

by Americans in foreign countries or on the seas, increasingly the rationale for the use of force was a government's economic policies.

Economic Interventionism, 1899-1918

The US began a policy of active interventionism in Central America and the Caribbean after its successful war with Spain won it a colony in Puerto Rico and a protectorate in Cuba. In addition to its geographic proximity, there were many economic factors that encouraged the drive for increased economic influence. Perhaps first and foremost, the decision to build the Panama Canal, motivated both by strategic and economic concerns, led to increased interest in the region. Second, since the early 1890s the US had sought to replace the British as the preeminent economic power in the region. When the US had been weaker, any desire to send the British packing in order to gain the dominant share in western hemispheric trade had to be reconciled with the overwhelming strength of the Royal Navy. Now that the British seemed to be willing to accommodate American interests, the Latin American trade could be exploited. Third, even as the US grew ascendant in the region, presidents still had to confront the British, French and German presence in many nations. In fact, it was the inability of many states, especially in the Caribbean, to settle their accounts with the Europeans that led the US to send in the Marines to take charge of local finances. The Roosevelt Corollary to the Monroe Doctrine was premised on this need to maintain stability in the hemisphere lest instability be used as a pretext for European interventionism. Still, there were many US bankers who stood to lose should these nations default on their loans. In addition, there were other, more pecuniary, economic interests, such as the need to protect US access to raw materials, particularly oil in Mexico.

American interventionism, especially the use of military force began with Theodore Roosevelt's style of nationalism, where the US presence in the region grew out of mutually reinforcing strategic and economic rationales. Roosevelt, an early admirer of Mahan, argued that the US had to behave like the great power that it was by expanding its economic ties and military presence. Each would bolster the other. President William Howard Taft, who authorized numerous military interventions, put even more of a commercial face on US policy with his 'dollar diplomacy'. According to Taft, his policy was, 'directed to the increase of American trade upon the axiomatic principle that the Government of the US shall extend all proper support to every legitimate and beneficial American enterprise abroad' (quoted in Schoultz, 1998 pp.208-209). He even encouraged American bankers by telling them that the US was ready to lend them a helping hand in their dealings with debtor nations to the South (Callcott, 1942, p.263). Woodrow Wilson consistently spoke out against the influence of big business in foreign policy and argued on behalf of the legitimate rights of the people of the western hemisphere. Yet, despite his rhetoric and occasional actions taken in contravention to the desires of the dominant US multinational corporations in Latin America, Wilson intervened more and for longer periods of time than did his predecessors.

There is a veritable explosion of uses of force at the end of the 19th century and in the first years of the 20th century. In fact, 26 of the uses of force (54

Economic Interests and the Political Use of Military Force 107

percent) during the first blossoming of US internationalism, 1899-1918, were aimed at protecting American business interests overseas. Presidents used force on average 1.23 times per year, the highest rate during any pre World War II period– double the rate of any other era (Table 3.1). 'Dollar Diplomacy', Wilsonian idealism, and American expansionism all combined with a strong and growing armed forces to encourage the US to intervene with more force and for longer periods of time. Many of these involved conflict/political unrest in the Central America/Caribbean region or China. In fact, 73 percent of all uses of force to protect or promote the interests of commerce during this era occur in Central America or the Caribbean (Table 3.3). The 'opportunity' to use force in this period seems to have expanded to meet American abilities and its newfound concern for the financial stability of its neighbors.

For example, in Honduras in 1912, Taft dispatched a military expedition to Honduras to prevent government nationalization of an American-owned railroad. US forces were sent into Nicaragua in 1912 and stayed on until the early 1930s, in part, to help the government run its financial affairs. The US sent the Marines and financial advisers into Haiti from 1915 through 1934 to run the customs house and keep Haiti from falling into the clutches of European bankers. In 1907 the US set up a customs receivership in the Dominican Republic. This was later expanded in 1916 when the Wilson ordered Marines ashore to seize control of the whole government. There were also repeated interventions to protect American property and provide stability in Cuba and Panama. Yet, according to Langley (1989, p.110), 'In all save Nicaragua, dollar diplomacy was a failure, though the private American economic presence, reinforced by stern diplomatic pressures and the occasional appearance of American warships, reminded the republics of Washington's policing role'. Luckily for the US, not to mention the nations of the region, foreign policymakers seemed to gradually learn that other, less aggressive instruments, (e.g., trade agreements) might work better, most of the time, to promote the American economy. As well, the decline of the European presence in the region after World War I decreased the need for military intervention to protect US security. Thus, the heyday of American-style economic imperialism in Central America and the Caribbean eventually ended after a period of frenetic activity. Perhaps to some degree we would expect that the number of military interventions would decrease to something approaching a more typical level. Nonetheless, even if some degree of 'overstretch' did ultimately cause foreign policy makers to reconsider the utility of such operations, long-term operations continued and even a few new ones were authorized. It really took the Great Depression to bring a halt to Yankee military imperialism in the Western Hemisphere.

The other region where the US gradually began asserting its newfound power throughout the late 19th and early 20th centuries was Asia. Presidents used force five times in Asia from 1899-1918 to advance economic interests (Table 3.3). The US, under Commodore Matthew Perry had earlier pried open the Japanese market with an impressive display of naval force, but always like today the China market loomed largest in the eyes of business and government. US commercial and political interest in China had continued to grow in the post Civil War period, but once again, it was the Spanish-American War in 1898 that served as the

108 *The Political Use of Military Force in US Foreign Policy*

catalyst to US imperialism. In the US Senate debate over how to manage the recent acquisition of the Philippines islands, Senator Albert Beveridge from Indiana and a prominent exponent of US power argued that, 'The Pacific is the ocean of commerce of the future and most future wars will be conflicts of commerce' (quoted in O'Connor, 1969, p.283). He, like many other nationalist politicians at the time, was eager for the US to assume a much more visible presence in the region, while staying aloof from the European quarrels over the spoils of trade. The Open Door Policy, initially a British suggestion like the Monroe Doctrine, seemed to satisfy the various and conflicting demands on US foreign policy at the time. In many ways, it is a quintessential American pronouncement. It sought to make up for a relative lack of US power through an appeal to an ostensibly universal and neutral principle–in this case open markets, access and fairness to all nations (with the notable exception of the Chinese themselves). It was a policy that sought to disguise substantial American business interests through idealistic rhetoric. And like many other noble-sounding policies with idealistic aims, the US ultimately wound up intervening with military force not just to protect its own, but to remake Chinese society into something that would more readily welcome US ideals, investment and exports.

The focus of the Open Door Policy, announced in September of 1899, was the differential treatment of the various trading nations in China. Van Alstyne (1973, p.78) summarized the main provisions of the US policy:

> Treaty rights in China were to be respected. Railway building, the development of mines and other capital investments might be of separate national origin; but differential tariffs on merchandise, discriminatory harbor dues in the leased ports and freight rates were not be tolerated.

The history books treat the policy as a victory for US idealism and trade, but in reality, the Chinese did not substantially reform the system by which outsiders exploited its weaknesses. Instead, the nation sank into chaos and the US, sometimes multilaterally, sometimes unilaterally resorted to using force to achieve what high-minded proclamations could not. President Taft ordered various US operations in 1911 during the initial stages of the nationalist revolution to defend US interests in Wuchang, Hankow, Shanghai, Nanking and elsewhere. The initial impetus for these missions was the immediate protection of US citizens and commercial interests, but they also served to remind the new government of Western economic and political privileges.

American Style Isolationism, 1919-1941

The US eventually tired of endless guerilla warfare in Nicaragua, long-term occupations of Haiti and the Dominican Republic, and ceaseless intervention into Chinese affairs. For in the end, it was not clear that even the strictly monetary benefits of such meddling paid off, a point made by one of the US's most famous military colonizers, General Smedley Butler (Butler, 1935). Like the use of force in general, gunboat diplomacy to advance American business largely fades away in

Economic Interests and the Political Use of Military Force 109

the late 1920s and 1930s. In the relatively isolationist years of 1919-1941, presidents used force only nine times to promote economic interests, for an average of .40 uses per year–the lowest of any of the eras examined here. And only 29 percent of all the uses in this period were directed at helping business in some fashion (Table 3.1). US forces did remain for many years in Haiti and Nicaragua keeping the peace. And though there were four, new uses of force in this era in the US backyard (44 percent of the total uses in this period to promote commerce), with the announcement of Franklin Roosevelt's 'Good Neighbor' policy, the US extracted its armed forces and downplayed its interventionist past (Table 3.3).

The other region where we do see some military activity in the interwar years is Asia. For example, in the early 1920s, Nationalist Chinese leaders announced that they would take part of the customs revenue, traditionally collected and held by outsiders, for various municipal projects. A combined fleet including ships of the US Navy collaborated in a demonstration off Canton to force the Chinese to relinquish control over the revenue (O'Connor, 1969, p.408). Throughout the 1910s and 1920s presidents had repeatedly used military force in or against China as civil war raged and the central government disintegrated. But, as was the case in Latin America, President Franklin Roosevelt retired the US from the active interventionism of the imperialist years. The Marine legation in Peking was brought home in 1934 and the Congressional Research Service study records no US military involvement again (except as it relates to World War II) in China until the communist revolution. In the isolationist years, presidents used force only twice in Asia to advance commercial interests. More often than not force was used to protect lives rather than property as we saw earlier.

In the first heady rush into imperialism, presidents, politicians and the public, imbued with progressivism and power, were ready to tackle the demands of remaking other societies, politically and economically. In the early days the US might charge into Cuba and the Philippines, convinced of its own moral superiority over the Spanish, but ultimately it would adopt the same violent and prolonged tactics to subdue the restless populations that resented colonialism no matter what the justification. Part of this increasing reluctance to use force was no doubt due to these lengthy commitments the US had undertaken in Central America, the Caribbean, China and the Philippines. As well, when the US faced a great many stronger, wealthier and more belligerent commercial competitors, it is not surprising that presidents resorted to the use of force to open markets and protect US citizens' property. In the 19th century, gunboat diplomacy was a perfectly acceptable method of protecting one's assets in a dangerous world. Whatever their rhetoric about avoiding entanglements in European politics, presidents could ill afford to remain entirely passive as others gobbled up markets and resources. Where in the heyday of imperialism, gunboat diplomacy was a perfectly appropriate and useful tool for managing 'the white man's burden', by the 1930s and certainly after World War II, the idea of sending a naval flotilla into a foreign harbor to force open trade or demand concessions seemed a bit antiquated. Other, less belligerent and equally as effective foreign policy tools, such as lending, foreign aid and economic sanctions, were becoming increasingly attractive.

US Hegemony and the International Economic System

The US emerged from World War II, not in cut-throat, economic competition with the major powers of Europe as it had been for so long, but in a vastly superior, economic position over them. The disruption brought about by the war, as well as the Great Depression were world wide and required global solutions. First, international trade had declined during the depression years as states pursued 'beggar thy neighbor' tariffs and trade restrictions. International trade declined an incredible 60 percent between 1929 and 1932 (Hathaway, 1984, p.278). Convinced that the survival of their domestic industries depended on protection from foreign competition, nations passed discriminatory trade regulations, like the Smoot-Hawley tariff in the US. The international monetary system was in a shambles as well as states dropped the gold standard and the United Kingdom relinquished its leadership position. The US was unwilling, until World War II, to accept responsibility for managing currencies and balance of payment issues. Finally, there was the economic and political devastation of the war. Europe and Japan would ultimately require enormous amounts of assistance to rebuild themselves. In short, the economic problems facing the world and its most powerful nation were massive and systemic. The health and wealth of the US economy would no longer depend on opening up trading outposts in the underdeveloped regions with gunboats and Marine expeditionary forces. Military force was fine for confronting localized problems, not managing a modern, global economy. As the key issues of the post war world were the structure and the rules of the economic system, international organizations and diplomacy would work much better.

It is instructive to contrast the military operations presidents authorized in the pre World War II era, especially in the 19th century, with those that were ordered in the Cold War to protect economic interests. One gets the sense that many of the older interventions occurred as US citizens and their property were caught up in violent events whose causes were local in origin. At other times, locals might target US interests for attack, but again such events were relatively isolated from any kind of larger foreign policy concerns on the part of national authorities in these countries. The US military was often called in to supply the kind of protection that local police and military personnel should have been providing. In the Cold War era, however, (non) violent attacks on American economic interests were often part of a deliberate government policy, as in Cuba, Chile, Iran, to name but a few. Foreign attacks on US property, whether with guns or government regulations, aimed at redistributing wealth and attacking symbols of it. Presidents did authorize military actions to provide protection against attack in the short-term, but also to effect change in the foreign policies of those hostile nations that targeted US economic interests. These modern uses of force occur more in an international context with both the US and its adversary conscious of the precedents they are setting both economically and politically. Thus, while there may be fewer uses of force occurring in the Cold War and its aftermath for the reasons discussed above, the stakes have often been significantly higher than in past eras.

At the same time because the US and the Soviet Union sought to extend both their power and their political-economic systems, there was a strong, economic caste to the Cold War and the superpower competition. While the Soviets promoted communism as the ideal, economic arrangement, so too did the US seek to win adherents to capitalism. Their allies tended to share the same economic system, and each superpower attempted to export its economic ideology along with its power into the uncommitted nations of the world. Thus, in one sense, economic philosophy and economic self-interest were omnipresent during the Cold War if one accepts the notion that the superpower competition was over control of the global, political-economic system. And certainly there were cases where the US took military action to protect or advance its economic interests against communist movements (e.g., Cuba in the early 1960s). But even if every military intervention was not a direct result of economic self-interest, such motivations provided an on-going fundamental basis of US foreign policy actions. On the other hand, if one believes that this ideological competition was merely a guise for more traditional security concerns and balance of power politics, the economic aspect of this contest is simply the latest rationale in the never-ending quest for power. Most scholars, like Krasner (1978), Gilpin (1975) and others conclude that anti-communism more than pro-capitalism led presidents to dispatch the military when economic interests were seemingly at stake. Yet, whether anti-communism was a modern label grafted onto old-time imperialism may never be untangled for US foreign policy was based on complementary set of political, economic and security objectives (Packenham, 1973).

Critics have certainly accused presidents of extensive meddling in the affairs of other nations to preserve or extend US business interests during the Cold War, but their favorite target has often been the Central Intelligence Agency. Critics and scholars have charged that, in addition to the 1953 Iranian operation, the CIA was heavily involved in Guatemala in 1954, Cuba in the early 1960s, the Congo in the early 1960s, and Chile in the early 1970s to protect US business interests by installing pliant governments. While CIA involvement in the internal politics of these nations is generally not disputed, scholars have argued over the extent to which pressure placed on the US government by business interests motivated the operations (i.e., United Fruit in Guatemala; various US business in Cuba nationalized by Castro; US mining interests in the Congo; US copper interests in Chile). But while presidents did authorize military missions against these nations, they were aimed more at achieving some general level of economic influence over the governments and internal developments than they were tailor-made operations on behalf of US multinational corporations.

In sum, we can see clear indications of the rise and fall of the prominence of economic interests in the use of force short of war throughout American history. The US was at first compelled to use force to protect its economic interests because its very survival seemed to be at stake. Such economic interests acquired greater influence throughout the 19th century as the US expanded economically and developed a navy that was capable of seizing opportunities to advance and protect economic interests throughout the globe. This sort of economic expansionism reached a culmination in the years between the Spanish-American War and US

112 *The Political Use of Military Force in US Foreign Policy*

entry into World War I with repeated interventions in the affairs of many Central American and Caribbean governments. These seemingly never-ending operations ultimately soured many in the Congress and the public on the benefits of reforming other governments and achieving economic gains at gunpoint. After this apogee of aggressive promotion of economic interests presidents became increasingly reluctant to reform the economies of other states and dispatch Marines to protect American businesses. In the post World War II era of American economic dominance, presidents more often relied on tools other than military force to protect and advance US economic interests. Since these economic interests were interwoven with the anticommunism in the Cold War, their juxtaposition suggested the US was once again acting like the colonial powers of old, aggressively dominating the world for its own benefit. As Boot (2002, p.xvii) argues, the old style gunboat diplomacy, '...served much the same function as World Trade Organization negotiations do today'. Nonetheless, particular, economic interests as well as the more general economic prosperity of the US continue to inform US foreign policy and motivate some critical uses of military force.

A Model of the Use of Force and Economic Interests, 1948-1998

We have seen that there are several diverse theories that pertain to the use of force and economic interests. The ideologically-inclined Marxist/world system/ dependency theory school of thought tends to view all or almost all US military interventions as driven by multinational corporations and the demands of a capitalist economic system. Interest group theory sees these businesses as one of a number of competing voices, albeit a privileged one, demanding special treatment in the foreign policy making process. Scholars who study the workings of the international economic system see hegemonic powers, like the US, as maintaining a particular set of international economic arrangements that are beneficial to its prosperity and continued leadership. We are interested in identifying specific factors in international crises that pertain to US economic interests as envisioned by these theories, and that increase the likelihood that a president will authorize the political use of military force. These factors may alert presidents to threats to specific American businesses and property, or to the general, economic prosperity of the US. They may also indicate the potential to advance private or more broadly conceived US economic interests.

Threats to American-owned businesses and other US economic interests overseas may take many forms, ranging from discriminatory taxation, laws against repatriation of profits, expropriation of property, and all the way to physical attacks on economic assets. Most disputes between US multinational corporations, or the US government itself and host governments are dealt with through diplomacy, arbitration, or perhaps economic sanctions by the US. We would not expect many disputes to escalate to the point at which the president begins to seriously entertain the idea of using military force to redress some financial grievance. Instead, as Krasner (1978) and Rodman (1988) show in their analyses of foreign government expropriation and nationalization, not only does the US government tend to shy

Economic Interests and the Political Use of Military Force 113

away from the use of force, it has often encouraged US-owned corporations to accept the best compensation they are likely to obtain, for fear that nasty, public battles between MNC's and foreign governments will harm larger US foreign policy interests. Many of the military coups in South America that brought to power governments that nationalized US-owned businesses in the 1950s and 1960s were dealt with through negotiation.

Conversely, when foreign governments physically attack US economic assets and economic interests, both business and the president are likely to view the events in an entirely different light. The use of armed force by a foreign government or its agents to attack, seize or destroy American-owned property escalates a dispute from arbitration to confrontation. In such instances, presidents may determine that protection of such assets or military retaliation against the aggressor is necessary to safeguard immediate, tangible interests, and signal a more general willingness to use force should other foreign governments consider such belligerent moves. Iranian attacks on US-flagged oil tankers transiting the Persian Gulf in the late 1980s are but one example of this sort of threat. Therefore, I expect that the president's response to international crises that involve threats to US economic interests will differ depending on the type of threat posed by the foreign government.

Hypothesis 6: Presidents will be less likely to use military force when an international crisis involves a non-violent threat against US economic interests.[14]

Hypothesis 7: Presidents will be more likely to use military force when an international crisis involves a violent attack against US economic interests.[15]

Instability or conflict in those nations that receive substantial amounts of economic assistance from the US may lead presidents to use force to protect such 'client' states. Especially if one subscribes to dependency theory arguments, the US has an interest in using force and economic aid to sustain favorable investment climates, promote American exports, and preserve access to valuable raw materials. Economic assistance might be viewed as just another tool designed to perpetuate a

---

[14] Each opportunity is coded for the presence or absence of several types of threats including: threatened or actual nationalization of US-owned businesses by government; attacks on US property or businesses by the government or non-governmental actors; protection of vital resources (e.g., oil); protection of shipping lanes, and several others. For this variable I consider all those events that are characterized by attempts to expropriate or nationalize US-owned property where there is no accompanying physical attack, as non-violent disputes.

[15] For this variable, I use the same information described in the previous footnote to determine when threats to US economic interests were present in an opportunity to use force. Only when the opportunity involved a physical attack on US property, or economic assets considered critical to the US economy (i.e., oil), did I code this second variable as "1"–a violent attack on US economic interests.

114   *The Political Use of Military Force in US Foreign Policy*

friendly client regime and foster a dependent relationship. When such nations undergo crises, presidents may use force to prevent changes in economic policies, defend the regime against rebel forces that may seek economic reforms, or to prevent other states from becoming the dominant power. Regardless of a particular, precipitating incident, presidents should be interested in protecting the investment of American economic assistance in such nations.

Hypothesis 8: Presidents will be more likely to use force during an international crisis, the greater the amount of US economic assistance to the target nation.[16]

One economic issue has been sufficiently important to inspire multiple uses of force in the Cold War and beyond–oil. As the US and its allies became increasingly dependent upon foreign oil, presidents have exerted tremendous pressure to maintain access to these supplies, especially in the Persian Gulf. In 1987, President Reagan authorized a sizeable US naval presence in the Persian Gulf to escort Kuwaiti and other oil tankers (flying under American flags) during the Iran-Iraq War. And of course, the deployment of US forces to Saudi Arabia in the summer of 1990 and again in the fall was intended, among other things, to prevent Kuwaiti, and ultimately Saudi Arabian oil supplies from falling into the hands of Saddam Hussein's Iraq. Even after the 1991 Persian Gulf War, presidents Bush and Clinton authorized several uses of force to protect Kuwait when it appeared Saddam Hussein was seeking to conquer that nation again. Iraq posed a variety of threats to the US and its allies in the region during the 1990s with its attempts to build weapons of mass destruction and dominate the region. But chief among these threats was the possibility that Saddam Hussein might one day control through force or intimidation enough of the oil in the region to wreak havoc on the economies of the West. Presumably the 2003 war in Iraq has removed this threat to Western interests. In addition to crises in the Middle East, however, the US has been involved in developments in many other oil-rich nations, most especially Indonesia and Venezuela. Because of US and Western interests in maintaining access to a steady supply of oil, we would expect that whenever crises threaten the stability of major oil-producing nations, or when such states take actions that disrupt the flow of oil, presidents would respond forcefully to protect this critical element of the US and indeed, the global economy.

Hypothesis 9: Presidents will be more likely to use force during an international crisis when the crisis locale is an OPEC state.[17]

---

[16] Data on foreign aid were taken from the Agency for International Development's (1994) US *Overseas Loans and Grants Series of Yearly Data from 1949-1994* and updates to these data from USAID thereafter.

[17] OPEC member states are: Algeria, Indonesia, Iran, Iraq, Kuwait, Libya, Nigeria, Qatar, Saudi Arabia, United Arab Emirates and Venezuela. I only measure OPEC membership from the first year in which the state was a member. Membership data is found at http://www.opec.org/homepage/frame.htm as of July 30, 2003.

Economic Interests and the Political Use of Military Force 115

To test the utility of the economic interest model of the US use of force, I again use probit analysis to test the hypotheses on US actions in international crises from 1948-1998. The overall fit of this model is rather modest. The χ^2 statistic testing the likelihood that all the coefficients are equal to zero, is statistically significant. The model predicts 54.5 percent of the cases correctly for a 4.2 percent proportionate reduction of error over guessing the modal category in every case. The model correctly predicts 12.5 percent of the non uses of force correctly, and 91 percent of the uses of force correctly–thus it is rather biased. The pseudo R^2 is extremely low at .017. The overall goodness of fit of this model is unfortunately, unimpressive, but that is not the only story.

Table 3.4 Predicting Uses of Force 1948-1998 Using Probit Analysis: The Economic Interest Model

Variable	Coeff.	Standard Error	T Statistic	P Value	Marginal Effect
Non Violent Economic Dispute	-.1704	.275	-0.62	0.536	-.0679
Attack on Economic Interests	1.063	.3622	2.94	0.003	.3501
US Economic Aid	.0007	.0003	1.80	0.072	.0002
OPEC Member State	-.0374	.1758	-0.21	0.831	-.0149
Constant	.0076	.0592	0.13	0.897	

N=605
$\chi^2 = 14.9$, p. < .01
Pseudo $R^2 = .017$
Percent Correctly Predicted = 54.5%
Proportionate Reduction of Error = 4.2%

Two of the four hypotheses are supported. Presidents are more likely to use force when there are violent threats or attacks made on US economic interests in an international crisis ('Attack on Economic Interests'). In fact, of the 21 cases that fit this description, presidents used force 18 times (85 percent). The probability of a political use of military force increases by 35 percent, *ceteris paribus*, according to the marginal effects coefficient. While these crises may be relatively infrequent, they also represent acute challenges to American economic hegemony. Some involved violent attacks on US commercial property, such as the Cuban seizure of an American-owned ship in 1961, or the Iranian attacks on shipping in the Persian Gulf in the late 1980s. Others concerned nationalization of US property accompanied by physical attacks, as occurred in Cuba in the late 1950s and early 1960s.

Crises that involve non-violent economic disputes, however, are neither more nor less likely to provoke a use of force. The coefficient for this variable is statistically insignificant. As I have argued, such foreign policy problems are most

The Political Use of Military Force in US Foreign Policy

likely dealt with by the State or Commerce departments rather than the Pentagon. Indeed, even many of the types of non-violent economic disputes that used to precipitate international crises are no longer very prevalent. In particular, government efforts to nationalize or expropriate American-owned businesses, or any foreign-owned enterprises for that matter, have almost gone the way of the dinosaur in international relations. As noted by the US State Department, 'Many countries have adopted policies other than expropriation in pursuing their efforts to gain greater control over their natural resources and to increase the benefits they derive from in-country economic activity' (Bureau of Intelligence and Research March 6, 1985, p.1). Placing restrictions on repatriation of profits, demanding technology transfer and requiring multinational corporations to establish joint ventures with local partners are more prevalent now. Such subtle tactics do not seem nearly as likely to precipitate an international crisis worthy of presidential consideration of the use of force.

As expected, we see in Table 3.4 that the greater the amount of US economic assistance provided to a nation, the more likely presidents will use military force when that nation experiences a crisis ('US Economic Aid'). As the variable is measured in million dollar increments, it is easier to interpret its impact by examining changes in aid by factors of ten. According to the marginal effects coefficient, and with the usual caveats, every one million dollar increase in economic aid results in a .07 percent increase in the likelihood of a use of force. Accordingly, nations that receive ten million dollars in assistance are .7 percent more likely to be the site of a use of force, while those allocated 100 million in aid are 7 percent more likely to attract a political use of military force by the US. Such evidence supports the arguments of many dependency theorists and other critics of US foreign policy, if we assume that the US is using force to sustain its client regime and protect its economic interests.

Lastly, despite the many problems the US has experienced with OPEC nations over the years, the mere fact that an OPEC state was involved in an international crisis does not make a use of force more likely ('OPEC Member State'). The coefficient for this variable was statistically insignificant. There were 72 crises in all in which OPEC states were involved, but presidents used force only 40 times (55.5 percent). Many of these, no doubt, concerned matters other than oil. Nonetheless, we might have expected presidents to be especially mindful of the (in)stability of these nations and their ability to bring oil to market. Especially when internal crises have occurred involving OPEC states, such as the 1979 Iranian revolution, the violent coup in Indonesia in 1965, and even more recent events in Venezuela, there have been noticeable if not significant disruptions in the supply of oil. Presidents did respond with a political use of military force in some of these types of cases, but not to the extent that we might have imagined. Perhaps presidents are more likely to use force to protect the flow of oil when it is physically threatened because of international events, as in the aftermath of the 1973 Yom Kippur War and in the war between Iran and Iraq in the 1980s. US foreign policy makers may choose to meet internal crises with economic and political measures instead, as in the various unplanned changes of government in Indonesia and Venezuela. I should note that there was some degree of correlation

Economic Interests and the Political Use of Military Force   117

between the OPEC variable and the variable, 'Attack on Economic Interest', but that there was still no bivariate relationship between OPEC nation involvement in a crisis and the use of force.

Conclusions

By now, the reader should be well familiar with the most important conclusions of this chapter. I have explained that presidents have often used force to promote economic interests, especially in the years from the founding of the Republic through the early part of the 20th century. More recently presidents have relied less on the use of force to achieve economic objectives, although sometimes nationalization of US property and threats to the supply of Persian Gulf oil have made the resort to force necessary. These operations were not undertaken to advance some grand, capitalist design at the instigation of multinational corporations. Instead, presidents engaged in such activities because practically all of them believed that the promotion of free markets was good for US businesses, and good for the US economy. As Leffler (1984, p.225) writes:

> American officials could extol the virtues of peace, support arbitration treaties, defend the rights of property, champion the sanctity of contracts, cultivate multinational efforts at cooperation in the private sectors, and oppose revolutionary movements abroad because they realized that efforts to avert war, disseminate American ideals, and encourage world economic progress were compatible with the interests of a net creditor, exporting nation, increasingly concerned with foreign supplies of raw materials.

Then and now the US has mostly pursued a global, open door policy. Whether through declaration, diplomacy, sanction or force, presidents have consistently sought to extend economic relations with other nations. As so many presidents viewed this as a right rather than a privilege, it is not surprising they were willing to take aggressive action to protect American economic rights. Whether it was the right to trade, the right of US multinational corporations to remain free of regulating and nationalizing local governments, or the right to access to raw materials, presidents have had occasion to use the military as a global, economic, police force. They have been most apt to do so when the US had sufficient, but not overwhelming power, and when economic interests dominated or complemented other military and political objectives. In the post World War II era presidents have not had much occasion to use force to advance economic interests, but when such things are attacked, they overwhelmingly tend to respond with force.

So why is the connection between economic interests and security policy such an understudied subject, as noted by Mastanduno (1988)? There are many possible explanations including the overall lack of communication between the fields of international security and international political economy, the influence of the now discredited, and empirically non-falsifiable Marxist/Leninist theories of imperialism, and the present dominance of diversionary and realist explanations of the use of force. I have shown, however, that economic interests have exercised a decisive impact on the use of force on many occasions. Indeed, the desire to protect or advance such interests has often been a necessary and/or a sufficient condition to use the military. Perhaps the reason why previous research overlooked this relationship is that scholars searched for a pervasive and prevailing influence of business interests in the foreign policy making establishment and not surprisingly found little evidence of such a deterministic relationship. I argue that economic interests are powerful not because the business elite dominates US foreign policy, but because specific threats to economic interests and opportunities to advance them are important to presidents. Such situations often call for a use of force to promote an even more fundamental objective–the continued prosperity of the US. Given that such a critical national interest provides the ultimate justification for some such military actions, we should expect all presidents to be willing to use force when necessary.

Economic interests have long been important in motivating the political use of military force. 90 uses of force–a majority–from 1798-1941 were designed to protect and/or advance the interests of commerce. Unfortunately, theories of economic interests in US foreign policy have not received the same level of attention and rigorous, empirical scrutiny as have other theories. Here we see just how important they have been across a considerable expanse of US history that should now make clear that any integrative theory of the political use of military force must include these goals. Because economic interests are such a critical and enduring impetus for the political use of military force it is important that they be better integrated into foreign policy models. The explanatory power of economic interests varies by the power capabilities of the US and the extent to which such interests compete with US security objectives. As power increases, so too should the use of force to protect and/or promote economic interests, but as power reaches hegemonic proportions, the use of force to realize economic objectives should decline in frequency. The influence of economic interests on a crisis by crisis basis is more likely to be dependent in part on event characteristics. When challenges to economic interests are more threatening than the security interests at stake, or when the latter are absent, the use of force is more likely. Perhaps the most important finding of this chapter has been that such occasions have been much more frequent than heretofore suspected. I will return to this theme in the final chapter when developing a more general model of decision making on the political use of military force.

Chapter 4

Liberal Idealism and the Political Use of Military Force

Introduction

The US is not unique in viewing the world influenced by its own experience, and partial to its ideals and seeking out converts. Many nations and empires have exported their religions and brand of government, but the US has done so more as proselytizer than conqueror. As Hans Morgenthau (1967, p.10) wrote, 'All nations are tempted–and few have been able to resist the temptation for long–to clothe their own particular aspirations and actions in the moral purposes of the universe'. Americans have been uniquely convinced of the righteousness of their cause so that the missionary zeal to reform has more often coincided rather than conflicted with the perceived national interest. What makes the world a better place, Americans believe, makes the US a more secure nation and vice versa. Increasingly, historians, political scientists and policymakers are acknowledging the importance of domestic values in foreign policies (Owen, 1994). Krasner (1978) regards the pursuit of ideological goals as among the most important, especially for dominant powers. In particular, if a state, such as the US, possesses overwhelming international power, there are substantial opportunities and incentives to remake the world in its own image (Krasner, 1978, p.340) and to socialize leaders in other states to its norms and values (Ikenberry and Kupchan, 1990). More so than any other political philosophy, liberal idealism has consistently and continually been the primary ideological rationale behind US foreign policy. By 'liberal idealism' I mean that philosophy that stresses the dignity of individuals using rationality to determine their political and economic destinies, and realized through procedural and substantive, democratic government. Whether sincerely intended or not, presidents have continually made reference to the US' unique role as a moral force in world politics, particularly in the promotion of democracy and human rights. According to Huntington (1999, p.236), 'In the eyes of most Americans not only should their foreign-policy institutions be structured and function so as to reflect liberal values, but American foreign policy should also be substantively directed to the promotion of those values in the external environment'. Political liberalism also has an economic counterpart in free

120   *The Political Use of Military Force in US Foreign Policy*

market capitalism that is sometimes promoted alongside democracy and human rights, but which was discussed in Chapter 3.[18]

How exactly is this abstract political theory turned into a method and an objective for US foreign policy and military intervention? I believe a useful methodology can be found in Peceny's (1999, p.15) definition of proliberalization foreign policies as, '...the combination of active support for 'free and fair' elections with the promotion of at least one of the following: centrist political parties, moderate interest groups, reductions in human rights abuses, and/or formal subordination of the military to civilian authority'. This is a sufficiently broad definition that captures more than just the supervision of elections since it also incorporates concerns like human rights that have long been a part of US foreign policy idealism. The purpose of this chapter is to evaluate the extent to which liberal idealism has informed the decision to use military force and the military intervention itself. Does the promotion of liberalism provide us with a unique and powerful explanation of foreign policy behavior, or is it superfluous to our understanding of this phenomenon?

In the first part of this chapter I discuss the burgeoning research on the role of liberal idealism, especially the promotion of democracy, in US foreign policy. I then review three, prominent occasions where we have strong reason to believe presidents used force on behalf of liberal idealism. Next, I provide an historical overview of the role of liberal idealism in US foreign policy and its impact on military intervention decisions. I show how presidents have understood that stressing liberal idealism could be a rational and effective foreign policy goal. It provided a weak nation with a principle by which to attract allies when its capabilities were insufficient to repel enemies. And liberalism gives a strong state an idealism (or perhaps a cloak to disguise its ambitions) when weaker nations might fear its ambitions. In addition to discussing the history of liberal idealism in US foreign policy, I also analyze the evidence for and against a liberal idealist basis for the use of military force in US foreign policy. I survey the available data from 1798 until World War II to assess the frequency with which presidents used military force on behalf of liberal idealist foreign policy goals, across both regions and various eras of American foreign policy. I find that while liberalism, especially the promotion of democracy, has not always been the driving force behind the use of military force short of war, there have been a number of prominent military interventions that have been justified on the basis of liberal foreign policy goals. I also develop a multivariate model of liberal idealist interests in the period 1948-1998, and find that under certain circumstances, presidents have deployed the military in situations where we might expect they

---

[18] There may be other ideological interests that the US has pursued through the use of military force, but as liberal values are the core of American political ideology, so too do they comprise the dominant ideological tendency in foreign policy. Other ideological interests grow out of liberalism, whether rightly or incorrectly justified, so it makes more sense to analyze this most powerful and popular tradition.

Liberal Idealism and the Political Use of Military Force   121

were seeking to promote liberal idealism. I conclude by assessing all the evidence presented in the chapter.

I show in this chapter that while liberal idealism is not 'the' dominant theory or 'a' dominant theory of the political use of military force by the US, it contributes to our understanding of the subject in several ways. First, the nation's foreign policy makers from the Founders to the present day have adhered to liberal political views, shared by their countrymen and expressed in their foreign policies in words and in deeds. It is impossible to understand the thinking and the goals behind American foreign policy without understanding the role played by liberal, political values. Second, liberal idealist uses of force do occur with some degree of frequency beginning in the very late 19th century. They are not isolated operations pursued by idealist presidents. There is substantial evidence to suggest that liberal idealist goals have significantly contributed toward the decision to use force.

Research on Military Force and Liberal Idealism

Research on the role and impact of liberal values in US foreign policy has become a popular subject of late in political science. Some have argued that domestic values permeate American external relations (Packenham, 1973; Huntington, 1981, 1999; Quester, 1982), while others agree that the US has shown a preference for liberal regimes, but explain it as a result of a broader favoritism toward stable, client states (Ferguson, 1972; MacDonald, 1992; Smith, 1994). Many have detected a messianic streak in US foreign policy that springs from Americans' conception of themselves as special and uniquely entitled to bring the benefits of the good news of liberalism (Whitcomb, 1998). Others have downplayed American exceptionalism (Lepgold and McKeown, 1995). The relationship between values and foreign policy, and in particular their impact on military intervention has grown dramatically since the end of the Cold War. Most scholars now agree on two, key issues. First, whatever their normative judgments, they recognize that the US has from time to time sought to remake other nations in its liberal image. Second, most researchers conclude that fostering democracy at gunpoint is a difficult task. Where scholars tend to differ is on the normative and practical wisdom of exporting democracy.

In an insightful essay on the dilemmas Americans face when they seek to remake the world in the image of a liberal democracy, Samuel Huntington (1999) finds that despite the difficulties involved, the world is much better off when the US is using its power on behalf of liberal principles. Huntington (1999, p.242) asserts that:

> The US is in practice the freest, most liberal, most democratic country in the world, with far better institutionalized protections for the rights of its citizens than any other society. As a consequence, any increase in the power or influence of the US in world affairs generally results–not inevitably, but far more often than not–in the promotion of liberty and human rights in the world.

122 *The Political Use of Military Force in US Foreign Policy*

Conversely, when American power internationally is weak, other states are unlikely to follow American leadership, let alone remodel their political regimes to suit US tastes. Huntington acknowledges that transforming the political institutions of other societies is a difficult task that requires an expansion of American power at home and abroad. It may antagonize some governments. But exporting liberalism also makes the world more stable, the US more secure, and will ultimately serve the interests of the reformed societies. While he does not evaluate the methods by which the US effects liberal change in these societies, the logical conclusion of his normative argument suggests that the US has every right and reason to export liberalism.

Whitcomb (1998) argues that interventionism in the 19th century was almost entirely limited to verbal support for revolutionary movements. Interventionism in the 20th century, while not without success, all too often resulted in narrow, self-centered and arrogant endeavors that bloodied and sullied the democratic reputation of the US. Others, such as Haass (1994, p.36) argue that, 'The US should largely stay outside or minimize its role in situations requiring...nation-building'. Robert Art (1991, p.42) concludes that while promoting democracy where it is feasible is in the US interest, military force is of little use in this effort. He argues (1991, p.42) that:

> The aim of spreading democracy around the globe...can too easily become a license for indiscriminate and unending US military interventions in the internal affairs of others. Democracies are best produced, rather, by stalemating aggressor states, by providing a stable international framework that facilitates economic development and the emergence of a middle class within states, and by using economic and other types of leverage to encourage internal liberalization.

Michael Mandelbaum (1996) asserts that intervention in the internal affairs of other states will not succeed because it does not have public support in the US and is unsustainable over the long run.

McDougall (1997) finds a variety of traditions in US foreign policy, most of them informed to some degree by liberal idealism. American exceptionalism, perhaps the oldest tradition, is based on the United State's unique history and mission in the world, and held sway primarily in the early years of the Republic. But it was a value foreign policy was supposed to '...defend [at home], not define [abroad]' (McDougall, 1997, p.37). It took the later, outwardly-directed traditions of Wilsonian Internationalism and Global Meliorism to give it some content in the foreign policy actions of the US government. Meliorism is premised on the notion that the US would be better off addressing the roots of international problems–lack of democracy and human rights, and poverty–than attacking its symptoms–war (perhaps terrorism today). Wilsonian internationalists wished to make the world safe for democracy–the Meliorists sought to make the world democratic (McDougall, 1997, p.174). McDougall derides those who would achieve liberalism and prosperity through coercive means because he argues these things cannot be implanted. As well, he argues that lack of democracy, human rights and economic prosperity do not necessarily lead to war and thus require eradication.

Nonetheless, McDougall does recognize that Americans have often found occasion to embark on ideological crusades throughout the globe. Like many, he simply doubts the wisdom of such enterprises.

Muravchik (1991) also distinguishes among different impulses in American foreign policy thinking–realism, isolationism and idealism. But within the group of idealists, he finds two additional schools of thought. He contends there are 'democratic idealists' and 'pacific idealists', who agree that moral considerations should guide foreign policy. The former are willing to act assertively by using force to realize these ambitions in the world, while the latter group is entirely reluctant to wage war on behalf of idealism. Muravchik (1991, p.6) asserts that advancing democracy is America's most effective foreign policy tool. Especially with the demise of communism, it should grow easier and assume preeminence in US foreign policy. He argues that the US can and should 'export' democracy and points to successful cases like Japan, Germany, Italy and Austria after World War II and the Dominican Republic and Panama during the Cold War. Muravchik acknowledges that force of arms should not be the preferred method, but neither should we dismiss its role in planting the seeds of democracy. He does conclude, however, by noting that more peaceful tools should be preferred in the future to help create an international system of institutions and laws. Smith (1994, p.3) refers to democratization as the 'central ambition of American foreign policy during the twentieth century'. He argues, like Muravchik, that liberal internationalism comports well with realist dictates because democratization enhances US security

Recently, many foreign policy scholars who emphasize applied analysis have investigated the merits of a proliberalization foreign policy. Carothers (2000) analyzes a variety of democratization programs the US government has conducted throughout the globe and demonstrates that liberal idealist programs have become embedded in the institutions and policies of American government. He argues that, 'American foreign policy of the past 100 years cannot be understood without serious attention to the democracy ideal' (Carothers, 2000, p.4). Carothers is primarily concerned, however, with foreign assistance programs rather than military intervention. He finds that annual US spending on proliberalization programs is approximately 600-700 million a year and that such programs have reached more than 100 countries (2000, pp.6-7). Despite the arguments made by skeptics and realists against such programs, Carothers concludes that democratization assistance is a worthwhile endeavor and has become increasingly important. He contends that the goals of democratization buttress other US economic and security objectives; that when such programs are carried out in the open they do not constitute an illegitimate form of intervention; and that democracy can be nurtured with outside support.

Larry Diamond writes that, 'Democracy should be the central focus–the defining feature–of US foreign policy' (1992, p.31). Hoffman (1998) argues that military intervention for nation building is in the national interest of the US, because it advances a world order more conducive to US interests. Allison and Beschell, however, conclude, 'The literature provides little advice for would-be promoters of democracy other than cautions about how little can be done' (1992, p.85). They go on, however, to provide readers with a lengthy list of suggestions the US government might follow to foster democratic growth, such as encouraging pluralization of societies, assisting in the development of market economies, and socializing military and security forces to respect democratic norms and values. Similarly, for Diamond (1992, p.27), promoting democracy '...means offering moral, political, diplomatic and financial support to individuals and organizations that are struggling to open up authoritarian regimes'.

There is also the immense literature on the democratic peace phenomenon. International relations scholars working from a variety of perspectives have conclusively demonstrated that democratic states rarely, if ever, war against one another (Maoz and Russett, 1993; Owen, 1994; Bueno de Mesquita and Lalman, 1992). In fact, one of the most fundamental characteristics of any state is its type of government, which researchers have found is predictive of all manner of intrastate and international policies. Democratic regimes tend to be more cooperative in general in their international behavior (Benoit, 1996; Leeds and Davis, 1999). Huth (1998) finds that major powers are more likely to intervene in conflicts when they share the same type of polity with a state that is threatened by a third, politically dissimilar nation. Thus, government type is highly predictive of how states treat one another because it represents the very core of their identity. If all the world were to become democratic, theoretically, international wars would never be fought again.

Political scientists have also studied the relationship between force and democracy using statistical methodologies. Peceny (1999) provides a thorough historical and empirical analysis of US efforts to export democracy 'at the point of bayonets'. He finds that in thirty-three of ninety-three 20th century interventions, the US has sought to advance liberal idealism. Peceny (1999, p.4) argues that when presidents initially consider military intervention, they will be more likely to act to support democracy when, '...the international system is least threatening, when it has the most leverage over the target government, and the conditions within the target country are most conducive to pursuing such reforms'. More specifically he finds that during the first and second world wars, as well as the Cold War, presidents were less likely to adopt proliberalization policies at the outset of a use of force. Toward the end of a military intervention, Peceny finds that, when a proliberalization Congress confronts presidents, they tend to resort to proliberalization goals in order to build domestic support for their actions. He argues that the US government promotes democracy at gunpoint because it is an attractive political option for presidents and that military intervention can be an effective method of promoting democracy when it is combined with support for free and fair elections. But few other researchers have sought to analyze the extent to which liberal idealism has motivated the use of force. Most political scientists who use empirical research methods examine the *consequences* rather than the causes of military intervention.

Meernik (1996) finds that in the majority of cases, regardless of the manner in which democratic change is measured, US military interventions did not lead to increased levels of democracy during the Cold War. Most nations retain

Liberal Idealism and the Political Use of Military Force   125

their current level of democracy. But, when he compares nations that have experienced intervention with those that have not, he finds that the former group is more likely to experience democratic growth. The use of ground forces and presidential statements on behalf of democratization also appear to lead to increased democratization during interventions. Hermann and Kegley examine a similar set of US military interventions, which aimed to promote liberalization, and find that they tend to leave nations more democratic (1998, p.97). When the US intervenes for reasons other than liberalization, nations tend to become more autocratic. Hermann and Kegley also distinguish between interventions aimed at protecting and those directed toward promoting democracy. The US is more likely to 'protect' regimes that are more democratic, and more likely to 'promote' liberalization in less democratic states. They also find that short interventions, minimally-sized commitments, agreement between the President and Congress regarding the liberalization goal of the intervention, and interventions occurring between 1975-1992 are all positively associated with democratization.

Most historians, policy analysts and political scientists have seemingly accepted the idea that the US has frequently sought to promote liberal idealism through force of arms. Based on presidential behavior and statements and the significant amount of research on this subject, it would appear that the promotion of liberalization has been an enduring concern in US foreign policy. Scholars then turn their attention to analyzing the effectiveness of military intervention in this regard and find that its impact is at best modest, and at worst potentially damaging to those involved. But, I would argue that we still have not adequately evaluated the extent to which presidents are motivated to use force in order to promote liberal goals. Peceny's (1999) analysis does an excellent job covering most of the 20th century in this regard, but we should also examine the earlier period, as well as more recent years. By evaluating the explanatory power of liberal idealist objectives using historical data and statistical analysis we can understand just when this core American political value contributes to the deployment of military force.

Three Case Studies of Military Force and the Promotion of Liberal Idealism

A Moral Crusade—Stopping the Slave Trade

Considering the history of American military intervention on behalf of liberal idealism in general and moral crusades in particular, perhaps no endeavor was more incongruous as the effort to halt the trafficking of human cargo in the years prior to the Civil War. This extensive naval operation involved squadrons of ships patrolling the Atlantic coasts of Africa and Latin America as well as the waters of the Caribbean. It is rather incongruous because it came at a time when the US had not resolved its own internal questions over slavery. Many of the foreign policy makers who developed the policy and the naval officers who implemented it were sympathetic to the interests of slave owners in the South, if not slave holders

126   *The Political Use of Military Force in US Foreign Policy*

themselves. Why then did the US embark on a major, military effort on behalf of such humanitarian ideals?

The roots of the US policy are located in British politics and foreign policy. In large part because of the efforts of abolitionists and church groups, in 1807 Great Britain passed the 'Act for the Abolition of the Slave Trade', and applied the extensive resources of the Empire to stop the slavery commerce entirely (Duignan and Gann, 1983, p.23). Once the British decided to deny themselves the right to profit from this trade, they had every incentive to deny other countries such benefits as well and so began patrolling the Atlantic in search of ships involved in that commercial traffic. Within a few days after the British outlawed the slave trade, so did the US Congress. The Constitution had originally allowed forbidding the importing of slaves after 1808, but in addition to making it illegal to introduce into the US any '...Negro, mulatto or person of color as a slave' the new law also prohibited US citizens from 'equipping or financing any slave ship, to operate from any port of the US' (Thomas, 1997, p.552). The act, however, did not contain any enforcement mechanisms, and so little was done at the time to actively put an end to the trade. In fact, contraband slaves continued to come into the US after the ban.

At the conclusion of the War of 1812, Great Britain was able to leverage into the Treaty of Ghent a clause committing the US to a more active effort to end the slave trade. Outside of abolitionist circles, however, the issue of slave trading was not a pressing concern to most Americans. Nonetheless, the US government was interested in ensuring reciprocal enforcement of the Treaty of Ghent and took seriously its commitment to make at least some effort to assist the British. And given the pitifully inadequate size of the US Navy, the fact that the US did send a small, naval force to the coast of West Africa is rather remarkable. According to Thomas (1997, p.617), 'All together, between May 1818 and November 1821, 573 Africans were captured by US Naval captains, from eleven ships'. The Africans were then repatriated to the West African coast.

But while the British were glad to see at least some American participation in their crusade, the US contribution was short-lived and difficult to sustain. US courts erected a number of legal impediments against an aggressive effort to stop the slave trade. The courts ruled that slaver ships could only be captured and considered slavers if there were slaves on board. When naval captains searched ships that turned out not to be slavers they could be held liable in US courts.[19] And the British, through their more extensive efforts, aroused resentment among the American naval officers and politicians. The British stopped and searched a large number of vessels in the waters off Africa from present day Angola to Ghana. While many of the ships were slavers, others were American-owned ships engaged in legitimate commerce whose owners protested vehemently against the strong-arm tactics of the British. To many, the British methods

---

[19] In fact, a lawsuit against one captain helped precipitate one of the most noteworthy cases of mass shirking of duties in US Naval history (Howard, 1963, 105).

Liberal Idealism and the Political Use of Military Force   127

resembled some of the very same attacks against the American merchant marine that had precipitated the War of 1812. Thus, not only did the Royal Navy arouse suspicion among many of the Americans involved in the anti-slaver efforts, it also caused the US government to divert some of the Navy's ships in the area to protect American commercial vessels. In fact, the US refused to grant the British the right to search vessels flying the American flag. After a few years of patrols, the US Navy returned from the African coast and from 1821-1839, the US was largely invisible on this issue (Duignan and Gann, 1983; US State Department Foreign Relations Series, various volumes).

It took considerable British diplomacy and the tireless efforts of humanitarian/abolitionist groups within the US before the American government made another effort to get serious about suppressing the slave traffic. Under Article 8 of the Webster-Ashburton Treaty, concluded with Great Britain in 1842, the US agreed to establish a permanent naval presence on the African coast that would, 'enforce, separately and respectively, the laws, rights and obligations, of each of the two countries, for the suppression of the slave trade' (Duignan and Gann, 1983, p.32). Indeed, in John Tyler's inaugural address (Presidential Papers Information Data Base, Vol. 3, 1903), he proclaimed, 'The highest considerations of public honor as well as the strongest promptings of humanity require a resort to the most vigorous efforts to suppress the trade'. The Africa Squadron was officially formed in 1843 and shortly thereafter, the first flotilla was dispatched under the command of Commodore Matthew C. Perry. Its four ships arrived on the African coast in August of 1843 and established a base in the Cape Verde islands. Although the US did station a number of ships off the coasts of Brazil and Cuba, the US largely confined itself to patrolling the waters north of the equator off the west coast of Africa. These hunting grounds were convenient to the US naval bases, but kept the Navy far away from Congo and Luanda further south where the traffic remained heavy. Altogether, the US Navy seized 28 ships from 1842 through 1853, but few American vessels were caught with slaves aboard because of the great reluctance among naval captains to stop such vessels and be tried in American courts for violating the owners' commercial rights (Duignan and Gann, 1984, p.33).

It was not until President Buchanan strengthened the African squadron and authorized a base in Angola closer to where the slavers were operating that the Navy captured many more vessels (Thomas, 1997). Throughout the rest of the 1850s, despite the best efforts of American courts and the malarial climate, the operation was fairly successful. But with the onset of the American Civil War, the African squadron was called home for the war effort and Secretary of State Seward suggested to Great Britain that it search and seize suspected slavers flying the American flag on both the African and Cuban coasts. Thus did the US end its involvement in the suppression of the slave trade.

The deployment of the Africa squadron stands out as perhaps the first extensive military effort on behalf of liberal idealism. There was no American territory to defend. No Americans were in need of protection. The British strongly encouraged US involvement, but never compelled it. The interests pursued largely benefited only those opposed to slavery and the slave trade. And while presidents

128   *The Political Use of Military Force in US Foreign Policy*

were not always wholly dedicated to the effort, when the US finally decided to commit its Navy, the efforts were fairly successful. Interestingly, this humanitarian effort has largely gone unnoticed in many histories of US military policy despite the similarities to many of today's naval operations. Many of these present day missions involving extensive maritime operations designed to punish international wrongdoing by naval blockades are quite reminiscent of the African squadron's mission. But because the US refrained from operations of this type and magnitude again for nearly a hundred years, the story of the slave trade patrols has generally been forgotten.

Elections in Panama

As the 19th century opened into the 20th, the US acquired an empire. The Spanish American War and the building of the Panama Canal turned the Western hemisphere into something more than just a target of the Monroe Doctrine. The Roosevelt Corollary to that longstanding, but only sporadically enforced expression of American beliefs, signaled that now the US had proprietary interests in managing the affairs of Central American and Caribbean nations. Teddy Roosevelt, through his Secretary of State announced:

> If a nation shows that it knows how to act with decency in industrial and political matters, if it keeps order and pays its obligations, then it need fear no interference from the US. Brutal wrongdoing, or an impotence which results in a general loosening of the ties of civilized society, may finally require intervention by some civilized nation, and in the Western Hemisphere the US cannot ignore this duty. (Quoted in Callcott [1942, p.192]).

A complex mixture of economic, strategic and liberal motives drew the US into the internal politics of these nations. The US had been investing in and trading with the Latin American nations for years, but as the British pulled up stakes and left the region, the US assumed a dominant, commercial role. The Spanish American War not only resulted in the acquisition of various territories, it highlighted the military and economic imperatives of building a canal. And certainly the American public and many politicians were outraged by the brutal Spanish policies in Cuba and looked upon the Cuban rebels (at least through the war's conclusion), as fighting for the same freedoms US citizens enjoyed. Once fully engaged in the politics of its new charges, the US formalized its protector status in treaties with these nations, which then led to numerous military interventions.

Panama and its canal were the crown jewels of the American dominion over Central America. The US treaty with Panama dealt mainly with the control and administration of the canal, but two key articles gave the US substantial power to oversee Panamanian affairs and take corrective action whenever its authority was challenged. Article I of the 'Convention for the Construction of a Ship Canal to Connect the Waters of the Atlantic and Pacific Oceans', signed in November of 1903, stipulated that the US would guarantee and maintain Panama's

Liberal Idealism and the Political Use of Military Force   129

independence.[20] Article XXIV stated that, 'No change either in the Government or in the laws and treaties of the Republic of Panama shall, without the consent of the US, affect any right of the US under the present convention...'[21] Furthermore, Article 136 of the Panamanian Constitution authorized the US to intervene anywhere in Panama, 'to re-establish public peace and constitutional order in the event of their being disturbed' (Major, 1993, p.119). Not surprisingly, Panamanian politicians realized that their futures would be shaped by the colossus to the North. Liberals and Conservatives alike (for those were the two, primary political parties) sought the favor of presidents and asked the US to monitor their electoral processes. Each believed the incumbent party would use its control of the Panamanian police to steal elections, and so both continually asked the American military to safeguard voting on election day. The US obligingly responded by using its military in several elections during the construction of the canal to prevent voter intimidation. At first Presidents Roosevelt and Taft viewed these interventions as necessary for the security and stability of a vital, new interest. A failure to retain control would have severe repercussions for US prestige and influence here and throughout the world. Over time, however, the US developed an interest in a smooth-running, and democratic Panamanian state. No episode better epitomized this trend toward interventionism in the name of democracy than the US military's involvement in the 1912 presidential elections.

The origins of US involvement in this particular election resulted from the incumbent Panamanian president's attempts to insure his re-election, despite constitutional injunctions against consecutive terms in office. The Liberal party president, Pablo Arosemena, took a six month, leave of absence from office in the first half of 1912, to make himself eligible for re-election. The man who thought he would be the next presidential nominee of the Liberal party, Belisario Porras, was outraged and complained to the US. But he was not a popular politician among the opposition or the US. The Conservative party viewed Porras with alarm and charged that he would bankrupt Panama with profligate spending. Porras had also charged the US with 'swallowing up' Panama after its revolution in 1903. The US, in turn accused him of being a 'thoroughly reckless soldier of fortune' (Mellander, 1971, pp.71-72). To prevent his election, the Conservatives planned to charge Porras with treason. Both sides, convinced the other would cheat on election day, pleaded with President Taft for intervention. Taft had in fact told the Panamanians when he visited the republic as Secretary of War in 1908 that, 'If fraud is to intervene in the election, so that a dispute arises as to who are the lawful elected authorities, then it becomes necessary for the US, in the discharge of its treaty and constitutional duty, to determine who are the lawfully elected officers...' (quoted in Mellander, 1971, p.149). For his part, Taft feared that the Conservative party would use the police to steal the election and get its candidate elected. When a supply of arms, presumably for use by the national police to intimidate voters, was discovered, President Taft elected to use the US military to guarantee the integrity

---

[20] Reprinted in Munro (1934, 275-283).

[21] Quoted in Munro (1934, 283).

130 *The Political Use of Military Force in US Foreign Policy*

of the elections. US intervention and supervision were crucial in insuring the police would not be used on election day in July of 1912. There was at least one representative from the US in each of the 61 electoral districts, who were, '…given authority not only to see that the election was properly conducted, but also that order was maintained and that there was no intimidation' (Munro, 1934, p.94). This resulted in a victory for the Liberal Party candidate, Belisario Porras, who had secured his party's nomination from the former president, Pablo Arosemena. That the US government acquiesced and its military aided in the election of a man known for his strong antipathies toward Yankees would seem to suggest that at some level it placed democratic principles above pure self interest.

Nation Building in Bosnia

Of all the military operations the US has embarked on in the 1990s, few have been more complex as the ongoing mission in Bosnia. After the General Framework, also known as the Dayton Accords, ended a bloody, three and one-half year war in the Balkans among Bosnian Muslims, Serbians and Croatians, President Clinton dispatched 20,000 US troops along with contingents from eighteen other nations to rebuild the shattered and divided nation. In December of 1995 the first units of the International Force, IFOR, arrived in Bosnia. During the Bosnian war from 1992-1995, both the Bush and Clinton administrations evinced great reluctance to insert US forces into what was believed to be a tangled imbroglio of ethnic, religious and political strife, punctuated by ethnic cleansing, mass murder and rape. But once the Clinton administration committed its armed forces, the US has taken the lead in creating a new, democratic Bosnia. The Dayton Accords produced a Bosnian nation with separate governmental entities. There was a Muslim-Croatian Federation and a Republika Srpska, each with substantial, autonomous powers and a national government with minimal powers. Bosnia was divided into a patchwork of ethnic communities each belonging to one of the two governments, roughly reflecting the division of territory at war's end. The various armies were separated, refugees were given the right to return home, and the international community set about rebuilding Bosnia. The most crucial element of the rebuilding effort was the deployment of an Implementation Force, IFOR, consisting of 60,000 troops from NATO nations as well as eighteen others, including Russia.

The first task of IFOR was to ensure the peace. A cease-fire had been in effect for several months before the troops began to arrive and IFOR was charged with enforcing 'zones of separation' (Dayton Accord, Military Annex, Article 6, Part 2, section A) between the armies. More importantly for our purposes, IFOR was authorized to:

> to help create secure conditions for the conduct by others of other tasks associated with the peace settlement, including free and fair elections; to assist the movement of organizations in the accomplishment of humanitarian missions; to assist the UNHCR and other international organizations in their humanitarian missions; to observe and prevent interference with the movement of civilian populations,

Liberal Idealism and the Political Use of Military Force 131

refugees, and displaced persons, and to respond appropriately to deliberate violence to life and person; and, to monitor the clearing of minefields and obstacles (Dayton Accord, Military Annex, Article 6, Part 3).

In terms of the promotion of liberal idealism, specifically democratization and human rights, I will address the effectiveness of the US and NATO in providing for safe and open elections.

The most direct action IFOR/SFOR (SFOR is the name given to the 'Stabilization' force, the smaller and reconfigured IFOR) has taken to further the cause of liberalism has been to assist in the electoral process. It provided protection for voters and for polling places; it helped identify voter registration centers and polling stations and operate the elections operations center. The main point of contention in the elections for all parties was the control of towns that had been ethnically cleansed. Under the Dayton Accords, all citizens were to be allowed to vote in their former places of residence. But since many of these citizens were refugees who had been ethnically cleansed, the physical act of voting in towns where their homes and businesses had been destroyed and where family members had been killed proved difficult. For example, in the town of Srebrenica, which had been the scene of the worst massacre of the entire war, those Muslims who escaped the carnage were almost all forced to vote by absentee ballot. SFOR could not guarantee their safety.

Elections for national office took place according to plan in September of 1996 and although there was little election day violence, observers found considerable evidence of voter fraud and other procedural irregularities. Still, since the election was mostly peaceful, IFOR was reduced to roughly 22,000 troops by the end of 1996 from a peak of nearly 60,000. Signs of progress were in evidence in the second round of national elections in September of 1998. There were fewer procedural problems and irregularities, less political violence (OSCE, Democratization Department Semi-Annual Report)[22], and evidence that multi-ethnic parties were increasing in strength, especially among Croatians. Local and international non-governmental organization participation in the election monitoring process was extensive and probably helped discourage attempts at violence and intimidation. This also led to a fairly high turnout of roughly 70 percent, which indicated a fair amount of voter confidence in personal safety (OSCE, Democratization Department Semi-Annual Report). Finally, municipal elections, which were to have been held in November of 1999, had to be postponed because of the NATO bombing of Serbia over the war in Kosovo. Political violence continued to decrease when the elections were finally held in April, 2000. General elections were then held in the fall of 2000. In Republika Srpska, Serbian nationalists of the SDS party still obtained a large majority in their parliament,

---

[22] http://www.oscebih.org/oscebih_eng.asp as found on August 15, 2003.

132   *The Political Use of Military Force in US Foreign Policy*

while in the Muslim-Croatian Federation there were signs of change as many reformers came to power.[23]

IFOR/SFOR efforts to guarantee a secure environment for the electoral process, although not perfect, have promoted proliberalization foreign policy goals. Election day violence was kept to a minimum. There were fewer violent attacks against parties and politicians during the campaigns with each succeeding election. And with some exceptions, the ballot box results were confirmed as candidates took their offices. The inability of the international community to ensure the return of refugees to vote and indications of voter fraud designed to consolidate control over ethnically cleansed areas, however, contributed to a perception, especially among Muslims, that the electoral process was flawed. To a remarkable degree, IFOR and SFOR operations have succeeded in restoring peace and stability to Bosnia, the most fundamental prerequisites to democracy. Judged solely in those terms the mission has achieved some of its primary objectives. According to Richard Holbrooke (1998, p.219), 'Without the backing of IFOR, the civilian parts of the agreement [the Dayton Accords]–the true test of peace–could not be carried out'.

At the outset, however, US military leaders sought to keep IFOR/SFOR objectives as limited as possible–what became known as the minimalist position. Keeping the peace, overseeing the demobilization of armies and other military tasks were most fundamental to IFOR/SFOR success. And since it was only given one year to complete its mission, minimalist objectives were probably all that were feasible initially. Later, policymakers in the State Department sought to expand IFOR/SFOR goals to include a greater role in the electoral process, the return of refugees and the capture of indicted war criminals. While the accomplishment of such goals is undoubtedly necessary for Bosnia's long-term viability, there was substantial disagreement over whether IFOR/SFOR should be responsible for realizing these 'maximalist' objectives. In particular, there were considerable divisions between the Pentagon under Secretary of Defense William Cohen and the Secretary of State, Madeleine Albright. This resulted in a compromise policy where SFOR became somewhat more involved in electoral politics and somewhat more aggressive in clamping down on hard-line Serbs, as well as arresting the occasional war criminal. SFOR stayed out of the much messier business of assisting in the return of refugees and making a concerted effort to arrest high-profile war criminals like Radovan Karadzic and Ratko Mladic. Predictably, few were happy with these sorts of half-way measures. The problem for the military is that as long as their leadership and the president resist making a *deep* dedication to resolving these thorny problems, they will probably have to make a *lengthy* commitment to Bosnia's future.

---

[23] See analysis of the elections at the SFOR website, http://www.nato.int/sfor/indexinf/126/p03a/chapter3.htm . As found on July 16, 2002.

Assessing the Evidence

Having described three historical examples where we have reason to believe presidents were motivated by liberal concerns, I now make a more rigorous assessment of the uniqueness and strength of the liberal rationale. First, identifying geopolitical interests in the slave trade patrols is problematic at best. For one thing, they took place not just off the coast of Africa, but also in South American waters and the Caribbean. Presidents had long asserted that the US had special interests in Latin America, but the same could not be said for Africa. Furthermore, the slave trade in no way materially affected US security, even in Latin America. One also looks in vain for some sort of economic rationale behind the decision to patrol for slavers. The trade advantages that Brazil, Cuba and other nations, where slave holding was legal, might have gained from further human imports do not appear to have been significant or sufficiently threatening to the US. Instead, one must look to another goal of the slave patrols, the protection of American commercial vessels from British searches and seizures, to identify a clear self-interest.

US concern, indeed, outrage at this practice had long been a matter of contention in US-British relations. From the time of the War of 1812 when British vessels had boarded American ships and impressed suspected, British naval deserters, Americans had strongly resented the lack of respect the British had shown for US sovereignty. The practice persisted for a number of years after the War of 1812, but had been stopped by the 1840s when the size and scope of the US anti-slaver patrols peaked. Still, Americans had not forgotten or forgiven Great Britain these abuses and continued to distrust British motives in stopping the slave trade. Many were more outraged that the Royal Navy would board American vessels and occasionally condemn them than they were that the slavers continued to ply their trade, often under cover of the American flag. For their part, because of intense pressure from abolitionist groups, the British government was committed to stopping the slave trade. And many of the ships involved in the trade on their route toward the West African coast flew the American flag precisely because the American government tried to forbid the British from stopping such vessels. If the Americans would not give them full permission to stop these ships, the British insisted the US take part in the slave trade patrols so that these vessels might be searched. Therefore, to ward off more aggressive British moves to gain power over US trading vessels, the US finally complied with British demands in the Webster-Ashburton Treaty and dispatched a naval squadron to begin the patrols. In fact, the same President Tyler who had expressed outrage over the slave trade and pledged that the US Navy would help end it, also stated, 'However desirous the US may be for the suppression of the slave trade, they can not consent to interpolations into the maritime code [i.e., search and seizure of US vessels] at the mere will and pleasure of other governments' (First Annual Address, Presidential Papers Information Data Base, Volume 3, p. 1931).

Thus, while there was a strong moral component to this use of force, we cannot conclude that liberal idealist aims provide a sufficient cause for the decision

134 *The Political Use of Military Force in US Foreign Policy*

to use force. Rather, concern among northern and southern politicians alike was over British actions on the high seas. Few were willing to place abolitionism over American rights at sea. Indeed, the Secretary of the Navy said in regard to the slave patrols, 'The rights of our citizens engaged in lawful commerce are under the protection of our flag. *And it is the chief purpose, as well as the chief duty of our naval power*, to see that those rights are not improperly abridged' (Duignan and Gann, 1984, p.32 [emphasis in original]). Even the noted abolitionist John Quincy Adams, defender of the slave mutineers of the *Amistad*, refused to be coerced into anti-slave patrols because of British pressure. Many members of Congress and presidents during these years were slaveholders as well and none too interested in doing anything that would been viewed as pro-abolitionist.

Nonetheless, although prompted by concerns over the behavior of the Royal Navy, the anti-slaver mission cannot be understood apart from the humanitarian values it sought to achieve. Such liberal underpinnings were not sufficiently powerful to precipitate these operations, but absent such concerns there would not have far less reason to commit the US Navy to such a long-term operation. And many commanders did take such actions at considerable financial and personal risk because of their commitment to the operation, even when their superiors did not support them as much they would like. And while presidents did stress the primacy of protecting US commerce, they ultimately authorized the naval patrols for many years to achieve if only secondarily, a humanitarian impulse.

The Panama Canal gave the US a truly vital and tangible interest in an area of the world that had preoccupied presidents dating back to the Monroe Doctrine. The enormity of the task, the tremendous commercial and military benefits the canal promised, as well as the considerable loss of prestige that a failure would entail gave Presidents Roosevelt and Taft every reason to be keenly interested in the stability and security of Panama, as well as the rest of Central America and the Caribbean. As the center of gravity of American interests in the western hemisphere, it is almost impossible to analyze US foreign policy toward Panama without reference to the canal. Had there been no canal, would the US have been sufficiently interested in democratic elections in Panama to intervene militarily? The question may be moot since without US interest in a canal through the Panamanian isthmus, an independent Panama probably would never have been born. So let us assume that the canal was a necessary and sufficient condition for US involvement in Panama in general. Can we then say that President Taft believed that the security and stability of Panama was dependent upon US military intervention in support of democratic elections?

US presidents had not exhibited much reluctance in the past to back Latin American dictators and otherwise countenance non-democratic methods of government selection. Elections were fairly messy and cumbersome processes in underdeveloped nations with little history of civil liberties and legitimate government. Certainly President Taft had every reason to be skeptical of democracy's prospects in Panama and desirous of a stable regime of whatever stripe. The nation had been created as a result of revolution and Taft feared the method might prove addictive. The two political parties were little more than personal cliques arguing over the system's spoils and tended to view elections

Liberal Idealism and the Political Use of Military Force   135

more as a method of ratification of the outcomes of power struggles than as an impartial tool for voter choice (Healy, 1988). Elections marred by vote fraud and voter intimidation might have precipitated the type of unrest with which the US was concerned. President Taft had the capability, the opportunity and most importantly given the canal, the incentive to install compliant leadership by force or diplomacy–democracy and free elections were not essential to this underlying task. In fact, Taft was so confident of US dominance over Panamanian affairs, and hence able to engineer whatever outcome it desired, he claimed, 'We have such control in Panama, that no government elected by them will feel a desire to antagonize the American government' (quoted in Major, 1993, p.126).

Despite the considerable incentives to impose a pliant government, the US took the time and energy to ensure a free and fair electoral process, when other less liberal means would have accomplished the same ends. As well, US officials on the spot favored a strong military presence on election day. In the end, the American minister to Panama, Percivil Dodge concluded that, '…the day of the election, passed off with perfect order and quiet…' and that the elections were the '…fairest which Panama has ever had' (State Department Foreign Relations Series, 1912, pp.1163-1164). Our conclusions regarding the influence of liberal idealism in the Panama operation must be more balanced. The desire to create a liberal democracy in Panama certainly did not lead to the US military presence that existed prior to the 1912 elections. The troops that were called out on election day had not initially been placed there to build democracy. However, their mission in Panama on that day was to assist the democratic process. Furthermore, this change in military responsibilities was determined not by any pervasive fear that the stability of Panama, and thereby the canal, was in jeopardy. Explanations based on military and/or commercial factors alone cannot tell us why the US forces were called upon that day to supervise the elections. Taft could have elected to not act and it is doubtful there would have been any severe repercussions for US foreign policy. He could have used alternative methods to ensure the selection of a friendly government, but he used his discretion to expend time, energy and resources to supervise elections instead. A proliberalization rationale cannot adequately explain why US forces were in Panama to begin with, but it can tell us why they acted as they did once present. Liberal values were a critical component of the decision to use force in Panama in 1912.

To what extent was the IFOR/SFOR intervention undertaken to promote liberal idealism? Unlike Panama, the US had no vital, national interests in Bosnia. Hence, the three years of dithering over how to end the conflict. To the extent that the war in Bosnia created instability in the Balkans and disunity in NATO, however, presidents Bush Sr. and Clinton were interested in resolving the ethno-political divisions. As the futility of US and European efforts to stop the war became more and more apparent, President Clinton acquired an interest in stopping the bloodshed in order to stanch the hemorrhaging of NATO's credibility. Outrage at Bosnian Serb violations of diplomatic agreements and their defiance of the West exacerbated this problem. The decision to bomb the Serbs into submission, which then led to the IFOR intervention, resulted from a constellation of forces that came together at one critical point in time. This was the turning point in American foreign policy in the Balkan wars. Once the US committed its military forces to bringing an end to the Bosnian war, it became committed to a peace settlement, which in turn would require a strong military presence to enforce. Immediate and long-term humanitarian concerns played a critical role in the air strike decision, but without the evidence of Serb weakness that demonstrated the air campaign would tip the scales in the conflict to the government of Bosnia, it is unlikely the West would have chosen that particular instant to become fully committed. Indeed, the massacres in Srebrenica, which had taken place just a few weeks before and that were the worst in Europe since World War II, did not lead to military intervention. Like Panama, however, once the US dispatched its forces, a crucial element of their mission was the advancement of liberal idealism.

In past interventions, the supervision of elections and other proliberalization measures were often viewed as, at best, helpful in enhancing security and annoying at worst. Today, foreign policy makers recognize that these measures are an indispensable and interconnected part of such military interventions. Those whom the US helps through such interventions are seen as entitled to a democratic form of government. It is difficult to imagine that the US and the international community could have sent troops into Bosnia only to countenance the creation of an autocratic form of government. Peace in the Balkans requires a political solution and for the nations implementing this strategy, it necessarily means a liberal, democratic solution. The proliberalization element of IFOR/SFOR's mission is as integral as its weapons–peace and democracy are merging into a single strategy. We must conclude that any explanation of military intervention in Bosnia that does not incorporate liberal idealism would be seriously incomplete. Liberal idealism played a unique and substantial role in this foreign policy decision, for as Richard Holbrooke, the US diplomat who engineered the Dayton Peace Accords argued, 'Strategic considerations were vital to our involvement, but the motives that finally pushed the US into action were also moral and humanitarian' (1998, p.359).

To summarize what we know about all three cases, if we take a conservative approach to ascertaining the importance of liberal idealism in presidents' decisions to use force, and set the evidentiary standard high, some factor other than liberal idealism likely precipitated initial US involvement. Once US forces were dispatched, however, the advancement of liberal idealism was a major and sometimes decisive impetus toward the continued use of military force, and in specific operations within the larger context of the military intervention. In all three cases presidents explicitly emphasized that the US was seeking to influence events to bring about a more humane (in the case of the anti-slave trade patrols) or more democratic (in Panama and Bosnia) outcome. This rationale was more muted in the case of the anti-slave trading patrols, but it was at the heart of the interventions in Panama and Bosnia. Liberal considerations informed military interventions, even if they did not always inspire them. We certainly cannot understand these three cases without reference to the liberal values that guided them. But what of the rest of the history of US foreign policy? How meaningful

Liberal Idealism and the Political Use of Military Force   137

were liberal idealist values in the conduct of American foreign policy? That is the subject we turn to next.

Liberal Idealism and the Use of Force: The Historical Record

Liberal Idealism and Restraint in the Use of Force, 1798-1898

We shall begin our review of the historical record of the use of force on behalf of liberal idealism in the one hundred year period between 1798 and 1898 when there were a number of notable opportunities to spread liberal values, but where presidents generally shied away from such actions. Yet, there is much to be learned from their unwillingness to use force in this regard for we cannot understand why presidents deploy the military by only examining those instances where such action took place. Indeed, many of the arguments offered in this era regarding why the US should *not* use force to advance democracy and human rights still resonate and are heard today. Nowhere was the opportunity to spread American liberal idealism through force of arms greater than in Latin America in the early 19th century. No sooner had the US gained its independence than the colonies to the South began agitating for freedom from Spain and Portugal. But while it might seem that US security, a common anti-colonial heritage and shared democratic ideals might have led to the forging of common bonds between the US and the rebel movements, more immediate interests militated against active US support for the revolutionaries. Certainly, most American leaders were hopeful that other nations and emerging states might emulate the US example, but even the most idealistic among them were not sanguine about the prospects for democracy outside of Europe. Even so committed a democrat as Thomas Jefferson favored a policy that extended US fellow feeling, but omitted any diplomatic or material assistance (Kaplan, 1987). Thus, the history of US involvement in Latin America begins not with a bang, but with a rebuff.

The problem for US foreign policymakers was that while they might have liked to remove the Spanish and the Portuguese from the hemisphere and advance democracy and trade, more immediate and material interests made any provision of assistance, let alone a military alliance, impractical. First, during the Napoleonic Wars the US was preoccupied with pursuing its neutralist, commercial policies and avoiding war with either of the two principal belligerents. Impressment of American sailors, Napoleon's Continental system and the British economic blockade, which severely endangered the US's nascent economy, were matters of the utmost urgency, while the cause of democracy in Latin America seemed at most a romantic pipe dream. Second, the US was at this time (1808-1819) attempting to wrest the Floridas away from Spain and was loath to take any action that might jeopardize the acquisition of territory much closer to home. Third, many were afraid that even if the revolutionaries did gain control, their power base (largely the wealthy, Creole elite), would be so weak as to require assistance from France or Great Britain. Certainly, a weak Spain was a better neighbor than either the French or the British. Foreign policymakers already viewed with concern many

138   *The Political Use of Military Force in US Foreign Policy*

of the commercial agreements concluded between the revolutionaries and the British (Langley, 1989). Then, as now, more immediate and material ends outweighed any inclination US foreign policy makers and presidents might have had to spread their system southward.

Lastly, despite the ostensibly shared democratic ideals between the US and the revolutionaries, most policymakers were at a minimum pessimistic about the chances of democracy and frequently, quite contemptuous of the Latin American leaders. Many, like John Quincy Adams, feared the influence of the Catholic Church and the military, and believed that whatever new governments were created would be unrepresentative, undemocratic and arbitrary in their exercise of power. Interestingly then, the US passed up what seemed, in many ways, to be an excellent opportunity to advance its liberal cause and aid friendly states. And even though it was the first nation to recognize one of these new governments (Columbia in 1822 [Langley, 1989, p.491]), presidents and their advisers saw more risks than potential gains in becoming a major player in Latin American politics. John Quincy Adams perhaps best summed up the feeling of the day when he declared:

> Wherever the standard of freedom and independence has been or shall be unfurled, there will America's heart, her benedictions and her prayers be. But she goes not abroad in search of monsters to destroy. She is the well-wisher to the freedom and independence of all. She is the champion and vindicator of her own. She will recommend the general cause by the countenance of her voice, and by the benignant sympathy of her example. Otherwise, she might become the dictatress of the world. She would no longer be the ruler of her own spirit (quoted in Graebner, 1964, pp. 88-89).

Adams' words epitomized for many the only path by which the US might see the community of democracies grow, while at the same time safeguarding the very values it wished to see emulated. They are echoed today in the writings of those who question the wisdom of embarking on military interventions to advance the cause of liberalism and destroy the dictatorial monsters of the world (Gholz, Press and Sapolsky, 1997; Haass, 1994; Mandelbaum, 1996; Smith 2000). Gholz, Press and Sapolsky (1997, p.41) argue that even though promoting democracy is a good thing, using force to do it is not. In words that echo Adams, they write, '...there is no surer way to turn millions of America's admirers into America's opponents than to force an unfamiliar social system on them'.

There were also a smattering of instances elsewhere in the world where the US might have acted to promote liberal idealism through the use of force. But even if presidents had wished to support democratic uprisings in Greece in the 1820s and Europe in the 1840s with more than sympathetic words, the US lacked even the most rudimentary of power projections capabilities. While the Navy possessed many fine ships, they were better suited to exploration and the occasional exercise of gunboat diplomacy to scare the locals rather than make them Jeffersonian democrats. More importantly, the US Army was weak and incapable of embarking on nation building exercises overseas. Domestic issues demanded the

Liberal Idealism and the Political Use of Military Force 139

nation's attentions throughout the period. The expansion westward and the settling of continental borders occupied a great deal of presidential attention during the entire century. As well, in the first half of the 19th century, the slavery question consumed the nation, much as the Civil War and reconstruction dominated policymaking in the second half. Still, there were some who believed that the US could achieve abroad, what it had created at home. In words that also seem applicable today, Henry Clay once said, 'I would not force upon other nations our principles and our liberty, if they do not want them. But, if an abused and oppressed people will their freedom; if they seek to establish it; if, in truth, they have established it; we have a right, as a sovereign power, to notice the fact, and to act as our circumstances and our interest require' (quoted in Talbot 1999 p.302). By the close of the 19th century, the US' industrial development, the solidity of the union, its security within the Western Hemisphere, and public confidence gave presidents the capability to assume a greater role for the US on the world's stage. Certainly there were plenty of opportunities in the world for presidents to pursue the ambitions Clay articulated. The only missing ingredient was a leader who was willing to use American power on behalf of its liberal ideals. It fell to William McKinley and his vice president and later president, Theodore Roosevelt to inaugurate an era of American international activism.

Liberal Idealism and the Use of Force, 1898-1941

Two pivotal events were responsible for bringing the US out of fortress America and into an extensive involvement in international relations and the domestic politics of other nations. First, the Spanish-American War led to the acquisition of territories in the Pacific and Caribbean. Second, the decision to build an American canal across Panama led to a sizeable US military presence in that country and a general interest in the politics of Central America and the Caribbean. Once the US obtained these physical assets, it developed a permanent and pressing interest in their protection from foreign meddling and domestic unrest. This then led to US involvement in the selection of leaders in the southern countries. Under McKinley, Roosevelt and Taft it was often fear–fear of leaders that would provoke civil war, foreign intervention and general unrest–rather than hope for a more democratic Latin America that led to interventionism. But if the ultimate goal of US interventions in Cuba, the Philippines, Panama, Haiti, Mexico, the Dominican Republic and Nicaragua in this era was a stability that suited US political and commercial interests, the promotion of liberal idealism was often the favored method.

At this point in US history as presidents begin to use the military to advance liberal idealism, it is appropriate to being examining the data we have on such uses of force. The types of military actions the US has taken to promote liberal idealism have been numerous and diverse. In this section I provide a broader analysis of the extent to which liberal idealism is predictive of presidential decision making. Once again, I analyze the data discussed in Chapter Two–the Congressional Research Service's, 'Background Information on the Use of US

140   *The Political Use of Military Force in US Foreign Policy*

Armed Forces in Foreign Countries' (1993). I examined each of the brief event descriptions and based on what was explicitly stated in the report as the goal or goals of each of the interventions, created several binary variables that measure whether or not a particular goal was pursued in each case. I did make one exception to my coding rule in this chapter. In some instances I supplemented these characterizations of US foreign policy goals with data from Peceny (1999) who analyzes the importance of liberal idealism in major, US military interventions. Peceny (1999, p.11) defines a major, military intervention as involving the direct or indirect use of force in order to change or preserve the political structure in another country. He relies on a variety of data sets to identify major interventions in the 20th century (Meernik, 1996; Pearson, Baumann and Pickering, 1994; Tillema, 1989, 1994). Peceny (1999, p.15) defines proliberalization policies as, '...the combination of active support for 'free and fair' elections with the promotion of at least one of the following: centrist political parties, moderate interest groups, reductions in human rights abuses, and/or formal subordination of the military to civilian authority'. Support for free and fair elections is further defined as at least one of the following:

> (1) active mediation with contending parties in the target state in setting the ground rules of an electoral contest, including assisting in the drafting of electoral laws and/or the creation or reformation of institutions like electoral boards, (2) the provision of financial and technical assistance for the voting process, including the payment of election workers, the management of voter registration lists, the creation of efficient procedures for the nonfraudulent counting of ballots, and/or (3) official participation in election observer missions to certify whether contests have been conducted in a free and fair manner (Peceny, 1999, p.17).

Whenever Peceny or the CRS report identifies a military intervention as designed to promote democracy, or supervise elections, I measure it as an intervention designed to promote liberal idealism. Peceny also includes other military operations that were not part of the CRS study, but which I have also included. I also code those few instances in the CRS Report where the mission is defined as patrolling for ships carrying on the slave trade as an intervention designed to promote liberal idealism.

Liberal Idealism and the Political Use of Military Force 141

Table 4.1 Uses of Force to Advance Liberal Idealism Across Historical Periods

Period	Number of Uses	Average Per Year	Number of all Uses	Percent of all Uses for the Period
1798-1866	2	.02	60	3%
1866-1899	0	na	33	na
1899-1919	20	1.0	48	42%
1919-1941	6	.26	31	19%
Total all years	28	.18	172	16%

Table 4.2 Uses of Force to Advance Liberal Idealism Across Regions

Region	Number of Uses	Percent of All Uses in Region	Total All Uses in Region
Continental US	0	na	12
Central America/ Caribbean	18	29%	62
South America	0	na	18
North Africa/ Middle East	0	na	12
Sub-Saharan Africa	2	50%	4
Europe/North Atlantic	1	12.5%	8
Asia	7	12.5%	56
Total all regions	28	16%	172

142 *The Political Use of Military Force in US Foreign Policy*

Table 4.3 Uses of Force to Advance Liberal Idealism Across Region and Time

Region	1798-1865	1866-1898	1899-1918	1919-1941
Continental US	0	0	0	0
	na	na	na	na
Central America/	0	0	15	3
Caribbean	na	na	75%	50%
South America	0	0	0	0
	na	na	na	na
North Africa/	0	0	0	0
Middle East	na	na	na	na
Sub-Saharan	2	0	0	0
Africa	na	na	na	na
Europe/	0	0	1	0
North Atlantic	na	na	5%	na
Asia	0	0	4	3
	na	na	20%	50%
Total	2	0	20	6
	100%	na	100%	100%

Total percentages are based on number of uses of force to advance liberal idealism in a region for each period of time.

Out of the 172 interventions in the 1798-1941 period given in the CRS Report and the Peceny data set, I find that on 28 occasions presidents used military force to promote liberal idealism, or 16 percent of the time across the entire period. Other than the anti-slave trade patrols, there is only one instance of such interventions before 1900, and that was in 1899. All the rest occurred in the period from 1900-1933. Not surprisingly almost all of these operations took place in Latin America. As we see in Table 4.3, 18 occurred in the Caribbean and Central America. Seven operations took place in the Philippines (all of the proliberalization uses of force in Asia) and one occurred in Russia after the Bolsheviks seized power. However, of all the uses of force that occurred in the period 1898-1918, 20 or 41.6 percent involved the promotion of democracy.

Liberal Idealism and the Political Use of Military Force   143

As we saw earlier, it was Teddy Roosevelt's corollary to the Monroe Doctrine that presaged more extensive US involvement in the affairs of its southern neighbors, especially to ensure order. But, in his approximately seven years in the White House, however, TR used force only three times to advance what we might term liberal idealism–in Panama in 1903 and 1904 and Cuba in 1906. William Howard Taft on the surface did not appear to be as energetic and assertive as Roosevelt, but he had extensive experience in governing colonized territories from his years as the chief US administrator in the Philippines. Taft used force six times in his four years in office to promote democratization. But it is Woodrow Wilson who is generally remembered as the most idealist of all and who embarked on crusades to uplift those nations who were not so politically fortunate as the US.

Of course, Woodrow Wilson inherited these foreign policy interests from his predecessors–he did not create interests in nations the US had never meddled in before, except Russia. But, unlike Roosevelt and Taft who were more likely to look upon democratic elections abroad as an instrument of US foreign policy, Wilson's crusading liberal idealism infused this policy with an emotional and idealist spirit. Wilson truly believed that the US was called upon to do good in the world. When he dispatched US forces into Central America to insure more orderly government, he strongly argued that he was acting in their best interest. In his own words, he would, '...teach the South American republics to elect good men' (quoted in McDougall, 1997, p. 131). Wilson often equated orderly regimes with pro-American governments, regardless of their democratic credentials, but he certainly preferred stable and democratic governments to all others. He authorized several uses of force against Mexico from 1914 through 1917 to realize his vision of a more democratic and stable Mexico. He sent US forces into Haiti, the Dominican Republic and Cuba for what became long-term occupations that oversaw the creation of various political regimes. Wilson directed the US military in Panama to supervise elections from 1918-1920. By today's standards the US operations appear overly domineering and occasionally violent. But by the standards of his day, Wilson sought to realize an American liberal ideal that seemed quite progressive and stood in marked contrast to the way in which Europeans treated their colonized peoples. In fact, according to Huntington (1999, p.243), 'In the second and third decades of this century, American intervention in Nicaragua, Haiti, and the Dominican Republic produced the freest elections and the most open political competition in the history of those countries'. Still, while such military interventions did contribute toward the holding of free and relatively fair elections, they could not sustain the advancement of democracy in many Latin American and Caribbean nations as dictators like Somoza in Nicaragua, Duvalier in Haiti and Trujillo in the Dominican Republic ultimately consolidated power.

But while I confine the data analysis to the limited uses of force Wilson authorized, we cannot ignore how Wilson's liberal idealism was put to the most extreme test in World War I. For it is the perceived failure of Wilson's efforts to make the world safe for democracies, and to promote self determination, the League of Nations and a more just and legal order in the world that helped bring about a US retreat from the internationalism of 1898-1918. Wilson believed that only through the creation of democratic polities in the remnants of the old empires

144   *The Political Use of Military Force in US Foreign Policy*

could Europe be stable and peaceful. Self-determination for the various nationalities of Central and Eastern Europe would be the first step. He argued that if these people were given their independence and the opportunity for democratic government, this would prevent war from engulfing the continent again. Following on the logic of the Founding Fathers, he strongly believed that the unchecked powers of the *ancien regimes* to make war, and their attempts to hold and gain dominion over other peoples made war likely. Destroy the governments of these empires and you dismantle the machinery of war. Destroy the empires and you destroy the reasons for war. As Wilson said in his 'Fourteen Points' speech:

> What we demand in this war, therefore, is nothing peculiar to ourselves. It is that the world be made fit and safe to live in; and particularly that it be made safe for every peace-loving nation which, like our own, wishes to live its own life, determine its own institutions, be assured of justice and fair dealing by the other peoples of the world as against force and selfish aggression. All the peoples of the world are in effect partners in this interest, and for our own part we see very clearly that unless justice be done to others it will not be done to us.

Wilson equated US security with democratic, self-determination for (most of) the peoples of the world. Only when nations were allowed the benefits of liberalism and were assured that other nations would treat them fairly (presumably because these other nations are also democratic), would the world, and thus the US, be at peace. While Woodrow Wilson has often been derided for his supposedly utopian plans for a new world order, there were (and are) strong practical reasons for his rejection of Old World politics. He was essentially correct in understanding that the root causes of World War I lay in the problems of empire. The European empires that denied the forces of self-determination made war more likely as they clung to their anachronistic forms of government. The longer these empires persisted, the more precarious European security was and the more likely the US would be sucked into its conflicts. Therefore, Wilson could argue that as he advanced his liberal plan for the world, so too did he advance US security and peace.

With the failure of the Versailles Peace Treaty to win Senate ratification, Wilsonianism became equated with a naive idealism. Few in the US were willing to trust American security to the promises of ideological crusades and collective security. And so for the next 20 years the US backed away from the assertive internationalism of this earlier period. The US used force to advance liberal idealism only six times in the period 1918-1941. Coolidge used force in the Philippines and Dominican Republic, while the Hoover administration attempted to promote democracy in the Philippines and twice in Nicaragua. Warren Harding used force only once on behalf of proliberalization aims. It should be noted, however, that some of these interventions in Central America and the Caribbean had been going on for many years, especially in Nicaragua. Ultimately, presidents and the public grew tired of these long-term commitments, and interventions in Latin America and the Caribbean became fewer until with the announcement of

Liberal Idealism and the Political Use of Military Force   145

Franklin Roosevelt's 'Good Neighbor' policy, the US rejected overt military intervention altogether. Then, as the Great Depression took hold, the fire of internationalism and crusading liberal idealism all but burned out. It took World War II to energize the nation and re-ignite the liberal idealist flame.

Liberal Idealism and the Use of Force, 1948-1998

The Allied victory in the war and the subsequent decision to force democratization upon Germany, Japan, Italy and Austria demonstrated that US leaders now saw a clear link between a nation's type of government and the foreign policies it pursued. Dictatorial regimes that treated some of their people as enemies that should be exterminated and the rest as little better than cogs in a machine could not be trusted to treat their international neighbors any better. The best hope for preventing the creation of genocidal and war-making machines was the creation of governments that represented the will of the people. That this experiment in forced democratization was such a success demonstrated (to many foreign policy makers) that when US foreign policy, and in particular its military, were put in the service of liberal idealism, all those involved gained. World War II and Harry Truman's vigorous leadership put to rest the notion that the US could afford to ignore the types of regimes other nations created and thus led to an abiding concern for preventing similar totalitarian systems from threatening the peace of the world.

The Cold War was in many ways a competition over ideological hegemony. To be sure, the Cold War was waged on two levels. On the one hand, the US and the Soviet Union possessed the world's most formidable militaries equipped with nuclear weapons, and fought each other via proxies throughout the globe. Questions of power, arms races, military security and political dominance permeated the conflict. But on another, more abstract level the superpowers fought for the loyalty of nations and publics with ideological rhetoric. For the US, liberal idealism was the paramount value foreign policy makers sought to protect and was often interwoven and conflated with its more material interests. Security and liberal idealism informed the major US, military interventions (short of war) of this era–in Lebanon in 1958, the Dominican Republic in 1965 and Grenada in 1983. The two goals were critical in the allocation of foreign aid (especially Title IX of the Foreign Assistance Act of 1961), the US-USSR negotiations that led to the Helsinki Accords, the Reagan Doctrine of assistance to those fighting illegitimate governments and so on.

This ideological war was first waged in Europe in the late 1940s and 1950s. The US sought to prop up the democratic governments of the West and undermine the communist governments to the East through ideological subversion, among other methods. The US was heavily involved, for example, in the Italian elections of 1947. But while friendly naval visits might be used to demonstrate US goodwill, often US foreign policy making operated in secret in both Western and Eastern Europe as the CIA attempted to influence the political climate. After the political and military battle lines hardened in Europe and conflict there became increasingly unlikely, the struggle shifted to the undecided regions of the world,

146   *The Political Use of Military Force in US Foreign Policy*

principally its most under-developed portions. These newly independent nations in Asia, Africa and elsewhere sought models and aid to lift them out of their economic poverty and provide the state-building tools to organize their inchoate societies. The US and the U.S.S.R. each trumpeted a political and economic system it argued offered the best life for these undeveloped and undecided nations of the world. US policymakers realized early on that the failure to encourage at least minimal socio-economic and political reform in highly inequitable societies risked provoking communist-inspired insurgencies. US foreign policy often sought to either reform these dictators or find some third way between right-wing and left-wing autocracies. The US preference was generally for democratic, stable and pro-American regimes, even if it often sacrificed the first for the other two on many occasions.

Throughout the 1960s and 1970s the superpowers sought partners in these underdeveloped societies. The US launched its Alliance for Progress in Latin America to attack simultaneously the problems of poverty, income disparity and lack of freedom. The Soviet Union provided aid to the emerging nations of Africa and elsewhere that sought gains through statist efficiencies. More often than not both sides offered aid in a rather cynical fashion to buy friends. More often than not the countries that sought such assistance were more interested in money than ideology. Over time, however, the President, Congress, and pressure groups became much more assertive about the need to tie US friendship to nations' internal policies. US involvement in Vietnam soured many on the implications of a foreign policy centered on simple anti-communism. Recalling the beliefs of the Founding Fathers, many argued that the US risked corrupting its own government and society by aligning itself with repressive regimes. Presidents Carter and Reagan distanced the US from a few of the more odious regimes in Asia, Africa and Latin America as a result of pressure from the public and reformers in Congress. By law, countries that favored human rights and democratization were to be preferred over those that did not. President Jimmy Carter made the promotion of human rights a centerpiece of his foreign policy and used the foreign aid program to encourage liberal idealism, albeit not always in a consistent manner. Even a committed Cold Warrior like President Reagan was forced to take these concerns into account and limit US involvement in Central America. As well, the Reagan Doctrine was premised on the right to assist those fighting illegitimate regimes and led to several uses of force short of war to assist anti-communists in Central America, Africa and Asia.

There were also some instances where liberal idealist policies were rejected. Presidents often aligned the US with some of the worst abusers of human rights in the name of anti-communism (and have been roundly criticized for sullying America's democratic credentials). Some have even overthrown elected governments and had them replaced with dictatorships (e.g., Iran, 1953; Guatemala, 1954). The US record is not unblemished. On balance, the promotion of liberal idealism has been an ongoing concern of foreign policy makers who realized that US security ultimately depended on friendly, stable regimes. This stability was, with varying degrees of intensity, often linked to open, political systems. This concern led to massive amounts of foreign assistance and the occasional use of force to promote liberalization. The Cold War environment of Mutual Assured Destruction and the competition for global hegemony, however, was not the ideal environment in which to make the world more democratic. Thus, when the communist political and military threat suddenly collapsed in the late 1980s it quickly became apparent that the US would be freed from these Cold War strictures. If ever there were an opportunity for liberal idealism to take center stage in US foreign policy, it was in the 1990s with the end of the Cold War and the emergence of a new generation of more idealistic foreign policy makers.

Initially, many scholars and pundits criticized the Clinton administration for failing to offer a convincing vision of US foreign policy in the post Cold War era. In response to those criticisms, President Clinton announced his policy of 'engagement and enlargement', as in engaging the world to enlarge the community of free market, liberal democracies. In a speech to the United Nations in September of 1993, Clinton pledged to foster and consolidate the new democracies in Eastern Europe, Latin America, Asia and Africa and to promote market economies where possible. Harkening back to the Reagan Doctrine, he also spoke of the US and international community's responsibility to check aggressor nations and support the liberalization of states hostile to democracy. Finally, he promised to help democracies develop in those parts of the world that had been scenes of some of the greatest humanitarian problems. Clinton argued:

> The US believes that an expanded community of market democracies not only serves our own security interests, it also advances the goals enshrined in this body's charter and its Universal Declaration of Human Rights. For broadly-based prosperity is clearly the strongest form of preventive diplomacy. And the habits of democracy are the habits of peace. Democracy is rooted in compromise, not conquest. It rewards tolerance, not hatred. Democracies rarely wage war on one another. They make more reliable partners in trade, in diplomacy, and in the stewardship of our global environment. And democracies with the rule of law and respect for political, religious, and cultural minorities are more responsive to their own people and to the protection of human rights.

Not since Woodrow Wilson has a president made liberal idealism such a center piece of his foreign policy. But then again, rarely have the benefits of enlarging the democratic community of states been so apparent. The discovery that democracies rarely if ever go to war against one another demonstrates that while anarchy, security and the concern for relative gains remain potent forces in global politics, the ever-expanding community of democratic nations is becoming equally important.

But, while liberal values might well color US foreign policy and have been part of the ideological competition between the US and the Soviet Union during the Cold War, to what extent did and do liberal idealist values motivate presidents to use force? Having described the frequency with which presidents deployed the military on behalf of liberal idealist objectives in the pre World War II era, I now turn to assessing their impact in the post World War II period using more sophisticated and multivariate statistical methodologies.

148   *The Political Use of Military Force in US Foreign Policy*

A Model of the Use of Force and Liberal Idealism, 1948-1998

Here, I attempt to explain what particular conditions, which are derivable from proliberalization theory and liberal idealist values, might lead presidents to use military force for political purposes, given the presence of an international crisis. In the earlier data analysis we knew, based on the research of Peceny and event descriptions from the Congressional Research Service, the specific aims sought by US foreign policy makers in the uses of force analyzed. Here, our task is more complicated. To make his determination regarding whether the US sought proliberalization objectives in a military intervention, Peceny examined the historical record and relied upon the rationales and reasoning provided by the US government largely during and after the military intervention occurred. When we wish to predict whether proliberalization interests contributed to a decision to use the military in the presence of an international crisis, however, we cannot rely on after the fact examinations of presidential deliberations to make our determination, or only those instances in which a president did use force. Rather we must construct our model of presidential decision making based on what we have reason to believe the president knew at the time, before force was used or not used, rather than what we as scholars find out later through an examination of historical documents. We must identify a set of conditions that we believe, based on our theory, will increase the likelihood a president will use force to advance liberal idealist interests and whose presence during an international crisis can be measured.

Accordingly, I argue in general that presidents will be more likely to use force to promote liberal idealist aims in crises either when such interests can be advanced or when they are threatened. We would not necessarily expect that presidents would be more or less likely to use force in or against (non) democratic nations generally speaking, for crises can occur anywhere at anytime and affect any country. Given the undemocratic state of much of the world, there are certainly a multitude of nations where there is room for improvement and where it is, in theory, possible for presidents to use military force to achieve greater levels of democracy and respect for human rights. Rather, if proliberalization accounts are plausible, presidential administrations must have sought, on occasion, to advance the cause of democracy and human rights when it was feasible and/or desirable. Presidents do not have the resources or the inclination to promote democracy and human rights everywhere, but we have reason to believe given the theoretical arguments above, that they do so in some places and at some times. Furthermore, it is plausible to suppose that there are some crises and some states that are more likely to benefit than others from a use of force to promote liberal idealist aims. I outline these specific scenarios below and construct liberal idealist hypotheses from them.

Nations that are undergoing a period of governmental transition represent prime opportunities to advance the cause of liberal idealism. Whether societies are in the process of throwing off the oppressive rule of a dictatorship, rewriting their constitution, or are involved in war, they are more malleable. Presidents can, through US military intervention, constrain, encourage and move the political process in a more democratic direction. The US military can be used to bolster pro-democracy advocates and restrain anti-democratic elements during a transition period to create a more hospitable environment for democracy. Military force can then be used to provide a secure environment in which political parties can form and campaign, in which voters can go to the polls without fear of intimidation, and oversee the electoral process to guarantee that it is fair. Presidents cannot authorize military interventions against just any or all nations where they might like to promote democracy. Rather, the proper conditions must exist before the president can justify such an intervention to the American people, and deploy military force.

To determine when these transitions occur, I rely on perhaps the most preeminent data set on democracy–the Polity IV Project (Monty G. Marshall and Keith Jaggers, principal investigators).[24] I use two indicators to capture regime transitions. First, Polity IV measures three types of regime transitions. Nations may be undergoing peaceful transitions that are largely planned, interregnums characterized by a collapse of political authority, or periods of 'interruption', usually associated with war time conquest.[25] I also include instances where the crisis took place in the context of an election. I consider all nations undergoing transitions as instances where presidents might use force to advance liberal idealist aims, and create a binary variable for all such situations. Second, I measure the difference in democracy between the year prior to the opportunity to use force, and the year of the opportunity to use force. I expect that the US will be more likely to use force the greater the decline in a nation's level of democracy. I take the difference between democracy at time 't' and 't-1'. Therefore:

Hypothesis 10: Presidents will be more likely to use military force when international crises occur in nations undergoing regime transitions.

Hypothesis 11: Presidents will be more likely to use military force during an international crisis the greater the decline of democracy from the previous year in a nation.

We might also expect that presidents would come to the aid of democratic states that are involved in wars. Whether these conflicts are of an international or intranational character, we would expect that the US would share many interests with these nations, and that presidents would wish to come to their assistance. The US and these nations share democratic forms of government, which make them more natural allies. Because their systems are similar, the US is more likely to have more extensive interaction with such states than with more autocratic regimes. Presidents may also wish to protect such nations in order to maintain the democratic zone of peace in the world. Given that these democratic states are

---

[24] http://www.bsos.umd.edu/cidcm/polity/ as found on August 15, 2003.

[25] These are coded as "-88", "-77", and "-66", respectively in the Polity IV data set. http://www.cidcm.umd.edu/inscr/polity/ as found on August 1, 2003.

involved in a militarized crisis already, presidents may view the political use of force as the most relevant and effective tool in their diplomatic arsenal to maintain democracy. Therefore:

Hypothesis 12: Presidents will be more likely to use military force during international crises when democratic states involved in international wars are the locale of the crisis.

Hypothesis 13: Presidents will be more likely to use military force during international crises when democratic states involved in civil wars are the locale of the crisis.[26]

In the aftermath of World War II, the international community began to take serious steps toward confronting widespread and systematic violence and human rights abuses, whether perpetrated in international or intranational wars. Liberal idealism, with its emphasis on the rights and freedoms all individuals ought to enjoy, is perfectly in keeping with the sentiment that the nations of the world, especially the major powers, ought to take measures to prevent or stop the kinds of atrocities such as Hitler and Nazism visited upon the Jews. Such high-minded goals may not always be pursued with the kind of dedication and resources that international agreements and the United Nations envision, but they nonetheless still lay a legal and moral claim on foreign policies. The end of the Cold War has renewed interest in the use of force as a tool to halt, or at least ameliorate widespread violence that harms civilian populations. The US has intervened in Somalia and Bosnian primarily on such humanitarian grounds. But to what extent did presidents show similar inclinations during the Cold War when military intervention might have damaged relations with US allies or provoked a superpower confrontation? As well, are the more recent interventions the more visible exceptions to US involvement in peacemaking and nation building exercises? If presidents are influenced by the tenets of liberal idealism, we would expect that they would be willing to intervene to prevent widespread death and destruction.

---

[26] Democratic regimes are those states that score "6" or higher in the Polity IV data set. I use Blechman and Kaplan (1978), Zelikow (1984), Job and Ostrom (1986), The Center for Naval Analyses: "The Use of Naval Forces in the Post-War Era: US Navy and US Marine Corps Crisis Response Activity, 1946-1990", and the Correlates of War data sets (Sarkes 2000) to identify international and civil wars.

Liberal Idealism and the Political Use of Military Force 151

Hypothesis 14: Presidents will be more likely to use military force during international crises in a nation when there are high levels of death and destruction.[27]

Table 4.4 Predicting Uses of Force 1948-1998 Using Probit Analysis: The Liberal Idealism Model

Variable	Coeff.	Standard Error	T Statistic	P Value	Marginal Effect
Regime Transition	.4365	.1290	3.38	0.001	.1699
Change in Democracy	.0684	.0273	2.50	0.012	.0272
Democracies & International War	.3758	.2831	1.33	0.184	.1449
Democracies & Civil War	-.7210	.2933	-2.46	0.014	-.2719
Widespread Societal Violence	-.2628	.1488	-1.77	0.077	-.1045
Constant	.0306	.0638	0.48	0.632	

N=605
$\chi^2 = 27.8$, p. < .001
Pseudo R2 = .03
Percent Correctly Predicted = 61.5%
Proportionate Reduction of Error = 18.9%

As in previous chapters, I use probit analysis to predict whether presidents will engage in a political use of military force, given some opportunity to use force, in the period 1948-1998. The overall fit of the model is good, although hardly outstanding. The χ^2 statistic, which tells the likelihood that all the coefficients are equal to zero, is statistically significant. The model correctly predicts, however, only 61.5 percent of the cases (both uses of force and non uses of force). If we had simply predicted that the president would use force every time, given an opportunity, we would have been correct 52.5 percent of the time. Thus, the simple model presented here does not improve substantially over what would be our best guess in the absence of any other information–the modal category. In fact, the proportionate reduction of error statistic, which tells us the degree to which our model improves over predicting the modal category in every case, is only 16.6 percent. The model successfully predicts only 29.6 percent of the non uses of force correctly, while it predicts 90.2 percent of the uses of force correctly. Given that the latter cases are the modal category, the model is necessarily predisposed to predicting this category.

---

[27] To determine where and when such levels of violence occurred, I use the "Major Episodes of Political Violence" data set. All those events that were rated as a level "5" or higher on the ten-point, "magnitude of societal-systemic impact" variable were designated as satisfying my criteria.

152   *The Political Use of Military Force in US Foreign Policy*

Recall that I predicted presidents would be more likely to use force when international crises occur in nations undergoing an interruption in the substance or form of their government, whether planned or unplanned. In those situations, presidents are more likely to use limited force ('Regime Transition'). In this case, when the opportunity to use force involves a regime transition, presidents are approximately 17 percent more likely to authorize military action than they would be if the situation were not so characterized. In fact, of the 138 opportunities to use force that fit this description, presidents ordered the use of force in 88 of those situations (63.7 percent). Since these transitions involve all manner of peaceful and occasionally violent transfers of power, I looked to see if presidents were more willing to use force during some types of transitions than others. First, there were 21 instances of what Polity IV considers to be 'interruption' of regime authority (coded '66' in the Polity IV data set), where the nation in question may have been occupied by foreign military forces, or 'short-lived attempts at the creation of ethnic, religious, or regional federations' (many of these occur in Bosnia during the 1990s).[28] The US used force 15 times during such periods. When the transition is largely peaceful and/or planned (coded '88' in the Polity IV data set), presidents are neither more nor less likely to use force. On these 54 occasions, presidents used force 25 times (46 percent), and chose not to intervene with force 29 times (54%). When the transition took place when there was a 'complete collapse of central political authority', however, presidents used force fairly regularly.[29] Of the 58 such opportunities to use force in my data set, presidents used force 44 times or 75.8 percent. The chaos and political instability accompanying such transitions may provide the additional rationale to use force that may not always be present in other types of regime transitions. Presidents may wish to promote democracy, but prefer that there be some additional reason for using force.

We see that presidents are more likely to use force in an international crisis the greater the *increase* in the level of democracy in a nation ('Change in Democracy'). I had hypothesized that as democratic conditions deteriorated within a country, presidents would wish to reverse the trend or at least stop the slide toward authoritarianism. Why would presidents use force when democracy appears to be on the upswing? And where did such incidents take place? These events take place across a broad swath of time and throughout much of the world. The US used force in the context of the Greek civil war in 1948 when democracy was improving; twice in Venezuela in 1958; multiple times in Central America in the early and mid 1980s as the first tentative moves were made there toward democracy, especially in Nicaragua, and in response to developments on the Korean peninsula as the government of South Korea opened up its political system. Perhaps some of these moves toward democratization are accompanied by other developments that threaten political liberalization. The US may act to consolidate democratization rather than promote it (although this is distinctly not the case in

---

[28] Polity IV Codebook, accessed at
http://www.cidcm.umd.edu/inscr/polity/index.htm on July 19, 2003.
[29] ibid

Nicaragua, which held elections in response to American pressure and despite US attempts to overthrow the Sandinista government). It is also interesting to note that most of the many nations that experienced a decline of democracy were becoming more autocratic rather than less democratic. That is, their level of democracy was already quite deficient to begin with, and grew worse.

Interestingly, we see that while presidents were apt to use force in crises where democratic nations were involved in international wars ('Democracies and International War'), they are less likely to use force when opportunities arise in democratic nations undergoing civil wars ('Democracies and Civil Wars'). The coefficient for the former variable, however, fails to obtain conventional levels of statistical significance. In the context of international wars, presidents are 14 percent more likely to use force according to the marginal effects coefficient and holding all other variables constant at their mean value. When democracies are involved in civil wars, presidents are 27 percent less likely to use force, with the usual caveats. In all, there were 23 opportunities to use force when democratic states were involved in international wars, and presidents authorized military action in 16 of these events (69.5 percent). There were 23 situations involving a democratic state experiencing civil war and presidents embarked on a limited use of force only six times (26 percent). While the data do not reveal why these situations are treated differently, we might speculate based on what we know of the democratic peace phenomenon.

Presidents may wish to use force to protect fellow democracies from attacks by other states because of the bonds that arise between nations with similar commitments to this type of regime. Presidents may fear that the adversaries of these states will either destroy the democratic regime, or replace it with a more authoritarian form of government. In either case, the desire to maintain the zone of democracy and democratic peace in the world may compel presidents to use the US military to tip the scales in favor of the fellow democracy. When the situation involves a civil war, we might expect that presidents would similarly wish to protect democratic regimes, but their decision calculus may be more complex. We see above that presidents typically refrain from intervening militarily when there is an unplanned interruption in political control because, as I speculated, conditions are probably not ripe for proliberalization policies. And while that result applied to all democratic and non democratic nations undergoing unplanned transitions, I believe there may be a similar sort of dynamic occurring here. Presidents may be reluctant to intervene because even though a democracy is under assault from within, a US military intervention to promote democratization at best might be premature, and at worst might inflame the situation. Presidents may use diplomacy instead to bring together the warring factions.

We also see that presidents are not more likely to intervene in an international crisis when there is widespread violence ('Widespread Societal Violence'). I had hypothesized that if presidents did subscribe to the belief that the US has an obligation to relieve such suffering, presidents would be more likely to act. While such idealism may be praised as a noble goal, in practice presidents are not substantially motivated by such concerns. The occurrence of such violence, despite being visible and highly destructive, but nonetheless occurring in isolation,

154　　　*The Political Use of Military Force in US Foreign Policy*

may not provide sufficient grounds on which to use military force. Presidents may believe that they require some sort of national security or other justification for using force in nations that are experiencing such widespread and systematic destruction. For example, the US recently intervened in the west African nation of Liberia, which has been at war for much of the past decade. Yet, several other nations in West African, such as Sierra Leone and the Ivory Coast have also experienced widespread violence, but the US never chose to intervene, except to protect its own citizens. The additional justification that is present in the case of Liberia is the long US association with that nation that was originally founded by freed American slaves in the 19th century.

In sum, the evidence for the liberal idealist model of presidential decision making is modest. We have some reason to believe that conditions conducive to a liberal idealist use of force contributed to presidents' willingness to deploy the military although only one of the hypotheses was statistically significant and in the predicted direction. Two of the hypotheses were not confirmed, and the direction of the coefficients was opposite what was expected. Part of the problem involved in studying the use of force to advance liberal idealism lies in determining just what international crises constitute opportunities to use force specifically for such purposes. Presidents may well use force often to advance democracy or stop human rights abuses, but identifying a 'stereotypical' international crisis in which such interventions occur may be difficult. Rather, the circumstances that make regime reconfiguration desirable may vary depending on the timing, location, feasibility, and other crisis-specific factors. The opportunity to promote democracy or human rights may be the added and even decisive impetus that leads to the political use of force, given the occurrence of a crisis. We should also remember that some of the largest military interventions of the last ten years have involved the promotion of democracy and/or human rights. The 1989 invasion of Panama, the 1994 invasion of Haiti and the ongoing operations in Bosnia and Kosovo all sought to replace authoritarian or unstable governments with pro-democratic forces. If we measure the importance of a foreign goal by the amount of resources devoted to it, liberal idealism would seem to be quite prominent. I return to this theme below.

Conclusion

From the time of Washington and Jefferson when liberal idealism was viewed by many as a core value of American exceptionalism to today's environment of ascendant liberal idealism throughout the globe, presidents have often found it useful to trumpet the liberal underpinnings of US interests. When the US was a new and weak nation, the principles of liberal idealism could be used to justify American behavior to the old regimes and gain adherents among the new ones. When the US became a strong and then hegemonic power, liberal idealism provided an altruistic vision of American interests when other nations might fear its power. Perhaps the key, unresolved issue regarding liberal idealism's place in US foreign policy is the degree to which presidents and policy makers have been sincere in their espousal of liberal values. Most scholars would agree that presidents have often used liberal rhetoric to explain their actions overseas. But has the rhetoric simply been a disguise for more selfish ends? We may never know presidents' true intentions, but the frequent resort to liberal rationales for military interventions and other foreign policies has at least served one important function. By continually justifying their actions in this way, the public has likely come to believe presidents and so expects US behavior overseas to reflect American values. In addition, it would be almost unthinkable for the US to intervene anywhere now with ground forces and not at least attempt to provide for more responsive government. For our more immediate purposes, however, we should like to know just how important liberal idealism has been in helping us understand why presidents use military force short of war. We should conclude that it is an enduring goal; that liberal idealism has assumed greater prominence over the years; and that at times it exercises a decisive influence on the decision to use force. I shall deal with each assertion in turn.

Liberalism is an enduring goal in US foreign policy because its values epitomize how Americans define themselves. The Founding Fathers first articulated an American foreign policy based it on a rejection of Old World values and a belief in the supremacy of liberty at home and liberty for all. Later presidents became convinced that the values that made America great would make other nations free and prosperous, and ultimately, similar to the US. The greater the power of the US and the liberal ideal, the more the US plunged into the business of reforming other nations. The Framers believed the American example would have to be sufficient to inspire freedom. The Wilsonians, Cold Warriors and the Meliorists (in McDougall's apt description [1997]) were not content with being spectators in this struggle, but became participants–something the Founding Fathers would have never intended. Liberal idealism's triumph in recent years can only encourage these activist beliefs.

More recently, international relations research has added to liberal idealism's growing luster by demonstrating that democratic states never war against one another (Maoz and Russett, 1992; Owen, 1994; Bueno de Mesquita and Lalman, 1992). With the collapse of Soviet-style communism, and the increasing recognition of all the good things that seem to accompany democracy, such as increased protection of human rights and economic growth, liberal idealist values have been given a huge boost in US foreign policy making. As discussed above, policymakers and presidents increasingly call attention to the merits of liberal idealism and justify military intervention in its name. Especially when the US intervenes in intra-state conflicts, it will become involved in liberal nation-building. It will become increasingly difficult, if not impossible, to justify US military intervention in other nation's politics without taking action to create more liberal, political institutions. Even in places as seemingly inhospitable to liberal idealism as Afghanistan and Iraq, the US is attempting to lay the groundwork for more democratic regimes. Indeed, these cases of imposing 'democracy at the point of bayonets' may well provide the critical tests of the merit of liberal idealism in US foreign policy for many years to come. Such nation building missions will necessarily include liberal aims, or as Peceny (1999) finds, the Congress will prod the President into proliberalization policies. Regardless, the democratic peace phenomenon seems to have convinced many in government that advancing liberal idealism means protecting American security. Liberal values in foreign policy today are more visible and sincere than ever before.

I would conclude that based on the case studies, broad, historical data, and the multivariate analyses that presidents have periodically used the military to help realize liberal goals, although they do not often dispatch the armed forces abroad on that basis alone. Yet, once US forces have landed on foreign shores to protect American security, property or citizens, their mission has often expanded to include things like election supervision and preventing human rights abuses. We cannot understand US foreign policy in general and many political uses of military force in particular without reference to liberal values. As I stated at the outset, conquering states have traditionally exported their political-economic systems, which in turn are a product of political belief systems. States bring this ideological baggage into diplomacy, trade, war and whatever else they do. A hegemon, however, can be more active and assertive in using its power to realize its proliberalization ambitions. The more threats to its interests and opportunities to advance them, the more likely it is a hegemon, like the US, will inject its values into foreign policy disputes. But rather than serving as the immediate pretext for military intervention, liberal idealism serves as both the method by which security is achieved, and the ultimate aspiration of the nation–a world that looks just like the US.

Chapter 5

Diversionary Theory and the Political Use of Military Force

Introduction

The general trend in both research on foreign policy and international relations has been to emphasize the ways in which domestic politics affect international behavior and vice versa (Keohane and Milner, 1996; Putnam, 1988; Rosecrance and Stein, 1993; Snyder, 1991). Previously, classical and more modern realists distinguished between the domestic bases of foreign policy making and international conduct (Kennan, 1951; Morgenthau, 1973; Waltz, 1979; Wolfers, 1962). They argued that the latter was the proper subject of international relations theory and that the study of foreign policy making should be the province of domestic politics research. Contemporary analysts have concluded that this distinction obscures the importance of reciprocal relationships between the two realms. Nowhere has the desire to locate a role for domestic politics in foreign policy been more prominent than research on the political use of force, especially the diversionary use of force (e.g., DeRouen, 1995, 2000; Fordham, 1998a, 1998b; Gelpi, 1997; James and Hristoulas, 1994; James and Oneal, 1991; Leeds and Davis, 1997; Meernik, 1994, 2000, 2001; Meernik and Waterman, 1996; Miller, 1995; Morgan and Bickers, 1992; Ostrom and Job, 1986; Richards et al, 1993; Smith, 1996a, 1996b 1998, 1999; Wang, 1996; Yoon, 1997). The essence of diversionary theory is that American presidents and other leaders use military force abroad to deflect public attention from problems at home. Although not without its theoretical and methodological weaknesses, diversionary theory has generated more empirical enquiry and has probably done more to elevate the study of the use of military force short of war than any other single, theoretical perspective.

Despite the scholarly attention and its intuitive plausibility, diversionary theory has not yet achieved widespread acceptance in the study of foreign policy making, especially US foreign policy. I believe that the ultimate reason for the lack of scholarly consensus is that insufficient effort (some notable exceptions include Levy [1989] and Morgan and Bickers [1992]) has been directed toward a systematic and critical inquiry into the theory itself and the methodological problems inherent in studying the subject. Many have focused their research designs on the impact of domestic politics and do not accord factors associated with international relations as much attention. It is my intention to address these problems while examining the assumptions of diversionary theory and data on domestic political conditions and the use of force by US presidents.

158 *The Political Use of Military Force in US Foreign Policy*

I first discuss the theory of the diversionary use of force and especially its assumptions about the relationships among international crises, presidential decision-making, public opinion and the use of force. More specifically, I seek to demonstrate where the internal logic of the theory is compelling and valid, and where it is problematic and weak. I next present three cases studies of presidential decision-making and the use of force in situations where presidents were accused of playing politics with the US military. I then examine research on the diversionary use of force and explain how these efforts might be improved. I briefly describe the evolving, historical role of domestic politics in the decision to use force. I follow this up by conducting a variety of bivariate and multivariate statistical tests of the relationship between the use of force and presidential popularity, the US economy and elections. I conclude by suggesting a revised conception of the role of domestic politics in foreign policy making.

The Diversionary Theory of the Use of Force

When we open the black box of foreign policy making we are confronted with a huge assortment of actors, institutions, issues, causes and effects that relate the internal context to the external environment. Interest groups, public opinion, and the media all figure prominently in many studies of US foreign policy. One might examine the role of the President, Congress, the bureaucracy, and the courts in foreign policy. Certainly the range of issues to be explored, when tracing the influence of intra state actors and forces, goes far beyond the scope of traditional realism to encompass trade policy, monetary policy, human rights, and the environment. The domestic factors that influence presidential decisions regarding the political use of military force are just as numerous and wide ranging. Members of Congress and Congress as an institution have played key roles in encouraging (Cuba at various times) and restraining (Dienbienphu, 1954) the use of force through informal discussion and formal legislation. Bureaucrats exercise important functions in creating and limiting the military options presidents choose from–a point made very evident in Allison and Zelikow's Essence of Decision (1999, 2nd ed.). Public timidity (the Vietnam syndrome) may discourage a president from embarking on military interventions. Media reporting may highlight crisis conditions in other countries and lead to demands for presidential action (Somalia 1992). Interest groups, whether ethnically (Haiti 1994), economically (Guatemala 1954) or ideologically based (Bosnia 1991-1995) may promote military action to satisfy constituent demands. Even the federal courts have played a role, often by supporting the president's war making powers (Adler and George, 1996; King and Meernik, 1999).

There is no one theory of domestic politics and foreign policy making to guide us in wading through all these dependent and independent variables. The absence of a general theory of domestic influences on the political use of military force, while it has led to an impressive array of studies freed from the strictures of an overarching framework, has resulted in an aggregation, not an integration of findings. Therefore, because I am interested in assessing the strengths and

Diversionary Theory and the Political Use of Military Force   159

weaknesses of the major theories of the political use of military force, I will confine my attention to the one theory that, although somewhat more narrow in conceptualization, has garnered a great deal of attention, particular from researchers using statistical analyses–diversionary theory. A great deal of effort has been spent investigating this linkage between domestic politics and the use of force, much of it in the last 20 years (DeRouen, 1995, 2000; Fordham, 1998a, 1998b; Gelpi, 1997; James and Hristoulas, 1994; James and Oneal, 1991; Leeds and Davis, 1997; Meernik, 1994; Meernik and Waterman, 1996; Miller, 1995; Morgan and Bickers, 1992; Ostrom and Job 1986; Richards et al, 1993; Smith, 1996a, 1996b 1998, 1999; Wang, 1996; Yoon 1997). The overwhelming attention given to this one theory would be reason enough to devote a chapter to it, but there are other reasons as well that make this theory particularly relevant to our subject. It is generally focused on the use of force short of war, while other international relations research often is concerned more narrowly with international war or just the most widely publicized cases of military intervention. Diversionary research is properly concerned with the forces that influence the president to undertake military action. A great deal of research on the use of force is historical in nature or focused on a few case studies, while diversionary research tends to be more comprehensive and empirically falsifiable. Accordingly, I focus on the diversionary theory of the use of force as the dominant, empirical research program in the area of domestic politics and the political use of force.

The theory of the diversionary use of force is fairly parsimonious, but it has grown more complex as research has become more sophisticated. The most fundamental axiom of the theory is that presidents (or executives of any political regime) engage in conflictual behavior abroad as a means of diverting attention at home from domestic problems. The four key elements of the theory are the president, the domestic environment, the conflictual behavior, and popular opinion. Each may be and has been conceptualized and measured in myriad ways, which in turn bears heavily on the assertions one makes and the evidence one uncovers. Thus, it is important at the outset that we review the role played by each element in the theory.

The role of the president is obviously key. Almost all diversionary theories of the use of force identify the president as the chief foreign policy maker who makes the final decision regarding whether or not to use force. I do as well. But as Ostrom and Job (1986) point out, the president plays more than just the role of commander-in-chief. He is also the national leader who must safeguard vital American interests and protect the nation. As such he will be attuned to the international environment and the characteristics of individual crises. He will consider the costs and benefits for US national interests of acting and not acting. More importantly for diversionary theory, however, the president is a politician who wishes to remain in office. The president will be mindful of the effect his (in) action will have on important domestic constituencies and the public at large. In particular, the president generally seeks to obtain favorable regard at home in order to increase the likelihood of enacting his legislative program, remaining in office (if he is in his first term), assisting his partisans in Congress and helping his party

160   *The Political Use of Military Force in US Foreign Policy*

in general. When the president is perceived to be meeting his responsibilities to provide for national security and the domestic welfare, his support among all sectors of society typically increases. If, however, the public's welfare is not being adequately addressed, the president's support generally decreases. As leader of an enormous bureaucracy with tremendous power and resources both at home and abroad, the president has at his disposal many tools for solving domestic problems. Fiscal policy, executive orders, speeches and the like can all be used at home to convince the public the president is attending to his responsibilities.

Rather than take action at home to address the nation's problems, diversionary theorists argue, for several reasons, that a president may use force to divert attention from his failings. First, it may be easier to act internationally than domestically. As commander-in-chief, the president has the power to order the military to undertake a variety of violent or peaceful activities that serve to demonstrate American power. He can often act quickly and without having to obtain the consent of other domestic actors. This is certainly not the case with legislation the president might wish to pass to address the country's problems. Second, his actions are likely to be widely reported and instantly visible to the American public, and thus the president may believe the public will rally behind his foreign policy and increase its support for the administration. Presidents may bank on the long tradition of bipartisanship and the 'rally-round the flag' effect in times of crisis to bolster their leadership.

There are, of course, some problems with these assumptions, most of which diversionary theorists have acknowledged. To argue that the military option has some attraction to it does not necessarily make it the preferable course of action. If the problem is the economy, the public would undoubtedly prefer a leader who is focused on slowing inflation or increasing jobs instead of attacking foreign governments. If there are domestic problems, the president's time may be devoted to addressing them rather than casting about for convenient opportunities to display American military might. In fact, presidents may not devote as much attention to international crises when confronted with problems at home.

The president's domestic status is the second, principal element of diversionary theory. Presidents are viewed as seeking to divert the public's focus on domestic problems by concentrating their attention on a foreign enemy or crisis and thus rallying the public behind their leadership. We typically find scholars utilizing at least one of the following as an indicator of the president's domestic political environment: presidential popularity, both current and changing levels, the unemployment and inflation rates, and election periods. Some researchers have also investigated a much broader array of negative, political developments, such as riots, civil strife and assassinations. But while there is agreement that these indicators are salient, there is considerable disagreement over precisely how and when these variables influence presidential decision-making. Are presidents more likely to use force when their popularity is high, low or somewhere in between–scholars have argued in favor of all three potential relationships. Are Democratic and Republican presidents essentially alike in their inclination toward diversionary behavior, or are there fundamental differences, especially contingent upon the state of the economy? Some researchers find that certain segments of public opinion

Diversionary Theory and the Political Use of Military Force 161

matter, while other scholars do not. Thus, while many scholars agree that in general a 'bad' domestic political environment is conducive to diversionary behavior, they disagree about what features predispose a president to use force.

The third, basic element in diversionary theory is the military intervention. Scholars generally agree that it is the use of military force short of war that is most relevant. Since the goal of a political use of force is to influence foreign actors without becoming embroiled in a war with them, these actions are comparably less risky than war. Many of these events are widely reported and noticeable to the public. As such, they possess many attributes that prove tempting to presidents who wish to rescue their declining political fortunes at home by demonstrating visible leadership abroad without running unnecessary risks. We believe that wars, due to their violence, duration and costs, are not as conducive to a quick, popular military strike. They are a wholly different beast.

The expectation that these activities will bolster a president's popular standing is the last and perhaps the key assumption of diversionary theory. It stems from sociological research on 'in-groups' and 'out-groups' (Coser, 1956; Simmel, 1955). Researchers discovered that people within groups tend to become more cohesive when confronted with a perceived threat from an 'out-group'. This increased solidarity became known in public opinion literature as the 'rally effect' (Mueller 1973). Mueller (1973, p.209) found that rally events, defined as an international incident that 'involves the US and particularly the president directly', and is 'specific, dramatic and sharply focused' typically lead to increases in the president's approval ratings among the public. Later, others found similar effects (Lee, 1977; Marra, Ostrom and Simon, 1990). Indeed, one can point to many occasions when international crises and in particular, the use of military force redounded to the president's political advantage (Cuban Missile Crisis 1962; Grenada 1983). Even those crises in which the US fared poorly, like the 1961 Bay of Pigs invasion and President Carter's failed 1980 hostage rescue mission in Iran still resulted in surges of support for the president. Most scholars recognize that these boosts are largely temporary, but they do provide enticing incentives for presidents looking for a quick fix to alleviate their domestic woes. Therefore, according to diversionary theory, the rally effect provides the incentive for presidents to use military force to divert attention from their domestic failings.

However, more recent and thorough research (Lian and Oneal, 1993) on the rally effect has indicated that the average gain in approval for presidents following a major and visible use of force is zero. In fact, Lian and Oneal find that prime time speeches to the nation have a greater impact on presidential popularity. Only when they restrict the universe of uses of force to just those occurring in major international crises and covered on the front page of the New York Times do they find evidence of an increase in support–but it is just 1 percent. Thus, we must wonder, would presidents commit American prestige, risk the lives of the men and women of the armed forces, and spend considerable sums of money for a 1 percent increase in popularity? If the press or Congress could show that a president did take such action for personal gain, there might well be calls for impeachment. Therefore, it is rather peculiar to base a theory of the use of force on the

162   *The Political Use of Military Force in US Foreign Policy*

assumption that presidents take the riskiest possible action for the most insignificant gains. The theoretical assumptions, as well as the practical and moral implications are quite troubling, but this has not diminished the popularity of diversionary theory.

In fact, academics are not the only ones who believe presidents are not above engaging in conflict abroad for political considerations. Pundits, politicians and ordinary Americans tend to look with suspicion on foreign adventures that occur when presidents are enmeshed in economic slumps, scandals or upcoming elections. Terms such as 'October surprise' and the 'wag the dog' scenario have entered popular culture, due in part to Americans' distrust and cynicism toward government. Thus, on one level the diversionary theory possesses a great deal of popular and intuitive appeal that has made it perhaps the most widely tested theory of the limited use of force. But has our willingness to embrace the theory, despite its flaws, interfered with our ability to examine objectively and analytically all the evidence regarding presidential decision-making and the use of force? The purpose of the rest of this chapter is to analyze the available historical and empirical evidence on the extent to which domestic problems increase presidents' incentives to use force. I begin with a more thorough review of research on diversionary theory.

Research on the Diversionary Use of Force

The literature on the political use of military force has grown in both quantity and quality over the last 20 years. In contrast to other theories of the use of force (e.g., realism and economic theories) in which many hypothesized relations can be abstract and sometimes non-falsifiable, research on diversionary theory has been fairly precise in specifying, measuring and testing hypotheses. Researchers working in this area have published many studies and advanced numerous, fascinating arguments about presidential decision making that have generated tremendous interest and further inquiry.

The ancient Greek scholar Plato was actually one of the first to note the tendency of governments to go to war to distract the people from their problems, which he commented on in *The Republic* (Republic, 556e, pp. 245-246). During the Russo-Japanese War, the Russian minister of the interior supposedly said, in an oft-cited statement, that, 'We need a little victorious war to stem the tide of revolution' (quoted in Blainey, 1973, p.76 [although Blainey disputes he ever said this]. Quincy Wright (1941) concluded in his massive study of war that there was a tendency among many states to go to war because of domestic ills. In an early statistical analysis of this phenomena, however, Rummel found in his correlations among domestic conflict and foreign conflict that, 'foreign conflict behavior is generally completely unrelated to domestic conflict behavior' (1963, p.24). Others using fairly simple, statistical techniques found similar results (Zinnes and Wilkenfeld, 1971; Wilkenfeld, 1972).

The study of the diversionary use of force really begins in earnest in the mid 1980s when greater data availability, more sophisticated statistical techniques

Diversionary Theory and the Political Use of Military Force 163

and the breaking down of the international/domestic divide in international relations theory resulted in a renewed interest in the subject. In perhaps the most widely cited study, Ostrom and Job (1986) found that presidents were more likely to use major levels of force during quarterly periods when their overall approval ratings were high, when their approval ratings declined over time, when the misery index rose and when elections were approaching (Stoll [1984], also found that uses of force occurred more during presidential elections in war time). James and Oneal (1991) challenged Ostrom and Job's assertion that collectively, domestic factors exercised the greatest impact on the likelihood the president would use force. They initially argued that Ostrom and Job had not adequately captured the importance of the international environment in presidential decision-making and so developed a more extensive measure of the severity of international crises. But with a few minor differences, they essentially replicated Ostrom and Job's work and found that domestic factors still exercised a greater statistical impact than the international ones.

James and Hristoulas (1994) developed a spatial model of incentives to engage in diversionary behavior that provides a stronger theoretical basis for much of the research, which previously was based more on anecdotal evidence and the 'in-group', 'out-group' research of sociologists. They argue:

> ...in a situation of highly escalated internal conflict, [presidential] reaction time is expected to become significantly shorter, resulting in the greater availability of projection. All other things being equal, a noteworthy increase in the level of internal conflict will result in an almost immediate reaction because the state is expected to shift from incremental to ad hoc decision making (James and Hristoulas, 1994, p.334).

James and Hristoulas also expand significantly the measurement of domestic conditions likely to produce diversionary behavior to include things like riots, protest demonstrations and assassinations. In an extensive analysis of the likelihood of US involvement in international crises, the authors found a positive relationship between popularity and the use of force, but a negative relationship between the misery index and the probability of diversionary behavior (although this relationship just misses statistical significance). It should be noted, however, that in their final, more parsimonious model, none of the domestic, political variables was found to be statistically significant.

Morgan and Bickers (1992) took notice of a growing gap between diversionary theory and the lack of consistent, statistical evidence to support it. They suggested that either the theory was incorrectly specified, or the statistical analyses were inappropriate for testing it. They, like Levy (1989) point out that the 'in-group', 'out-group' sociological research on which diversionary theory is premised pertains to small group behavior that may not be generalizable to an entire society, especially one as large and diverse as the US. As well, they argue that researchers have failed to adequately account for the time lag between domestic conflict and diversionary behavior, the level of domestic conflict that precipitates a use of force, and the likelihood that the relationship between domestic conditions and diversionary activity is non-linear. Morgan and Bickers hypothesize that leaders will be more concerned about their standing within important, domestic political constituencies, than society at large. They argue that, 'If support among members of the ruling coalition is eroding, we can expect the leader to mollify them or to use an external threat to rally their support' (1992, p.33). They suggest that when aggregate presidential approval is high, and partisan support is low and declining, presidents will be most likely to engage in militarized, interstate disputes. They find that, '...the likelihood of a US initiated action increases sharply as the level of partisan support for the president falls' (Morgan and Bickers, 1992, p.41). As well they find that the level of partisan support is more important than changing partisan approval.

DeRouen (1995, 2000) suggests a more sophisticated method of modeling the relationships among the US economy, presidential popularity and the political use of military force. We know that the unemployment and inflation rates are important predictors of presidential popularity. There is also some evidence that some uses of force have led to increases in public support for the president (notwithstanding the Lian and [1993] findings). DeRouen sensibly concludes that the most appropriate method for modeling these interrelationships is through a simultaneous equation system in which he models the determinants of public support before and after the use of force decision. In his analysis, DeRouen finds that increases in the misery index are associated with decreasing levels of presidential approval. When he models the level of force employed by the president in an international crisis, DeRouen finds that while the misery index is not a statistically significant predictor of presidential behavior, approval ratings are negatively related to force levels and statistically significant. He concludes that the economy indirectly affects the use of force by influencing approval ratings and that approval ratings directly affect the use of force decision. This finding, however, contradicts some previous research, which found a positive association between approval and the use of force. Differences in data and methodology may very well account for this discrepancy, but DeRouen's findings are more in keeping with the logic of the diversionary hypothesis. That is, if presidents do wish to deflect attention from poor job performance, it only makes sense that they would do so when the public indicates it is dissatisfied with their leadership. Interestingly, few researchers have delved into this crucial paradox in the diversionary literature. Others have made arguments similar to DeRouen's (Levy, 1989; Russett, 1990), but few have taken the time to explore the issue in any great detail.

Wang uses an expected utility approach in modeling presidential uses of force and argues that, '(1) the expected value for war, (2) the reputational costs leaders anticipate facing for backing down in a crisis (*capitulation*), (emphasis in the original), and (3) the expected domestic political costs for using force' determine the propensity to use force (1996, p.72). He also improves upon previous research that, '...portray US strategic considerations in crises almost entirely as functions of the U.S.-Soviet relationship' (Wang, 1996, p.81) through the inclusion of more information about the international situation in the president's decision. Wang finds that the greater the expected value for war and the greater the costs for backing down, the higher the level of the US military response in a crisis. He also

Diversionary Theory and the Political Use of Military Force 165

finds a positive relationship between presidential popularity, elections and a worsening economy and the likelihood of a use of force, given a crisis. Interestingly, Wang finds that partisan support and changing support among the general public are positively related to the level of the US response. The former contradicts Morgan and Bickers (1992), while the latter contradicts Ostrom and Job (1986) and James and Oneal (1991). But, he concludes that, 'presidential popularity, at both the aggregate and the partisan levels, has little substantive impact in determining the severity of US responses in foreign policy crises' (Wang, 1996, p.86). The usual caveats regarding data and methodology apply, but clearly we can see the growing number of unresolved discrepancies in the literature.

Fordham (1998a) explores potential differences between Republican and Democratic presidencies in their willingness to use diversionary force. He argues that the two parties pursue different macroeconomic policies that can be expected to influence when each is more likely to resort to diversionary behavior. Democratic elites have been more concerned with maintaining high employment, while Republican elites strive to keep inflation down. According to Fordham, Democratic presidents have devoted more attention and domestic resources to fighting unemployment, while Republican presidents have done the same to address inflation. Democratic presidents have been more reluctant to take action to combat inflation, because such measures typically hurt important political constituencies, while Republican presidents have been more unwilling to adopt measures to address unemployment for the same political reasons. Therefore, when Democratic presidents preside over inflationary periods, or Republicans preside over times of high unemployment, rather using macroeconomic policy, Fordham predicts they will engage in diversionary behavior. As expected, Fordham finds that Republican presidents are more likely to use force than Democratic presidents when unemployment is high. However, he finds that inflation dampens the enthusiasm to use force for both political parties. It is negatively related to the number of uses of force, but there is little difference between Democratic and Republican proclivities to use force (he also finds that this may be partially explained by the effects of the Vietnam War which generated both high inflation and fewer uses of force). Fordham (1998, p.437) concludes that, 'There is now abundant empirical evidence to suggest that some presidents have succumbed to this temptation [to use diversionary force]'.

Fordham (1998b) also looks at the role of opportunities to use military force, and in particular, the supply of such events as produced by the domestic and international environments. He argues that presidents' ability to use force will be dependent upon domestic resources, including the level of employment, investor confidence, election years and US involvement in wars. He finds that the unemployment rate is positively related to the number of quarterly and yearly uses of force, because military action may be seen as a useful way of absorbing excess labor. On the other hand, investor confidence is positively related to the use of force, because when perceptions of economic performance are negative, '...investors will have greater difficulty accommodating losses [which presumably

166   *The Political Use of Military Force in US Foreign Policy*

result when force is used internationally] when the value of their investments is already diminished (Fordham, 1998b p.574). In addition, Fordham finds that there is a significant degree of what he terms, 'motivated bias and threat perception'. That is, presidents are more likely to search for opportunities when they possess the necessary resources to use force. He claims, 'The influence of domestic political and economic circumstances on threat perception underlines the reality that 'national interests' are not given by the international system. Instead, they are chosen by individuals...' (Fordham, 1998b, p.585).

Then there are those who argue that there is little evidence of diversionary behavior. Meernik (1994) and Meernik and Waterman (1996) find that the effects of presidential approval ratings, economic conditions and elections on the probability of a use of force and increasing levels of force are trivial. Because their models are based on the opportunity to use force as the unit of analysis (crises in which there is reason to believe the president considered using force instead of quarterly time units, they were able to use crisis-specific instead of only environmental characteristics as independent variables, which proved more predictive of presidential behavior. In a follow-up study, Meernik (2000) also finds that the timing of crisis occurrence affects the decision to use force. Foreign leaders are more likely to use force when times are bad for presidents at home because they seek to exploit distracted leaders. The more frequent occurrence of crises during such periods just makes it seem that presidents use force more often under these conditions.

Other studies use different conceptualizations of US crisis involvement, while still investigating the impact of domestic conditions on presidential decision making. Yoon (1997), in a study of US intervention in civil wars in the third world, examined the impact of a variety of factors pertaining to US strategic interests, and the domestic context. Yoon finds that presidents are less likely to intervene during election periods and as the misery index increases. Lindsay, Sayrs and Steger (1992) look at the degree of cooperation/conflict in US-Soviet relations during the Cold War. They find that none of their domestic variables, including presidential approval, business expectations, and first year in office, is statistically significant in predicting the level of conflict. However, business expectations were negatively and significantly related to the level of cooperation. They conclude, 'The estimation results indicate that international politics matters more than domestic politics in determining presidential foreign policy choice' (Lindsay et al, 1992, p.15). Using a formal model, Richards and others (1993) look at diversionary behavior as a form of the principal-agent model, where the leader is the agent designated by the public (the principal) to provide good governance. The likelihood of diversionary behavior is dependent upon the competence of the leader and the degree of risk she is willing to assume. They write, 'Good executives have an incentive to divert more often than incompetent executives simply because it provides them with an additional opportunity to prove their abilities. Bad managers have an incentive to divert, however, if they are sufficiently risk acceptant or if they can mislead the public as to the abilities required to manage the operation successfully' (Richards et al, 1993, p.527).

Additional formal theoretical research has been done by Smith (1996a, 1998). He assumes, like Richards et al (1993) that voters in democratic societies seek competent executives and will retain those who preside over good economies. Smith suggests that successful foreign policy actions can slightly influence voters' perceptions of executive competence. Specifically, when voters' evaluations of leaders' foreign policy performance is likely to affect election results, leaders are apt to engage in unnecessary foreign policy activities (Smith, 1996a, p.147). In a follow-up article, Smith (1998) demonstrates that leaders are unlikely to undertake military intervention when their competence is high–because there is little to be gained–and when their competence is low–because such interventions will only serve to underscore their ineptitude. More specifically, he suggests that competent leaders during close elections possess the greatest incentives to retaliate, but will generally not be able to do so because leaders in other states will refrain from initiating crises to avoid near-certain retaliation.

There has also been an increasing amount of cross-national research on the diversionary use of force. Scholars studying the democratic peace phenomenon have shown that domestic institutions and values matter greatly in determining foreign policy behavior. Gelpi (1997) argues that democracies should be more likely to use force for domestic consumption because of the 'rally round the flag' effect among the public and because they cannot use repressive measures at home to quell discontent. The use of force becomes a convenient alternative. He asserts, 'My results indicate that the diversionary initiation of force is generally a pathology of democratic states' (Gelpi, 1997, p.277). In another cross-national study, Miller (1995) argues and finds that leaders who possess more revenue and resources to address public discontent will be less likely to engage in diversionary behavior, while those whose nations are not as wealthy will have more of an incentive to act aggressively abroad to divert attention at home. In addition, Miller also finds that political institutions influence the likelihood of the use of force to distract publics. 'All other things being equal, if autocratic leaders expect to incur fewer domestic political costs for the use of force, they should be more willing than their democratic counterparts to employ diversionary tactics' (Miller, 1995, p.767).

While there are a number of unresolved theoretical and methodological issues in this research program, many of these problems can be addressed. The most straightforward explanation for the disparity in findings is simply that there are many intuitively plausible, but contradictory assumptions about what presidents might do during international crises. There is at least one compelling reason as to why leaders would wish to engage in diversionary behavior–they wish to remain in office. Conversely, there are institutional and ethical grounds for believing presidents would not engage in such risky behavior. Democratic leaders might be viewed as possessing greater incentives to engage in diversionary behavior because they cannot use repression at home to deal with public discontent. On the other hand, democracies have numerous checks on the power of executives to engage in conflict that authoritarian leaders do not face. None of these arguments will be entirely true or false because they are all suppositions based on an array of political

168 *The Political Use of Military Force in US Foreign Policy*

incentives and impediments nationally and cross-nationally. Given that there are equally plausible reasons to expect and not expect diversionary behavior, our findings mirror this confusion.

Researchers also share a substantial portion of the blame for the confusion in the field because few scholars use the same data to test their hypotheses. This lack of comparability makes it difficult to generalize across studies and develop a common theoretical framework. The most obvious example can be seen in the measurement of the use of force. DeRouen (1995, 2000), Fordham (1998a, 1998b), James and Oneal (1991), Meernik (1994, 2000, 2001), Meernik and Waterman (1996), Ostrom and Job (1986) use data on the political use of military force originally collected by Blechman and Kaplan and supplemented later by others. Leeds and Davis (1997), Miller (1995) and Morgan and Bickers (1992) use the Militarized Interstate Dispute data set to measure conflictual behavior. Gelpi (1997), James and Hristoulas (1994) and Wang (1997) utilize the International Crisis Behavior data set to determine whether or not the US was a 'crisis actor' in an international dispute. Yoon codes US intervention based on the Brecher and Wilkenfeld criteria in the International Crisis Behavior data set, but does not use their data. Lindsay, Sayrs and Steger use the Conflict and Peace Data Bank to measure US foreign policy behavior. Richards et al (1993) and Smith (1996a, 1998) use formal modeling techniques. We would expect that when researchers gather data on specifically US military activity (e.g., Blechman and Kaplan, 1978), they will identify more such events than those who focus on international wars and conflicts (e.g., the Militarized Interstate Dispute data set) (see Fordham and Sarver, 2001). Since the variables measuring domestic political conditions (which are also measured in manifold different ways) are never overwhelmingly statistically significant in these models, it is quite possible that differences in data could account for the discrepant findings.

Research on the timing of international crises suggests a very different explanation to account for these perplexing findings. International relations and foreign policy scholars have increasingly taken notice of the problems created by what are known as 'selection effects' in the study of conflictual behavior (Clark, 2003; Leeds and Davis, 1997; Meernik, 2000; Morrow, 1989; Reed, 2000; Smith, 1998). Problems of selection effects arise when the occurrence of one event is dependent upon the occurrence of a prior event. If the conditions that determine whether or not this prior event obtains are systematic and explainable, our explanations of the subsequent phenomenon will be tainted.

In research on the use of force, the event that determines whether or not the president uses force is the opportunity to use force. Absent an international crisis, there will be no situation for the president to direct the military. Thus, we must ask, are international crises either constantly or randomly occurring events in the global environment? If they are, there is nothing systematic about their occurrence and little reason to be concerned that our explanations of the use of force will be biased in some manner. But if crises occur for predictable reasons, perhaps because foreign leaders time crises to occur when they believe they are most likely to emerge victorious, then our models will not give us an accurate picture of presidential decision making.

Scholars are of two minds regarding crisis initiation and the diversionary use of force. Some argue that crises are *least* likely to be instigated when the initiator perceives that the target has an increased incentive to respond with military action. In particular, if the economy in the target state is performing poorly, or support for the government is lacking, leaders of such states will have an incentive to engage in conflict overseas to distract their publics. Knowing this, the potential initiator refrains from starting a crisis with states whose leaders have incentives to retaliate (Leeds and Davis, 1997; Smith, 1996a, 1998). These authors argue that fewer crises should arise when target states possess incentives to engage in diversionary behavior. Others (Meernik, 2000) argue that if US adversaries do strategically time crisis initiation, they will be more apt to do so when the president's domestic performance is poor. US adversaries should be more likely to cause trouble when they believe the president is too consumed with problems at home to be drawn to trouble abroad. Why would one nation initiate a crisis against another nation whose leader is focused and competent, when it could wait to exploit incompetent, distracted leaders? Again, there is conflicting evidence on this question. But while they disagree about the factors that lead to crises, Leeds and Davis (1997) and Meernik (2000) both agree that when scholars do take selection effects into account, the evidence for diversionary behavior diminishes.

As we see there are several methodological problems facing the diversionary theory research program. While we cannot hope to reconcile all the competing claims, we can more systematically investigate the explanatory power of the theory, and we can use our better understanding of the problems of diversionary theory to guide us in this examination. First, we should utilize different methodologies and different forms of data to evaluate the likelihood that presidents use force for domestic purposes. I use relatively simple, bivariate data analysis to test diversionary theory to identify whether there are simple and straightforward relationships regarding diversionary behavior that might have been hidden in more sophisticated statistical analyses. I employ the domestic conditions associated with diversionary theory in a more sophisticated statistical analysis using a probit model to test diversionary hypotheses on international crises in the post World War II era. By the end of this investigation we should be able to make a much better judgment regarding the plausibility of diversionary theory and thereby determine more thoroughly the applicability of diversionary theory.

Three Case Studies of the Diversionary Use of Force

Of all the explanations regarding the use of force by American presidents, the diversionary theory may be the most difficult to verify. It is difficult because it is so unlikely presidents would ever allow evidence of such calculations to become part of the public record. There is little likelihood of ever finding a smoking gun. For the same reason it is also difficult to disprove diversionary motives for it is always possible a president kept his personal, political considerations private, and because some will always see conspiracy in shows of military might at politically

170 *The Political Use of Military Force in US Foreign Policy*

opportune moments. But if some scholars and pundits would see the lack of documentation as evidence of nefarious motives, undoubtedly other scholars would turn elsewhere for explanations of the use of force. Since it is never difficult to find at least some political/military rationale for using force, it would be relatively easy to point to a number of other, presumably more important reasons in the decision to use force. I refrain from doing so precisely because finding alternative causes is too simple. Therefore, I do not seek either to verify diversionary theory by searching for smoking guns, or disprove it by introducing alternative explanations. The former is too difficult to be feasible, while the latter is too easy to be fair. In keeping with my emphasis on using cases where there is at least prima facie evidence for the theory in question, below I describe three cases where there was much speculation that the president used force to distract the public from his domestic problems. After describing the historical events, I attempt to make the case for domestic politics as a major factor in the decision to use force. I then try to marshal counter-evidence against such arguments.

Perdicaris Alive or Raisuli Dead

As he began his first campaign for the presidency, Theodore Roosevelt faced formidable obstacles. He had earned the presidency in 1901 when an assassin's bullet felled William McKinley, and so to many Republican Party stalwarts TR was still an accidental president. The Old Guard was inherently opposed to the young progressive reformer and continually cast about for some party veteran, like Mark Hanna (and after his death in the winter of 1904, others), to take over the reins and return the party to its conservative, pro-business ways. Many felt the trust-busting TR did not support big business and the monied interests of Wall Street strongly enough. Others viewed him as crude and his indecorous behavior, such as skinnydipping in Rock Creek Park, as unbecoming of a president (Morris, 2001, pp.319-320). In private, Roosevelt agonized, 'over what he feared might be his impending defeat at the polls' (Dalton, 2002, p.261).

In the run-up to the campaign, the Old Guard tried to hang on to its power. They dictated selection of the vice-presidential candidate and the party platform (Dalton, 2002, p.259). They were incensed when Roosevelt handpicked his man, George Cortelyou, to serve as Republican Party Chairman, perhaps the most important, patronage dispensing post in the party (Morris, 2001, p.330). Despite his near complete control of the proceedings of the Republican Convention in Chicago that summer of 1904, TR still faced a last minute rebellion from the Old Guard, which still tried to find an alternative candidate. In fact, TR's stage management had left the Convention almost completely bereft of any excitement and public interest that might give him a boost going into the presidential campaign. The ground swell of support Roosevelt was counting on seemed to be slipping away. But half a world away in an odd throwback to the days of the Barbary pirates, events were conspiring to provide TR with just the lift he needed if the media-savvy president played his cards right.

The rampant piracy on the high seas off the North African coast might be a thing of the past, but there were still plenty of pecuniary and political enticements for local war lords to kidnap foreigners. Ahmed ben Mohammed el Raisuli, a tribal leader in Morocco opposed to both French domination and to the rule of the Sultan Mulay Abd al Aziz IV, was one such combination brigand and insurgent. On May 18, 1904 he kidnapped Ion Perdicaris, an American expatriate and his stepson (a British subject) from their villa outside Tangier for ransom, and to strike a blow against the Sultan's government (Morris, 2001, p.324). In exchange for his hostages, Raisuli demanded an end to government military interventions in the lands he controlled, release of all political prisoners from his region, dismissal of a local Tangier ruler who once had Raisuli chained to a prison wall for four years, 70,00 Spanish silver dollars, and control over two of Morocco's richest districts (Morris, 2001, pp.326-327). Until then he held Perdicaris, his stepson and other members of his entourage in the Er Riff mountain region to wait for pressure to build on the Sultan to pay his ransom.

When the American Consul General in Tangier, Samuel Gummere, got wind of the kidnapping he immediately cabled his superiors in the State Department and requested that a warship be sent. At the time, 16 ships of the US Navy were on a goodwill cruise in the Mediterranean, and several were diverted to Tangier where they arrived by the end of May (Morris, 2001, p.325). But as more of the flotilla steamed into the Moroccan harbor, Raisuli's demands escalated. Roosevelt grew increasingly frustrated at the lack of progress and believed that any further negotiation, even though this was largely carried out by those within the Moroccan government, would be futile and unfitting of a great power. To make matters worse, investigations in the State Department revealed that Perdicaris was not even an American citizen! He had traded away his citizenship at the beginning of the Civil War to avoid taxation (Morris, 2001, p.337). Roosevelt seemed to be employing a sizeable portion of the US Navy and engaging American reputation all to save a man who was not entitled to any kind of American protection. What purpose would such an action serve?

The purposes such a timely and visible display of military might and American power might serve became perfectly obvious at the Republican Convention as negotiations over Perdicaris's ransom were concluding. Protests in the press about incident were building (Gould, 1991, p.136). The convention lacked any drama, and Roosevelt feared the consequences for his campaign. At that point and after even more wrangling over the ransom, Secretary of State John Hay sent one last telegram to Tangier as American warships there gathered in force for a potential invasion. While the telegram itself contained much of the appropriate diplomatic niceties, it is remembered more for the one phrase that best encapsulated American demands: 'We want Perdicaris alive or Raisuli dead'. Hay sent off the cable to Tangier, and allowed it to go out over the press wires (Morris, 2001, p.335). But while the telegram reached Tangier after a settlement had finally been reached, it was read with great drama and effect at the Republican Convention that afternoon on June 22. The *New York Times* was led to write, 'Roosevelt and Hay at last had succeeded in creating artificial respiration and heart action in the convention through saline treatment' (quoted in Gould, 1991, p.136).

Nixon, Watergate and the 1973 Middle East War

For six years, since the Six Day War of 1967, Egypt, Syria and Jordan had sought to recapture the lands they had lost in that conflict. Soviet assistance, diplomacy and saber rattling had accomplished almost nothing and so Egypt and Syria resorted to force, if only to demonstrate that Israel was not invincible. On October 6, 1973 Egyptian forces crossed the Suez into Israeli-occupied Sinai, and Syrian forces attacked in the direction of the Golan Heights. The two nations achieved an incredible measure of tactical and strategic surprise, for most observers predicted they would never strike first given the reputation of the Israeli Army. Indeed, most of the diplomatic efforts in the days leading up to the war centered around trying to convince the Arab states that Israel was not about to attack. Initially the Egyptian and Syrian forces did quite well and threw back the Israeli army. After Israel recovered from the initial shock, it halted the Arab advance and the tide of battle seesawed for several days. As the belligerents quickly used up their weapons stocks, the US began airlifting supplies to Israel while the Soviet Union assisted its Arab allies. The US and the USSR also began to negotiate a cease fire bilaterally and among their proxies. By this point in the conflict, the Israeli forces were on the offensive and Egypt especially was losing ground. Believing that he had achieved his political objectives, Egyptian President Anwar Sadat was ready to halt the war. A fragile truce was arranged on October 22 in the United Nations, but almost immediately both sides began charging the other with violating it.

The focal point of these cease-fire violations was the Israeli encirclement of the Egyptian Third Army in the Sinai. Whether it was the Egyptians seeking to break out of their position or Israel attempting to cut off all hope of retreat may never be clear, but it became apparent to both the US and the Soviet Union that Egypt was in a desperate position. Both the Soviets and the Americans had been mostly content to let the war play out as long as neither side achieved a decisive advantage. But at this juncture, Israel was threatening to demolish a substantial portion of the Egyptian military–something the Soviets could never countenance. As the Third Army's plight became more dire, the Soviet General Secretary Leonid Brehznev sent a letter to Richard Nixon on October 24. To resolve this crisis, he proposed that both the US and the Soviet Union send military forces to the region to guarantee the cease fire and the diplomatic settlement. Failing American participation in such a force, the Communist leader asserted the Soviets were ready to act unilaterally. In addition to their diplomatic signals, the Russians were building up their military forces in the region and increasing their alert status. The Nixon administration crafted a diplomatic response to the Soviet missive rejecting their proposal, but foreign policy makers felt that the words needed to be backed up with physical action.

Accordingly, on the night of October 24-25, the National Security Council decided to ratchet up the alert status of US military forces. Normally most of the military, with the exception of the Strategic Air Command, were on Defense Condition 5, where DEFCON 1 is war. The NSC decided that it would have to order DEFCON 3 if the Soviets were to notice the change in status. Since the alert put all US forces, including its strategic ones in a heightened readiness, the NSC

Diversionary Theory and the Political Use of Military Force   173

was explicitly escalating the crisis to nuclear levels. The US also placed the 82nd Airborne on alert, sent 60 B-52's based in Guam back to the US, and dispatched the aircraft carrier, *Franklin Delano Roosevelt* to the eastern Mediterranean along with carriers *Independence* and *John F. Kennedy* (Betts, 1987, p.124). In fact, Richard Nixon (1978, p.938) characterized the situation in his memoirs as the most serious US-Soviet altercation since the Cuban missile crisis. All the military muscle and blustery threats, however, did not change the fact that the US and the USSR shared a common interest–a cease fire before the Third Army was wrecked. Recognizing the seriousness of the situation its ally had gotten itself into, Washington pressured Israel into allowing relief to reach the Egyptians and then a cease fire. In fact, the US alert was lifted very shortly thereafter on October 26th. The crisis was essentially resolved when Sadat requested an international military force, not a US-Soviet one, to patrol the cease fire.

Few presidents in modern times were confronted with as many incentives to engage in a diversionary use of force as Richard Nixon in the fall of 1973. The most significant was the Watergate scandal. That domestic crisis was reaching a boiling point as testimony in congressional committee hearings implicated Richard Nixon in all manner of dirty, campaign tricks. At issue in October of 1973 were the tapes Nixon had surreptitiously recorded in the White House and which the Special Prosecutor investigating the matter, Archibald Cox, was trying to obtain. Negotiations among the White House, Congress and Cox were getting nowhere. Finally, in response to Cox's refusal to accept White House summaries of the tapes' contents, Nixon ordered his Attorney General, Eliot Richardson, to fire Cox on Saturday, October 20th. Richardson refused and resigned instead. The second in command at the Justice Department, William Ruckelshaus, similarly refused Nixon's order to remove Cox and he was fired. Finally, the Solicitor General, Robert Bork, carried out the order and the FBI sealed off Cox's office and took away his work. What came to be known as the 'Saturday Night Massacre' was viewed at the time as one of the most serious constitutional crises in US history. Even Nixon's supporters were taken aback by the audacity of his actions. Support among the public for his job performance dropped to 17 percent in some polls (Summers, 2000, p.459). Eight impeachment resolutions were introduced in the House Judiciary Committee in short order. At this point in his administration, few presidents in American history were as disliked as Richard Nixon. And just a few days later Nixon ordered the nuclear alert.

At the time of the Saturday Night Massacre, Secretary of State and National Security Adviser, Henry Kissinger was in Moscow working for a negotiated settlement to the war. As he returned home, a cable sent by White House Chief of Staff, Alexander Haig, reached him in mid air. According to Kissinger (1982, p.567), Haig wrote, 'Because the situation (the Saturday Night Massacre) is at a state of white heat, the ramifications of the accomplishment in Moscow have been somewhat eclipsed and their true significance underplayed. For this reason it is essential that you participate fully in maintaining the national perspective and *that a major effort be made to refocus national attention on the President's role in the Middle East settlement*' (emphasis added). While presidents

174 *The Political Use of Military Force in US Foreign Policy*

routinely try to direct the nation's attention toward their successes and away from failures, the implication in Haig's letter was that Kissinger should take action that would call attention to the president's involvement in the Middle East conflict. The Middle East war provided Nixon with the perfect opportunity to do what he loved best–act assertively and unilaterally on the world's stage.

And if this were not enough, Nixon was suffering through a host of other problems that fall. The war inspired the Arab oil embargo against the US, later resulting in an energy crisis and escalating gas prices. Vice-President Spiro Agnew had pleaded *nolo contendere* to a charge that he had received kickbacks on building contracts while governor of Maryland. As part of the deal, he resigned from office at this time. A few days before the Soviet challenge the Congress had passed the War Powers Resolution, which attempted to reinterpret the president's powers as commander-in-chief of the armed forces and make the deployment of military force more of a joint executive-legislative endeavor. While unemployment levels hovered around 5 percent at this time, inflation was still a problem and running at approximately 7 percent. In fact, the only incentive to engage in a diversionary use of force not present was an upcoming election. The 1973 Middle East War provides us with a compelling case for presidential motive and opportunity to use military force for domestic consumption.

The Invasion of Grenada

The US-led invasion of the tiny Caribbean island nation of Grenada to overthrow a hard-line Marxist government may seem like small potatoes today, but at the time it was a big deal. Coming after the 1982 US intervention in Lebanon, President Reagan's Star Wars speech in March of 1983, the KAL 007 shoot down by the Russians in September, and the ongoing controversy over the increase in US nuclear forces in Europe, the invasion heightened already high Cold War tensions. Despite the fact that almost no government in the world outside of the few microstates in the Caribbean that took part, supported the operation, it did restore some degree of faith in the United State's capacity for action at home and abroad. Looking back, however, Operation Urgent Fury pales in comparison to more recent US interventions in Panama, the Persian Gulf, Somalia, Bosnia, Kosovo and other areas. Still the invasion was fairly controversial in the US and many members of Congress, the media and other public figures claimed Reagan was using the military to divert public attention from his failings elsewhere, principally in Lebanon.

The government of Grenada was controlled by the Marxist-Leninist, New Jewel Movement that had seized power in 1979 and was closely allied with Cuba and the Soviet Union. In early October of 1983, a more radical faction of the New Jewel Movement, led by Bernard Coard and General Hudson Austin attempted to wrest power from the more moderate, but popular prime minister, Maurice Bishop. Bishop was placed under house arrest on October 14, but at the same time Coard resigned from government, perhaps because he did not want his fingerprints on any action taken against the charismatic leader. Regardless, Bishop's imprisonment and Coard's resignation threw the nation into chaos. A few days later, on October 19, a

Diversionary Theory and the Political Use of Military Force 175

crowd marched on the residence where Bishop was being held and demanded his release. They succeeded in freeing their leader, who then led them on a march to a military base where Bishop wrested control of some small arms from the troops. It is not clear if government troops then fired on Bishop and the crowd following him, if Bishop fired first in an attempt to capture the fort, or if Bishop was simply recaptured. Regardless, he and several of his supporters were killed by government forces. Some accounts have depicted what followed as a 'raging civil war' (Meese, 1992, p.214), but other than a 24-hour curfew on the island, neither the government nor the opposition took any significant action.

The US had been watching Grenada carefully for several years and had even staged military maneuvers in the Caribbean that simulated an invasion of a small island, but it was members of the Organization of Eastern Caribbean States who sounded the alarm bells. The State Department then engineered an invitation from the OECS asking for a US intervention in Grenada. On Saturday, October 21, Secretary of State George Schultz was informed that there had been an official request for intervention. The administration would have to act quickly before word of the request and planning for the invasion leaked out. The Reagan administration diverted a naval task force that had been heading to the Mediterranean to bolster US forces in the aftermath of the bombing of the Marine barracks in Lebanon. Reagan then gave the go-ahead for the operation on Sunday, October 22, after he learned of the attack on the US military compound in Lebanon (O'Shaughnessy, 1984).

Operation Urgent Fury began on Wednesday, October 25. US Marines were sent in to take the north part of the island, while Army Rangers captured the southern portion, which included the medical school where 800 US citizens took classes. Elite teams of Navy Seals slipped into the capital, Georgetown, to find and protect the Governor General of Grenada, Sir Paul Scoon, capture the radio station and free political prisoners. Later Army paratroopers were flown in to mop up, secure the island and prepare the way for the token, OECS force. While OECS participation was important politically, for it gave the operation some legitimacy, the contribution of OECS forces was limited almost exclusively to police duties and guarding captured Cuban and Grenadian forces. The operation was mostly over by midday on October 27. In all, approximately 6000 US forces took part in the intervention (O'Shaughnessy, 1984). Urgent Fury was described mostly as a resounding military and political success, although problems with equipment, communications and bad intelligence (the US demolished a mental hospital and killed most of its patients after mistaking it for a military fort) and some initial resistance from Cuban and Grenadian troops all created problems. In some respects, the more important battle for public opinion took place later as the Reagan administration attempted to justify the massive assault on the obscure, tiny island. It is the inadequacy of these explanations and the timing of the event so closely on the heels of the debacle in Beirut that led many to charge the Reagan administration with using military force for domestic political purposes.

In a speech before the nation, Reagan cited three reasons for invading Grenada. First, he claimed that the lives of 1000 Americans on the island, most of

176   The Political Use of Military Force in US Foreign Policy

them medical students, were at risk. Reagan did admit that while the students' lives were not in any imminent peril, the chaos on the island and the government's willingness to use violence against its own people created a situation rife with danger. Reagan argued that the invasion was necessary because the students and others had no way off the island. On Monday, October 23 two days before the invasion, however, four flights had come and gone at the international airport taking some foreigners and a small minority of the medical students who wished to leave (Speakes, 1988). Most stayed behind because they did not feel they were in any danger. On Sunday, October 22, US officials in the Caribbean reported back to Washington that the students did not want to interrupt their studies and leave the island. Furthermore, the US mission in Barbados, which handled US relations with many of the small eastern Caribbean islands, had not even told Americans to leave Grenada (O'Shaughnessy, 1984, p.166). The president's press secretary, Larry Speakes, had said the day before the invasion that US citizens were in no danger. In his memoirs, Speakes doubted the wisdom of the invasion and whether the students were in any danger (1988, p.161). Thus, many in the US were skeptical at first of Reagan's claims about endangered Americans. The image of a student kissing American soil upon arrival in the US shortly after the invasion, however, seemed to vanquish doubts about the necessity of the invasion. 'I don't want to hear anyone criticize those American soldiers. They saved our lives, man', one student proclaimed (O'Shaughnessy, 1984, p.176). Still, the lives of US citizens were never really in jeopardy until the invasion and fighting began on their campus. It was never clear if their relief was a result of being evacuated out of a war zone or the events preceding the invasion.

Reagan also argued that the invasion was justified to prevent further chaos and assist in restoring law and order. Yet, with the exception of the killing of Bishop and his followers, there was hardly any bloodshed on the island. The twenty-four hour curfew saw to that. There was no raging civil war. Instead, as events developed, it became clear that the Reagan administration was mostly concerned about the presence on the island of several hundred Cubans who were helping to expand Grenada's international airport. Among the 784 Cubans were 47 military advisers (O'Shaughnessy, 1984, p.15). The rest were construction workers who had received training in the Cuban army reserves, although the Reagan administration charged that they were all heavily armed and dangerous (Burrowes, 1988, p.87). Interestingly enough, the Reagan administration acknowledged the necessity of expanding the runway at the airport when it later helped fund the project. But, Fidel Castro was just as opposed as the other Caribbean states to the deaths of Bishop and his associates and did not support the change in government (O'Shaughnessy, 1984, pp.150-151). The violence of October 19 represented a timely pretext for confronting a minor, but manageable nuisance to US foreign policy in the Western Hemisphere. According to one contemporary report of the invasion:

> In a sense, the Reagan administration has been looking for a situation like Grenada from the day it took office. Senior foreign policy officials say that this is an administration that has felt a need–indeed, a compulsion–to demonstrate the use of

Diversionary Theory and the Political Use of Military Force 177

American power, especially in the Western Hemisphere...Despite official statements that the prime motivation was to protect American citizens in Grenada, this operation, more than anything else, sends a strong message to both Nicaragua and Cuba that this is an administration that is ready and willing to use military force to achieve its objectives.[30]

The communist beachhead in Grenada may have appeared to some Reagan administration officials as a major Soviet/Cuban asset, but in the global balance of power, Grenada barely registers.

Few watching international events at this time could not help but draw a connection between the bombing of the US Marine barracks in Beirut, Lebanon and the invasion of Grenada, which took place just three days later. The bloody incident took the lives of 241 Americans, but other US soldiers had been killed previously in Lebanon and the US embassy had been leveled, killing another 63 people. To many it seemed the Reagan administration was attempting to deflect public criticism of its confused, and now costly Middle East policy with an easy foreign policy victory elsewhere. Reagan himself tied the two events together in his speech to the nation on October 26 when he charged that both had their ultimate root causes in Soviet support for international communism and terrorism. Support for Reagan's policies in the Middle East was extremely low and it looked to many like the US was sinking into the same sort of quagmire that had engulfed the US in Vietnam. The Pentagon initially was resistant to the Grenada mission and wanted to focus only on rescuing American citizens because of the deepening involvement in Lebanon. The impetus for the invasion seems to have come more from the State Department, which was looking for an opportunity to hand the communists a setback and assert American power in the wake of the debacle in Lebanon. To what extent their desire to use force was motivated more by domestic public opinion rather than international credibility is difficult to say. Both were important to an administration that was so identified with increasing American strength and respect for its military.

Assessing the Evidence

The Moroccan affair of 1904 certainly demonstrates the president's ability to profit domestically from events overseas. President Theodore Roosevelt did not necessarily enter into this hostage crisis conniving to exploit the events for his political advantage in an election year. Yet, once events rose to the level that military force would likely be needed, he did make a show of his actions for public consumption and perhaps went further in his actions than was necessary because of a desire to play to the grandstands. Indeed, some critics have even charged that 'TR hoodwinked the conventioneers and the public–and spent taxpayers' money–for political gain' (Chapman, 2002, p.14). We also know that TR knew when he sent his final ultimatum to Tangier that Perdicaris was not an American citizen, and yet

---

[30] *Newsday*. October 10, 1983, p. 6.

178   *The Political Use of Military Force in US Foreign Policy*

he was still willing to continue pressing the case militarily and was prepared to launch an invasion of Morocco. Furthermore, the State Department had declined an opportunity to free Perdicaris earlier in the negotiating process. Raisuli had indicated that Perdicaris would be let go, although other non-US citizens would remain. The State Department declined because it did not wish to guarantee Perdicaris's safety on the return journey (Foreign Relations of the US, 1904, 499). Other options for resolving the crisis short of massive displays of force were available. Thus, once the crisis was underway, some of TR's decisions did seem to reflect a domestic political calculus.

But while TR did clearly profit politically from his assertion of American military power, it is more difficult to conclude that domestic political incentives significantly contributed to the decision to use force or that they provide a unique perspective toward understanding US foreign policy in this case. Presidents had used force to protect and rescue Americans overseas many times in the past. British warships were also sent to Tangier for the same reason. In fact, Raisuli was certainly counting on this sort of international action and pressure to assist him in gaining his ransom. Furthermore, Roosevelt did not know at the time that he ordered the first deployment of naval vessels to Tangier that the crisis would drag out all the way to the Republican Convention and allow him to rally the party. And when he learned that Perdicaris was not an American citizen he decided to continue with the show of force and threaten invasion because he believed American credibility had already been engaged. Those watching the events unfold at home and abroad believed Perdicaris was a US citizen, and because Raisuli had 'done deliberate violence to the whole concept of American citizenship' (Morris, 2001, p.334), Roosevelt took action. What does seem fairly obvious is that the extremely media savvy TR seized a great opportunity and some choice words from his Secretary of State to demonstrate American power to the world and his own power and energy to the American people. Thus, while political motives may color presidential and even military decisions regarding the manner in which a military operation is presented to the public, this sort of stage management does not therefore imply that diversionary motives inspired the military action. The public relations aspect of many government policies is, we would suspect, important to presidents.

The use of force in the 1973 Yom Kippur War illustrates another important feature of many crises in which we may suspect diversionary behavior. To what extent is the president actually involved in the crisis decision-making? Far from being ready to seize the Middle East war as a pretext for diverting public attention from the Watergate juggernaut, in October of 1973 Richard Nixon was a president obsessively distracted by his troubles and disengaged from the nation's foreign policy. It was Henry Kissinger who was in charge of the day-to-day running of diplomacy. Nixon would *sometimes* sign off on the diplomatic proposals and military maneuvers engineered by his subordinates, but often he was indisposed when the crucial decisions were made. Kissinger routinely made decisions on his own, and occasionally even ignored Nixon's instructions. As well, some of Brehznev's dispatches were addressed to Kissinger and not Nixon. This exchange in Kissinger's (1982, p.585) account of the night of the Soviet threat to

Diversionary Theory and the Political Use of Military Force   179

intervene militarily is telling: 'I asked Haig whether I should wake up the President. He replied curtly: 'No'. I knew what that meant. Haig thought the president too distraught to participate in the preliminary discussion. It was a daunting responsibility to assume. From my own conversation with Nixon earlier in the evening, I was convinced Haig was right'. While Kissinger and Haig described Nixon as distraught over Watergate, others were not so charitable in their depictions of his mental state. Summers (2000, p.460) cites Kissinger aides as claiming the president was drunk at the time the decision was made to go to DEFCON 3. Others describe him during this period as sitting in White House rooms with the air conditioning cranked up so he could enjoy a soothing fire. Even Nixon's own memoirs make no mention of his involvement in the NSC deliberations. The president was deliberately left out of the meeting in which the US military response to one of the most critical Cold War crises was formulated.

Is it possible that Nixon's aides and advisers sought to use the crisis to Nixon's advantage? Could they have engaged in a diversionary use of force on Nixon's behalf? Interestingly, Kissinger notes in his account that he wished the change in alert status to be visible to the Russians, but not to the American people. As in the September, 1970 Middle crisis, he wanted the change in status kept secret until after the crisis was over. He did not want a public showdown with the Soviet Union that might force the Russians to dig in their heels rather than lose face in front of the world. As he wrote in his memoirs (1982, p.591), 'This unexpected publicity would inevitably turn the event into an issue of prestige with Moscow, unleashing popular passions at home and seriously complicating the prospects of Soviet retreat'. The NSC wanted to underscore US opposition to any potential Soviet moves in the region, not engage in brinkmanship diplomacy. Kissinger was angered when news of the nuclear alert splashed all over the newspapers the next day. Rather than wishing to use the military alert to distract the public, Kissinger and the NSC did not even want the public to notice the action.

In the final analysis, Nixon's standing and trust among the public and media was so low at this point in time that probably nothing could have rescued him. In fact, Kissinger was quite convinced that it was the Soviets who were exploiting the crisis because of Nixon's domestic problems. He wrote, 'I could not avoid the conviction that Nixon's evident weakness over Watergate had not a little to do with the Politburo's willingness to dare so crass a challenge' (Kissinger, 1982, p.584). A failure to respond under such circumstances could only embolden adversaries to exploit one's weaknesses even more. Presidents may find it necessary to use force in moments of domestic crisis not because they wish to appear strong to the American public, but because they need to appear resolute to the international community. Thus, while there is circumstantial evidence that might well lead one to conclude Richard Nixon resorted to military force because of domestic troubles, the more convincing evidence would seem to indicate that he

180   *The Political Use of Military Force in US Foreign Policy*

was not directly involved in the decision and those who made the choice did not even want the operation to become visible to the public.[31]

In the case of Grenada there are few, compelling reasons, other than the Reagan administration's fear of communism in the Caribbean and aversion to looking weak to the world to adequately explain the intervention. Few would doubt that Reagan and his advisers were passionate about communism in the region and flexing America's military might. But, aside from its location in the Western Hemisphere there is nothing really about Grenada, except the timing of its upheaval, to explain why it suddenly became so important. There was Soviet-Cuban involvement on Grenada, but this tiny speck of land was not about to tip the balance of power, even in the East Caribbean.

Additionally, when we seek to find exculpatory evidence that domestic politics did not affect the decision, we come up short. We do know that the crisis on Grenada and planning for the invasion began before the bombing in Beirut, but the decision by Reagan was made only after the terrorist attack had occurred. Thus, we cannot escape the possibility that Reagan was influenced by the attack to intervene. Perhaps the most accurate characterization of the justification for the Grenada invasion that we can draw is that the Reagan administration in its ceaseless striving to project an image of strength abroad and at home, conflated the two. Reagan may not have invaded Grenada because he wanted a quick boost in his public approval ratings, but because he had long portrayed himself as a resolute defender of American interests, a failure to respond may well have been portrayed as timidity. Having created expectations in the public, Reagan was not in a position to disappoint. The attack in Lebanon made this all the more imperative for he was well aware of how the Middle East had contributed to his predecessor's image of weakness. Reagan's standing among the public was on the rebound from its nadir during the 1982 recession, but it still stood at only 47 percent at the time of the October troubles. Rather than using force to boost his approval ratings, Reagan may have acted in part to prevent a decline in them. This sort of calculation is undoubtedly in the back of most presidents' minds when they are confronted with international crises. But perhaps no recent president was so responsible himself for creating the expectation of strong action. The evidence is stronger here that domestic politics played an important role in the invasion of Grenada. Unfortunately, we cannot readily decipher whether it was the president's need to avoid a loss to his personal reputation, or the president's desire to enhance his domestic standing.

Based on the evidence from these three case studies, I would conclude that the evidence regarding the effect of domestic politics on presidents' decisions to use force is weak to modest. Diversionary political incentives were not a necessary or sufficient for the use of force. The evidence in the Grenada case was

---

[31] It is possible that Kissinger's recollections of the events are self-serving and designed to highlight his importance and protect his former boss. Still, all accounts of the decision making leading up to the decision to go to DEFCON 3 indicate that Nixon was not at the meeting and only signed off later on the proposal.

Diversionary Theory and the Political Use of Military Force   181

strongest, but still falls short of what we might consider to be empirically falsifiable findings. Nonetheless, we still must be mindful of the fact that domestic political considerations may remain obscured from us, and that we should not reach any final conclusions on their impact based upon case studies. It may also be the case that while the evidence may be slight in any one case, when viewed across hundreds of cases presidential decision making, their impact is more noticeable. These summaries do illustrate several important points regarding presidential decision making in the domestic context.

First, we see that crises at home may demand the president's energies to the exclusion of almost all other matters, providing little time for foreign policy. Crises and subsequent uses of force may, however, be exploited for domestic consumption, especially by media savvy presidents like Teddy Roosevelt and Ronald Reagan. Perhaps the efforts of presidents who wage such effective public relations campaigns on behalf of a use of force help contribute to the suspicion that public opinion motivated the use of force. In general, presidents who demonstrate expertise in managing the public and press may find their motives for using force questioned precisely because of their cleverness. Lastly, the case studies illustrate that domestic crises may encourage international ones and create greater foreign policy incentives to use force. Still, diversionary scholars might argue that we are missing the forest for the trees by engaging in case study analyses. The custom in diversionary theory research has been to use aggregated data on crisis decision making to search for an increased likelihood of using force during troubled times. I next turn to an examination of these data to analyze the evidence for diversionary theory.

The Evolving Role of Domestic Politics in US Foreign Policy

We cannot speak of a 'history' of the diversionary use of force in American foreign policy in the same way we can discuss the history of the liberal idealist tradition. It is not a strategy for engaging the outside world so much as it is a tactic for avoiding internal problems. It is not a foreign policy doctrine that has been or even could be debated and analyzed openly such that the scholarly community could assess its causes and consequence. When we look for historical evidence of diversionary behavior, we look for the revealed secrets of presidential decision-making, for few presidents would ever wish their ignoble political ambitions to become a matter of public record. Such a muckraking exercise makes little sense since, if presidents do use force for domestic political purposes, the greater their motivation to do so, the more reason there is to believe they will keep their deliberations entirely private. If it is unlikely we will find the 'smoking gun' that would prove the existence of diversionary behavior, we must look instead for circumstantial evidence. We must examine how conducive the domestic political environment has been to diversionary behavior.

In theory, leaders of all countries possess incentives to engage in diversionary behavior–some more so than others–because all rely on the continued support of some constituency. Even dictatorships of the one or the few must have the backing of some group(s), however small for their continued tenure and may resort to aggressive action abroad to rally their supporters. Witness the Argentinean government's 1982 assault on the Falkland Islands in the midst of a regime crisis. Democratic governments, however, *may* be more susceptible to such behavior. Democratic leaders face regular, popular elections and a constant barrage of opinion polls that serve as continuing referenda on their leadership. Ever mindful of the need to maintain popular support to further power, policy and electoral goals, these leaders may seek out opportunities to demonstrate their competence abroad. In theory then, George Washington faced the same basic motives to use force as Bill Clinton. But are the domestic conditions necessary for diversionary behavior constant across time and space? Or, are there reasons to suppose that the incentives and the opportunities to engage in diversionary behavior have varied over the course of US history?

At a minimum, diversionary behavior requires motive, opportunity and capability. Presidents must wish to act aggressively to deflect attention from their failings and they must show some demonstrable cause for using force, although such things may occasionally be manufactured. The ability to use force to affect domestic politics, however, was more limited prior to the 20th century, principally because of the difficulties of communication. If a president wished to use force to deflect attention from a particular, domestic problem, or to create an image of strength for an upcoming election, he would need some method by which to transmit information and orders to and from his military officers about foreign events, learn their location, and relay his commands regarding the actions they should take. In almost all cases this would have been quite difficult. The transmission of such information in the days before radio communication or even the telegraph were fairly limited. When naval vessels were out to sea, their captains were often incommunicado from the White House. As well, their vessels might be far away from the scene and require substantial time to reach a crisis hot spot. The President might not receive word about some international crisis until it had been resolved. If he were made aware of troubles in South America or Asia, he would have to find some way to send orders to his commanders in time for them to act before it was too late. And even if the President received word about some crisis and was able to order a military response, he still would have found it difficult to be sure that word of the US military action would spread through the American press in time to rescue him from his political troubles at home. Identifying an international crisis to exploit, ordering the military into action in a timely manner, and getting word of a (hopefully) successful military action back to the American public in time to affect the president's political fortunes was a fairly tall order in the 19th century.

Diversionary behavior also assumes that there are domestic problems a president would like the public to overlook. Economic problems are the most obvious type, especially issues like unemployment and inflation. The 19th century witnessed a number of extreme swings in the business cycle and a host of other problems that accompanied industrialization. But if the excesses of expansion and retraction at one time or another affected almost all Americans, they did not always affect people across the nation simultaneously. Before the US developed a fully integrated, *national* economy, inflation and recession were often regional problems. Farmers in the Midwest might be suffering from a drop in agricultural prices, but the manufacturing sector in the Northeast could be doing quite well. Hence, if economic problems were often local, there would be fewer incentives for a president to engage in diversionary behavior aimed at a national audience.

In addition, for much of American history, presidents were not as knowledgeable about the depth of their support in the country. Public opinion polls did not come onto the scene until the 1930s and did not become reliable until the 1950s. Before then presidents could gauge their public support from personal sources, newspapers, and election results, but nothing as systematic, timely and reliable as public opinion polls. Absent good and continuous information about the depth of public dissatisfaction with his leadership, the typical 19th and early 20th century president would have less cause to engage in diversionary behavior. I do not mean to suggest that economic problems were unimportant or that presidents were ignorant about their popular standing before the modern era, just that presidents had less reliable and simply less information about their national audience that would have provided them with the proper incentives to engineer a diversionary use of force. As well, because information traveled so slowly, presidents might not always be cognizant of their domestic woes soon enough for them to take action to change popular perceptions. And if the president might be somewhat ignorant about the level of his national, public support, so too was the Congress. And if the Congress was not so attuned to the shifting political winds of the nation, the incentives for individual members of Congress to not support the president because of public attitudes were diminished as well.

Nonetheless, while the president's ability and need to *order* the use of force for diversionary purposes and profit from such actions may have been more limited in the 19th century, it was not altogether impossible to *exploit* military actions for political gain. When some international crisis was brought to the attention of the public, the president might make a big show at home of the dispatch of military forces to resolve the dispute. The press could also be manipulated to presidential advantage to a greater extent in those days as well. One such crisis arose during the Andrew Jackson administration. On February 7, 1831, the US ship, *Friendship* of Salem, Massachusetts, captained by Charles M. Endicott was docked at Quallah Batoo in what is now Malaysia. Captain Endicott went ashore with some of his men to buy pepper and left a subordinate in charge. Unfortunately, the officer let some armed Sumatrans on aboard who then killed three merchantmen, injured six, and looted the ship. The captain recaptured the ship with the aid of some of the merchantmen who escaped, but was not able to gain restitution from the local chiefs for the $41,054 worth of goods that had been plundered (Long, 1973). When the American public learned of this, it clamored for revenge and '...immediate redress of this outrage' (Long, 1973, p.149). President Jackson ordered the frigate, *Potomac,* under the command of Captain John Downes, to sail half way around the world to Quallah Batoo to demand compensation from the natives. Failing that, Captain Downes was to punish the

Sumatrans for their lack of respect to the commercial interests and honor of the US. The *Potomac* sailed from New York City and cheering crowds on August 26, 1831 with fifty mounted guns and 500 sailors (Long, 1973). Such flag-waving parades of tall ships leaving the harbor to exact revenge on the enemies of America no doubt bolstered support for the president among the patriotic crowds. But such cases were more about presidents exploiting rather than using force for domestic gain.

Several developments in the 1930s and 1940s, however, made the presidency a much more public office, and made presidents more aware of the effects of their actions on the nation. The rise of mass media–radio, television and film–that could reach nearly all Americans made the president much more of a public figure. Simultaneously, the creation of national opinion polling made the president and everyone else constantly aware of the effect of his actions on the people. The perpetual election that the mass media and polling created encouraged presidents to undertake far more public activities to maintain support (Kernell, 1993). Knowing that their actions would be instantly known, and thus could be turned into political capital in relatively short order, presidents possessed substantial incentives to engage in highly visible actions that would rally the nation. In the days before a mass media could report on the activities of military units half-way around the world in a timely fashion, presidents had little hope an exercise in gunboat diplomacy could deflect attention from immediate and pressing concerns at home. But with near instantaneous communication of words, and especially pictures, presidents could undertake actions abroad for the audience at home with the hope of an immediate, political payoff. The essential elements were all finally in place for diversionary behavior beginning in the Cold War era. The US possessed greater capabilities for power projection than at any time in its history. A national economy, greater and continual presidential awareness of his standing with the American public, and a media that reported his every move all created substantially greater domestic incentives to engage in diversionary behavior. The superpower competition with the Soviet Union encouraged presidents to develop numerous foreign policy interests throughout the world, which made it easier to find a convenient pretext for using force.

One final feature of this most recent era deserves comment. Before the Vietnam quagmire and the Watergate scandal created a great deal of cynicism and skepticism about national politics in general and the president in particular, the public tended to look upon presidents more favorably and the press tended to report more positively on their activities. At a minimum, greater deference was given to their office and their statements. The country was more likely to trust the president's explanations for using force and accept the need for action. This was also the era of congressional bipartisanship in foreign policy. The Congress often provided near-unanimous support for operations like the 1958 invasion of Lebanon and the 1964 Tonkin Gulf Resolution. This changed with Vietnam when the public and the press discovered that official Washington had been deceptive about US involvement in that conflict and the likelihood of success. Watergate further soured the national mood and increased public and media skepticism about presidential explanations for their foreign policy actions. Facing a cynical and savvy audience, presidents in the post Vietnam era would find it more difficult to engage in military operations designed primarily for domestic consumption. As Rose (1991, p.9) points out, the media can, 'put the White House on trial any night of the week'. In a sense, there may have been something of a 'golden age' of opportunity for the diversionary use of force between 1945 and 1973 when the public was more likely to uncritically rally around presidential leadership. Absent that loyalty, presidential motivations for using force are often challenged by a nation wise to 'October surprises' and the 'wag the dog' scenario.

A Statistical Overview: Diversionary Theory and the Use of Force

I believe it is quite useful to analyze diversionary theory using more descriptive statistics, especially regarding relationships and hypotheses where there is significant scholarly disagreement. While such numbers can neither falsify nor confirm that domestic politics play a significant role in decision making, they can reveal simple trends in the data that are often obscured in more complex analyses. I examine the relationship between presidential popularity, the unemployment rate, the inflation rate and elections and the use of force. As the unit of analysis, I use data on international crises from 1948-1998 to which presidents may or may not have responded with a use of force for these simple descriptive statistics, as well as in the probit analysis that follows. By doing so, we can distinguish how presidents were influenced to respond to international events in different ways depending on domestic politics. I begin by briefly reviewing our expectations regarding the influence of domestic conditions on the use of force.

Presidential Popularity

Perhaps the most visible and critical indicator of presidential support is the president's approval rating as measured by numerous polling organizations. The percentage of the public that expresses its approval of the way in which the president is handling his job provides a quick and reliable gauge of popular sentiment. Researchers who claim that presidents use military force to increase their approval ratings have argued that we should find an inverse relationship between popularity and the use of force (e.g., DeRouen, 1995, 2000). Other researchers, however, have argued that presidents will be more likely to use force when their popularity ratings are high because they will not wish to act in the absence of support (e.g., James and Oneal, 1991; Morgan and Bickers, 1992; Ostrom and Job, 1986). Other scholars, including the author, have concluded that there is little relationship between popularity and the use of force (Meernik, 1994; Meernik and Waterman, 1996). I will posit the standard diversionary hypothesis:

186   *The Political Use of Military Force in US Foreign Policy*

Hypothesis 15: There will be a negative relationship between presidential approval ratings and the use of force.[32]

First, I ran a simple bivariate correlation between approval ratings and the likelihood of a use of force, given some opportunity or international crisis from 1948 through 1998. The simple bivariate correlation between presidential approval ratings and the likelihood of a use of force is .07, but is not statistically significant at the .05 level (results not shown). This relationship is, however, directly at odds with what we would expect from diversionary theory. Presidents should be more likely to use force as their approval ratings decline if they are attempting to deflect public attention from their failings. This result suggests instead that more popular presidents are more likely to use force, and although others have found this same relationship (Morgan and Bickers, 1992; Ostrom and Job, 1986), it would seem to contradict the notion of a diversionary use of force. As these scholars have argued, presidents may believe that the authorization of military action is politically more palatable when they enjoy public support, but such a view of presidential decision-making suggests that presidents are actually risk-averse–precisely the opposite of the risk-acceptant diversionary theory of decision making.

---

[32] I use presidential approval ratings obtained from the Gallup organization web site at http://www.gallup.com for all years to create a monthly average. Since accessing this web page originally, however, the Gallup organization has now begun to charge users for access to their data. Other organizations, however, such as Roper, do provide these same data. http://roperweb.ropercenter.uconn.edu/

Diversionary Theory and the Political Use of Military Force

Table 5.1 Presidential Popularity and the Use of Force, 1948-1998

Approval Ratings	Use of Force	All Cases
20-29%	4 25%	16
30-39%	28 60.9%	46
40-49%	80 58%	138
50-59%	87 49.7%	175
60-69%	73 54.5%	134
70-79%	55 58.5%	94
80-89%	1 50%	2
TOTAL	318 52.5%	605

$\chi^2 = 12.1$, p. > .05
gamma = .097, p > .05

188   *The Political Use of Military Force in US Foreign Policy*

Table 5.2 Presidential Popularity, the Use of Force and Presidential Administration, 1948-1998

Approval Ratings President	Less Than 50%		50% or Greater	
	Force	All Cases	Force	All Cases
Truman	7 28%	25	4 26.7%	15
Eisenhower	1 100%	1	49 60.5%	81
Kennedy	0	0	35 63.6%	55
Johnson	11 50%	22	28 63.6%	44
Nixon	6 37.5%	16	10 26.3%	38
Ford	7 36.8%	19	1 16.7%	6
Carter	15 46.9%	32	5 38.4%	13
Reagan#*	32 82.1%	39	42 59.2%	72
Bush	8 53.3%	15	16 44.4%	36
Clinton	15 48.4%	31	26 56.5%	46
Total	102 51%	200	216 53.3%	405

= Statistically significant χ^2
* = Statistically significant gamma coefficient / For RWR = -.519

This slight, positive relationship is noticeable in Table 5.1, which presents the percentage of the time presidents used force across various levels of popularity. I collapsed the approval measure into six categories (0 percent thru 29 percent, 30-

Diversionary Theory and the Political Use of Military Force 189

39 percent, 40-49 percent, 50-59 percent, 60-69 percent, and 70-100 percent. When popularity falls below 40 percent, presidents are slightly less likely to use force. Most noticeably, when presidential popularity is between 20 percent and 29 percent, presidents use force only one quarter of the time. When their approval ratings are 40-49 percent, presidents are generally more likely to use force. All the percentages vary only slightly between 49 percent and 58.5 percent in these categories, which mirrors their overall likelihood of using force–53 percent. The trend in presidents' willingness to use force because of their standing among the public is slight.

Perhaps the relationship between popularity and the use of force varies among presidents because of personal, historical or idiosyncratic causes–some individual presidents may have been willing to use force for diversionary purposes, while others have not been. I undertook an examination of presidential popularity for each president, but instead of measuring presidential popularity by the decile (which resulted in many empty cells), I collapsed the Gallup measure into two values–below 50 percent and 50 percent or greater. These results are presented in Table 5.2. For Truman, Eisenhower and Kennedy we see little evidence of any trends. Truman was equally unlikely to use force whether his popularity ratings were above or below 50 percent. There was only one crisis during the Eisenhower administration when the president's approval ratings fell below 50, while John Kennedy never had to confront a situation in which his approval ratings fell below 50 percent. It is not until Lyndon Johnson's administration that we detect a slight trend. LBJ was more likely to use force when his approval ratings were above 50 percent—he used force 63.6 percent of the time on these occasions–than he was when his popularity dipped below 50 percent—he used force only 50 percent of the time in these cases. Richard Nixon did not use force that often in either case–he used force 37.5 percent of the time when his performance did not meet with general approval, and 26.3 percent of the time when he was supported by a majority of the public. There is little data from which to drawn any solid conclusions about Gerald Ford's behavior. Jimmy Carter, however, was somewhat more likely to use force when his popularity ratings fell below 50 percent—he used force 46.9 percent of the time in these cases versus the 38.4 percent of the time he used force when his ratings were above 50 percent. Ronald Reagan exhibits a similar and even more pronounced proclivity to take action when he is suffering in the polls. Reagan used force 82.1 percent of the time when a majority of the public disapproved of his job performance, and 59.2 percent of the time when the public did back him. President Reagan used force quite frequently early in his administration at the same time he was suffering in the polls because of serious economic problems. In 64 crises in his first term in office, Reagan used force 46 times (71.8 percent), while in his second term he used force on 28 occasions in 46 crises (60.8 percent). George Bush also used force more often when he was down in the polls–53.3 percent of the time–than when he was doing well–44.4 percent. But the relationship reverses during the Clinton administration. Clinton uses force slightly more often when he is doing well in the polls. We see slight evidence of a trend in support of the diversionary theory–presidents Carter through Bush tended

190   *The Political Use of Military Force in US Foreign Policy*

to use force more often when they were supported by less than a majority of the public. Nonetheless, with the exception of the Reagan administration, there were no statistically or substantially significant relationships between this measure of presidential popularity and the use of force according to the χ^2 statistics and the gamma coefficients.

Table 5.3 Change in Presidential Popularity and the Use of Force, 1948-1998

Change in Approval	Use of Force	All Cases
-33 thru -20	8 33.3%	24
-19 thru -10	46 59.7%	77
-9 thru -1	108 54.8%	197
0	28 68.3%	41
1 thru 9	116 51.6%	225
10 thru 19	10 28.6%	35
20 thru 30	2 33%	6
Total	318 52.5%	605

$\chi^2 = 19.0$, p. $< .01$
gamma $= -.10$, p. $> .05$

Next, I examined the relationship between change in approval (the difference in approval at the time of the international crisis minus the approval rating six months prior) and the use of force. The simple correlation coefficient between change in approval and the likelihood of a use of force is -.04, which is statistically insignificant (results not shown). Table 5.3 displays the frequencies of uses of force across various levels of change in approval ratings. I grouped together the change in approval ratings measure into various categories: -33 percent through -20 percent; -19 percent through -10 percent; -9 percent through -1 percent, 0 percent, 1 percent through 9 percent, 10 percent through 19 percent, and 20 percent through 33 percent. Negative values indicate that a president's approval ratings are

Diversionary Theory and the Political Use of Military Force   191

falling. This ordinal measure of change in popularity, however, is statistically significant according to the χ^2 statistic. In addition, the gamma statistic, which measures the strength of the relationship is negative (-.10), indicating that presidents are more likely to use force when their approval ratings are falling (although it is not statistically significant). We see that when a president's popularity has been falling precipitously (-33 percent through -20 percent), he is unlikely to use force (only 33 percent, given an international crisis), but when the fall is not quite so severe, presidents become more likely to use force. Presidents use force 59.7 percent when the decline in their approval ratings is between 19 percent and 10 percent. The trend fluctuates up and down in the range between -10 percent and 9 percent, but generally presidents are more likely to use force when changes in popularity are moderate in size. When the president's political situation is improving dramatically—when change in popularity is between +10 percent and +30 percent—presidents are distinctly less likely to use force. Presidents use force 28.6 percent of the time when the increase is between 10 and 19 percentage points, while they use force two times in six when the increase is between 20 and 30 points. This does accord with diversionary theory and the findings of other scholars (James and Oneal, 1991; Ostrom and Job, 1986). We would expect presidents whose reputation is declining might take action to reverse the downward slide.

Unemployment and Inflation

We find a similar variety of argument and evidence when we study the relationship between the US economy and the limited use of force. On the one hand we might suspect presidents would wish to deflect public concern over increasing unemployment and inflation rates by capturing their attention with a popular display of military force. This might rally the public behind the president and against the American adversary and cause people to forget their differences and problems to confront the external threat. On the other hand, if the economy is the problem, the President may be focusing his time and energy and the government's resources to address the nation's ills. It may be the President is too absorbed in repairing the economy to seek out enemies abroad. He may even fear that military diversions in search of monsters to destroy will be greeted with skepticism and complaint rather than flag-waving applause. The evidence mirrors these contrasting arguments. There are those who report a direct and positive relationship between unemployment and inflation and the use of force (James and Oneal, 1991; Ostrom and Job, 1986); there are scholars who find an indirect relationship between the economy and the use of force mediated by presidential popularity (DeRouen, 1995; 2000), the president's political party (Fordham, 1998a, 1998b), or democratization and wealth (Miller, 1995); and still other researchers report a negative relationship (James and Hristoulas, 1994). And, of course, there are some, including the author, who find no relationship (Meernik, 1994, 2000, 2001; Meernik and Waterman, 1996). Once again, I will restate the standard diversionary hypotheses:

Hypothesis 16: Increasing unemployment rates will be positively associated with the use of force.

Hypothesis 17: Increasing inflation rates will be positively associated with the use of force. [33]

I begin with the simple correlation coefficient between each variable and the likelihood of a use of force. The correlation between unemployment and the use of force is .12 and is statistically significant, while the correlation between inflation and the use of force is -.11, and is also statistically significant (results not shown). The negative relationship in the latter case runs counter to what almost all scholars hypothesize–that a worsening economy makes presidents more likely to engage in diversionary behavior. In fact, many combine the inflation and unemployment rates into a single misery index, despite the fact that their relationships to the use of force are different. Fordham (1998a), however, does argue that the effects of these indicators will differ depending on which party occupies the White House. He argues that Democratic presidents should be more likely to use force during times of high inflation, while Republican presidents have been more likely to engage in diversionary behavior during periods of high unemployment. To test the validity of this hypothesis I computed correlation coefficients between each economic indicator and the use of force for Democratic and Republican presidents. The direction of the relationships stayed the same for Democratic presidents, but both coefficients became statistically insignificant. On the other hand, the relationships between the economy and the use of force for Republican presidents retain their direction and statistical significance. The correlation between unemployment and the use of force is .15, while the correlation between inflation and the use of force is -.141 (results not shown). These findings support Fordham's hypothesis (1998a) that Republican presidents would be more likely to use force during times of high unemployment, and less likely in times of high inflation.

Perhaps, however, some Republican presidents have been especially prone to use force and preside over periods of high unemployment. To investigate this possibility and to determine if there were any other peculiar relationships among presidents, the economy and the use of force in the data, I created several tables that distinguish between high, medium and low levels of inflation and unemployment to create an ordinal measure based on the 33rd and 67th percentiles of these data. This allows us to determine the propensity of individual presidents, as well as Democratic and Republican presidents in general, to use force during these different periods. I begin by looking at the relationship between unemployment and the use of force for each president.

---

[33] Data on unemployment were downloaded from the Department of Labor's Bureau of Labor Statistics web page at http://stats.bls.gov/top20.html. The inflation rate was calculated from Consumer Price Index data downloaded from the Department of Commerce's Bureau of Economic Analysis web page at http://www.bea.doc.gov/.

Diversionary Theory and the Political Use of Military Force 193

Table 5.4 Unemployment and the Use of Force By President, 1948-1998

| | Unemployment | | |
	Low Force/All Cases	Medium Force/All Cases	High Force/All Cases
Truman	7/32 21.9%	4/6 66.7%	0/2
Eisenhower	26/48 54.2%	17/25 68%	7/9 77.8%
Kennedy	0/0	26/42 61.9%	9/13 69.2%
Johnson*	32/58 55.2%	7/8 87.5%	0/0
Nixon	9/30 30%	7/24 29.2%	0/0
Ford	0/0	1/3 33%	7/22 31.8%
Carter	0/0	13/24 54.2%	7/21 33.3%
Reagan	1/2 50%	15/22 68.2%	58/86 67.4%
Bush Sr.	5/10 50%	9/19 47.4%	10/22 45.5%
Clinton	15/28 53.6%	21/37 56.8%	5/12 41.7%
Total	95/208 45.7%	120/210 57.1%	103/187 55.1%

= Statistically significant χ^2
* = Statistically significant gamma coefficient / For LBJ = .701

Table 5.5 Inflation and the Use of Force By President, 1948-1998

| | Inflation | | |
| | Low | Medium | High |
	Force/All Cases	Force/All Cases	Force/All Cases
Truman	5/15	0/6	6/19
	33.3%		31.6%
Eisenhower	34/58	16/24	0/0
	58.6%	66.6%	
Kennedy	35/55	0/0	0/0
	63.6%		
Johnson*	28/39	8/20	3/7
	71.8%	40%	42.9%
Nixon	0/0	3/8	13/46
		37.5%	28.3%
Ford	0/0	0/0	8/25
			32%
Carter	0/0	0/0	20/45
			44.4%
Reagan	12/14	39/62	23/34
	85.7%	62.9%	67.6%
Bush Sr.	0/0	10/20	14/31
		50%	45.2%
Clinton	10/18	31/59	0/0
	55.6%	52.5%	
Total	124/199	107/199	87/207
	62.3%	53.8%	42%

\# = Statistically significant χ^2
* = Statistically significant gamma coefficient / For LBJ = -.507

Diversionary Theory and the Political Use of Military Force   195

Table 5.6 Presidential Party, Unemployment and the Use of Force, 1948-1998

		Republicans Use of Force	Democrats Use of Force
	Low	4/90 45.6%	54/118 45.8%
Unemployment	Medium	50/95 52.6%	70/115 60.9%
High		81/137 59.1%	21/49 42.9%
Total		172/322 53.4%	145/282 51.4%

For Republicans

$\chi^2 = 4.0$, p. $> .05$

gamma $= .18$, p. $< .05$

For Democrats

$\chi^2 = 7.1$, p. $< .05$

gamma $= .06$, p. $>$ .05

Table 5.7 Presidential Party, Inflation and the Use of Force, 1948-1998

		Republicans Use of Force	Democrats Use of Force
	Low	47/74 63.5%	77/125 61.6%
Inflation	Medium	67/112 59.8%	39/86 45.3%
	High	58/136 42.6%	29/71 40.8%
Total		172/322 53.4%	145/282 51.4%

For Republicans

$\chi^2 = 11.2$, p. $< .01$
gamma $= -.29$, p. $< .001$

For Democrats

$\chi^2 = 9.6$, p. $< .01$
gamma $= -.29$, p. $< .001$

Table 5.4 presents evidence on the relationship between unemployment and the use of force for individual presidents. Harry Truman had the good fortune to preside over a period of high employment, and consequently the vast majority of the opportunities occur during such times. He only used force approximately 22 percent of the time when unemployment was low. Data on his propensity to use force at higher levels of unemployment are too sparse to draw any reliable conclusions. Eisenhower was more likely to use force regardless of the level of unemployment, although he is more apt to use the military in times of medium and high unemployment. There is almost no difference in JFK's willingness to use force, although the national economy was more prone to medium and high unemployment during these years. LBJ is more likely to use force when unemployment is at low levels, and nearly always uses the military when the unemployment rate is moderate (87.5 percent of the time). There were no opportunities that occurred during Johnson's tenure when unemployment was high. Richard Nixon also held office during years of high employment, but he is generally unlikely to use force regardless of the state of the economy. Again, there

Diversionary Theory and the Political Use of Military Force 197

is little data on Gerald Ford's administration, but during the Carter administration we once again see a period of economic retraction. Carter confronted opportunities to use force only when unemployment was at moderate or high levels. He appears to be the only Democratic president whose behavior supports Fordham's (1998a) hypothesis. Carter is more likely to use force when unemployment is at moderate levels and less likely to deploy the military when a significant percentage of the public is out of work. Ronald Reagan, whose presidency also occurred at a time when unemployment was never low, is very consistent in his propensity to use force. During times of moderate unemployment, he deploys the military 68.2 percent of the time while during periods of high unemployment that figure is 67.4 percent. President George Bush was equally likely to use or not use force during periods of low and medium unemployment, and slightly less likely to use force when unemployment rates were high. We see more fluctuation in the likelihood of a use of force during the Clinton administration. Clinton uses force 53.6 percent of the time when unemployment is low, 56.8 percent when unemployment is moderate, and 41.7 percent of the time when it is high. Most of these individual relationships were neither statistically insignificant nor strong based on the χ^2 and gamma statistics, with the exception of LBJ.

We see in Table 5.6 that in general, Democratic presidents are most likely to use force when unemployment is moderate–60.9 percent of the time, and use force at almost exactly the same level when unemployment is either low or high–42-45 percent of the time. Contrarily, Republican presidents demonstrate an increasing willingness to use force as unemployment increases in keeping with Fordham's arguments. When unemployment is low, they tend slightly not to use force, and when it is moderate, Republicans tend to slightly favor using force. When unemployment is high, Republican presidents generally prefer to use force. Presidents Eisenhower and Reagan demonstrate the greatest willingness to use force during these periods. Thus, there appears to be a simple bivariate relationship between unemployment and the likelihood of a use of force for Republican presidents using this ordinal measure of unemployment. However, the χ^2 is statistically significant only for the Democratic presidential table. The gamma statistics are never significant. We will see later if this relationship holds up in the presence of other variables.

Many of the same patterns that were in evidence in the previous tables are apparent when we look at how presidents' propensity to use force is affected by inflation. Harry Truman is still unlikely to use force, regardless of the level of inflation. Dwight Eisenhower generally does use force, but did not have to contend with periods of high inflation. Even luckier is President Kennedy, whose term coincided with one of the most non-inflationary periods during the Cold War. Opportunities to use force only occurred when inflation was low. LBJ, however, occupies office during a time of varying inflation. He was unlikely to use force during times of medium and high levels of inflation, but often used force (71.8 percent), given the opportunity when inflation was low. Undoubtedly, this period of low inflation occurred before the Vietnam War led to a decline in the use of force elsewhere, but during the crisis-laden years of the mid 1960s. Richard Nixon

198 *The Political Use of Military Force in US Foreign Policy*

was in the Oval Office when the full inflationary effects of the Vietnam War hit home. There were a few opportunities to use force when inflation is moderate–most occur when inflation is high. Nixon is distinctly unlikely to use force on these occasions perhaps due to the war effort. Gerald Ford, who launched the infamous, 'Whip Inflation Now' campaign, is president only when inflation is quite high. Jimmy Carter met a similar fate–inflation was always high during his presidency. As was noted previously, he was slightly less likely to use force in general. We see variation once again during the Reagan administration. He generally used force regardless of whether inflation was moderate or high, but he demonstrates a pronounced tendency to engage in military action when inflation is low–85.7 percent of the time. This would also tend to support Fordham's thesis that Republican presidents will be more apt to take domestic economic measures to confront inflation than engage in aggression abroad. Finally, neither George Bush nor Bill Clinton exhibit any unusual patterns. Both tend to use force at roughly the same rate regardless of the level of inflation.

Finally, I again look at the general trends among Republican and Democratic presidents to use force, contingent upon inflation in Table 5.6. Republican presidents are likely to use force when inflation is low or moderate and unlikely to use force when it is high, as Fordham suggests. The χ^2 is statistically significant, as is the gamma, which is -.31. This indicates a marked decrease in Republican presidential willingness to use force when inflation is on the rise. Democrats are most likely to use force when inflation is low, but unlikely to use it when inflation is moderate or high, which runs counter to Fordham's thesis. Clearly, the differing impact of the unemployment and inflation rates on the use of force require further investigation for they support the research of some (Fordham, 1998a; Yoon, 1997), but contradict the findings of other scholars (James and Oneal, 1991; Ostrom and Job, 1986; Wang, 1996). More importantly, we see that unemployment and inflation have different effects on the use of force. Therefore, we cannot assume that economic problems, regardless of their nature (as diversionary theory implies), increase the likelihood of diversionary behavior.

Elections

Perhaps the most enduring, popular image of the diversionary use of force is the 'October surprise'–that specially timed display of military might designed to rally the nation just before it goes to the polls. Do presidents seek out enemies overseas or stage foreign adventures during such times? Some scholars find evidence of an increased willingness to use force during these times (Ostrom and Job, 1986; Smith, 1996a, 1998; Stoll, 1984; Wang, 1996), but most of the researchers cited previously find the relationship to be weak or non-existent. Presidents confront the same sorts of incentives and disincentives for a diversionary use of force. A well-timed, quick, relatively painless, effective and justifiable use of force could well cause the country to unite behind its leader and his party. How difficult would it be for a president to pull off such a use of force? The operation would have to occur in fairly close proximity to the election, or the public would probably forget about it later (witness George Bush in 1992). The use of force would have to be over in a short period of time lest it appear the nation was being dragged into some sort of protracted conflict that might conjure up images of Vietnam. There would have to be relatively few casualties given the public's aversion to loss of American lives. The use of force would have to result in some sort of tangible benefit or at least appear effective. A military strike against terrorists would work best to rally the public if the targets were actually hit. And finally, the military operation would have to be justifiable, which is perhaps the most significant hurdle. Given a skeptical public warned all too often about 'October surprises', and a suspicious, scandal-seeking national press, presidents will have to provide compelling evidence that vital interests were at stake. In the absence of such justification, there might well be a public backlash against the president. Nonetheless, I restate the diversionary hypothesis:

Hypothesis 18: Presidential election periods will be associated with the use of force.

I briefly examine presidential willingness to use force using several measures of elections periods, including: 1) presidential election years, 2) presidential election periods [August, September and October of presidential election years], 3) presidential *re*-election years, and 4) presidential and congressional election periods [August, September and October of all even-numbered years].

First, presidents are not more likely to use force in any kind of election year or election period according to the correlation coefficients (not shown). None of these coefficients was even remotely close to statistical significance. In Table 5.8 we see that they use force 51.2 percent of the time during presidential election years; 46.5 percent of the time during presidential election periods; 53.6 percent of the time during presidential re-election years and 57 percent of the time during all presidential and congressional election periods. Of all the domestic political relationships we have examined thus far, these are the most trivial. With all the usual caveats regarding the possibility of conditional and indirect relationships, we must conclude that there is virtually no evidence of a relationship between election periods and the use of force.

In general, there is only ambiguous evidence of bivariate relationships among domestic conditions and the use force. Even though I found some evidence to indicate presidents were more likely to use force when their popularity was declining and when unemployment was on the rise, the size of their impact is quite small. In addition, when approval levels are high, presidents are very slightly more likely to use force, which runs completely counter to the logic of the diversionary theory. In general, when we strip the hypothesized relationships down to their most basic elements, we see that whatever trends do exist are slight. While the statistics are simple and the data on the use of force do differ slightly from some studies, there would appear to be few obvious and simple relationships between domestic politics and the use of force.

Table 5.8 Presidential Elections and the Use of Force, 1948-1998

Presidential Election Years	Use of Force
Yes	86/168 51.2%
No	232/437 53%

Presidential Election Periods	
Yes	20/43 46.5%
No	298/562 53%

Presidential Re-election Years	
Yes	67/125 53.6%
No	251/480 52.2%

Presidential and Congressional Election Years	
Yes	45 / 79 57%
No	273/526 51.9%

No statistically significant χ^2 statistics or gamma coefficients.

Testing Diversionary Theory, 1948-1998: Probit Analysis

Having studied the link between domestic factors and presidents' inclination to use force through fairly simple bivariate analyses, I now examine these same relationships through probit analysis. I use the same data on the use of force from 1948-1998 that I used above and in previous chapters where the international crisis is the unit of analysis. The overall fit of the diversionary model is modest–the

Diversionary Theory and the Political Use of Military Force   201

likelihood that all the coefficients are equal to zero is extremely slight, but the pseudo R^2 is only .02. The domestic factors associated with the diversionary model correctly predict 58.8 percent of the cases for a 13.2 percent proportionate reduction of error. The model predicts 38.3 percent of the non uses of force correctly and 77.3 percent of the uses of force correctly.

Table 5.9 Predicting Uses of Force 1948-1998 Using Probit Analysis: The Diversionary Theory Model

Variable	Coeff.	Standard Error	T Statistic	P Value	Marginal Effect
Presidential Popularity	.0046	.0046	0.99	0.321	.0018
Unemployment	.1310	.0344	3.81	0.000	.0521
Inflation	-.0496	.0183	-2.70	0.007	-.0197
Election	-.1052	.2033	-0.52	0.605	-.0419
Constant	-.7603	.3767	-2.02	0.044	
N=605					

$\chi^2 = 23.5$, p. < .001
Pseudo $R^2 = .02$
Percent Correctly Predicted = 58.8%
Proportionate Reduction of Error = 13.2%

The coefficient for the unemployment variable ('Unemployment') is statistically significant and positive, which is what we might expect given the assumptions of diversionary theory. With every one-unit increase in the unemployment rate, presidents become 5 percent more likely to use military force. This is the one finding that does lend credence to diversionary theory. Presidents may wish to deflect the attention of those concerned or affected by joblessness to the international arena through a timely display of military force. As I discussed earlier, however, the first term of the Reagan presidency during which there were many uses of force and very high levels of unemployment might be partially responsible for this trend. I entered a control variable for this period, but the relationship between unemployment and the use of force held up (results not shown). Presidents, particularly Republican ones, show a marked tendency to use force during times when a significant percentage of the population is out of work. In fact, there are four distinct periods when unemployment has been high while Republicans have been in office. These are the late 1950s, the mid 1970s, the early 1980s and the early 1990s. During the Eisenhower and Reagan administrations, force was used quite often, while during the Ford administration, force was rarely employed. President George W. Bush tended to use force at levels near the historic average.

As we saw earlier, presidents are increasingly *unlikely* to use force as inflation rises. With each one point increase in the rate of inflation, presidents are correspondingly .019 percent less likely to use force according to the marginal effects coefficient. This finding runs counter to what most researchers have argued. If presidents are led to use force for diversionary purposes, we ought to find that as the US economy suffers, uses of force become more attractive. That we find presidents do not behave in this manner is good from the perspective of the general public and the economy. Most citizens would prefer and the economy would presumably recover better if the president was fully engaged in addressing the inflationary pressures instead of casting about for foreign enemies to attack. Like Fordham, I also created interaction variables for unemployment rates during Republican presidential administrations and inflation rates during Democratic presidential administrations to assess the degree to which economic causes of diversionary force are contingent on the party occupying the White House. When these variables were entered into the model, however, all coefficients save the inflation rate itself became statistically insignificant. The inflation rate and the interaction affect with Democratic presidents was jointly significant, but that relationship was opposite what Fordham hypothesizes. Democratic presidents are distinctly less likely to use force when inflation is on the rise. We do know that the 1970s were a time of high inflation and few uses of force. Presidents Nixon, Ford and Carter were among the least likely to authorize military operations. The only president who matches their unwillingness to use the military is Harry Truman, who also presided over times of high inflation (especially in 1948, and during the Korean War).

Presidents are neither more nor less likely to use force as their popularity level rises or falls. Contrary to the expectations of those who believe that presidents are more likely to use force as their approval ratings decline, and those who believe that presidents will be more apt to use force when they have strong public support, I find that the relationship between these two measures is close to zero. Perhaps this occurs because of these conflicting incentives and necessities. Perhaps the contradictory effects of these competing dynamics average out the aggregate relationship to very little. I would argue, however, that while popularity may in *some* instances encourage or discourage a use of force, it is not powerful enough in a particular situation to cause a use of force and not influential enough across all opportunities to register a consistent impact. I also checked to see if there was a relationship between change in popularity and the use of force, but this coefficient too was statistically insignificant. This variable was left out of the model because of its collinear relationship with the level of popularity measure.

Finally and once again, upcoming elections do not seem to provoke diversionary behavior. The coefficient for this variable is also statistically insignificant. Of the 43 opportunities to use force that occurred in the months leading up to presidential elections, presidents used force on 20 occasions (46.5 percent). It seems reasonable to suppose that given public skepticism and media scrutiny, an 'October surprise' might actually do more harm than good. In addition, what president would want to be forced to attend to foreign policy matters in the middle of the most time-consuming and stressful part of an election campaign?

Diversionary Theory and the Political Use of Military Force   203

Once we examine the (dis)incentives for this type of diversionary behavior, it seems apparent that the logic behind this hypothesis, while theoretically defensible, is in a practical sense, quite dubious.

Conclusion

Domestic politics do affect presidential decision making in foreign policy, although it is not obvious here. But what can we say with confidence about the nature of the relationship between a president's domestic standing and the likelihood of a use of force? First, it is highly unlikely that domestic politics are sufficient or necessary conditions for using force. Such conditions probably never exercise a decisive impact on presidential decision making either. Without any plausible national security objective, presidents would find it perilous to use force. Threats to national interests may be exaggerated to bolster the justification for dispatching the military, but they cannot be conjured up out of whole cloth especially in the age of mass media and a skeptical public. Domestic political incentives probably do not exercise a decisive impact on the use of force–they are unlikely to move any president to use force, except perhaps those who are already *almost* willing to authorize a military deployment. Second, it is highly unlikely we will find a smoking gun to provide the crucial evidence to prove a president used force for diversionary purposes. The diversionary theory can probably never be verified or falsified. Third, I would argue that it is presidents who appear to be most distracted by their domestic problems. Foreign policy is probably an afterthought to presidents who must deal with scandal, recession and elections. Fourth, given that one can reconcile diversionary theory with any manner of positive, negative, conditional or non-linear relationships between domestic conditions and the use of force, it is unlikely we will find compelling and consistent evidence of statistically significant relationships. The cumulative weight of the difficulties inherent in testing diversionary theory should make us cautious about asserting the primacy of any one particular relationship.

As I argued at the beginning of this chapter, I believe that if we wish to understand how domestic conditions generally affect presidential decision making regarding the political use of military force, we should reframe the question. Instead of seeking to explain when domestic conditions encourage presidents to use force, we should study when domestic conditions *allow* presidents to use force. In other words, when are domestic politics quiescent enough, the domestic economy prosperous enough, and public opinion internationalist enough to make the political use of military force feasible? Obviously there will always be occasions in which the president will be compelled to use force to respond to severe threats to national security. Conversely, there will be some international events when the threat to US interests is weak or non-existent and where presidents will almost never use force. Presidential decisions in these cases will be largely automatic and unlikely to be influenced by domestic, political considerations. It is the large, discretionary realm of decision making in between these extremes that concerns us.

204 *The Political Use of Military Force in US Foreign Policy*

What do presidents do when international conditions are neither so threatening as to demand action nor so innocuous as to be unsuitable for military force? The characteristics of the international event to which the president is considering dispatching military personnel will weigh heavily and may ultimately determine what he does. But under those circumstances where the president's decision is not already dictated by the international environment, there exists room for domestic politics to exercise some influence. In general, I believe that presidents will more likely be constrained by domestic conditions from using force. If unemployment and inflation are on the rise, the president's approval ratings are sinking, or an election is in the offing, presidents will be too absorbed with these matters to seek out foreign enemies. Such conditions may make a use of force somewhat less attractive and thus slightly less likely. On the other hand, if the economy is doing well, the president enjoys the support of the public, and the country is not in the midst of a fall campaign, we would not expect the president to be predisposed to either use force or not use force because of the state of the domestic environment. Rather, its influence would seem to be neutral. It would permit him the ability to focus more on foreign policy and to use force when he saw fit. Thus, domestic conditions either constrain or merely 'allow' presidents to use force, but per se, do not increase the likelihood of a use of force.

I would suggest viewing the president's decision making during international crises the following way. First, domestic politics create a fundamental parameter governing the latitude with which presidents may act internationally. At one end of this continuum is an isolationism, which permits little executive action (e.g., the US in the 1930s), while the opposite end is marked by a body politic demanding of action (e.g., the US prior to the Spanish-American War). Next, within such eras, domestic conditions may be characterized as more or less constraining the use of force. Presidents who are well-regarded already, preside over a prosperous economy and do not face upcoming elections are better equipped to convince the public of the need to use force in the broad range of moderately important crises. At a minimum the domestic political environment would not militate against a political use of military force. Those presidents who are concerned more with a further erosion of public confidence because they preside over a troubled nation, should be less likely to use force in general.

Finally, we should consider the ease with which the president can justify a use of force with reference to national security interests. The greater the challenge to US interests, or the more odious the international perpetrator, the easier it will be for the president to 'sell' the use of force to the public. I would argue that the more severe the domestic threat to the president, the more severe the international crisis will have to be to plausibly justify an American response. For example, the public would probably be unwilling to countenance a massive invasion of an obscure country to avenge a single loss of American life if the president was in the process of being impeached (although stranger things have happened). The difficulty for the president is that while his domestic woes may make a high-level use of force politically untenable, a low-level use of force that is entirely commensurate with the nature of the threat may go unnoticed by the public and do him little good.

Paradoxically the president has the greatest latitude for acting when he least needs it domestically, and the least discretion when he most needs it.

Having circumscribed the president's options, we could estimate a tentative baseline of domestic acceptability for a political use of military force. This baseline may help us account, in part, for presidents' proclivity to use force across time and in specific situations. The public's level of internationalism/isolationism and its support for the president should help us estimate the frequency of uses of force over time. Measuring the severity of the threat to national security, and the extent to which it makes a 'discretionary' a use of force for diversionary purposes more/less likely can best modeled on a case-by-case basis. Having accounted for these conditions in specific situations, we may then assess the degree to which the domestic environment constrains or allows a political use of military force. The evidence thus far would suggest that the impact of these conditions is marginal at best, but we still have further tests to perform.

Chapter 6

Comprehensive Analysis of the Political Use of Military Force in US Foreign Policy

Introduction

We have discussed and analyzed the four, most prominent theories of the political use of military force short of war in US foreign policy. Through argumentation, descriptive statistics and preliminary model testing, I have sought to explain the strengths and weaknesses of these explanations. These theories are both complementary and competitive. They are complementary in that no one theory claims a near perfect and complete accounting of the use of force, and thus it is possible for each theory to be 'right' about some cases. They are competitive in that some of their claims are mutually incompatible. For example, many realists and neorealists would deny that the president's popular approval ratings are an important determinant of military security policy. Many Marxist/Leninist and dependency theory scholars would argue that economic imperialism dominates US foreign policy to the exclusion of other factors. Comprehensive understanding of the reasons why presidents use force demands all four theories be analyzed and assessed together. Too often our research on the political use of military force has focused on the testing of single theories to the detriment of other perspectives. In this chapter I hope to show that hypotheses derived from each of the four theories should be tested together and that the variables from these theories add to the overall explanatory power of our predictions of presidential decision-making.

First, I briefly review the data on the use of force in the pre World War II years, 1798-1941 to assess the relative performance of the four models. Then I analyze the four models in the Cold War and beyond, 1948-1998. I review the results of the individual hypothesis tests and the joint hypothesis tests for the groups of variables. I assess the successes and shortcomings of the model by examining its ability to correctly predict presidential decision-making. Next, I examine the importance of other factors that might affect the likelihood of a use of force. I conclude by assessing how the theories might be improved or modified, and where future research should concentrate.

Comprehensive Analysis of the Political Use of Military Force 207

Assessing the Theories, 1798-1941

Here I briefly review what we have learned about the frequency with which presidents have used force for various objectives in the pre World War II era. In Table 6.1 I have grouped the Congressional Research Service (1993) data according to the type of foreign policy goals pursued across time periods, while in Table 6.2 I group the data on use of force objectives by region. It bears repeating that it is possible that multiple foreign policy objectives can be associated with any one use of force. Therefore, the column percentages in both tables may exceed 100 percent.

Table 6.1 Uses of Force to Advance Foreign Policy Goals Across Historical Periods

	1798-1865	1866-1898	1899-1918	1919-1941	Total
Protect US Citizens	34 56.7%	25 75.8%	29 60.4%	15 48.3%	103 60%
Protect/Expand Territory	10 16.7%	1 3%	4 8.3%	4 12.9%	19 11%
Protect Govts.	1 1.7%	2 6.1%	12 25%	10 32.2%	25 14.5%
Protect US Honor	3 5%	0	0	0	3 1.7%
Prevent War	0	0	0	1 3.2%	1 .6%
Promote Commerce	35 55%	20 66.7%	26 54.2%	9 32.2%	90 52.3%
Promote Liberal Idealism	2 3.3%	0	20 41.7%	6 19.4%	28 16.3%

Note: column percentages exceed 100 percent because multiple goals may be involved in uses of force.

Table 6.2 Uses of Force to Advance Foreign Policy Goals Across Regions

	US	Central America/ Caribbean	South America	Middle East	Africa	Europe	Asia
Protect US Citizens	1 9.1%	30 47.6%	15 83.3%	12 100%	2 50%	1 12.5%	42 75%
Protect/Expand Territory	10 90.9%	3 4.8%	1 5.6%	0	0	2 25%	3 5.4%
Protect Govts.	0	12 19%	3 16.7%	0	0	5 62.5%	5 8.9%
Protect US Honor	0	2 3.2%	0	0	0	0	1 1.8%
Prevent War	0	1 1.6%	0	0	0	0	0
Promote Commerce	1 9.1%	41 65.1%	14 77.8%	5 41.7%	1 25%	3 37.5%	25 44.6%
Promote Liberal Idealism	0	18	0 28.6%	0	2 50%	1 12.5%	7 12.5%
Total Uses of Force in Region	11 6.4%	63 36.6%	18 10.5%	12 7%	4 2.3%	8 4.7%	56 32.6%

Note: column cell percentages may exceed 100 percent because multiple goals may be involved in uses of force. Column totals reflect the total number of uses of force in the region. Column cell frequencies may sum to greater numbers because multiple goals may be involved in uses of force.

As we can readily see in Table 6.1, the two most commonly pursued objectives of the use of force short of war in the pre-modern era were the protection of American lives (60 percent) and the protection/advancement of American commerce and property (52.3 percent). Often, the US pursued these two objectives in tandem, and so there is a fair degree of overlap between them. Altogether, these two objectives account for 132 of the uses of force, or 76.7 percent across all these years. Both objectives were pursued jointly on 61 occasions. Presidents used force to protect lives, but not commerce in 42 instances. They used force 29 times to protect commerce, but not lives. Presidents used force

Comprehensive Analysis of the Political Use of Military Force 209

to advance liberal idealist interests on 28 occasions in total (16.3), mostly in the 1899-1918 time period. They also used force 25 times to protect friendly governments (14.5 percent). Territorial integrity or expansion accounted for 19 uses of force (11 percent). The other foreign policy goals were sought in only a small number of instances.

That we should find the need to protect American lives is the most frequent objective of the use of military force should come as no surprise since it is perhaps the ultimate purpose of any military. When presidents use force for such purposes they are following the dictates of the US Constitution, which makes the President as Commander-in-Chief responsible for the protection of the nation and its peoples. If presidents left Americans overseas to the mercies of local governments, rebel fighters or terrorist groups, they may well signal a dangerous degree of disengagement and weakness in international affairs that might tempt further violence and attacks. Any president who would allow US citizens to become helpless victims of violence overseas would not only endanger all Americans living overseas, he would imperil American properties and other interests as well.

That we find the protection of commerce and property itself to be such an important objective of US foreign policy throughout this period is somewhat more unusual or surprising. As I argued in Chapter Three, many analyses of the limited use of force, especially quantitative ones, have given such economic objectives short shrift. In fact, presidents have been keenly interested in protecting American economic assets throughout history. They have done so more as the strong friend rather than the lackey of American business interests as some scholars have alleged. Throughout the period 1798-1941, the US military functioned as sort of a global police force for Americans and their property abroad. When local police or national authorities could not be relied upon to provide such protection, presidents believed they must. If a government could not control its own territory, the US has traditionally believed it then forfeited some measure of sovereignty and must accept international assistance. This was also, of course, the same argument the US used to acquire territory from Spain when that country would not control (to US satisfaction at least), the Floridas.

But while uses of force designed to protect US lives and commerce served both a short-term interest in physical protection, and a long-term interest in deterring future attacks, there were also multiple uses of force aimed at *promoting* commerce. The former type of operation tended to be more reactive in nature, while the latter style of the use of force has been more proactive. Perry's mission to Japan, the 1871 operation to Korea, and many of those interventions in the 1899-1918 era aimed to change the economic policies of foreign governments as well. Thus, in contrast to the many policing type uses of force designed to protect/prevent harm, these uses were aimed at promoting change. As such, they had much more profound consequences for both the US and the nations that were targeted for they involved larger military forces, were much more sustained operations, and sought more fundamental and long-term change in regime policies. The military operations aimed at achieving liberal idealist ends share these traits

210   *The Political Use of Military Force in US Foreign Policy*

for here as well presidents sought to change some of the basic policy goals and institutional designs of foreign governments. For this reason and because of their frequency, the historical uses of force that sought to promote commerce deserve much more scrutiny. Peceny's analysis (1996) on proliberalization military operations by the US provides a rich history of this type of endeavor. An analogous study of pro-commerce operations is also needed.

A geographical overview of the use of force shows once again that most such operations took place in Central America and the Caribbean (63, or 36.6 percent), and Asia (56 or 32.6 percent). A considerably smaller number were authorized in South America (18, or 10.5 percent), and the Middle East (12, or 7 percent). Conversely, very few uses of force occurred in Sub-Saharan Africa (4) and Europe (8). Eleven uses of force took place on or around the continental US. Overall, the geographical distribution of uses of force in terms of foreign policy goals tends to mirror what we saw in Table 6.1, although there are some interesting exceptions. First, notice that the vast majority of uses of force that occurred in South America pertained to the protection of American lives (83.3 percent) and/or commerce (77.8 percent). We see similar numbers in the case of Central America. Presidents used force in this region for few very other reasons. They also generally used force for the same such purposes in Asia, although the promotion of commerce is a distinctly secondary goal (44.6 percent) compared to the protection of US citizens (75 percent). When force has been used in the continental US, it has almost always been to protect or expand US territory (90.9 percent).

The geographical distribution of uses of force in this era tends to reflect several important trends in the location of US interests. First, the use of force tends to follow where private US citizens and their assets were going, but also where they were most likely to come into danger. There has generally been a significant amount of trade, as well as turbulent politics in Central America, South America and Asia. Thus, we see presidents using force to provide protection to Americans and their commercial interests. Where the American presence was smaller, as in the whole of the African continent, there is much less need for the use of force. Second, relative American power, particularly vis a vis its major European competitors, may explain the relative lack of such operations there. Given the weakness of the US Navy compared to those of the major European nations, as well as the US's almost complete inability to field ground troops that might come ashore in Europe and contest local forces, it would have been foolish, if not suicidal for presidents to authorize military operations against the European powers for whatever reason. Indeed, five of the eight military operations that did take place in and around Europe occurred as the US prepared for World War II–some of the last uses of force in the pre-modern era.

In general, we might say that presidents tended to use force primarily in reaction to foreign events for much of the pre Spanish-American War era. Just as nations reserved the right to deal with lawlessness on the high seas as they saw fit, presidents believed they had the right to deal with restive natives in parts of the world where there was no government, as they needed to protect lives and property and occasionally exact revenge. This same conception of a right to defend its interests was also extended to those countries that, while they might have

Comprehensive Analysis of the Political Use of Military Force 211

governments, their leaders were incapable of safeguarding US interests, or were viewed as not sufficiently 'advanced' to be trusted with such responsibilities, as in the Americas and China. While the US certainly had a foreign policy strategy premised on what we might consider to be its national interests, presidents tended to use the military more often for short-term, tactical goals. The economic interest model and the protection of American lives dominate the rationale for using force before 1898. After the Spanish-American War, those interests are still dominant, but increasingly we see presidents using force for more long-term strategic goals. Whether it is in the development of stable, free market democracies in Central America, or in the protection of friendly governments, the growth of US influence and its acquisition of global interests demanded that presidents be cognizant of US power and responsibilities in the world. Traditional 'realist' type foreign goals, as well as liberal idealist interests assume increased importance in the first age of US internationalism, and even into the isolationist years before World War II. Now we must turn to analyzing what degree of impact all such foreign policy goals exercised in the years of American hegemony when presidents have had the power and opportunity to pursue all manner of objectives.

Comprehensive Analysis of the Modern Era, 1948-1998

I use the statistical software package, Intercooled Stata 8.0, to generate the results.[34] The dependent variable–measured as the presence or absence of a

---

[34] In previous research (Meernik 2000, 2001), I have employed selection models that predict when crises will occur, and given the occurrence of a crisis, when the president will use force. Selection effects are a serious issue in the study of the political use of military force, but confronting this issue also creates substantial modeling costs. Because crises can potentially arise anywhere at anytime, predicting their occurrence is difficult. We end up having to utilize variables related to the international or domestic environment at the time of a crisis (e.g., presidential popularity, unemployment, US involvement in war [Clark, 2003; Meernik, 2000, 2001]). Predicting multiple crises in a given period of time is even more difficult. The upshot is that when using selection models or Zero Inflated Poission models, our ability to make use of information relating to a particular crisis when predicting the use of force is severely limited by the level of analysis we use in predicting crises. We must either predict one crisis for a given month, quarter or year, and ignore instances where there are multiple crises occuring (e.g., Meernik, 2000, 2001), or we can utilize only environmental factors and ignore crisis-specific factors (e.g., Clark, 2003). Because my interest in this research is to predict why presidents use force, I am most interested in analyzing all potential explanations and uses of force, and thus the modeling strategies just described are not appropriate. I would note that there are strong similarities between what is found here and what I have found in other research regarding crisis occurrence and the use of force.

212   *The Political Use of Military Force in US Foreign Policy*

political use of military force given an opportunity to use force–is measured in the same manner and using the same data from the period 1948-1998 as in the previous four chapters. Table 6.3 contains the results of the model predicting the decision to use force using all the same variables from the previous four chapters. One of the most important indicators of the explanatory power of the entire model is the percentage of correctly predicted cases. I predict 75.2 percent of the cases–both uses of force and non uses of force–correctly using the probit estimates. The model predicts 73.8 percent of the non uses of force correctly and 76.4 percent of the uses of force correctly. While this indicates that the model performs better than simply guessing that 50 percent of all cases result in a use of force, a better benchmark to evaluate the results against would be the modal prediction. In this case, if we were to predict the modal category of the dependent variable in each instance, we would be correct 52.5 percent of the time–the percentage of time presidents used force. If we compare the predictive accuracy of the model against this benchmark, there is a 47.7 percent proportionate reduction of error. The likelihood ratio statistic, which tells us the probability that all the coefficients are equal to zero, is quite large and thus the probability of a poor fit is extremely low. The pseudo R^2 is .23. The reader may note that the results in the comprehensive model differ somewhat from the results obtained when the hypotheses were tested separately in the previous four chapters. In particular, a few of the coefficients lose their statistical significance in the presence of other variables. I have indicated with an asterisk those coefficients that had been found to be statistically significant previously.

The Security and Power Model

The dominant variables in the analysis are those pertaining to US security interests. All five coefficients are statistically significant, and with the exception of 'US Power', are in the predicted direction. In addition, the likelihood that all these coefficients are equal to zero is infinitesimally small according to the likelihood ratio test. As we saw in Chapter 2, 'Prior Use of Force', 'Number of Crisis Actors' and 'Anti-US Violence' are all strongly positive predictors of the likelihood of a use of force. All indicate the extent to which US interests and credibility have been engaged in an opportunity to use force. A prior use of force increases the probability of a current use of force by 9 percent in any given crisis, according to the marginal effects coefficient. In a sense, this variable measures the degree of US commitment to a particular nation or an ongoing, international dispute. During the Cold War presidents and other foreign policy makers continually asserted that American credibility and/or its reputation as a guarantor of another nation's security was at stake whenever some regime threatened the US or an ally. Having once used force against these adversaries, presidents often felt compelled to respond again to prevent an erosion of confidence in the American security system, both locally and globally. This need or willingness to respond with force time and again helps explain why we find many of the same nations involved in crises with the US. I return to this point later.

Table 6.3 Testing All Four Theories, 1948-1998

Variable	Coefficient	Standard Error	T Statistic	P Value	Marginal Effect
*US Relative Power	-5.278	1.777	-2.97	0.003	-2.093
*Prior Use of Force	.2300	.1400	1.64	0.100	.0904
*Number of Crisis Actors	.3177	.0426	7.45	0.000	.1260
*Anti US Violence	.9307	.1374	6.77	0.000	.3421
*US War Deaths	-.0627	.0219	-2.86	0.004	-.0249
Non Violent Economic Dispute	.2734	.3284	0.83	0.405	.1058
*Attack on Economic Interests	.8130	.3763	2.16	0.031	.2822
*US Economic Aid	.0005	.0002	2.05	0.041	.0002
OPEC Member State	-.1860	.2010	-0.93	0.355	-.0740
*Regime Transition	.2649	.1534	1.73	0.084	.1037
*Change in Democracy	.0507	.0297	1.71	0.088	.0201
Democracies & International Wars	.3610	.3042	1.19	0.235	.1379
*Democracies & Civil Wars	-.2581	.3167	-0.82	0.415	-.1027
*Widespread Societal Violence	-.2725	.1666	-1.64	0.102	-.1083
Popularity	-.0034	.0054	-0.63	0.532	-.0013
*Unemployment	-.0119	.0566	-0.21	0.833	-.0047
*Inflation	-.0803	.0226	-3.55	0.000	-.0318
Presidential Election	-.2155	.2463	-0.87	0.382	-.0858
Constant	.4062	.7933	0.51	0.609	

N=605
χ^2 = 196.2, p. < .0001
Pseudo R^2 = .23
Percent Correctly Predicted = 75.2%
Proportionate Reduction of Error = 47.7%
* = previously found to be statistically significant

Security Variables Likelihood Ratio χ^2 = 125, p. < .001
Economic Interest Variables, Likelihood Ratio χ^2 = 11, p. < .05
Liberal Idealist Variables, Likelihood Ratio χ^2 = 10, p. < .06
Diversionary Variables, Likelihood Ratio χ^2 = 14.6, p. < .001

Anti-US violence, or the threat of it, increases the likelihood that a president will use military force in a crisis by 34 percent, holding other variables constant at their mean value. Previously we had seen that the protection of American lives was the most frequent aim of limited uses of force from the early years of the Republic through the beginning of World War II. In the post Cold War world and in the aftermath of September 11, 2001, the protection of US

214   *The Political Use of Military Force in US Foreign Policy*

citizens abroad is still one of the top US foreign policy objectives.[35] Interestingly, the reader will recall that we saw in Chapter 2 that anti-American violence and threats of it increased the probability of a use of force in the modern era by 34 percent. Thus, regardless of the presence of many other conditions related to the limited use of force, the size of the effect of anti-American violence remains virtually identical.

Each additional crisis participant increases the chance of a use of force by 12 percent, all other things being equal. The number of state actors involved in a given crisis may range from between one and 10. Thus, even though each additional crisis participant may increase the probability the president will use force by a modest amount, the cumulative effect is considerable. The critical turning point in the effect of this variable on the use of force occurs as the number of crisis actors moves from three to five states. Presidents more often do not use force when the number of crisis nations is three (force is used 47 percent of the time); they are just slightly more willing to use force when four nations are involved (force is used 59 percent of the time); but they are quite likely to use force when five nations are involved (85 percent of the time force is used). Thereafter, presidents use force at least 66 percent of the time as the number of nations involved increases. This variable perhaps best measures the severity or importance of a crisis in the international environment by indicating, in effect, the 'demand' for some sort of visible and powerful response by the US. The laws of probability ensure that as state involvement increases, that at some point, an important US ally, or key US adversary will become involved as well and engage US interests.

As we saw in Chapter 2 there is a negative relationship between US power in the world and the political use of military force. But when we remove the years 1948-1953 from the analysis because of the exceptionally and temporarily high level of US power in the post World War II era, this coefficient no longer approaches statistical significance. The US has been as or more powerful than every adversary it has faced since World War II, but its power has not always been relevant in every international crisis. Concerns related to power, however, have been important. Credibility and depth of commitment in particular have been critical to presidents and are both causes and consequences of American capabilities. Hence, that is why we find that the most powerful predictors of presidential decision making are those crisis-specific factors that indicate to the president the degree and nature of the threat to US national security interests. As I have been arguing, to understand why presidents use force we must differentiate between explaining the use of force in the aggregate and the use of force in particular international crises. Explaining increases and decreases in the political use of military force across time is best accomplished with reference to changing systemic and international environmental conditions. Predicting presidential decision making during particular opportunities to use force, as demonstrated here,

---

[35] It is listed as one of the foremost US interests and objectives in the Quadrennial Defense Review Report (2001, p.2).

Comprehensive Analysis of the Political Use of Military Force 215

is best accounted for by situation-specific information. I will return to this theme later.

The results also indicate that uses of force become less likely as cumulative US casualties in the Korea and Vietnam wars mount–the coefficient for this variable is negative and statistically significant ('US War Deaths'). Public fear of further costly military operations combined with the financial and logistical strains wars place on the foreign and defense policy machinery make other uses of force, even limited ones, much more difficult. Thus, even when the opportunity arises, presidents avoid using force. Interestingly, this inability or unwillingness to authorize additional military actions was one of the consequences feared by some realist thinkers who opposed US involvement in Vietnam especially. If the US was distracted by a war fought over comparatively trivial stakes, some feared that the Soviet Union or other US adversaries would be tempted to make trouble elsewhere. While no crises erupted during these wars that radically altered the balance of power, given the general reluctance to use force during war, these fears may have been justified.

As we would have expected from Chapter 2, we see that the variables derived from power and security considerations perform extremely well. With these variables included, the model explains over 75 percent of the cases correctly, while without them it can only account for 65.4 percent of the cases. All the hypotheses related to this model are convincingly supported, save that regarding US power. No explanation of the political use of military force can be complete without a thorough consideration of the power and security interests that are threatened in the events surrounding an international crisis.

Economic Interest Model

The hypotheses derived from the economic interest model fare slightly better in this set of estimates. The likelihood ratio test for the joint statistical significance of all the economic interest variables indicates that we can conclude that their coefficients are jointly distinguishable from zero. The additional boost in the model's predictive success rate gained by adding the economic interest variables, however, is slight. We explain 74.3 percent of the uses of force without these variables and 75.2 percent with them for an additional pickup of four cases. There are no changes in the direction or statistical significance of any of the variables from this model.

The positive relationship between the level of US economic aid and the use of force is still present and statistically significant. The greater the amount of US economic assistance provided to the target nation, the greater the probability of a use force. For every hundred million dollars in US economic aid provided to the nation at the origin of the international crisis, presidents are 2 percent more likely to use force, with the usual caveats. The economic assistance variable may be functioning principally as an indicator of the depth of US ties to the nation at the center of the opportunity to use force. The nations that receive the most such assistance, controlling for inflation, such as Germany in the late 1940s and early

216 *The Political Use of Military Force in US Foreign Policy*

1950s and Egypt in the 1980s are more likely to be assisted by a US use of force. Interestingly, one of the few international crises that occurred among the top aid recipients and where the president elected not to use force, involved the US's Cold War nemesis, Russia (regarding the 1994 war in Chechnya).

Presidents are also more likely to use force in an international crisis when there has been violence directed at US economic interests. Under such circumstances, presidents are 28 percent more likely to use force, holding other variables constant at their mean value. As we saw in Chapter 3, though such events are somewhat infrequent, when they do occur, there is a high degree of probability the president will use force. As well, the relationship between non violent economic disputes and the political use of force continues to be statistically insignificant. Finally, we still find that there is no relationship between crises that arise in OPEC nations and the political use of military force.

The overall performance of the economic interest model is not especially noteworthy in this set of analyses. However, there is compelling evidence that threats and attacks on US economic interests significantly increase the likelihood of a use of force. Such circumstances may not occur frequently, but these events do comprise a specific subcategory of uses of force that cannot generally be accounted for by other theories. We should continue to investigate these events within the context of the limited use of force. Additionally, such international crises should be examined with other foreign policy disputes that involve specific threats to US economic interests, and in conjunction with US foreign policy behaviors that involve coercive economic diplomacy, such as sanctions. Even though attacks on US economic interests should be considered when we study the political use of military force, crises involving economic threats and attacks should also be analyzed in the context of other economic disputes and the use of coercive, economic foreign policy tools. Krasner's (1978) and Rodman's (1988) analyses of US foreign policy behavior during such events is instructive, but are becoming somewhat dated. Analyses of more recent uses of force, such as the reflagging of the Kuwaiti oil vessels and the economic blockades the US has taken part in, are also needed.

The Liberal Idealist Model

The results regarding the effects of the hypotheses derived from the liberal idealist theory are fairly similar to those obtained in Chapter 4. The only difference is that the coefficient for the variable, 'Democracies and Civil Wars', which had been negative and statistically significant in the estimates in Chapter 4 is now statistically insignificant. First, note that the likelihood ratio test for this model, which tells us whether or not a group of coefficients is distinguishable from zero, barely misses statistical significance. The probability value for the LR test is actually .059. Theoretically and practically we may believe these variables are adding crucial information to our understanding of these phenomena, but in terms of their contribution to the overall fit of the model, they are not that critical. Other variables can explain many of the same uses of force that this group can. In fact, the predictive accuracy of the model minus the liberal idealist variables is actually

Comprehensive Analysis of the Political Use of Military Force 217

higher (75.3 percent) than it is with their inclusion (75.2 percent), albeit not by much. It is possible that one or more of these variables is collinear with other measures, and that this may account for the poor overall effect. I tested for multicollinearity by creating a correlation matrix of all variables. While there was some degree of minor correlation among the liberal idealist measures, the only noticeable correlation between one of these measures and those derived from other theories was between opportunities involving nations in a period of regime transition, and opportunities to use force where force had been used in the past year ($\rho = .32$).

In Chapter 4 we saw that presidents were more likely to use force when a democracy was undergoing a regime transition and when a nation was moving in a more democratic direction. Both hypotheses are still supported here. Using the marginal effects coefficient, we can see that when a nation is undergoing a polity transition ('Regime Transition'), presidents are 10 percent more likely to use force, given an opportunity and holding all other variables constant at their mean value. The more democratic a nation is becoming ('Change in Democracy'), given some international crisis, the more likely the president is to use military force. For each unit change of improvement in the Polity IV scale of democracy, presidents become 2 percent more likely to use force, holding other variable constant at their mean value. As noted in Chapter 4, this finding contradicts our expectation that presidents would use force to rescue or bolster democracy after it had declined in some nation. Instead, it is possible they use force to help 'push along' democratization as it occurs. I return to the issue of the timing of the use of force during such changes below.

Presidents are statistically neither more nor less likely to use force when democracies are involved in international or civil wars ('Democracies and International Wars'; 'Democracies and Civil Wars'). In Chapter 4 we saw that presidents had been statistically less likely to use force when democracies were involved in civil wars. That result, however, had contradicted the hypothesis that presidents would come to the aid of democratic states involved in such conflicts. While the coefficient for this variable is no longer statistically significant, it is also no longer directly contradicting our predictions. Presidents are apparently not influenced to use force by the nature of the regime when that nation is involved in any kind of war.

Presidents are still less likely to use force when a crisis occurs in the context of a widespread violence ('Widespread Societal Violence'). The reader will recall that I defined widespread violence as occurring when a conflict in a nation that was the origin of an opportunity to use force was scored at least a '5' on the 'societal-systemic' impact indicator in the 'Major Episodes of Political Violence' data base. Presidents are not apparently moved for practical or humanitarian reasons to use force when such violence is occurring. Part of the explanation for this finding may be a difference in attitudes toward such violence visited on societies in the Cold War and post Cold War eras. During the Cold War presidents may have refrained from getting involved in many such disasters for fear of a confrontation with the Soviet Union or China, because international outrage at such events was not as manifest, or perhaps because information regarding the magnitude of the problem was lacking. Certainly these three impediments are not nearly as germane today. Thus, we may find that presidents have used force when such widespread violence occurs in the post Cold War era. To test for this possibility I created an interactive variable for widespread societal violence in the post Cold War era (I consider the post Cold War era as beginning in 1990). Not only was the coefficient for this variable positive, it was also statistically significant (results not shown). Presidents have become more likely to use force now under such circumstances than they were before. In fact, according to the marginal effects coefficient for this variable, presidents are 37 percent more likely to use force, holding other variables constant at their mean value, when the opportunity occurs in the context of widespread societal violence after the end of the Cold War. Of the 38 opportunities to use force that occurred in the context of widespread and massive violence in the post Cold War era, presidents used force on 26 occasions (68.4 percent). During the Cold War, opportunities to use force arose in the context of such violence on 56 occasions. But presidents only used force 34 percent of the time. This is something of a remarkable turnaround in foreign policy thinking and behavior that seems to indicate that the US has begun to take on the role of enforcer of certain human rights norms. Nonetheless, because the post Cold War era consists principally of the Clinton administration years, further evidence is necessary to determine if this tendency results from the policy preferences of a particular administration .

Ultimately, though we do find support for two of the hypotheses derived from the liberal idealist model, its overall explanatory power leaves something to be desired. We would not expect this model to have nearly the predictive accuracy as the power and security variables, but we would certainly prefer that it not detract from the overall model performance. There are several possibilities that may account for these problems. First and foremost, we may simply have an incomplete understanding of what political/social events in other nations are most likely to lead presidents to use force to advance liberal idealist aims. Let us assume that US foreign policy makers are led, from time to time, to use force to advance democracy. But are they more interested in helping countries that are moving toward democracy, or preventing democracies from backsliding? Would they rather target authoritarian nations whose people suffer from the greatest deficit in democracy, or would US policymakers rather help nations whose systems are partly free already and more susceptible to US pressure? And more specifically, at what point(s) exactly in these transformations do presidents and their advisers begin to actively consider using force? Does this occur when a regime has become a failed state, or when it takes the first steps down the slippery slope to dictatorship or chaos? Does it occur only when US national security interests are also engaged, or when other nations have sanctioned such US action? These are just some of the many questions that deserve greater attention than I can provide here. A more in-depth study of presidential decision-making pertaining to the post Cold War liberal idealist uses of force is needed to gain better understanding of pro-democracy uses of force, as well as those designed to stop widespread violence.

Comprehensive Analysis of the Political Use of Military Force 219

Another, and related explanation as to the relatively poor performance of the liberal idealist model is that the uses (and non uses) of force it predicts are also characterized by events that pertain to the objectives of other foreign policy interests/theories. For example, during the 1990s, the full model predicts most uses of force in connection with the Bosnian war correctly because such events were characterized both by a regime in transition, and by a situation in which force had been used previously. Presidents may 'need' some additional justification for using force to promote democracy or advance human rights. Since these interventions entail US forces and the US government exercising domestic, political powers in the target nations, presidents may wait to use force until other US interest are engaged because of the still powerful norm of state sovereignty. Finally, it may be that liberal idealist goals are advanced later during the course of a military intervention at the behest of the President or by other actors, such as the US Congress (Peceny, 1996). This may make it more difficult to predict such interventions in advance. Thus, while the effect of the liberal idealist model on the use of force may not be wide, its influence may still be felt deeply enough in critical military interventions to warrant more scrutiny. We do know that US foreign policy makers have placed increased emphasis on liberal idealist aims, and so we might proceed initially by developing stronger explanations of when and where the US utilizes proliberalization tools and in what order. Military force is unlikely to be the initial choice of a prodemocratization campaign, except perhaps in the most extreme circumstances, and thus by better understanding its place in the sequence of policy making choices, we can predict when force will used. In short, we need more theoretical development regarding the time and mechanics of promoting democracy.

Diversionary Model

The likelihood ratio test indicates that the probability that all the coefficients from the diversionary model are equal to zero is quite small. In the aggregate, knowledge of these domestic conditions improves our ability to correctly predict presidential decision making. When the diversionary variables are left out of the analysis, the model correctly accounts for 73.7 percent of the cases, while their inclusion boosts the percentage of correctly predicted cases to approximately 75.2 percent. Thus, we are able to predict an additional eight cases of the use or non use of force. Most of the results we saw in Chapter 5 continue to hold here. We continue to find that there is no statistically significant likelihood of a relationship existing between approval ratings ('Presidential Popularity'), a presidential election ('Election') and the use of force.

In the case of the diversionary theory hypotheses we find that only one result from Chapter 5 no longer obtains. Where previously 'Unemployment' and the political use of military force were positively related, now we see that presidents are no longer statistically more likely to use force as unemployment increases. Yet, at the same time there still is a negative relationship between 'Inflation' and the use force that is statistically significant. The greater the rate of

220 *The Political Use of Military Force in US Foreign Policy*

inflation, the less likely presidents are to use the military for political purposes. Support for the principal hypotheses of the diversionary model is weak. Presidents are not more likely to use force as unemployment increases; less likely to use force as inflation increases; and neither more nor less likely to use force as their popularity ratings decline. While there is some degree of multicollinearity among these three measures, each is still independently related to the use of force. We also know, however, from research by Fordham (1998a, 1998b) and the results of the bivariate analyses in Chapter 5 that the relationship between unemployment and the use of force tends to occur during Republican administrations. Support for diversionary theory must remain qualified.

Once again, the overall performance of the model is not great and must be treated with some degree of caution, for it is actually the domestic *variables* that provide the additional explanatory power, not generally diversionary *theory* since its predictions are not entirely borne out. Presidents are not led to use force because of rising inflation, upcoming elections or their own political misfortunes. Those who subscribe to the diversionary model might argue that political incentives are not sufficient conditions, but rather they add to the attractiveness of military operations. Yet, the public's evaluation of the president's handling of the macro economy and every individual's assessment of his or her own economic situation is perhaps the most important determinant of presidential support. Every chief executive is keenly aware that his performance and place in history are closely linked to the performance of the US economy. As economic conditions worsen, the public expects the president to devote more time and resources to addressing the problems (Nincic, 1998). Should the president immerse himself in foreign affairs at such times, not only will such matters detract from his attention to domestic policy, it may further erode his standing among the public. Furthermore, the 'rally effect' in public opinion following a use of force is quite slight and ephemeral (Lian and Oneal, 1993). The benefits are few and the costs are high for attempted diversionary behavior.

Although the findings here do not lend substantial support to any of the liberal idealist, economic interest or diversionary theory models, I would nonetheless argue that more research is needed on the first two and less on the last. Diversionary theory has been tested and retested multiple times in political science journals using quantitative techniques despite a paucity of evidence to support. The liberal idealist and economic interest model have not enjoyed nearly as much attention, especially from scholars employing more sophisticated, empirical methodologies. It is time to rectify this imbalance.

Overall Assessment

Clearly, the most convincing evidence supports the superiority of the power and security variables over the other theories of the political use of force by the US. We saw that they significantly enhances the overall predictive capacity of the model, while the contribution of the other models is slight, or even detrimental to model performance in the case of the liberal idealist variables. The power and security model is best at capturing the characteristics of specific events that seem to weigh mostly heavily in the president's decision making. The economic interest, liberal idealist and diversionary theories add to our knowledge of such decision outcomes, but do not appear to provide us with information that consistently and decisively influences whether the president chooses to use force. Realistically, it would appear that we may derive indicators of the importance of some opportunity to use force from these three other theories that facilitate or encourage uses of force on a number of occasions. The measures we derive from realism and other theories where concerns regarding security, the national interest and power are preeminent, more frequently seem to determine what the president will do in a more causative sense. Simply put, the power and security variables provide the best explanation of the political use of military force in the 1948-1998 period.

The next tables and figure present information on the comprehensive model's ability to correctly predict cases across presidential administrations and the Cold War/Post Cold War divide. In all, the model incorrectly predicted 75 cases as non uses of force where presidents did, in fact, use force. The model incorrectly predicted 75 cases as uses of force when the president did not authorize military action. Table 6.4 is reproduced from Chapter 1 to remind the reader of frequency with which presidents used force. Table 6.5 presents the results of the model's predictive success across presidential administrations. While there is not wide variation in the prediction rates among administrations, we do see some fluctuation in Table 6.5. The model performs least well when predicting presidential decision making during the Eisenhower, Carter, Reagan and Clinton administrations, while its performance peaks with the Truman, Nixon and Ford presidencies (total predictive success exceeds 80 percent in all three cases). The most obvious, distinguishing characteristic between these two groups is the frequency with which these presidents used force. Truman, Nixon and Ford used force far less often than all other presidents. While the model performs reasonably well predicting the behavior of presidents who seem to be more predisposed to use force, it clearly performs better when explaining the decision outcomes of those who tend not to use force. What might explain this tendency?

Table 6.4 Presidents, Opportunities and the Use of Force

President	Opportunities	Uses of Force	Frequency
Truman	40	11	27.5%
Eisenhower	82	50	60.9%
Kennedy	55	35	63.6%
Johnson	66	39	59.0%
Nixon	54	16	29.6%
Ford	25	8	32.0%
Carter	20	45	44.4%
Reagan	110	74	67.2%
Bush	51	24	47.0%
Clinton	77	41	53.2%
Total	605	318	52.5%

Table 6.5 Predictions by Presidential Administration

	Percent Correct Total cases	Percent Correct Non Uses of Force	Percent Correct Uses of Force
Truman	85% (40)	90% (29)	80% (11)
Eisenhower	68.3% (82)	59.3% (32)	74% (50)
Kennedy	76.4% (55)	65% (20)	82.9% (35)
Johnson	72.7% (66)	63% (27)	79.5% (39)
Nixon	81.5% (54)	92.1% (38)	56.3% (16)
Ford	80% (25)	76.5% (17)	87.5% (8)
Carter	73.3% (45)	84% (25)	60% (20)
Reagan	74.5% (110)	55.5% (36)	83.8% (74)
Bush	76.4% (51)	77.7% (27)	75% (24)
Clinton	72.7% (77)	72.2% (36)	73.1% (41)
Total	75.2% (605)	73.8% (287)	76.4% (318)

Comprehensive Analysis of the Political Use of Military Force 223

Table 6.6 Predictions before and after the Cold War

	Percent Predicted (Total Uses)	Percent Predicted Non Uses of Force	Percent Predicted Uses of Force
Cold War Era	74.9% (494)	73.5% (234)	76.1% (260)
Post Cold War Era	76.5% (111)	75.4% (53)	77.5% (58)
Total	75% (605)	73.8% (287)	76.4% (318)

Perhaps the model performs better when predicting presidential decision making when US economic conditions are particularly bad and presidents are more focused on domestic policy, and thus reluctant to focus on foreign policy and the use of force. We know that high inflation was particularly salient during parts of the Truman, Nixon and Ford administrations. But this does not explain why the model does not perform as well during the Carter administration where inflation was high and the president also tended to use force at below historic levels. A second, more plausible theory is that the model performs better when explaining presidential decision making in severe international crises. If presidents Truman, Nixon and Ford tended to use force only in major, international crises, these cases may be fairly easy to predict given that they are over determined by any number of security and power considerations. Other presidents may be relatively more likely to use force in crises that are not so severe and demanding of a use of force, and which may also exhibit more idiosyncratic traits. Predicting decision making in these crises where the threats are not so severe, and perhaps where the president responds with lower level uses of force, may be more difficult.

For example, President Jimmy Carter dispatched elements of the US Air Force to assist in the transportation of armed forces during the end of the civil war in what was then Rhodesia. The US had never targeted a use of force in Rhodesia before, there were no threats to any of the US interests identified in the overall model, and thus the predicted probability of a use of force is quite low at 23 percent according to the probit estimates. President Eisenhower used force in 1957 in regard to a military coup in Haiti even though there were few, if any, concrete US interests at stake. The probability of a use of force in this case is 18 percent. Finally, I note the occurrence of a coup in the Maldives in 1988, which precipitated a use of force, even though there seemed to be few US interests at stake and no history of US involvement in that island nation. In each of these cases, however, the president did respond with force, but only low level uses. The model seems to have the most difficulty predicting uses of force where we can identify few US

224 *The Political Use of Military Force in US Foreign Policy*

interests, but where presidents perceive that a low level display of force may be just the right measure to back up US diplomacy.

The model also tends to perform more poorly when predicting presidential decisions during those administrations that use force quite frequently. For example, both the Eisenhower and Reagan administrations used force often, but also confronted a number of other opportunities in which they chose not to use force. The model tends to keep predicting uses of force across a good many of these opportunities, especially when important US interests are at stake. The model predicts that there was a 97 percent probability that President Reagan would use force in response to the bombing of the Marine barracks in Lebanon in 1983, but he chose not to (at least in the context of a specific operation in response to that event). The model also assumes that the US would continue to use force in Laos in the 1960s no matter what the crisis, as well as in Berlin in the late 1950s and early 1960s. The US did use force in most of the crises that occurred in these two areas, but presidents also passed up several opportunities as well.

We also see, in Table 6.6, that the model reassuringly predicts well in both the Cold War and the post Cold War eras. The model's performance in this period is satisfactory, but as the influence of Cold War thinking on US foreign policy wears off and new interests and strategies develop, especially with regard to terrorism, we may have to accord greater theoretical and empirical attention to the differences in US foreign policy thinking and behavior. For example, the model as it is specified performs reasonably well at predicting US responses to terrorist incidents such as the violence directed against the US in Lebanon in the mid 1980s and the bombing of the US embassies in Tanzania and Kenya in 1998. Most of the incidents that we would consider to be terrorist attacks involve violence directed against US citizens or property, which the model already accounts for. The model does not account for the types of terrorist threats that were used to justify, in part, the build-up of forces in the Persian Gulf that preceded the 2003 war in Iraq. Another potential problem area is in humanitarian or peacekeeping operations. As I demonstrated earlier, when we look at the likelihood of a US response to human rights disasters across the entire 1948-1998 time span we find that presidents are less likely to use force under such circumstances. But when we restrict the period of analysis to just the post Cold War era, we see that presidents are more likely to use force. To an extent we can credit the end of that 'war' and the uncontested ability of the US to deploy forces wherever, whenever and to some extent for whatever reasons it pleases for this change in decision making. Yet we also need to develop a better understanding of why presidents intervene in some such humanitarian disasters and not in others. Ideally, we would need some sort of measure of the salience of the disaster and/or the degree of pressure placed on the president to intervene. Thus, responses to terrorism and humanitarian operations need to be better accounted for in our theories of presidential decision making in the post Cold War era.

Additional Analyses

Not all of the potentially interesting and revealing people, places and things that might help us better understand the use of force are derived from one of the four theories I outlined in this book. The purpose of the next analysis is to provide additional insights into where presidents use force. In particular, I examine whether there are some countries that seem to attract more than their fair share of US military operations. Especially in recent years it seems presidents have singled out certain regimes and their leaders as international pariahs, and have became fixated on developments in these nations. For John Kennedy it was Fidel Castro and Cuba; for Jimmy Carter it was the Ayatollah Khomeini and Iran; for George Bush it was Saddam Hussein, and for the Bill Clinton it was North Korea and Slobodan Milosevic's Yugoslavia. Research on enduring rivalries in international relations has shown that many of the crises and most of the wars that have occurred involve the same pairs of states (Bennett, 1998; Goertz and Diehl, 1993, 1995). According to Bennett (1998, p.1200), 'Rivalries are dyads with a long history of repeated conflict, within which conflicts are repeated over time'. We might expect the US, as hegemon, to be involved in multiple crises with the types of states just described. While some states may refrain from future crisis involvement if they fare poorly in their initial encounter(s) with the US, others may not be willing to acquiesce to the hegemon. Their areas of disagreement may remain unresolved to their satisfaction. Some regimes may believe their domestic and international status depends on an adversarial relationship with the hegemon, while others come to depend on their hostile relationship with the hegemon to maintain power and even wealth at home (e.g., Iraq under Saddam Hussein and Yugoslavia/Serbia under Milosevic). As long as the US is not provoked into replacing the regime, its defiance may continue over a series of confrontations and crises. The US might also be involved in a number of crises, or use force repeatedly over the years in certain countries because, having earlier invested resources, personnel and energy into dealing with events in a country, presidents may continue to remain involved because of these sunk costs. Several states in Central America, such as El Salvador and Honduras, as well as Zaire/Congo come to mind. Thus, repeated uses of force may occur both within the context of an adversarial as well as an amicable relationship.

First, to assess to what extent presidents were likely to use force against prominent American adversaries, I created a series of binary variables for North Korea, Cuba, Iran, Iraq and Yugoslavia,[36] and used them to predict uses of force,

---

[36] The North Korea variable is coded "1" for all years and all opportunities in which North Korea was involved. The Cuba variable is coded "1" for all opportunities in which Cuba was involved from 1959-1998. The Iran variable is coded "1" for all opportunities in which Iran was involved from 1979-1998. The Iraq variable was coded "1" for all opportunities in which Iraq was involved from 1990-1998. The Yugoslavia variable was coded "1" for all opportunities in which Yugoslavia or the former republics of that nation were involved from 1991-1998.

226   *The Political Use of Military Force in US Foreign Policy*

but without the variables derived from the four theories. The results are shown in Table 6.9. Apparently, some states are more deserving of repeated uses of force than others, even among pariah regimes. Presidents have been significantly more likely to use force against Cuba, Iraq and the former Yugoslavia, but not North Korea and Iran. With the other variables held constant at their mean values and according to the marginal effects coefficients, president were 32 percent more likely to use force against Castro's Cuba; 24 percent more likely to use force against Saddam Hussein's Iraq; and 28 percent more likely to use force during the Balkan wars of the 1990s.

Table 6.7 Pariah States and the Use of Force, 1948-1998

Variable	Coefficient	Standard Error	T Statistic	P Value	Marginal Effect
North Korea	-.3086	.3240	-0.95	0.341	-.1223
Cuba	.9389	.2584	3.63	0.000	.3229
Iran	-.1156	.2865	-0.40	0.687	-.0460
Iraq	.6845	.3452	1.98	0.047	.2481
Yugoslavia	.8146	.3288	2.48	0.013	.2865
Constant	-.0100	.0560	-0.18	0.858	

N=605
$\chi^2 = 26$, p. < .0001
Pseudo R^2 = .03
Percent Correctly Predicted = 54.2%
Proportionate Reduction of Error = 3.5%

When we examine the frequency with which the US is involved in international crises with particular nations in Table 6.8, we see several interesting trends. In Table 6.8 notice that seven nations of the top 20 account for 25 percent of the total number of crises. These nations are in rank order: Lebanon, Cuba, the former Yugoslavia, North and South Korea, Iran, Iraq and the Congo/Zaire. When we examine the frequency with which the US uses force against particular nations, given an opportunity, in Table 6.9, we see that seven nations of the top 20 account for 31 percent of all uses of force. Many of them are the same nations that account for most of the crises. Fourteen nations account for almost 50 percent of all uses of force. While these findings confirm what most of us would have already suspected, the reasons why presidents keep using force against these regimes is perhaps more interesting. First, presidents, like the American public, seem to concentrate their energies on and direct their wrath against readily identifiable villains. This tendency has been noted by foreign policy scholars who have criticized the emotional basis of some policies and much foreign policy rhetoric (e.g., Kennan

Comprehensive Analysis of the Political Use of Military Force 227

and Kissinger). The public desire for an emotional or ideological justification for costly foreign policies has, of course, been a traditional American affliction.

Table 6.8 Top 20 Nations Involved Most Frequently in Opportunities to Use Force

Nation	Frequency	Percent of Total
LEBANON	33	5.5%
CUBA	24	4.0%
FORMER YUGOSLAVIA	23	3.8%
NORTH & SOUTH KOREA	22	3.6%
IRAN	20	3.3%
IRAQ	18	3.0%
CONGO/ZAIRE/CONGO	15	2.5%
HAITI	14	2.3%
VIETNAM	14	2.3%
WEST & EAST GERMANY	14	2.3%
HONDURAS	12	2.0%
TAIWAN	12	2.0%
LAOS	12	2.0%
INDONESIA	12	2.0%
DOMINICAN REPUBLIC	11	1.8%
NICARAGUA	11	1.8%
LIBYA	11	1.8%
EGYPT	11	1.8%
PANAMA	10	1.7%
VENEZUELA	10	1.7%
	309	51%

The Former Yugoslavia includes all opportunities associated with the Federal Republic of Yugoslavia prior to 1991 and all events associated with its successor states thereafter.

Second, however, even regimes that are friendly to the US are likely to continue to attract US military involvement, perhaps because their internal/external political and military problems are equally as unsolvable. The state that was involved in the most opportunities to use force, as well as actual uses of force, is Lebanon. The US has had a long history of military intervention there dating back to 1958. At times the US has acted as a friend of Lebanon, or attempted to provide a stabilizing force, as in the deployment of the early 1980s. At other times, the US relationship was more adversarial, as during the hostage situations of the mid and late 1980s. Many of the other states became 'clients' of the US whose security comes to depend upon a strong US military presence or a consistent willingness to

228 *The Political Use of Military Force in US Foreign Policy*

use limited force to protect the client. This certainly characterized the US relationship with Mobutu's Zaire from the 1960s through the 1980s, with Taiwan particularly in the 1950s when it was threatened quite often by mainland China, and the states of Central America that came under threat of communist insurgencies in the early 1960s and 1980s. Their dependence on US security guarantees, coupled with the significant investment of American resources and credibility in their defense, made the US commitment to such states difficult to break. Force tends to be used against or on behalf of the same set of state actors over time as the US develops its own set of enduring rivalries and ongoing friendships.

Table 6.9 Top 20 Nations Involved Most Frequently in Uses of Force

Nation	Frequency	Percent of Total
LEBANON	23	7.2%
CUBA	19	6.0%
FORMER YUGOSLAVIA	16	5.0%
HAITI	11	3.5%
VIETNAM	11	3.5%
CONGO/ZAIRE/CONGO	10	3.1%
TAIWAN	10	3.1%
IRAN	9	2.8%
IRAQ	9	2.8%
WEST & EAST GERMANY	9	2.8%
NICARAGUA	8	2.5%
NORTH & SOUTH KOREA	8	2.5%
DOMINICAN REPUBLIC	7	2.2%
HONDURAS	7	2.2%
CYPRUS	7	2.2%
EGYPT	7	2.2%
JORDAN	7	2.2%
LAOS	7	2.2%
VENEZUELA	6	1.9%
LIBYA	6	1.9%
	197	61.9%

The Former Yugoslavia includes all opportunities associated with the Federal Republic of Yugoslavia prior to 1991 and all events associated with its successor states thereafter.

Conclusion

Explaining and predicting whether presidents will use force or not across six hundred international crises spanning over 50 years is a challenging enterprise. We are aided by the guidance of four different theories of these activities, but still the final analysis is only as good as the data one employs and the hypotheses one tests. In the aggregate, the results are solid, but not outstanding. The model predicts roughly 75 percent of the cases, which is a respectable improvement over predicting the modal category. Thus, as we so often do in the social sciences, we conclude that while our results are good, they could be improved and we need to continue to pursue this research topic. The manner in which we improve our understanding of presidential decision making is best managed by evaluating the strengths and weaknesses of the four theories.

The results demonstrate that the power and security model performs best in explaining presidential decision making during international crises. Each of the other theories contributes toward our overall knowledge of when presidents use force, but the collective impact of any one model is not especially powerful. The economic interest and liberal idealist models help us identify certain important predictors of presidential decision making. These are attacks on or violence directed toward US economic interests, US economic assistance to target nations, and opportunities where regimes are undergoing some sort of transition. Yet, it would be difficult to conclude that any of the theories associated with these models has been supported. Nonetheless, both the economic interest and liberal idealist models deserve additional scrutiny and analysis. The economic interest model performs best in the pre modern era where it has been subject to few large N analyses. A more in-depth data collection project on the use of force in the pre World War II era is needed to obtain a better understanding of these events. The liberal idealist model should be analyzed more in the post Cold War era as its 'star' seems to be rising in both academic and policymaking circles. Indeed, in President Bush's recent, 'U.S. National Security Strategy', the foreign policy goal listed first is to, 'champion aspirations for human dignity'. Additional research is also required to better integrate the threats from terrorism and the proliferation of weapons of mass destruction into realist theories of US foreign policy making, and power and security models of the political use of military force.

Further analysis is also needed to explain what sorts of nations and what types of events are most likely to generate the conditions associated with opportunities to use force. Much research has focused on the manner in which domestic conditions in one state influence the crisis strategies of other states. No doubt many shrewd world leaders monitor conditions inside the US to gauge its potential reaction to events and provocations. Yet, Meernik (2000, 2001) finds that US domestic factors generally do not predict the occurrence of international crises, and concludes that, 'Foreign governments are no doubt aware of the economic health of the US and the political health of presidents, but these may not be their primary considerations. Rather their own interests and convenience may dictate the timing of crises' (Meernik, 2001, p.899). We might expect that a nation's

230 *The Political Use of Military Force in US Foreign Policy*

propensity to become involved in conflicts with the US is better explained by international and local conditions, rather than the US economy. We would expect that the US would be most likely to become involved in crises with nations that fit a certain profile, such as regimes that are politically dissimilar, are militarily capable of confronting the US, and have a history of adversarial relationships with their neighbors and/or the US. Thus, a better understanding of when and where crises occur will help us to explain why presidents use force. This can also help us to untangle the relationships that exist among US foreign policies that may induce or contribute to instability in other countries, which then necessitates a use of force. Such complex interactions among US foreign policy, the behavior of pariah regimes, failed states, and other unstable nations, and the subsequent use of force by the US need to be examined in more detail to help us sort out US foreign policy goals. Does the US intervene in such situations to rescue failed states and promote democracy as part of a liberal idealist agenda, or has it merely exploited such problems for its own realpolitik considerations?

In general, our findings regarding the political use of military force by the US have accumulated in an additive, rather than an integrative manner. Many political science scholars have analyzed data and tested diversionary theory, but few have sought to test together diversionary hypotheses and those derived from other theories. I have argued that research is better served by the testing of diverse models of US foreign policy interests. Whatever direction future research progresses in it is always better to test other explanations of the limited use of force alongside the principal theory, and perhaps even integrate these theories together.

Chapter 7

Conclusion

Introduction

In this book I have sought to weave together various strands of thinking on the political use of military force in US foreign policy so that we might understand more thoroughly the causes behind these events. I have combined different methodological and theoretical approaches to provide a more comprehensive review of these visible and sometimes violent events in the nation's history. I have tried to shed light on one very simple question: 'why do presidents use US military forces to influence foreign actors?' The short and direct answer to this question is that presidents use force primarily to protect/advance US security, often to promote economic interests, occasionally to advance liberal idealist ambitions, and seldom to advance their own domestic political interests. My answer challenges the arguments of many other scholars identified with a particular theoretical approach, but supports those who believe that theoretical integration rather than segregation is the best method of discovery. Specifically, I disagree with those who would argue that only those concepts derived from classical realism or neorealism, including power, the national interest, security, the balance of power and so forth deserve to be included in a theory of military force in the international arena. I disagree with those who would argue that the interests of big business and capitalism dictate US foreign policy. And I disagree with those who contend that the domestic political interests of presidents exercise substantial influence over the political use of military force.

While I believe that US security and power interests are generally the dominant motivating force behind these phenomena, I believe, and the evidence strongly suggests, that during many periods in US history and during particular international crises, presidents have been strongly motivated by the need to protect economic interests and the desire to advance democracy and human rights. It may be rare that these two interests would be sufficiently compelling to lead a president to act in opposition to US national security interests, but there are many occasions when US security interests are not engaged or reinforce liberal idealist and economic interest objectives. We have not accorded these two interests the theoretical importance they are due or recognized the important influence they exercise on presidential decision-making. Specifically, we have not analyzed the effect of economic interests on the political use of military force in the 19th century, nor the influence of liberal idealist goals in the post Cold War using more advanced statistical analyses. In contrast, the scholarly community has overemphasized the development and empirical testing of diversionary theory.

232   *The Political Use of Military Force in US Foreign Policy*

There are other and better ways in which we can account for the inhibiting and encouraging tendencies within the US body politic than through diversionary theory.

In this conclusion I summarize, critique and extrapolate from the findings of the analyses. First, I assess the utility of each of the models as it was tested alone and with the others. I also discuss how valid or useful these theories will be in the future as the world changes. I conclude by deriving three essential lessons from all we have discovered about the political use of military force.

Security Interests

International relations theories, like realism, that focus on security interests in driving state behavior have provided critical insights into the use of force. Even the diversionary model, which has tended to garner most of the political science journal space, is in large part a reaction to this perspective. But, how useful are general theories of international relations in explaining the behavior of one state? International relations theory has typically conceptualized the dominant forces of world politics, such as the distribution of power and anarchy, as systemic features that encourage or inhibit the behavior of states, such as their proclivity to become involved in armed hostilities. As I have stated before, we can use this type of knowledge to explain general tendencies of states to, for example, become internationally active or use military force across time. Such explanations are not intended to explain what nations do in a given crisis or toward other particular states–they are constrained in their spatial applicability. Hence, we may use such concepts, preeminently the US share of global power, to predict general trends in the political use of military force by the US across time.

Power as the dominant currency in world politics is requisite for the use of force, although it is not a sufficient condition. We observe a positive relationship between US relative capabilities and the political use of military force over time, although there are exceptions. The isolationist phase from 1919-1941 when the US used force less often than its level of power would predict, and the Cold War period when there appears to be no relationship between the two are anomalies. But, as I have shown and others have argued, capabilities themselves generate interests, which lead to the use of force. As a state's capabilities expand, so too do its political and economic contacts with the rest of the world. Such contacts create interests and commitments, which in turn require protection and proaction. Power also creates expectations. When the US became a major power at the end of the 19th century, the public's and presidents' attitudes changed. They believed it was time for the US to take its rightful place in world politics and that the major powers should accommodate the new member of their club. Power also leads to a desire to use it. Few states seem to be able to resist the temptation to diligently conserve the sources of their power. Most states, like businesses, seem to expand continually until met with obstacles. For the US this obstacle was a significant imbalance between resources and commitments toward the end of the Cold War. Only when it hit this limit did the US begin to retrench, albeit temporarily. To put it succinctly,

Conclusion 233

capabilities help substantially to predict when force is used, but on an aggregated level. We can agree to some extent with Zakaria (1998), that capabilities are first filtered through state power, structure and decisions-makers' perceptions. Nonetheless, their influence is ubiquitous. And as power is the central component of realism and security-oriented theories of foreign policy, it provides important explanatory power to any general account of the limited use of force.

Based on the statistical analyses I conducted in Chapters 2 and 6, security and power interests provide a consistently useful guide to explaining and predicting the political use of military force in specific, international crises. The dominant variables in the comprehensive model of Chapter 6 are those that measure specific threats to US security interests. Here we found that security concerns such as credibility, the number of crisis actors and anti-American violence are strong predictors of the use of force. Presidents are also especially prone to use force against the same set of states over and over again. They continually seek to threaten some states that any behavior antithetical to American interests will be met with some sort of reprisal, while they seek to remind other states friendly to the US that their American security commitment is credible. Those systemic factors identified with realism and its variants, especially power, and those situational factors associated with security interests provide the most powerful explanation of the political use of military force across time and space, respectively.

But how well will power and security interests, and their theoretical parent, realism, fare in accounting for US foreign policy behavior in general, and the political use of military force in particular, in this new age of American hegemony? One of the principal strengths, as well as one of the most problematic weaknesses of power and security concerns as we have seen, has been their malleability. Theoretically and operationally, they can be stretched to fit any number of types of threats and definitions of foreign policy interests. This type of looseness contributes toward theoretical vagaries and empirical non-falsifiability. Nevertheless, these concepts should continue to prove useful in the post Cold War international environment, and should help us explain when and where presidents use force to confront the critical threats of today and tomorrow, such as terrorism and the proliferation of weapons of mass destruction. For example, one fundamental security interest is the protection of American lives at home and abroad. Security considerations account for this well; as does the operational model I developed and tested here.

However, there are several other areas in which we may find that security and power interests will be severely tested, both theoretically and empirically in accounting for the limited use of force. First, predicting US responses to one of the principal threats of the 21st century–the development of weapons of mass destruction–may be more difficult than predicting US responses to other types of international crises. Often these programs are run under a veil of extreme secrecy so that predicting the exact timing of an American response may be problematic. Much US diplomacy on this subject may be carried out covertly, particularly regarding the development of nuclear weapons, since both the US and many

234   *The Political Use of Military Force in US Foreign Policy*

nuclear aspirants have, or have had, strong incentives to keep such research programs quiet (e.g., Israel, Taiwan, South Africa). Additionally, when confronted with clear evidence of nuclear capability (e.g., the Indian and Pakistani nuclear tests of 1998), or a strong intent to develop such weapons (e.g., North Korea in 1994; Iraq during the 1990s), the US either did not use force even in a very limited way (India, Pakistan and North Korea), or used force massively (Iraq). Predicting when force will be used when the stakes and dangers are so high will prove formidable. As well, assessing when such long-simmering crises turn into opportunities to use force is complicated; although in the case of North Korea there have been readily identifiable flashpoints.

Scholars may also find it challenging to employ security and power interests in the age of the Bush Doctrine of 'preemption'. According to this policy:

> The US has long maintained the option of preemptive actions to a counter a sufficient threat to our national security. The greater the threat, the greater is the risk of inaction–and the more compelling the case for taking anticipatory action to defend ourselves, even if uncertainty remains as to the time and place of the enemy's attack. To forestall or prevent hostile acts by our adversaries, the US will, if necessary, act preemptively.[37]

President Bush used this doctrine of preemption to justify the buildup of forces in the Persian Gulf to counter Iraqi leader Saddam Hussein's perceived intentions to develop WMD. To a certain extent we can still explain such uses of force because we would expect that they would occur in relation to those long-running adversarial relationships the US has with a select number of nations. Predicting the timing of these military operations may prove problematic. More importantly, the doctrine of preemption highlights an even more fundamental problem with security and power interests, realism and their ability to explain foreign policy actions. At what point does a nation's efforts to protect itself, especially a hegemon with overwhelming power, move from prudent measures to maintain its sovereignty and protect its people and interests, to aggressive strategies designed to dominate the international system beyond what is necessary for its security?

Since the end of the Cold War, foreign policy makers, and scholars, have debated the wisdom of maintaining America's international 'primacy' (Huntington, 1993; Jervis, 1993). During the Bush administration, a leak of the draft document of the 'Defense Planning Guidance' report stated that:

> Our first objective is to prevent the re-emergence of a new rival. This is a dominant consideration underlying the new regional defense strategy and requires that we endeavor to prevent any hostile power from dominating a region whose

---

[37] From "US National Security Strategy" (2002, p.15).

Conclusion 235

resources would, under consolidated control, be sufficient to generate global power.[38]

After a considerable flap arose over such bald assertions of US dominance, the draft was rewritten. More recently, however, in the 'US National Security Strategy' report, it was declared that, 'our forces will be strong enough to dissuade potential adversaries from pursuing a military build-up in hopes of surpassing or equaling, the power of the US'.[39] Certainly the US does wish to maintain its hegemony, but toward what end? As I discussed in Chapter Two, as states are able to satisfy their more immediate security needs, such as the protection of physical assets like as people, land and resources, they may move on to consider how other, more distant developments may impinge on their national security. Hegemons may become increasingly engaged in maintaining the economic and political 'rules' or regimes that govern international relations to perpetuate their dominance. They may grow more interested in the internal developments of other nations, especially as external policies such as international war, are posing less of a threat. Thus do we find the US interested in promoting democracy, human rights and free markets, not just as liberal idealist goals or ends in themselves, but as a way of ensuring global order and stability. Soon, there may be few issues that escape the attention of the US, for as we saw with the Munich syndrome and domino theory during the Cold War, policy makers are ready to perceive and believe an inter-connectedness of threats. But while presidents and their advisers may believe in such inter-connected patterns of international and intranational developments, and act upon these assumptions by using military force to counter challenges, the rest of the world may not share their perspective. A world suspicious of or hostile to a hegemonic US may breed more threats to its interests. The challenge for the US is still to identify where its true interests lie without resort to universalist doctrines that ultimately demand continual sustenance lest the US perceive itself as failing to uphold the web of commitments it has created.

Making such distinctions between real interests where force is necessary, and more ephemeral interests where force would prove helpful is fraught with complications. In an era when military budgets are once again rising and the military is expected to handle more and more diverse duties, and when one must use the rhetoric of 'war' and 'national interest' to gain attention, special interests will have a strong incentive to cast their agendas in terms of national security and threats. And when the Secretary of Defense announces that, 'This nation can afford to spend what is needed to deter the adversaries of tomorrow and to underpin our

---

[38] "Defense Planning Guidance" (1992) Draft document as found at http://www.pbs.org/wgbh/pages/frontline/shows/iraq/etc/wolf.html on August 8, 2003.

[39] From, "U.S. National Security Strategy: Transform America's National Security Institutions To Meet the Challenges and Opportunities of the 21st Century".

236   *The Political Use of Military Force in US Foreign Policy*

prosperity',[40] we may expect that the use of force will increase with the expansion of the definition of national interests. Whether such rhetoric and subsequent actions will go the way of JFK's call to 'pay and price, bear any burden', remains to be seen. The challenge for scholars is to maintain a power and security or realist theory of foreign policy that can adapt as necessary to incorporate new threats, while we avoid the passing fads and stretching theory to the point of non-falsifiability.

Economic Interests

When we examine the record of military force deployed on behalf of economic interests, we encounter an interesting and sometimes overlooked history. Economic factors were often important and even critical throughout the last 220 years, but not generally for the reasons we find asserted in many texts. Presidents used the military primarily to defend American commerce, and occasionally to give it a helpful push. Neither presidents nor the military appear to have been the tools, unwitting or otherwise, of industry, or some capitalist ruling elite. Though they often shared many of the same values and views of the world, presidents rarely, if ever, acted to support big business at the expense of national security interests. Rather, presidents believed that trade; the protection of US economic interests overseas and the national interest went hand-in-hand. Presidents authorized the political use of military force to advance economic interests more than any other specific goal in the period 1798-1941, with the exception of protecting American lives. When specific, economic interests were attacked in the period 1948-1998, presidents almost always used force, even if they did not use force as often as in the past. Therefore, any explanation of the political use of military force in US foreign policy history that overlooks the enduring and critical role played by economic interests is seriously flawed.

Even when US capabilities were weak, what little navy the nation had was mostly devoted to protecting commercial vessels on the high seas. As US trade flourished, the US naval presence expanded and presidents used the military not just to take action on the waters, but on land too when fractious societies endangered American property and businesses. Later, when the US built a navy to match its economic power, presidents became more aggressive about asserting and protecting US economic interests. Taft's 'dollar diplomacy' and Wilson's crusading idealism were much more than brief exercises in gunboat diplomacy. Wilson especially relied on the military to engineer thoroughgoing economic reforms in other nations. In the post World War II era, the US had all the capabilities it needed to promote commerce, but military power *mostly* became too blunt an instrument to shape the economic policies of other nations. Diplomacy was more effective, less expensive and certainly more politically correct.

---

[40] Quadrennial Defense Review Report (2001, VI).

Conclusion 237

The will to use force for economic gain has been present throughout American history. All presidents from the framers of the Constitution through the present have seen the virtue and necessity in using force to defend/advance the wealth of the nation. Whether it was to protect the merchant marine or insure access to oil, when diplomacy failed, force was called in. Even presidents like Woodrow Wilson who claimed to be above such materialistic ambitions, certainly understood that American values could be threatened by those who did not play by the economic rules of the game. Against such nations and leaders, force was an appropriate tool. The only time when we see a conspicuous absence of will was in the global imperialism of the 1860s through 1880s. Presidents generally resisted the temptation to inject the US into the scramble for colonies. Only when it could be joined with a practical and morally uplifting crusade, could presidents rationalize sacrificing these ideals. Presidents most often used force to defend tangible interests like property and promising markets, not for the greater glory of commerce.

The world has provided the US with ample opportunity to exploit foreign peoples and resources overseas. Until World War II, the choice concerned which among these numerous opportunities offered the greatest profit at the least cost; or which presented the most compelling threat to America's own properties and resources. Opportunities still abound if presidents wished to demand fair trade or cheap resources at gunpoint. But these are not truly opportunities for presidents possess little choice in such matters as I have argued previously. Opportunities exist today only when states seek to deny or control those resources or markets presidents believe are vital to the health of the nation. Because the US has become so powerful, most states are behaving mostly as the US would wish. The vast majority of US trade and investment in the world is with nations with whom the US enjoys good relations. The exceptions continue to be many of the oil-exporting nations of the Middle East and perhaps China. While we cannot rule out the possibility that an issue like the trade deficit with China may one day cause a rupture in the relationship, the source of contention is generally political-military issues (e.g., the future of Taiwan). Currently in the Middle East the US enjoys fairly good relations with the major oil exporters. Even some of its former adversaries, such as Libya and Iran, seem to be moving away from some elements of past extremism. Nevertheless, the continuing Arab-Israeli conflict, power transfers to potentially hostile leaders in places like Saudi Arabia, and terrorism make this region unpredictable and potentially dangerous. Indeed, oil crises appear to occur with some regularity (1973, 1980, 1990). Until the autocratic regimes of the Middle East make democratic transitions, there exists the possibility that political and military conflicts will spill over into the economic realm.

If we assume that trade, investment, currency values and other economic issues will increasingly come to dominate global politics, the utility of military force in such a world may be either quite high or quite low. If present trends continue and more countries open their markets and subscribe to the basic tenets of capitalism, presidents will have little reason to use force to either open markets or protect US economic interests in them. Host governments will, presumably do

238 *The Political Use of Military Force in US Foreign Policy*

those things that force accomplished in years past. This trend ought to diminish the value of force. Furthermore, if the major, economic actors of the world continue to assume that economic issues are to be resolved through negotiation and that even the threat of force is disruptive to the international economy, the utility of military power should decline even further. This is one possible world future. But what if the US trade deficit or the balance of payments problems grows to be of such importance and intractability, that the diplomats cannot envision a solution and the soldiers must take over? If US, or any other nation's prosperity becomes so threatened by the interests and actions of its trading partners, military force may be employed to force concessions. The answer regarding which future is the more likely hinges on the fungibility of military force in economic matters. We can only assume that force is always a last resort option when all else fails. Nonetheless, given that presidents almost always use force when there are threats or attacks on specific, US economic interests, we should expect economic interests to continue to play a critical role in explaining key, political uses of military force.

Liberal Idealist Interests

Liberal idealist interests retain a storied place in the annals of US military intervention. Although largely absent from presidents' decisions in the 18th and 19th centuries, its values still lay at the ideological core of US foreign policy. Liberalism anchored the belief systems of the Framers and guided the international practices of subsequent leaders. Liberal idealism led earlier presidents toward restraint in the use of force as military action would corrupt the nation's ideals and enmesh the US in the anti-liberal machinations of the European empires. But as US power and the influence of progressivist thinking grew in the late 19th and early 20th centuries, presidents set aside the old reluctance to go abroad in search of monsters to destroy, to paraphrase John Quincy Adams. Liberal values played a prominent role in the spate of military interventions in the Western hemisphere, and later permeated the US-USSR competition for client states. As the tensions of the Cold War abated then ended, presidents became more likely to use the military to promote democracy and human rights. Freed from the zero-sum competition of superpower rivalry where a regime's external allegiance meant more than its internal policies, presidents now have the opportunity to realize the ideals to which so they have so often referred. For even though presidents may not always be sincere in their espousal of liberal values to justify military operations, the increasing frequency with which they make such arguments may well make such justifications a real and necessary, political requirement for using military force.

The role of liberal idealism in the political use of military force is varied and complex. The need to protect liberal institutions and way of life at home is a core value of US foreign policy that all presidents pursue. As US strength and confidence has grown, so too has the willingness to export these ideals, even at gunpoint. Although liberal values did not always cause military interventions earlier in the 20th century or during the Cold War, proliberalization aims often become central to operations once they were underway. More recently, some of the

Conclusion 239

most massive, military interventions of the 1990s involved such objectives. Over the last one hundred years it has become increasingly difficult for US forces to intervene in substantial numbers in another government's affairs without attempting to instill or advance liberal values and institutions. If the US military presence is to be strong and pervasive in a foreign nation, the US cannot help but act in ways mostly in keeping with liberal idealist values. We can conclude that liberal values are embedded deep enough in US foreign policy to substantially influence an important number of major political uses of force. They have become critical enough to recent major interventions to demand their inclusion in any comprehensive theory of the use of force as a foreign policy tool.

It is at times difficult to discern when US foreign policy aims to satisfy primarily the interests of its own citizens, and when it is truly looking out for the welfare of people in other nations. We continually see those in charge of its policies injecting the rhetoric of liberal idealism into foreign policy debates, justifying US actions on such grounds and seeking to remake the world in its own liberal idealist image. In fact, it is when the use of force is contemplated that we truly see foreign policy makers attempting to come to grips with what the US seeks in the world, and what image the nation wishes to project. The consideration of military action raises the most profound questions a people consider regarding their national identity, and so it is at these times that we can learn the most about a country. If force is to be used, US citizens have demanded that the reasons be just. While notions of what is 'just' have continually evolved, the need to frame the exercise of military power as a 'police' force seeking to right wrongs, and not as a conquering army, has remained constant and grown stronger.

Opportunities to use military force to advance the aims of liberal idealism abound at the moment. The personal liberties and human rights that are the rewards of democracy are attracting more and more people. Many non-democratic regimes are loosening their reigns on power and so inspire their citizens to ask for more freedom. The US seeks to expedite these trends, largely through words and material incentives. But when dictators' repressive policies cause massive human rights violations within or threaten surrounding nations, presidents have found that military force can be an effective tool to promote liberal idealism and restore stability. Democracy, or at least government legitimated in the eyes of its people, has come to be seen as a right of all people. Presidents from Woodrow Wilson to Harry Truman; from Ronald Reagan to Bill Clinton have claimed for the US a right, even a responsibility to help these people. If these current experiments in proliberalization policies in the former Yugoslavia, and in many African and Latin American nations succeed, and the lesson learned is that external assistance is vital to the genesis of democracy, we can expect that when similar opportunities arise in the future, similar models will be followed.

It is therefore extremely important for theorists and those who conduct empirical analyses of US foreign policy to explore the liberal idealist underpinnings of US foreign policy and develop better methods of verifying the causes and consequences of proliberalization, military interventions in this new age. We must be especially mindful of the timing and choice of US military

240   *The Political Use of Military Force in US Foreign Policy*

intervention in the context of regime change and widespread human rights abuses and violence. What types of regimes and what kinds of regime changes are most likely to make military intervention more attractive to a president who may be reluctant to embark on a major nation building exercise. At what point in the cycle of violence in some failed state do presidents find it most appropriate, both from a political as well as a humanitarian perspective, to intervene? At present, we know that presidents are increasingly likely to use force in some such circumstances, but we do not know nearly enough about when they become so inclined, and perhaps most importantly, where they will intervene. Given the prevalence of civil wars and other forms of political violence and abusive regimes around the world, the 'opportunities' to use force to come to the aid of oppressed people are abundant. Deciphering where the 'demand' is greatest and when the 'supply' of force is acceptable is the challenge for scholars here.

Domestic Political Interests

The influence of domestic, political forces on presidents' willingness to use force is perhaps the weakest of all the interests we examined. Across time, and even within the last 50 years, which scholars have analyzed the most intensively, we see do not see the level of empirical evidence that we might expect given the immense popularity of this particular theory. I will first review this evidence, but then suggest that perhaps we should expand our search for domestic political linkages beyond presidential popularity, elections and the economy.

Diversionary theory holds that opportunities for diversionary behavior arise when presidents' popularity and the economy are in a downswing or when elections are approaching. Given US power and the advent of mass media technology, we would expect that the Cold War era and beyond would provide presidents with a plethora of opportunities to engage in diversionary behavior. For most of this time the public and the Congress accepted the notion that the country was under siege the world over, thus providing presidents with an ongoing rationale for using force in a variety of settings. The rise of public opinion polls created awareness of the president's political situation, while the use of instantaneous communications made it possible to both order the military into battle on a moment's notice and for word of these events to make it back in time for the evening news. Yet, the statistical evidence presented in both Chapter 5 and Chapter 6 indicates that domestic conditions exercise little impact on the likelihood of a use of force. Indeed, when we look at the wide body of research in this field, as well as the statistical analyses here, it is never really clear if presidents are supposed to use force when times are good or times are bad. Scholars make both arguments. That both arguments could coexist within one theory is, to coin a phrase, highly illogical.

What does the future hold for diversionary theory and diversionary behavior? Since the US is the dominant power in the world, its ability to use force has never been greater. Presidents will have the capability to use force for diversionary and all manner of purposes. We can assume there will always be

Conclusion 241

upswings and downswings in the president's domestic political fortunes, but what of the targets he might attack? Will presidents always have a convenient set of targets against whom a quick, visible military strike is a plausible option? If the US uses force to settle internal conflicts, assist in humanitarian endeavors and anchor emerging democratic regimes, the rally round the flag effect would probably not be all that great. The rally seems to occur in response to a shared sense of threat, but if there are no enemies (with the exception of the usual suspect states), only nations to be assisted or governments to be reformed, where is the need to close ranks? On the other hand, there is always the possibility that new enemies could arise. Many of the same rogue nations the US has always confronted, along with terrorist organizations and the looming Chinese challenge may still provide plenty of opportunity for diversionary behavior. I should add, however, that diversionary theory says little about such developments. I can only extrapolate from it and attempt to find some justification to continue to test this theory. The only question left to be answered would seem to be, why are scholars so focused on what is arguably the weakest theory of the use of force?

I would suggest that instead we concentrate our energies on looking for other, potential linkages between domestic politics and the use of force. The role the domestic environment plays in *discouraging* uses of force would seem to be ripe for theoretical exploration and empirical testing. We have seen that presidents generally would rather focus on domestic issues that are important to their party and constituents than foreign policy, especially when times are bad. For example, Chanley (1999) finds that as the public increasingly identifies domestic, economic problems as the most important problem facing the nation, public support for foreign policy internationalism in general, as well as militant internationalism in particular, decrease. Presidents do not possess strong enough incentives to ignore public demands to devote resources to problems at home while seeking to divert public attention away from such matters. The benefits are few and the costs are high for attempted diversionary behavior. Instead, it is the president who is diverted from foreign policy to domestic matters. If we assume that presidents are most interested in succeeding in office and maintaining the support of voters and members of Congress, they will be strongly encouraged to spend their time and money on those problems at the top of the public agenda. Far from rescuing a president from declining approval ratings and a slumping economy, a diversionary use of force may well generate public suspicion and criticism. In fact, the worse the problems at home, and hence the greater the incentive to distract the public according to diversionary theory, the more likely the public would presume the president was seeking to hoodwink it. Given a domestic polity afflicted with political or economic problems, we would expect that only when the threat to the US was so severe that the justification to use force was obvious to all, might today's savvy and cynical public accept the military deployment. But such urgent uses of force would no longer really qualify as diversionary uses of force given their necessity. A theory of domestic politics and the use of force should be premised more on estimations regarding costs and less on calculations about benefits and their relationship to the timing of military action. Diversionary theory

242   *The Political Use of Military Force in US Foreign Policy*

as it is currently applied is far too limited, for it is concerned only with the latter. We should focus on the manner in which the domestic environment either limits or 'allows' presidents to use the military to influence foreign actors. Public opinion, political institutions, media activity, and a host of other domestic actors and factors certainly shape presidential decision-making. Congressional support of the president, public fear of casualties, and the CNN factor, just to name a few of the more obvious candidates, should be thoroughly researched. The scholarly community would be best served by developing a broader model of these forces than one that is so narrowly focused. We should examine the wide range of conditions that set the broad parameters on foreign policy, thereby serving to make possible or discourage particular activities.

Three Final Points

From all the major and minor points I have raised thus far, I see three more encompassing lessons we can extract that any reader, scholar or practitioner should remember if she remembers nothing else. First, the US, for a variety of reasons, seems especially prone to use military force to influence rather than compel foreign actors to undertake some action. Unlike other major powers that have conquered or occupied foreign lands to achieve their objectives and were prepared to sustain the financial, political and military costs required to dominate other lands, the US has mostly eschewed such policies as violative of the values of freedom and liberty. Granted there have been notable exceptions to the US aversion to the occupation of foreign lands, such as the military interventions in Central America and the Caribbean early in the 20th century and the post Cold War operations in Somalia, Haiti, Bosnia and now Iraq. The influence of liberalism, mostly though not always, contributes to a reluctance to become involved in the affairs of other nations to the extent required were the US to compel change. And certainly the US generally seems desirous of exiting these nations as quickly as possible. Yet, even these thoroughgoing interventions were designed in principle to promote rather than supplant liberal values. In addition, we see a typical American distaste for prolonged occupations as messy, burdensome and corrupting of its own values. One senses a profound reluctance rather than an eager desire to play the role of military overseer. Perhaps this has deep roots in American isolationist tendencies or perhaps it stems from a desire to make money rather than make war. Thus, in contrast to those major powers that sought to influence nations, peoples and the world through military conquest, the constant use of limited, military force to achieve limited political objectives is the preferred, American method. Whatever the reason, presidents have authorized such missions hundreds and hundreds of times, while waging war on just a few occasions. The degree to which this trend continues in the post September 11 world is a vital issue for all to ponder and examine.

     Second, (and perhaps even as a result of the previous assertion) the US tends to remain in recurring patterns of behavior when using military force. Once it has begun using the military to achieve a type of objective or to influence a

Conclusion 243

particular nation, it typically continues to engage in such behavior until some major event disrupts the pattern or a new crisis redirects its attention toward other interests and places. For example, throughout the 19th century, presidents repeatedly used force to protect and advance US commercial interests abroad. It continually intervened in events in Latin America, the Caribbean and Asia to protect propertied interests until the 20th century when the US developed a diplomatic corps and later other bureaucracies to manage many of these tasks. Then, in the years 1898-1919, and again since the end of the Cold War, the US repeatedly used military force to advance the cause of democracy and human rights. The carnage of World War I put a stop to nation building exercises that had once been embarked upon with great frequency and zeal in the Progressive era. And as we saw in Chapter 6, the US has often singled out certain pariah nations for aggressive assertion of its interests. Presidents have repeatedly used force against these states and especially their leaders until there was a regime change. Absent some drastic improvement in leadership in these nations, however, the US tends to become involved in what scholars term an 'enduring rivalry' where often presidents perceive the only foreign policy option strong enough to signal US interests and demonstrate US credibility is the use of military force. And there are even times when the recurring pattern in the use of force is the disinclination to use it, as in the isolationist period from 1920-1941. Thus, there is a strong tendency toward predictability in the reasons for which military force is employed, and the frequency with which presidents use force. Having become convinced of the need to use force to achieve some end or thwart some dictator, and perhaps even developed a 'doctrine' to publicly justify their actions, presidents become committed to a course of action that they do not waiver from until some watershed event convinces them that the old ways are no longer appropriate.

Last, because of the increasing interconnectedness of its foreign policy goals, it is becoming more difficult to ascertain which particular objectives lead to which specific political uses of military force. As hegemon the US has broad interests geographically and substantively. It is interested in events the world over and has the capacity to project force to the most remote corners of the earth. Even though the US tends to use force much more often against particular regimes, geographically it tends to use force everywhere. Probably no place on earth escapes US notice and given sufficient cause, presidents would probably not hesitate to use force against any particular nation. More importantly, the US has deep and varied interests in the military, economic and ideological relations among nations, the military, economic and ideological policies within nations and the formal and informal international rules and regimes that structure relations. As the guarantor of global stability it has an interest in deterring or stopping those nations and those international and intranational developments, whether military, economic or political, that put this equilibrium at risk. As Colin Powell, no proponent of the continual use of military force once said, 'The real threat is the unknown, the uncertain. In a very real sense, *the primary threat to our security is instability…*'

(emphasis added).[41] Threats to any of the elements of the hegemonic world order implicate the others. For example, war damages the global economy, while the threat of war creates uncertainty that prevents growth in the economy. Disruptions in the essentials of a modern, global economy, such as oil shortages, affect the security and stability of the system. And increasingly when presidents do authorize major, military interventions they either do so to change the policies of another regime, or are expected to do so in the course of the intervention. Each of the major US foreign policy objectives reinforces the others and is an interlocking element of its hegemonic order. They do not exist in isolation from each other, geographically or substantively, and could not long be pursued in opposition to one another without jeopardizing the global framework of order they constitute. As more nations of the world come to accept the US-led global military, economic and ideological system, these elements become even more fused together. Any explanation of the political use of military force requires that all be considered even when one objective appears to be dominant. As long as the US remains the hegemon, we can expect this trend to continue.

---

[41] General Colin Powell, testimony, Committee on the Budget, US Senate, February 3, 1992.

Bibliography

Adler, David G. and Larry N. George (1996), *The Constitution and the Conduct of American Foreign Policy*, Lawrence, Kansas: University of Kansas Press.

Allison, Graham T. Jr. and Robert P. Beschel, Jr. (1992), 'Can the US Promote Democracy?' *Political Science Quarterly*, vol. 107, pp. 81-98.

Allison, Graham and Philip Zelikow (1999), *Essence of Decision*, Boston: Little, Brown Company.

Art, Robert (1999), 'The Strategy of Selective Engagement' in *The Use of Force*, (Robert Art and Kenneth Waltz (eds). New York, New York: Rowan and Littlefield.

Axelrod, Robert (1984), *The Evolution of Cooperation*, New York, New York: Basic Books.

Axelrod, Robert (1991), 'A Defensible Defense'. *International Security*, vol.15, pp.5-53.

Ayabar de Soto, Jose M. (1978), *Dependency and Intervention: The Case of Guatemala in 1954*. Boulder, Colorado: Westview Press.

Barnet, Richard (1968), *Intervention and Revolution: The US in the Third World*, New York, New York: World Publishing Company.

Bennet, D. Scott (1998), 'Integrating and Testing Models of Rivalry Duration', *American Journal of Political Science*, vol. 42, pp. 1200-1232.

Benoit, Kenneth (1996), 'Democracies Really are More Pacific (In General): Reexamining Regime Type and War Involvement'. *Journal of Conflict Resolution*, vol. 40, pp. 636-57.

Berk, Richard A. (1983), 'An Introduction to Sample Selection Bias in Sociological Data.' *American Sociological Review*, vol. 48, pp. 386-398.

Betts, Richard (1987), *Nuclear Blackmail and Nuclear Balance*, Washington D.C. The Brookings Institution.

Blainey, Geoffrey (1973), *The Causes of War*, New York, New York: The Free Press.

Blechman, Barry and Stephen Kaplan (1978), *Force Without War*, Washington D.C.: The Brookings Institution.

Boettcher, William (1995), 'Context, Methods, Numbers, and Words: Prospect Theory in International Relations'. *Journal of Conflict Resolution*, vol. 39, pp. 561-583.

Boot, Max (2002), *The Savage Wars of Peace*, New York, New York: Basic Books.

Brands, H.W. (1987), 'Decisions on American Armed Intervention: Lebanon, Dominican Republic and Grenada', *Political Science Quarterly*, vol.102, pp. 607-624.

Brecher, Michael and Jonathan Wilkenfeld (1997), *A Study of Crisis*, Ann Arbor, Michigan: University of Michigan Press.

Brewer, Thomas L. (1991), 'Foreign Direct Investment in Developing Countries', World Bank Working Paper, Policy, Research and External Affairs Complex.

Bueno de Mesquita, Bruce and David Lalman (1992), *War and Reason*, New Haven, Connecticut: Yale University Press.

Buhite, Russell D. (1995), *Lives at Risk: Hostages and Victims in American Foreign Policy*, Wilmington, DE: Scholarly Resources Books.

Burkhart, Ross E. (1997), 'Comparative Democracy and Income Distribution: Shape and Direction of the Causal Arrow', *Journal of Politics*, vol. 59, pp.148-164.

246 *The Political Use of Military Force in US Foreign Policy*

Burkhart, Ross E. and Lewis-Beck, Michael S. (1994), 'Comparative Democracy: the Economic Development Thesis', *American Political Science Review*, vol. 88, pp. 903-910.

Burrowes, Reynold A. (1988), *Revolution and Rescue in Grenada*, New York, New York: Greenwood Press.

Butler, Smedley (1935), *War is a Racket*, New York.

Calhoun, Frederick S. (1986), *Power and Principle*. The Kent State University Press.

Callcott, Wilfrid Hardy (1942), *The Caribbean Policy of the US, 1890-1920*, Baltimore, Maryland: The Johns Hopkins University Press.

Carothers, Thomas (2000), *Aiding Democracy Abroad*, Washington D.C.: The Carnegie Endowment for International Peace.

Carr. E.H. (1946) (2nd ed.), *The Twenty Years Crisis: 1919-1939*, London: Macmillan and Company.

Center for Naval Analyses (1991), 'The Use of Naval Forces in the Post-War Era: US Navy and US Marine Corps Crisis Response Activity, 1946-1990', Alexandria, Virginia: Center for Naval Analyses.

Chanley, Virginia A. (1999), 'U.S. Public Views of International Involvement from 1964-1993: Time series Analyses of General and Militant Internationalism', *Journal of Conflict Resolution*, vol. 43, pp. 23-44.

Chapman, Michael (2002). 'TR: No Friend of the Constitution', *CATO Policy Report*, vol. XXIV, pp. 1 and 14-16.

Christenson, Thomas J. (1996), *Useful Adversaries: Grand Strategy, Domestic Mobilization and Sino-American Conflict, 1947-1958*, Princeton, New Jersey: Princeton University Press.

Clark, David (2003), 'Can Strategic Interaction Divert Diversionary Behavior? A Model of US Conflict Propensity', *Journal of Politics*, vol. 65, pp. 1013-1039.

Clark, David and Patrick Regan (2003), 'Opportunities to Fight: A Statistical Technique for Modeling Unobservable Phenomena'. *Journal of Conflict Resolution*, vol. 47, pp. 94-115.

Congressional Research Service. (1993), *Background Information on the Use of US Armed Forces in Foreign Countries: 1993 Revision*, Washington D.C.: US Government Printing Office.

Coser, Lewis. A. (1956), *The Functions of Social Conflict*, New York, New York: Free Press.

Dalton, Kathleen (2002), *Theodore Roosevelt*. New York, New York: Alfred A. Knopf.

DeRouen, Karl (2000), 'Presidents and the Diversionary Use of Force: A Research Note', *International Studies Quarterly*, vol. 44, pp. 317-328.

DeRouen, Karl (1995), 'The Indirect Link: Politics, The Economy and the Use of Force', *Journal of Conflict Resolution*, vol. 39, pp. 671-695.

Destler, I.M., Leslie Gelb and Anothy Lake (1984), *Our Own Worst Enemy*, New York, New York: Simon and Schuster.

Deutsch, Karl W. (1974), 'Theories of Imperialism and Neocolonialism', (35-56) in Steven J. Rosen and James R. Kurth (eds) *Testing Theories of Economic Imperialism*, Lexington, Massachusetts: Lexington Books.

Diamond, Larry (1992), 'Promoting Democracy', *Foreign Policy*, vol. 87, pp. 25-46.

Dos Santos, Theotonio (1970), 'The Structure of Dependence', *American Economic Review*, vol. 60, pp. 231-236.

Duignan, Peter and L.H. Gann (1984), *The US and Africa: A History*, Cambridge: Cambridge University Press.

Facts on File (1948-1998), *Yearbook*, New York, New York: Facts on File Inc.

Bibliography 247

Federation of American Scientists. US Military Operations, Found at http://www.fas.org/man/dod-101/ops/#post on July 22.

Ferguson, Yale (1972), 'The US and Political Development in Latin America', in *Contemporary Interamerican Relations: A Reader in Theory and Issues*, Yale Ferguson (ed.), Englewood Cliffs, New Jersey: Prentice Hall.

Field, James A. (1984), 'All Economists, All Diplomats', in (pp. 1-54) William H. Becker and Samuel F. Wells (eds), *Economics and World Power*, New York, New York: Columbia University Press.

Fordham, Benjamin (1998a), 'The Politics of Threat Perception and the Use of Force: A Political Economy Model of US Uses of Force, 1949-1994', *International Studies Quarterly*, vol. 42, pp. 567-90.

Fordham, Benjamin (1998b), 'Partisanship, Macroeconomic Policy, and the US Uses of Force, 1949-1994', *Journal of Conflict Resolution*, vol. 42, pp. 418-439.

Fordham, Benjamin O. and Christopher C. Sarver (2001), 'Militarized Interstate Disputes and US Uses of Force', *International Studies Quarterly*, vol. 45, pp. 455-466.

Fossedal, Gregory A. (1989), *The Democratic Imperative*, New York, New York: Basic Books Inc.

Frank, Andre Gunder (1969), *Latin America: Underdevelopment or Revolution*, New York, New York: Monthly Review Press.

Gaddis, John (1982), *Strategies of Containment*, New York, New York: Oxford University Press.

Galtung, Johan (1971), 'A Structural Theory of Imperialism', *Journal of Peace Research*, vol. 2, pp. 81-98.

Gelpi, Christopher (1997), 'Democratic Diversions: Governmental Structure and the Externalization of Domestic Conflict'. *Journal of Conflict Resolution*, vol. 41, pp.255-282.

George, Alexander and Richard Smoke. 1974. *Deterrence in American Foreign Policy: Theory and Practice*. New York, New York: Columbia University Press.

Gholz, Eugene, Daryl G. Press and Harvey M. Sapolsky (1997), 'Come Home, America: The Strategy of Restraint in the Face of Temptation', *International Security*, vol. 21, pp. 5-48.

Gibbs, David N. (1991), *The Political Economy of Third World Interventions*, Chicago, Illinois: University of Chicago Press.

Gilpin, Robert (1987), *War and Change in World Politics*, 2nd ed. Cambridge: Cambridge University Press.

Gilpin, Robert (1975), *US Power and the Multinational Corporation*, New York, New York: Basic Books.

Gleijeses, Piero (1991), *Shattered Hope: The Guatemalan Revolution*, Princeton, New Jersey: Princeton University Press.

Goertz, Gary and Paul F. Diehl (1995), 'The Initiation and Termination of Enduring Rivalries: The Impact of Political Shocks', *American Journal of Political Science*, vol. 39, pp. 30-52.

Goertz, Gary and Paul F. Diehl, 'Enduring Rivalries: Theoretical Constructs and Empirical Patterns', *International Studies Quarterly*, vol.37, pp.147-171.

Gould, Lewis L. (1991), *The Presidency of Theodore Roosevelt*, Lawrence, Kansas: University Press of Kansas.

Graebner, Norman A. (1964), *Ideas and Diplomacy: Readings in the Intellectual Tradition of American Foreign Policy*, New York, New York: Oxford University Press.

Greene, William (1993), *Econometric Analysis* (2nd Ed.), Englewood Cliffs, New Jersey: Prentice Hall.

Grieco, Joseph M. (1988), 'Realist Theory and the Problem of International Cooperation: Analysis with Amended Prisoner's Dilemma Model', *Journal of Politics*, vol.50, pp. 600-624.

Grieco, Joseph, Robert Powell and Duncan Snidal (1993), 'The Relative Gains Problem for International Cooperation', *American Political Science Review*, vol. 87, pp. 729-743.

Haass, Richard (1994), *Intervention: The Use of American Military Force in the Post Cold War World*, Washington D.C.: Carnegie Endowment for International Peace.

Hagan, Kenneth J. (1991), *This People's Navy: The Making of American Sea Power*, New York, New York: Free Press.

Hamilton, Alexander, James Madison and John Jay (1787-1788), originally. *The Federalist Papers*, Bantam Classic Edition, 1982, New York, New York: Bantam Books.

Hannigan, Robert E. (2002), *The New World Power*, Philidelphia, Pennsylvania: University of Pennsylvania Press.

Hathaway, Robert M. (1984), 'Economic Diplomacy in a Time of Crisis', in (pp. 277-332) William H. Becker and Samuel F. Wells (eds), *Economics and World Power*, New York, New York: Columbia University Press.

Haydock, Michael D. (1999) *City Under Siege*, Washington D.C.: Brassey's.

Healy, David (1988), *Drive To Hegemony*, Madison, Wisconsin: University of Wisconsin Press.

Heckman, James J. (1976), 'The Common Structure of Statistical Models of Truncation, Sample Selection and Limited Dependent Variables and a Sample Estimator for Such Models', *Annals of Economic and Social Measurement*, vol. 5, pp. 475-492.

Henkin, Louis (1990), *Constitutionalism, Democracy and Foreign Affairs*, New York, New York: Columbia University Press.

Hermann, Margaret and Charles Kegley (1998), 'The Use of US Military Intervention to Promote Democracy: Evaluating the Record', *International Interactions*, vol. 24, pp. 91-114.

Hobbes, Thomas (1968), *Leviathan*, London: Penguin Books.

Hobson, John A. (1965), *Imperialism, A Study*, Ann Arbor, Michigan: University of Michigan Press.

Hoffman, Stanley (1998), *World Disorders*, Lanham, MD: Rowan and Littlefield Publishers.

Horowitz, David (1955), *The Free World Colossus*, New York, New York: Hill and Wang.

Horsman, Reginald (1985), *The Diplomacy of the New Republic*, Arlington Heights, Illinois: Harlan Davidson, Inc.

Howarth, Stephen (1991), *To Shining Sea*, New York, New York: Random House.

Huntington, Samuel P. (1999), 'American Ideals versus American Institutions', Reprinted in *American Foreign Policy*, G. John Ikenberry (ed.), New York, New York: Longman Press.

Huntington, Samuel P. (1993), 'Why International Primacy Matters'. *International Security*, vol. 17, pp. 68-83.

Huntington, Samuel P. (1981), *American Politics: The Promise of Disharmony*, Cambridge, Massachusetts: Belknap Press of Harvard University.

Huth, Paul K. (1998), 'Major Power Intervention in International Crises', *Journal of Conflict Resolution*, vol. 42, pp. 744-770.

Ikenberry, G. John (1988), 'Conclusion: An Institutional Approach to American Foreign Economic Policy', *International Organization*, vol. 42, pp. 219-243.

Ikenberry, G. John and Charles A. Kupchan (1990), 'Socialization and Hegemonic Power', *International Organization*, vol. 44, pp. 283-315.

Immerman, Richard (1982), *The CIA in Guatemala*, Austin, Texas: University of Texas Press.

Bibliography 249

Jackson, Robert (1988), *The Berlin Airlift*, Wellingborough, United Kingdom: Patrick Stephens Press.

James, Marquis (1938), *The Life of Andrew Jackson*, New York, New York: The Bobbs-Merrill Company.

James, Patrick and Athanasios Hristoulas (1994), 'Domestic Politics and Foreign Policy: Evaluating A Model of Crisis Activity for the US', *Journal of Politics*, vol. 56, pp. 327-348.

James, Patrick and John R. Oneal (1991), 'Influences on the President's Use of Force', *Journal of Conflict Resolution*, vol. 35, pp. 307-332.

Jervis, Robert (1993), 'International Primacy', *International Security*, vol. 17, pp. 52-67.

Jessup, P.C. (1938), *Elihu Root*, New York, New York: Dodd, Mead and Company.

Job, Brian L. and Charles W. Ostrom Jr. (1986), 'Opportunity and Choice: The US and the Political Use of Force: 1948-1976', Paper presented at the 1986 Annual Meetings of the American Political Science Association, Washington D.C.

Johnson, Loch K. (1989), *America's Secret Power*, Oxford: Oxford University Press.

Johnson, Robert (1985), 'Exaggerating America's Stakes in Third World Countries', *International Security*, vol. 10, pp. 32-68.

Jones, Daniel M. Stuart A. Bremer and J. David Singer (1996), 'Militarized Interstate Disputes, 1816-1992: Rationale, Coding Rules, and Empirical Patterns', *Conflict Management and Peace Science*, vol. 15, pp. 163:213.

Kaplan, Lawrence S. (1987), *Entangling Alliances with None: American Foreign Policy in the Age of Jefferson*, Kent, Ohio: The Kent State University Press.

Kaufmann, William (1954), *The Requirements of Deterrence*, Princeton, New Jersey: Center for International Studies.

Katzenstein, Peter (1976), 'International Relations and Domestic Structures: Foreign Economic Policies of Advanced Industrialized States', *International Organization*, vol. 30, pp.1-45.

Keesing's Limited, Various years (1948-1986), *Keesing's Contemporary Archives*, London: Keesing's Limited.

Kennan, George F. (1985/1986), 'Morality and Foreign Policy', *Foreign Affairs*, vol. 64, pp. 205-218.

Kennan, George F. (1951), *American Diplomacy*. Chicago, Illinois: University of Chicago Press.

Kennedy, Paul (1987), *The Rise and Fall of Great Powers*. New York, New York: Random House.

_____ (1974), *The Samoan Triangle*, New York, New York: Barnes & Noble.

Keohane, Robert O. and Helen Milner (1996), *Internationalization and Domestic Politics*, Cambridge, United Kingdom: Cambridge University Press.

Keohane, Robert, and Joseph Nye (1989), *Power and Interdependence* (2nd edition), New York, New York: HarperCollins.

Kernell, Samuel (1993), *Going Public* (2nd edition), Washington D.C.: Congressional Quarterly Press.

King, Kimi L. and James D. Meernik. (1999), 'The Supreme Court and the Powers of the Executive: The Adjudication of Foreign Policy.' *Political Research Quarterly*, vol. 52, pp. 801-824.

Kissinger, Henry (1994), *Diplomacy*, New York, New York: Simon and Schuster.

Kissinger, Henry (1982), *Years of Upheaval*, Boston, Massachusetts: Little, Brown and Company.

Kolko, Gabriel (1988), *Confronting the Third World*, New York, New York: Pantheon Books.

250   *The Political Use of Military Force in US Foreign Policy*

Kolko, Gabriel (1969), *The Roots of American Foreign Policy*, Boston, Massachusetts: Beacon Press.

Krasner, Stephen D. (ed.) (1983), *International Regimes*, Ithaca, New York: Cornell University Press.

Krasner, Stephen D. (1978), *Defending the National Interest*, Princeton, New Jersey: Princeton University Press.

Kurth, James R. (1974), 'Testing Theories of Economic Imperialism', (3-14) in Steven J. Rosen and James R. Kurth (eds), *Testing Theories of Economic Imperialism*, Lexington, Massachusetts: Lexington Books.

Lafeber, Walter (1978), *The Panama Canal: The Crisis in Historical Perspective*, New York, New York: Oxford University Press.

Lake, David. (1988a), *Power, Protection and Free Trade*, Ithica, New York: Cornell University Press.

Lake, David A. (1988b), 'The State and American Trade Strategy in the Pre-Hegemonic Era', *International Organization*, vol. 42, pp. 33-58.

Lake, David A. (1987), 'Power and the Third World: Toward a Realist Political Economy of North-South Relations', *International Studies Quarterly*, vol. 31, pp. 217-234.

Langley, Lester D. (1989), *America and the Americas: The US in the Western Hemisphere*. Athens, Georgia: University of Georgia Press.

Lee, Jong (1977), 'Rallying Around the Flag: Foreign Policy Events and Presidential Popularity', *Presidential Studies Quarterly*, vol. 7, pp. 252-256.

Leebaert, Derek (2002), *The Fifty Year Wound: How America's Cold War Victory Shapes Our World*, Boston, Massachusetts: Little, Brown and Company.

Leeds, Brett Ashley and David Davis (1999), 'Beneath the Surface: Regime Type and International Interaction, 1953-78', *Journal of Peace Research*, vol. 36, pp. 5-21

Leeds, Brett Ashley and David Davis (1997), 'Domestic Political Vulnerability and International Disputes', *Journal of Conflict Resolution*, vol. 41, pp. 814-834.

Leffler, Melvyn P. (1984), 'Expansionist Impulses and Domestic Constrainst', in (pp. 225-276) William H. Becker and Samuel F. Wells (eds), *Economics and World Power*, New York, New York: Columbia University Press.

Legro, Jeffrey W. and Andrew Moravcsik (1999), 'Is Anybody Still a Realist?', *International Security*, vol. 24, pp. 5-55.

Lenin, Vladimir Ilich (1939), *Imperialism, the Highest Stage of Capitalism*, New York, New York: International Publishers.

Lepgold, Joseph and Timothy McKeown (1995), 'Is American Foreign Policy Exceptional', *Political Science Quarterly*, vol. 110, pp. 369-384.

Lewis, William S. and Murakami Naojiro (1923), *Ranald McDonald: The Narrative of His Early Life*, Spokane, Washington: The Eastern Washington State Historical Society.

Levy, Jack (1989), 'The Diversionary Theory of War: A Criqique'. In Manus Widlarsky (ed.) *Handbook of War Studies*. Boston, Massachusetts: Unwin Hyman.

Lian, Bradley and John R. Oneal (1993), 'Presidents, the Use of Military Force and Public Opinion', *Journal of Conflict Resolution*, vol. 37, pp. 277-300.

Lindbloom, Charles E. (1977), *Politics and Markets: The World's Political-Economic Systems*, New York, New York: Basic Books.

Lindsay, James, Lois W. Sayrs and Wayne P. Steger (1992), 'The Determinants of Presidential Foreign Policy Choice', *American Politics Quarterly*, vol. 20, pp. 3-25.

Lipset, Seymour Martin (1991), *Political Man* (Revised Ed.), Baltimore, Maryland: Johns Hopkins University.

Bibliography

Lipson, Charles (1985), *Standing Guard: Protecting Foreign Capital in the Nineteenth and Twentieth Centuries*, Berkeley, California: University of California Press.

Long, David F. (1973), 'Martial Thunder: The First Official American Armed Intervention in Asia', *Pacific Historical Review*, 143-162.

MacDonald, Douglas (1992), *Adventures in Chaos: American Intervention for Reform in the Third World*, Cambridge, Massachusetts: Harvard University Press.

Machiavelli, Niccolo (1999), *The Prince* (George Bull, translator), London: Penguin Books.

Mahan, Alfred Thayer (1898) (15th ed), *The Influence of Sea Power Upon History*, Boston, Massachusetts: Little, Brown and Company.

Major, John (1993), *Prize Possession: The US and the Panama Canal*, Cambridge, UK: Cambridge University Press.

Mandelbaum, Michael (1996), 'Foreign Policy as Social Work', *Foreign Affairs*, vol. 75, pp. 16-32.

Mansfield, Edward D. (1992), 'The Concentration of Capabilities and International Trade'. *International Organization*, vol. 46, pp. 731-763.

Maoz, Zeev and Bruce Russett (1993), 'Normative and Structural Causes of Democratic Peace 1946-1986'. *American Political Science Review*, vol. 87, pp. 624-638.

Marra, Robin, Charles Ostrom and Dennis Simon (1990), 'Foreign Policy and Presidential Popularity'. *Journal of Conflict Resolution*, vol. 34, pp. 588-623.

Marshall, Monty G. Major Episodes of Political Violence. Data base, Available at http://members.aol.com/CSPmgm/warlist.htm as found on July 14 2002.

Maslow, Abraham (1970), *Motivation and Personality*, New York, New York: Harper and Row Publishers.

Mastanduno, Michael (1998), 'Economics and Security in Statecraft and Scholarship', *International Organization*, vol. 52, pp. 825-854.

May, Ernest (1973), *Lessons of the Past*, New York, New York: Oxford University Press.

McDougall, Walter A. (1997), *Promised Land, Crusader State*, Boston, Massachusetts: Houston Mifflin Company.

Mearsheimer, John (1990), 'Back to the Future: Instability in Europe after the Cold War', *International Security*, vol.15, pp. 5-56.

Meernik, James D. (2000), 'Modeling International Crises and the Political Use of Military Force by the US', *Journal of Peace Research*, vol. 37, pp. 547-562.

Meernik, James D. (1996), 'U.S. Military Intervention and the Promotion of Democracy'. *Journal of Peace Research*, vol. 33, pp.391-402.

Meernik, James D. (1994), 'Presidential Decision Making and the Political Use of Military Force', *International Studies Quarterly*, vol. 38, pp.121-138.

Meernik, James D. (1992), 'Presidential Decision Making and the Political Use of Military Force', Ph.D. Michigan State University: East Lansing.

Meernik, James D. Eric L. Krueger and Steven C. Poe (1998), 'Testing Models of US Foreign Policy: Foreign Aid During and After the Cold War', *Journal of Politics*, vol. 60, pp. 63-85.

Meernik, James and Peter Waterman (1996), 'The Myth of the Diversionary Use of Force by American Presidents', *Political Research Quarterly*, vol. 49, pp. 573-590.

Meese, Edwin (1992), *With Reagan*, Washington D.C.: Regnery Gateway.

Mellander, G.A. (1971), *The US in Panamanian Politics*, Danville, Illinois: The Interstate Printers and Publishers Inc.

Miller, Ross A. (1995), 'Domestic Structures and the Diversionary Use of Force', *American Journal of Political Science*, vol.39, pp.760-785.

Morgan, T. Clifton and Kenneth N. Bickers (1992), 'Domestic Discontent and the External Use of Force', *Journal of Conflict Resolution*, vol. 36, pp. 25-52.

Morgan, T. Clifton and Glenn Palmer (1997), 'A Two-Good Theory of Foreign Policy', *International Interactions*, vol.3, pp.225-244.

Morgenthau, Hans J. (1984), 'Human Rights and Foreign Policy', in Kenneth W. Thompson (ed.), *Moral Dimensions of American Foreign Policy*, New Brunswick, New Jersey: Transaction.

Morgenthau, Hans J. (1982), *In Defense of the National Interest*, Washington D.C.: University Press of America.

Morgenthau, Hans J. (1973), *Politics Among Nations* (5th ed.), New York, New York: Alfred A. Knopf.

Morris, Edmund (2001), *Theodore Rex*, New York, New York: Random House.

Morrow, James D. (1989), 'Capabilities, Uncertainty and Resolve: A Limited Information Model of Crisis Bargaining', *American Journal of Political Science*, vol. 33, pp. 941-972.

Mueller, John (1994), 'The Catastrophe Quota', *Journal of Conflict Resolution*, vol. 38, pp. 355-375.

Mueller, John (1973), *War, Presidents and Public Opinion*, New York, New York: Wiley.

Muller, Edward N. and Seligson, Mitchell (1994), 'Civic Culture and Democracy: the Question of Causal Relationships', *American Political Science Review*, vol. 88, pp. 635-652.

Munro, Dana (1934), *The US and the Caribbean Area*, Boston, Massachusetts: World Peace Foundation.

Muravchik, Joshua (1991), *Exporting Democracy: Fulfilling Ameria's Destiny*, Washington D.C.: AEI Press.

Newsday, New York edition, October 26, 1983, 'Made to Order Action', page 6.

Nixon, Richard M. (1978), *RN: The Memoirs of Richard Nixon*, New York, New York: Grosset and Dunlap.

NSC-68, April 14, 1950, FR: 1950 I., 263-264.

New York Times, Various years (1948-1998), *New York Times Index*, New York, New York: New York Times Company.

O'Connor, Richard (1969), *Pacific Destiny*, Boston, Massachusetts: Little, Brown and Company.

O'Shaughnessy, Hugh. (1984), *Grenada: An Eyewitness Account of the US Invasion and the Caribbean History That Provoked It*, New York, New York: Dodd, Mead and Company.

Odell, John S. (1974), 'Correlates of US Military Assistance and Military Intervention', in Stephen Rosen and James R. Kurth (eds), *Testing Theories of Economic Imperialism*, Lexington Massachusetts: D.C. Heath.

Olson, Mancur (1993), 'Dictatorship, Democracy, and Development', *American Political Science Review*, vol. 87, pp. 567-576.

Olson, Mancur (1982), *The Rise and Decline of Nations*, New Haven, Connecticut: Yale University Press.

Olson, Mancur (1965), *The Logic of Collective Action*, Cambridge, Massachusetts: Harvard University Press.

Oneal, John R. and Russett, Bruce (1997), 'The Classical Liberals were Right: Democracy, Interdependence, and Conflict, 1950-1985', *International Studies Quarterly*, vol. 41, pp. 267-293.

Ostrom, Charles W. Jr. and Brian L. Job (1986), 'The President and the Political Use of Force', *American Political Science Review*, vol. 80, pp. 541-566.

Ostrom, Charles W. and Dennis M. Simon (1988), 'The President's Public', *American Journal of Political Science*, vol. 32, pp. 1096-1119.

Bibliography

Owen, John M. IV (2002), 'The Foreign Imposition of Domestic Institutions', *International Organization*, vol. pp. 375-409.

Owen, John M. IV (1994), 'How Liberalism Produces Democratic Peace', *International Security*, vol. 19, pp. 87-125.

Packenham, Robert (1973), *Liberal America in the Third World: Political Development Ideas on Foreign Aid and Social Science*, Princeton, New Jersey: Princeton University Press.

Political Handbook of the World, Various years. New York, New York: McGraw Hill.

Palmer, Michael A. (1987), *Stoddert's War: Naval Operations During the Quasi War with France, 1798-1801*, Columbia, South Carolina: University of South Carolina Press.

Paterson, Thomas G., J. Garry Clifford and Kenneth J. Hagan (2000), *American Foreign Relations*, Volume 1 (4th Ed.), Lexington, Massachusetts: D.C. Heath and Company.

Pearson, Frederic, Robert Baumann, and Jeffrey Pickering (1994), 'Military Intervention and Realpolitik', in Frank Wayman and Paul Diehl (eds), *Reconstructing Pealpolitik*, Ann Arbor, Michigan: University of Michigan Press.

Peceny, Mark (1999), *Democracy At The Point Of Bayonets*, University Park, Pennsylvania: Pennsylvania State University Press.

Peceny, Mark (1995), 'Two Paths to the Promotion of Democracy During US Military Interventions', *International Studies Quarterly*, vol. 39, pp. 371-401.

Poe, Steven C. and C. Neal Tate (1994), 'Human Rights and Repression in the 1980s: A Global Analysis', *American Political Science Review*, vol. 88, pp. 853-872.

Pollins, Brian M. and Randall L. Scweller (1999), 'Linking the Levels: The Long Wave and Shifts in US Foreign Policy, 1790-1993', *American Journal of Political Science*, vol. 43, pp. 434-464.

Pratt, Julius W. (1955), *A History of US Foreign Policy*, New York, New York: Prentice Hall.

Prins, Brandon C. and Christopher Sprecher (1999), 'Institutional Constraints, Political Opposition, and Interstate Dispute Escalation: Evidence from Parliamentary Systems, 1946-89', *Journal of Peace Research*, vol. 36, pp. 271-287.

Putnam, Robert (1988), 'Diplomacy and Domestic Politics', *International Organization*, vol. 42, pp. 427-460.

Quester, George (1982), *American Foreign Policy: The Lost Consensus*, New York, New York: Praeger.

Reed, William (2000), 'A Unified Model of Conflict Onset and Escalation', *American Journal of Political Science*, vol. 44, pp. 84-93.

Remini, Robert V. (1977), *Andrew Jackson and the Course of American Empire, 1767-1821*, New York, New York: Harper and Row.

Richards, Diana, T. Clifton Morgan, Rick K. Wilson, Valerie L. Schwebach and Garry D. Young (1993), 'Good Times, Bad Times and the Diversionary Use of Force', *Journal of Conflict Resolution*, vol. 37, pp. 504-535.

Rodman, Kenneth A. (1988), *Sanctity Versus Sovereignty: The US and the Nationalization of Natural Resource Investments*, New York, New York: Columbia University Press.

Rose, Gideon. (1998), 'Neoclassical Realism and Theories of Foreign Policy', *World Politics*, vol. 51, pp. 144-172.

Rose, Richard. (1991), *The Postmodern President*, 2nd ed. Chatham, New Jersey: Chatham House.

Rosecrance, Richard and Arthur A. Stein (eds) (1993), *The Domestic Bases of Grand Strategy*, Ithica: Cornell University Press.

Rosen, Steven J. (1974), 'The Open Door Imperative of US Foreign Policy,' in *Testing Theories of Economic Imperialism*, Stephen Rosen and James R. Kurth (eds), Lexington Massachusetts: D.C. Heath.

Rosenberg, Emily (1982), *Spreading the American Dream*, New York, New York: Hill and Wang.

Rummel, Rudolph (1963), 'Dimensions of Conflict Behavior With and Between Nations', *General Systems*, vol. 8, pp. 1-50.

Ryden, G.H. (1933), *The Foreign Policy of the US in Relation to Samoa*, New Haven, Connecticut: Yale University Press.

Sarkees, Meredith Reid (2000), 'Correlates of War War Datasets: An Update', *Conflict Management and Peace Science*, vol. 18, pp. 123-144.

Schattscneider, E.E. (1935), *Politics, Pressures and the Tariff*, New York, New York: Prentice Hall.

Schell, Jonathon (1976), *Time of Illusion*, New York, New York: Random House.

Schelling, Thomas (1966), *Arms and Influence*, New Haven, Connecticut: Yale University Press.

_____ (1960), *The Strategy of Conflict*, Cambridge, Massachusetts: Harvard University Press.

Schlesinger, Stephen and Stephen Kinzer (1999), *Bitter Fruit: The Story of the American Coup in Guatemala*. Cambridge, Massachusetts: Harvard University Press.

Schoultz, Lars (1998), *Beneath the US*, Cambridge, Massachusetts: Harvard University Press.

Schroeder, John. H. (1985), *Shaping A Maritime Empire*, Westport, Connecticut: Greenwood Press.

Schweller, Randall (1994), 'Bandwaggoning for Profit: Bringing the Revisionist Back In', *International Security*, vol. 19, pp. 72-107.

Simmel, Georg (1955), *Conflict and the Web of Group Affiliations*. New York, New York: Free Press.

Singer, J. David, Stuart Bremer, and John Stuckey (1972), 'Capability Distribution, Uncertainty, and Major Power War, 1820-1965.' in Bruce Russett (ed.) *Peace, War, and Numbers*, Beverly Hills, California: Sage, 19-48.

Singer, J. David, and Melvin Small (1972), *The Wages of War, 1816-1965: A Statistical Handbook*, New York, New York: John Wiley.

Skidmore, David (1994), 'Explaining State Responses to International Change: The Structural Sources of Foreign Policy Rigidity and Change', in Jerel A. Rosati, Joe D. Hagan and Martin W. Sampson (eds), *Foreign Policy Restructuring*, Columbia, South Carolina: University of South Carolina Press.

Small, Melvin, and J. David Singer (1982), *Resort to Arms: International and Civil Wars, 1816-1980*, Beverly Hills, California: Sage Publications.

Smith, Alastair (1999), 'Testing Theories of Strategic Choice: The Example of Crisis Escalation', *American Journal of Political Science*, vol. 43, pp. 1254-1283.

Smith, Alastair. (1998), 'International Crises and Domestic Politics', *American Political Science Review*, vol. 92, pp. 623-638.

Smith, Alastair (1996a), 'Diversionary Foreign Policy in Democratic Systems', *International Studies Quarterly*, vol. 40, pp. 133-153.

Smith, Alastair (1996b), 'To Intervene or Not to Intervene', *Journal of Conflict Resolution*, vol. 40, pp. 16-40.

Smith, Tony (2000), 'Morality and the Use of Force in a Unipolar World: The Wilsonian Moment?', *Ethics and International Affairs*, vol. 14, pp. 11-22.

Bibliography 255

Smith, Tony (1994), *America's Mission: The US and the Worldwide Struggle for Democracy in the Twentieth Century*, Princeton, New Jersey: Princeton University Press.

Smith, Tony (1981), *The Paterrn of Imperialism*, Cambridge: Cambridge University Press.

Snyder, Jack (1991), *Myths of Empire:Domestic Politics and International Ambition*, Ithica, New York: Cornell University Press.

Speakes, Larry (1988), *Speaking Out*, New York, New York: Charles Scribner's Sons.

Sprout, Harold and Margaret (1944), *The Rise of American Naval Power*, Princeton, New Jersey: Princeton University Press.

Stoll, Richard (1984), 'The Guns of November', *Journal of Conflict Resolution*, vol. 28, pp. 231-246.

Summers, Anthony (2000), *The Arrogance of Power*, New York, New York: Viking Press.

Talbot, Strobe (1996), 'Democracy and the National Interest', in G. John Ikenberry (ed.), *American Foreign Policy*, New York, New York: Addison Wesley.

Thomas, Hugh (1997), *The Slave Trade*, New York, New York: Simon and Schuster.

Thucydides (1996), *History of the Pelopennesian War* (Robert Strassler, ed.), New York, New York: Free Press.

Tillema, Herbert (1994), 'Cold War Alliance and Overt Military Interventions, 1945-1991', *International Interactions*, vol. 20, pp. 249-278.

Tillema, Herbert (1989), 'Foreign Overt Military Intervention in the Nuclear Age', *Journal of Peace Research*, vol. 26, pp.179-195.

Tillema, Herbert (1973), *Appeal to Force*, New York, New York: Thomas Y. Crownwell Company.

Tucker, Robert W. and David Hendrickson (1990), *Empire of Liberty*, New York, New York: Oxford University Press.

Tusa, Ann and John Tusa (1988), *The Berlin Blockade*, London: Hodder and Stoughton.

US Air Force (1993), 'Toward the Future: Global Reach-Global Power, US Air Force', White Papers, 1989-1992, Available upon request.

US Department of Defense (2001), 'Quadrennial Defense Review Report', As found online at http://www.defenselink.mil/pubs/qdr2001.pdf on August 8, (2003).

US State Department, Bureau of Intelligence and Research, Various years 1980-1987, 'Disputes Involving US Private Direct Foreign Investment', Microfiche.

US Department of State (2002), 'U.S. National Security Strategy', As found online at http://www.state.gov/r/pa/ei/wh/15421.htm on August 8, (2003),

US Department of State, Various Years, State Department Foreign Relations Series, Washington D.C.: US Government Printing Office.

US Senate (1854), 33rd Congress, Second Session, *Correspondence Relative to the Naval Expedition to Japan*, Senate Executive Document Number 34.

Van Alstyne, Richard W. (1973), *The US and East Asia*, New York, New York: W.W. Norton and Company.

Wallerstein, Immanuel (1988), *The Modern World System III: The Second Era of Great Expansion of the World Capitalist System, 1730-1840*, San Diego, California: Academic Press.

Wallerstein, Immanuel (1974), 'The Rise and Future Demise of the World Capitalist System: Concepts for Comparative Analysis', *Comparative Studies in Society and History*, vol. 16, pp. 387-415.

Wang, Kevin H. (1996), 'Presidential Responses to Foreign Policy Crises', *Journal of Conflict Resolution*, vol. 40, pp. 68-97.

Weisskopf, Thomas E. (1974), 'Capitalism, Socialism and the Sources of Imperialism' (57-86) in Steven J. Rosen and James R. Kurth (eds) *Testing Theories of Economic Imperialism*, Lexington, Massachusetts: Lexington Books.

Whitcomb, Roger (1998), *The American Approach to Foreign Affairs*, Westport, Connecticut: Praeger Publishers.

Wilkenfeld, Jonathan (1972), 'Models for the Analysis of Foreign Conflict Behavior of States, in Bruce Russett (ed.), *Peace, War and Numbers*, Beverly Hills, California: Sage Publications.

Williams, William Appleman (1959), *The Tragedy of American Diplomacy*, Cleveland, Ohio: The World Publishing Company.

Wolfers, Arnold (1962), *Discord and Collaboration: Essays on International Politics*, Baltimore, Maryland: Johns Hopkins University Press.

Wright, Quincy (1941), *A Study of War*, Chicago, Illinois: University of Chicago Press.

Yoon, Mi Yung (1997), 'Explaining US Intervention in Third World Internal Wars, 1945-1989', *Journal of Conflict Resolution*, vol. 41, pp. 580-602.

Zakaria, Fareed (1998), *From Wealth to Power*, Princeton, New Jersey: Princeton University Press.

Zelikow, Phillip D. (1984), Force Without War, *Journal of Strategic Studies*, vol. 70, pp. 29-54.

Zinnes, Dina and Jonathan Wilkenfeld (1971), 'An Analysis of Foreign Conflict Behavior of Nations', in W.F. Hanrieder (ed.), *Comparative Foreign Policy*, New York, New York: David McKay.

Index

Acheson, Dean 13
Adams, John 51, 52, 101
Adams, John Quincy 32, 33, 133,
   137–8, 238
Afghanistan 63, 155
Africa
   economic interests 98, 99, 100
   liberal idealism 141, 142, 239
   number of operations in 210
   policy goals 208
   security interests 48, 49
Agnew, Spiro 174
Albania 17
Albright, Madeleine 132
Allison, Graham T. Jr. 123–4, 158
American Civil War 53–4, 104, 127,
   138
Angola 16
anti-communism 26, 146
   Cold War 16, 60, 62, 63
   economic interests 81, 97, 111, 112
Arbenz, Jacobo 92, 93, 94, 97
Arevalo, Juan 92, 97
Argentina 17
Armas, Castillo 94, 95
Arosemena, Pablo 129, 130
Art, Robert 122
Asia
   economic interests 99–100, 103–4,
      107–8, 109, 242
   liberal idealism 141, 142
   number of operations in 210
   policy goals 208
   security interests 48, 49, 55
assurance 6
Austin, Hudson 174
Austria 123, 145

balance of power 23, 24, 111
Bennett, D. 225
Berlin Airlift (1948) 36–40, 42, 43
Berlin Wall 61
Beschell, Robert P. Jr. 123–4
Betts, Richard 26
Beveridge, Albert 108
Bickers, Kenneth N. 157, 163–4,
   165, 168
Bishop, Maurice 174, 176
Blechman, Barry 3, 4, 5–6, 11,
   13–14, 27, 168
Bolivia 16
Boot, Max 27, 112
Bork, Robert 173
Bosnia 3, 17, 65, 242
   interest groups 158
   liberal idealism 8–9, 130–2, 135–6,
      150, 154, 219
   see also Yugoslavia, former
Brands, H.W. 27
Brazil 16, 103, 133
Brecher, Michael 14, 168
Brehznev, Leonid 172, 178
brinkmanship 28
Bryan, William Jennings 91
Buchanan, James 127
Bush, George Sr. 65, 74, 114, 222
   approval rating 188, 189
   Bosnia 130, 135
   elections 198
   inflation 194, 198
   opportunities and the use of force
      15, 17, 221
   Panama 5
   Saddam Hussein 225
   unemployment 193, 197

258   *The Political Use of Military Force in US Foreign Policy*

Bush, George W. 20, 201, 229, 234
Butler, Smedley 108–9

Calhoun, John 31
Cambodia 17, 62, 63
Camp David negotiations 6
capital-ship theory 105
capitalism 8, 76, 77, 81, 117, 231
  Cold War 111
  dependency theory 79–80, 84–5,
    112
  economic liberalism 120
  hegemony 83, 84
  Marxism 78–9, 85, 112
  open markets 237
  see also economic interests;
    multinational corporations; trade
Caribbean 3, 242
  economic interests 8, 87, 96,
    98–100, 103, 106, 107, 112,
    242
  liberal idealism 141, 142, 144
  Monroe Doctrine 52
  number of operations in 210
  pirates 102
  policy goals 208
  security interests 44, 48, 49, 53, 56
Carothers, Thomas 123
Carter, Jimmy 63, 146, 161, 222
  approval rating 188, 189
  inflation 194, 198, 202, 223
  Iran 225
  opportunities and the use of force
    15, 17, 221
  Rhodesia 223
  unemployment 193, 196–7
Castro, Fidel 111, 176, 225, 226
Center for Naval Analyses 12
Central America 6, 16, 242
  economic interests 8, 98–100, 103,
    106, 107, 112
  liberal idealism 141, 142, 143, 144,
    152
  number of operations in 210
  pirates 102
  policy goals 208

  Reagan interventions 17, 62, 63,
    146
  security interests 48, 49, 53, 56–7
  see also Latin America
Central Intelligence Agency (CIA) 2,
  16, 93–5, 111, 145
Chad 17
Chanley, Virginia A. 241
Chapman, Michael 177
Chile 80, 110, 111
China 16, 17, 35, 55, 103, 240–1
  Open Door policy towards 57, 108
  trade with 102, 107–8, 109, 237
  US-Sino relations 25
Christensen, Thomas J. 25
Churchill, Winston 60
CIA *see* Central Intelligence Agency
citizen protection 13, 207–9, 210,
  211
  post Cold War 213–14
  security interests 44, 46–7, 49–50,
    67, 70–1, 75, 213, 233
civil wars 151, 152–3, 166, 174–5,
  217, 239
  see also American Civil War
Clay, Henry 138–9
Clay, Lucius 37, 39
Cleveland, Grover 34, 41, 55
Clifford, Garry 51
Clinton, Bill 64, 65, 114, 181, 222,
  225
  approval rating 188, 189
  Bosnia 130, 135
  democracy 239
  inflation 194, 198
  Iraq 1, 2
  liberal idealism 147, 218
  opportunities and the use of force
    15, 17, 221
  unemployment 193, 197
CNN factor 241
Coard, Bernard 174
Cohen, William 132
Cold War 10, 16, 18, 150, 166
  Berlin 37
  commitments 28, 70

containment strategy 24
costs of war 27
credibility 62–3, 70, 212
diversionary behavior 184
domino theory 235
economic interests 77, 97, 110–11, 112
exporting democracy 123, 124
Grenada invasion 174
ideology 145–7
liberal values during 238
nuclear diplomacy 26
power 232
predicted uses of force 223, 224
security interests 21, 29, 60–4
widespread societal violence 217–18
see also anti-communism; communism; Soviet Union
Colombia 56, 57
colonialism 41
communism 13, 16, 17, 26, 27
Central America 95
collapse of 64, 80, 147, 155
credible commitment against 28
Grenada invasion 75, 177, 179
Guatemala 93
likelihood of US involvement 29
see also anti-communism; Cold War
compellence 5–6
Conflict and Peace Data Bank 168
conflict strategy 28–9
Congo (Zaire) 17, 18, 61, 111, 225
civil war 16
economic interests 82
frequency of uses of force 226, 227, 228
Congressional Research Service (CRS) 11, 44–5, 98, 109, 139–40, 207
Coolidge, Calvin 144
Correlates of War project 5
Cortleyou, George 170
costs of war 27
Cox, Archibald 173

credibility
abstract nature of 55
Cold War 62–3, 70, 212
security interests 28–9, 44, 66, 69–70, 75, 214
crisis escalation 14, 28
critical theories 77, 78–81, 84–6
CRS *see* Congressional Research Service
Cuba 17, 56, 106, 109, 225–6
acquisition of 54, 57
CIA involvement 111
Cold War 110
Congress influence 158
economic interests 90, 115
frequency of uses of force 226, 227, 228
goal of intervention 139
liberal idealism 143
missile crisis 3, 6, 16, 161
Platt Amendment 59
slave trade 133
Spanish policies 128
Wilson 143
Cyprus 228

Davis, David 168, 169
Dayton Accords 130, 131, 132, 136
decision-making restraints 26
defensive realism 22, 25
democracy 1, 2, 65, 167, 231, 242
Bosnia 131, 132, 136
Clinton 147
diversionary behavior of politicians 181
global order 235
Latin America 137, 138
liberal idealism 8–9, 119–25, 136, 140, 142, 148–55, 217–19, 238–9
Panama 129, 130, 134–5, 136
Wilson 58, 143–4
Democratic presidents 165, 192, 195–6, 197, 198, 202
democratization 123, 125, 145, 146, 152, 153, 217

260 *The Political Use of Military Force in US Foreign Policy*

see also proliberalization policies
dependency theory 78–81, 84–5, 112, 113–14, 116, 206
DeRouen, Karl 29, 164, 168
deterrence 5–6
Deutsch, Karl W. 79
Diamond, Larry 123, 124
diplomacy 6–7, 153, 236
  'dollar diplomacy' 79, 91, 96, 106, 107, 236
  gunboat 3, 20, 53, 102, 108–9, 112, 138, 184
  nuclear 26
diversionary use of force 1, 7–11, 20, 157–205, 221, 240–1
  case studies 169–81
  dominance of 117–18, 231–2
  elections 2, 163, 198–200, 201, 202–3
  evolving role of domestic politics 181–4
  model of 185–203, 219–20
  presidential popularity 160–1, 163–6, 185–91, 201, 202, 240
  probit analysis 200–3
  research 162–9
  testing the theory 230
  unemployment and inflation 164, 165, 174, 182, 191–8, 201–2, 219–20
Dodge, Percivil 135
'dollar diplomacy' 79, 91, 96, 106, 107, 236
domestic politics *see* diversionary use of force
Dominican Republic 16, 26, 57, 59, 63, 108
  democracy 123
  economic interests 90–2, 96, 107
  frequency of uses of force 227, 228
  goal of intervention 139
  liberal idealism 144, 145
  Wilson 143
domino theory 62, 66, 73, 235
Downes, John 183

Dulles, Allen 93, 94, 95
Dulles, John Foster 93, 94

Eastern Europe 17, 64
economic assistance 113–14, 115, 116, 215–16
economic growth 104–5
economic interests 1, 7–11, 76–118, 220–1, 231, 236–8, 242
  case studies 87–97
  critical theories 77, 78–81, 84–6, 112
  hegemony 83–4, 85, 110–12
  imperialism 20, 79–81, 84–5, 97, 103–6, 107–8, 109
  interest groups 25, 81, 82–3, 84–6, 112
  interventionism 106–8
  isolationism 104, 105, 108–9
  model of 112–17, 215–16, 229
  navy 100–3
  promotion of commerce 98, 100–3, 207–9, 210, 211
  see also capitalism
Egypt 1, 171–2, 216, 227, 228
Eisenhower, Dwight 37, 62, 222
  approval rating 188, 189
  Guatemala coup 93–4, 97
  Haiti 223
  inflation 194, 197
  opportunities and use of force 15–16, 221, 224
  unemployment 193, 196, 197, 201
El Salvador 225
elections 2, 163, 198–200, 201, 202–3, 204
Endicott, Charles M. 183
'enduring rivalry' 243
Ethiopia 17, 18, 63
Europe
  Cold War 61, 145
  economic interests 98, 99, 100, 106
  imperialism 104
  liberal idealism 141, 142
  number of operations in 210
  policy goals 208

Index 261

post-war economic recovery 84,
110
security interests 48, 49, 55, 56, 58,
59
stability 64
US troop deployments 6
Wilsonian idealism 144
exceptionalism 121, 122, 154

Falkland Islands 53, 181
Far East 57
Federation of American Scientists 12
Field, James A. 103
Fillmore, Millard 88, 95
Florida 30–3, 40–1, 42–3, 51, 52,
137, 209
Ford, Gerald 222
approval rating 188, 189
inflation 194, 198, 202, 223
opportunities and the use of force
15, 17, 221
unemployment 193, 196, 201
Fordham, Benjamin O. 5, 165–6,
168, 192, 197–8, 202, 220
foreign aid 113–14, 115, 116,
215–16
foreign policy prudence 43, 50–5
France, Quasi War 51, 52, 101
friendly governments 44, 46–7, 49,
59, 207–9, 211

Gaddis, John 28
Gelpi, Christopher 167, 168
Germany
anti-German sentiment 58
Berlin Airlift 36–40, 42, 43
democracy 123, 145
economic assistance to 215–16
frequency of uses of force 227, 228
Nazi 59, 60
Samoa 33, 34–6, 41–2
Gholz, Eugene 138
Gibbs, David N. 82
Gilpin, Robert 77, 81, 84, 85, 97,
111
Gleijeses, Piero 97

Gore, Al 20
Grant, Ulysses 103–4
Great Depression 79, 107, 110, 145
Greece 17, 18, 60, 152
Grenada 3, 17, 63, 75
diversionary use of military force
174–7, 179–80
liberal idealism 145
presidential approval ratings 161
threat to US citizens 71
Guatemala
1954 coup 13, 80, 92–5, 96–7, 111,
146
interest groups 158
Gulf War (1991) 2, 7, 65, 114
Gummere, Samuel 171
gunboat diplomacy 3, 20, 53, 102,
108–9, 112, 138, 184

Haass, Richard 122
Hagan, Kenneth J. 51
Haig, Alexander 173, 178
Haiti 3, 17, 57, 59, 223, 242
economic interests 90, 96, 107
frequency of uses of force 227, 228
goal of intervention 139
interest groups 158
liberal idealism 8–9, 154
long-term occupation of 108, 109,
143
Wilson 143
Hamilton, Alexander 54, 101
Hanna, Mark 170
Harding, Warren 59, 144
Hawaii 35, 55, 56
Hay, John 171
hegemony 234, 235, 243, 244
Cold War 145, 146
economic interests 83–4, 85,
110–12
foreign policy goals 211
liberal values 156
security interests 44, 64, 66, 71, 73
see also power
Hermann, Margaret 125
Hitler, Adolf 60, 150

Hobson, John A. 79
Hoffman, Stanley 123
Holbrooke, Richard 132, 136
Honduras 57, 90, 107, 225, 227, 228
honor 44, 46–7, 49, 54–5, 207, 208
Hoover, J. Edgar 144
Hristoulas, Athanasios 29, 163, 168
human rights 1, 2, 231, 242
  Carter 146
  Clinton 147
  global order 235
  liberal idealism 8–9, 119–22, 140,
    148, 154–5, 218–19, 238–9
humanitarian disasters 150, 224
Hungary 16
Huntington, Samuel 64, 119, 121–2,
  143
Hussein, Saddam 1–2, 6, 114, 225,
  226, 234
Huth, Paul K. 124

idealism
  democratic 123
  pacific 123
  Wilsonian 58, 107, 143–4, 155,
    236
  see also liberal idealism
ideology 119, 120, 145
Ikenberry, G. John 77, 82, 83
Immerman, Richard 95, 97
imperialism 20, 84–5, 97, 103–6,
  107–8, 109
  critical theories 79, 80, 81, 117,
    206
  global 237
'in-group / out-group' research 161,
  163
India 17, 18, 234
Indonesia 16, 62, 114, 116, 227
inducement 6
inflation 164, 165, 174, 182, 191–8,
  201–2, 204, 219–20, 223
influence 4, 6
instability 27
interest groups
  diversionary theory 158

economic interests 81, 82–3, 84–6,
  112
liberal idealism 120
realism 25
International Crisis Behavior project
  5, 168
internationalism 56, 145, 205, 241
  economic interests 105, 107
  foreign policy goals 211
  liberal 123
  Wilsonian 122, 143
interventionism
  economic 106–8
  liberal idealism 122, 139
  security interests 26, 43, 55–8
Iran 71, 93, 116, 225–6
  attacks on US economic interests
    110, 113, 115
  dictatorship 146
  frequency of uses of force 226,
    227, 228
  Iran-Iraq War 114, 116
  trade with 237
Iraq 155, 225–6, 234, 242
  2003 war against 65, 224
  continued use of force against 66
  frequency of uses of force 226,
    227, 228
  Gulf War 2, 7, 65, 114
  Iran-Iraq War 114, 116
  threat to Kuwait 1–2, 6
isolationism 204, 205, 211, 232, 242,
  243
  economic interests 104, 105, 108–9
  security interests 33, 43, 58, 59–60
Israel 171–3, 234, 237
Italy 123, 145
Ivory Coast 153

Jackson, Andrew 31–3, 40, 43, 101,
  183
Jaggers, Keith 149
James, Patrick 29, 163, 165, 168
Japan
  democracy 123, 145

Perry's mission to 3, 87–90, 95–6, 209
post-war economic recovery 84, 110
Russo-Japanese War 56, 57, 162
US troop deployments 6
Jefferson, Thomas 51, 52, 54, 58, 101, 137, 154
Jimenez, Horacio 91
Job, Brian L. 12–13, 14, 29, 68, 159, 163, 165, 168
Johnson, Lyndon B. 5, 222
  approval rating 188, 189
  inflation 194, 197
  opportunities and the use of force 15–16, 221
  unemployment 193, 196
Johnson, Robert 28, 66
Jordan 1, 171, 228

Kaplan, Stephen 3, 4, 5–6, 11, 13–14, 27, 168
Karadzic, Radovan 132
Kautz, Albert 35
Kegley, Charles 125
Kennan, George 23–4, 226
Kennedy, John F. 222, 235
  approval rating 188, 189
  Castro 225
  inflation 194, 197
  opportunities and the use of force 15–16, 221
  unemployment 193, 196
Kennedy, Paul 33
Kenya 224
Keohane, Robert 77
Khomeini, Ayatollah 225
Khrushchev, N. 61
Kinzer, Stephen 95
Kissinger, Henry 23, 173, 178–9, 226
Kolko, Gabriel 80
Korea 55, 62, 63, 64, 104, 209
  see also North Korea; South Korea
Korean War 26, 69
  casualties 29, 68, 71, 215

high inflation 202
Kosovo 17, 65, 131, 154
Krasner, Stephen 77, 81, 83, 97, 111, 112–13, 119, 216
Kurth, James R. 79–80
Kuwait 1–2, 6, 7, 17, 114, 216

Lake, David 77, 80, 82–3
Lansing, Robert 91
Laos 62, 224, 227, 228
latent goals 6
Latin America
  Alliance for Progress 146
  economic interests 87, 242
  liberal idealism 137–8, 142, 144, 239
  Monroe Doctrine 52, 53
  political instability 96
  security interests 44, 56
  slave trade 133
  US multinational corporations 106
  see also Central America; South America
League of Nations 58, 143
Lebanon 4, 16, 17, 26, 224
  Cold War 61, 63
  Congress support for 1958 invasion 184
  frequency of uses of force 226, 227, 228
  Grenada invasion as diversion from 174, 175, 177, 180
  liberal idealism 145
Leeds, Brett Ashley 168, 169
Leffler, Melvyn P. 117
Lenin, Vladimir Ilich 78–9
Leninism 78–9, 117, 206
Levy, Jack 157, 163
Lian, Bradley 161
liberal idealism 7–11, 119–56, 207–10, 221, 231, 238–40
  case studies 125–36
  historical record 136–47
  model of 148–54, 216–19, 229
  research on 121–5
  US internationalism 211

see also democracy; idealism
Liberia 153
Libya 3, 17, 63, 227, 228, 237
Lindsay, James 166, 168
Lodge, Henry Cabot 105
Louisiana Purchase 51, 54

McDougall, Walter A. 122–3
McKinley, William 139, 170
Mahan, Alfred T. 105
Maldives 223
Mandelbaum, Michael 122
Manifest Destiny 54
Mansfield, Edward D. 84
Marshall, George 39
Marshall, Monty G. 149
Marx, Karl 78
Marxism
  economic interests 8, 77, 78–9, 81, 85, 112
  Grenada 174
  imperialism 117, 206
Mastanduno, Michael 77, 78, 117
Mata'afa 34–5, 41–2
Mearsheimer, John 64
media 158, 183, 184, 240, 241
Meernik, James D. 29, 124–5, 166, 168, 169, 229
Meliorism 122, 155
Mexico 17, 52, 53, 57
  democracy 143
  goal of intervention 139
  Mexican-American War (1848) 54
  oil 106
Middle East
  economic interests 98, 99, 100
  liberal idealism 141, 142
  number of operations in 210
  policy goals 208
  Reagan's policies 177
  security interests 48, 49, 56
  Six Day War (1967) 171
  trade 237
  Yom Kippur War (1973) 3, 17, 116, 171–4, 178–9
  see also Gulf War; Persian Gulf

Militarized Interstate Dispute project 5, 168
Miller, Ross A. 167, 168
Milosevic, Slobodan 225
Mladic, Ratko 132
Monroe Doctrine 50, 52–3, 55, 59, 128, 134, 143
Monroe, James 30–1, 32, 40, 41, 52
Montgomery, General Bernard 37
Morgan, T. Clifton 72, 157, 163–4, 165, 168
Morgenthau, Hans 22, 23, 81, 119
Morocco 170–1, 177–8
Mozambique 63
Mueller, John 68, 161
multinational corporations 8, 76, 77, 91, 112–13, 117
  CIA missions 111
  dependency theory 79, 80
  Guatemala coup 92–5, 96–7
  joint ventures 116
  Latin America 106
  see also capitalism
Munich syndrome 62, 66, 235
Muravchik, Joshua 123

national interest 64, 66–7, 211, 235
  Cold War 63
  diversionary use of force 203
  economic interests 118
  maximalist security 73
  nation building 123
  realism 22, 23, 24, 25
national security *see* security interests
National Security Strategy 229, 235
nationalism 106
NATO *see* North Atlantic Treaty Organization
navy
  British 50–1, 52–3, 100, 101, 106, 126–7, 133
  economic interests 76, 100–3, 105, 236
  naval security in Samoa 33–4, 35, 36, 41–2

slave trade 125–8, 133–4
weakness of 138, 210
neorealism 22, 24, 25, 206, 231
Nicaragua 53, 55, 57, 63
democracy 152
dictatorship 143
economic interests 90, 107
frequency of uses of force 227, 228
goal of intervention 139
guerilla warfare 108
long-term occupation of 108, 109, 144
Nixon Doctrine 63
Nixon, Richard 23, 171–4, 178–9, 222
approval rating 188, 189
inflation 194, 197–8, 202, 223
opportunities and the use of force 15, 17, 221
unemployment 193, 196
Noriega, Manuel 5
North Atlantic Treaty Organization (NATO) 39, 42, 61, 130, 131, 135
North Korea 6, 21, 225–6, 227, 228, 234
nuclear diplomacy 26
Nye, Joseph 77

Odell, John S. 81
offensive realism 22, 24–5
oil
crises 237
economic interests 84, 87, 114, 116–17
Mexico 106
Persian Gulf 1–2, 64, 87, 113, 114, 117
Olney, Richard 55–6
Olson, Mancur 83
Oneal, John R. 29, 161, 163, 165, 168
'Open Door' policy 57, 80, 108, 117
Operation Urgent Fury 174, 175
Operation Vigilant Warrior 2
opportunity to use force 11–15

Ostrom, Charles W. Jr. 12–13, 14, 29, 68, 159, 163, 165, 168

Pacific Ocean 36, 102, 103
Pakistan 17, 234
Palmer, Glenn 72
Panama 3, 5, 17, 59, 123
Canal 56–7, 74, 106, 128, 134, 139
Colombia control over 56
elections 128–30, 134–5
frequency of uses of force 227
goal of intervention 45, 139
liberal idealism 8–9, 136, 143, 154
threat to US citizens 71
pariah states 225–7, 242–3
Paterson, Thomas G. 51
Peceny, Mark 45, 120, 124, 125, 139–40, 148, 155, 210
Perdicaris, Ion 170–1, 177–8
Peron, Juan 17
Perry, David 54–5
Perry, Matthew 3, 87–90, 95–6, 107, 127, 209
Persian Gulf 6, 8, 17
oil 1–2, 64, 87, 113, 114, 117
war against Iraq 224, 234
see also Gulf War; Middle East
Peurifoy, John 94, 95
Philippines 35, 56, 108, 109
goal of intervention 139
liberal idealism 142, 144
Taft 143
pirates 101, 102
Plato 162
pluralism 82–3, 84–6
Polity IV Project 149, 152, 217
Polk, James 54
Porras, Belisario 129, 130
Powell, Colin 64–5, 243
power 69, 232–3
economic interests 86, 118
realism 8, 23, 25, 66, 73, 233
security interests 20, 21, 73–4, 75, 214, 215, 220–1
wealth relationship 76, 85
see also hegemony

preemption 234
presidential popularity 160–1, 163–
  6, 185–91, 201, 202, 204, 206,
  240
  see also public opinion
Press, Daryl G. 138
proactive foreign policy 72, 73
proliberalization policies 123–5,
  144, 148, 155, 210, 219, 239
  Bosnia 132, 136
  Cold War 238
  definition of 120, 140
  hegemons 156
  Panama 135
  see also democratization; liberal
    idealism
prudence 43, 50–5
public opinion 24, 29, 158, 182–4
  diversionary theory 159, 160, 161,
    181, 240, 241
  Grenada invasion 175
  see also presidential popularity
Puerto Rico 54, 56, 106

quantitative research 9–10, 29–30
Quasi War 3, 51, 52, 101

Raisuli, Ahmed ben Mohammed el
  170–1, 177–8
rally effect 160, 161, 220, 240
rational choice models 29
Reagan Doctrine 63, 145, 146, 147
Reagan, Ronald 13, 114, 180–1, 222,
  239
  approval rating 188, 189, 190
  Cold War 62, 63, 146
  Grenada invasion 75, 174–7,
    179–80
  inflation 194, 198
  opportunities and the use of force
    15–16, 17, 221, 224
  unemployment 193, 197, 201
realism 8, 20–5, 65, 71, 221, 231
  Cold War 64
  commitments 28
  domestic politics 157

dominance of 117–18
foreign policy goals 211
international relations theories 232
power 8, 23, 25, 66, 73, 233
preemption 234
presidential popularity 206
terrorism 229
Vietnam War 215
see also neorealism
regime transition 148–9, 151–2, 217,
  243
Republican presidents 165, 192,
  195–6, 197, 198, 201, 202
reputation 44, 62, 70
  see also credibility
Rhodesia 223
Richards, Diana 166, 168
Richardson, Eliot 173
risk 28
Rodman, Kenneth A. 82, 112–13,
  216
Rogers, John 104
Roosevelt, Franklin D. 58, 59–60,
  109, 144
Roosevelt, Theodore 96, 105, 106,
  128
  Corollary to Monroe Doctrine 59,
    90, 106, 128, 143
  diversionary use of military force
    170–1, 177–8, 180
  international activism 139
  Panama 57, 129, 134
  Russo-Japanese War 56, 57
Rose, Gideon 24
Rose, Richard 184
Rosenberg, Emily 105
routine troop deployments 6
Ruckelshaus, William 173
Rummel, Rudolph 162
Russia 142
  see also Soviet Union
Russo-Japanese War 56, 57, 162

Sadat, Anwar 172, 173
Saddam Hussein 1–2, 6, 114, 225,
  226, 234

Samoa 33–6, 41–2, 43, 55, 56, 103
Sapolsky, Harvey M. 138
Sarver, Christopher C. 5
Saudi Arabia 1, 6, 114, 237
Sayrs, Lois W. 166, 168
Schattschneider, E.E. 82
Schell, Jonathon 28
Schelling, Thomas 28
Schlesinger, Stephen 95
Schroeder, John H. 102–3
Schultz, George 175
Scoon, Paul 175
security interests 1, 7–11, 20–75, 204, 231, 232–6
  case studies 30–43
  Cold War 60–4, 111
  definitions of security 71–4
  economic interests relationship 86–7, 117, 118
  foreign policy prudence 43, 50–5
  hierarchy of 44
  importance of 220–1
  instability 243
  interventionism 43, 55–8
  isolationism 43, 59–60
  model of 65–71, 212–15, 229
  objectives of military force 43–4, 45, 46, 47, 49–50
  post Cold War 64–5
  research 26–30
  see also realism
selection effects 168, 169, 211
self-determination 144
Sierra Leone 153
Six Day War (1967) 171
slavery 54, 138
  crusade against 9, 125–8, 132–4, 136
  Florida 31, 33, 40
Smith, Alastair 166–7, 168
Smith, Tony 81, 97, 123
Smith, Walter Bedell 93
Snyder, Jack 25
Social Darwinism 41
Somalia 4, 17, 63, 150, 158, 242
South Africa 234

South America
  economic interests 98, 99, 100, 103, 113
  liberal idealism 141, 142, 143
  naval deployments 102
  number of operations in 210
  policy goals 208
  security interests 48, 49, 53
  see also Latin America
South Korea 6, 13, 152, 226, 227, 228
sovereignty 44, 72, 219
Soviet Union (USSR)
  Berlin Airlift 36–40, 42
  Cold War 16, 60–4, 111, 145–7
  likelihood of US involvement 29
  Middle East War 172–3, 179
  nuclear diplomacy 26
  support for Arab states 171, 172
  see also Russia
Spanish Florida 30–3, 40–1, 42–3, 51, 52, 137, 209
Spanish-American War 35, 41, 56, 128, 139, 204, 210–11
Speakes, Larry 176
Steger, Wayne P. 166, 168
subnational groups 23
Suez crisis 61
Summers, Anthony 178–9
Syria 171–2

Taft, William Howard 57, 59, 108, 139
  'dollar diplomacy' 79, 96, 106, 107, 236
  liberal idealism 143
  Panama 129, 134–5
Taiwan 227, 228, 234
Taiwan straits 61
Tanu 34, 35
Tanzania 224
territorial integrity 12, 44, 46–7, 49, 75, 207–9, 210
terrorism 13, 65, 73, 75, 199, 224, 229, 237
Thomas, Hugh 126

Tibet 16
Tillema, Herbert 26
Tonkin Gulf Resolution (1964) 184
trade 82, 84, 110, 236, 237
  imperialism 104
  Japan 88, 89, 95
  naval security 100–3, 105
  see also capitalism; economic
    interests
Truman, Harry S. 60, 69, 145, 222,
  239
  approval rating 188, 189
  Berlin Airlift 38, 39, 42
  inflation 194, 197, 202, 223
  opportunities and use of force 15,
    221
  unemployment 193, 196
Turkey 17, 18, 45, 60
Tusa, Ann 38
Tusa, John 38
Tyler, John 54, 127, 133

UFCO *see* United Fruit Company
uncertainty 65, 243
unemployment 164, 165, 174, 182,
  191–8, 201, 204, 219–20
United Fruit Company (UFCO) 92–
  5, 97
United Kingdom
  Berlin Airlift 36, 37–8
  Central America 53
  impressment of US sailors 50–1,
    137
  liberal economic system 83
  Royal Navy 50–1, 52–3, 100, 101,
    106, 126–7, 133
  Samoa 33, 34, 35, 41–2
  slave trade abolition 126–7, 133
  threat to US security 40–1
  Venezuela dispute 55–6
United Nations 150
USSR *see* Soviet Union

Valdes, Jose Bordas 91
values

American 19
  economic interests 236
  liberal 119, 121, 147, 154–6, 238,
    242
Van Alstyne, Richard 108
Venezuela 17, 18, 55–6, 152
  frequency of uses of force 227, 228
  oil 114, 116
Vietnam 62, 227, 228
Vietnam War 5, 16, 26, 62, 63, 165
  casualties 29, 68, 71, 215
  inflationary effects 197–8
  public opinion 184

Wallerstein, Immanuel 84
Waltz, Kenneth 24, 25
Wang, Kevin H. 29, 164–5, 168
war definition 3–5
war prevention 46–7, 49–50, 207,
  208
Washington, George 51, 52, 58, 74,
  76, 154, 181
Watergate scandal 173, 178, 184
Waterman, Peter 29, 166, 168
weapons of mass destruction 229,
  233–4
Weeks, Ronald 37
Whitcomb, Roger 122
Wilkenfeld, Jonathan 14, 168
Williams, William Appleman 80
Wilson, Woodrow 57, 58, 59, 106
  Dominican Republic 91–2, 96, 107
  liberal idealism 9, 143–4, 236, 239
Wilsonian idealism 58, 107, 143–4,
  155, 236
Wolfers, Arnold 72
Woolsey, James 64
World War I 56, 58, 112, 124, 143–
  4, 242
World War II 60, 69, 124, 145
world-systems theory 78, 79–81, 112
Wright, Quincy 162

Yom Kippur War (1973) 3, 17, 116,
  171–4, 178–9
Yoon, Mi Yung 29, 166, 168

Yugoslavia, former 225–6, 227, 228, 239

see also Bosnia

Zaire see Congo

Zakaria, Fareed 20–1, 25, 104–5, 233

Zanzibar 16

Zelikow, Phillip D. 11, 13, 158

Zhukov, Marshall 37